As You Law It – Negotiating Shakespeare

Law & Literature

Edited by
Daniela Carpi and Klaus Stierstorfer

Volume 15

As You Law It – Negotiating Shakespeare

Edited by
Daniela Carpi and François Ost

DE GRUYTER

ISBN 978-3-11-059082-1
e-ISBN (PDF) 978-3-11-059151-4
e-ISBN (EPUB) 978-3-11-059089-0
ISSN 2191-8457

Library of Congress Cataloging-in-Publication Data
A CIP catalog record for this book has been applied for at the Library of Congress.

Bibliographic information published by the Deutsche Nationalbibliothek
The Deutsche Nationalbibliothek lists this publication in the Deutsche Nationalbibliografie; detailed bibliographic data are available on the Internet at http://dnb.dnb.de.

Printing and binding: CPI books GmbH, Leck

www.degruyter.com

Table of Contents

Part Three Legal Theory

Part Four Performance

Introduction

Daniela Carpi

Shakespeare and the Law: State of the Art

> Shakespeare shows us repeatedly what it is to fail in justice.
> Regina M. Schwartz, *Loving Shakespeare, Living Justice*, vii

This volume sets itself within a flourishing production on Shakespeare featuring legal problems, which has characterized the last twenty years and more, in the wake of the parallel flourishing of studies on law and literature. The seminal interdisciplinary topic of law and literature, born in the United States, has seeped into Europe giving rise to innovative studies and researches branching out into many more comparative studies that have connected law to the most varied disciplines. The Shakespearean texts, in their endless interpretations and over-interpretations, have very often been the focus of these analyses linking law and literature, surprising the readers and viewers with the many legal perspectives that had gone unnoticed so far in the Shakespearean texts.

With any attempt to produce yet another book on Shakespeare and the law, we must necessarily start with an assessment of the state of the art of the latest critical studies. This brief survey will hopefully provide the background to show how the present volume can contribute to the never ending fascination with the legal aspects of Shakespeare's plays. For this purpose, a number of recent books have been singled out for their insightful scrutiny into Elizabethan legal problems in dramatic productions of the time.

I shall begin with Regina Mara Schwartz's *Loving Shakespeare, Living Justice*[1], a very interdisciplinary text that weaves together literature, psychology, philosophy, and personal experience. The book starts from the observation that all books on justice written from a political perspective never mention the question of love because this emotion is considered to be private and not public; while all books on religion have love as their focal point. The connection between love and justice has never been taken into consideration so far.

Another consideration that has so far prevented this connection is that duty and obligation pertain to the realm of reason, while love is emotional. Even for Kant the moral act follows the dictates of duty and not of emotion.

---

1 Regina M. Schwartz, *Loving Shakespeare, Living Justice* (Oxford: Oxford University Press, 2016).

https://doi.org/10.1515/9783110591514-001

> We understand justice to be a universal value of impartiality, all persons, whatever differences of race, gender, religion, or abilities, deserve to be treated with impartiality. The Kantian ideals of universality and impartiality have informed theories of justice as fairness.[2]

How can we define justice? Justice has to do with impartiality, it is a universal value that goes beyond the distinction into religions and races. It derives from Kant's idea of fairness. All this entails a universal ethical theory.

In most of Shakespeare's plays justice is a central question: they widely debate problems concerning law, ethics and equity, justice, legitimacy and authority. Schwartz observes that most often the tragic result of his tragedies stems from lack of love, while the happy ending of comedies consists in the recovery of loving relations and the redress of justice through love.

Why does love not appear in theories of political justice? Justice can be enforced, while love asks for no constrictions. Still one of the many rhetorical devices Elizabeth I used in her speeches was the recourse to the love for her subjects. She used love as a rhetorical device to fascinate her people and draw their consensus. She said that she was married to England and her subjects would never again have a queen that loved them more. Elizabeth I, who skillfully used strategies of self-promotion so to create a favourable iconic image of herself, focused her power not on force and control, but on loving and communal sharing.

> The power of love was not underestimated by Shakespeare, whose romances depict the moral order righted when love prevails and whose tragedies often suggest that the dissolution of order accompanies a loveless world.[3]

The biblical tradition and the Kantian tradition are at variance: the former contemplates giving as an act of love, while the latter considers giving as duty. Therefore love and justice coincide in the former, love is compassion and duty in the latter.

Our contemporary societies are based on contracts that have been considered a solution to domination. Even the principles of justice are forged by an imagined original agreement: societies come together on principles of cooperation and on the assignment of rights and duties. Therefore we can speak of contractual justice as the basic principle of societies. One enters a contract freely; it marks mutual benefit.

---

2 Schwartz, *Loving Shakespeare, Living Justice*, 12.

3 Schwartz, *Loving Shakespeare, Living Justice*, 38.

> The contract marks the relational character of legal rights and exemplifies social relationships within the modern world. The form of the contract allows people to overcome any juridical limitation through the dialectics of single wills.[4]

But Schwartz correctly asserts that contracts cannot create trust between the parties.

Coming to a more general statement concerning retributive justice, Schwartz asserts that hardly ever does the criminal law system take into consideration the social disadvantage of the culprit in criminal actions. We tend to equate bad behaviour to bad person, as if the moral life could be measurable. What prevails is an economic perspective. The sort of punishment attributed must be in proportion to the offense: in this case the judge appears to be the equalizer. What Schwartz calls retribution can after all be compared to the rigorous application of the law, while we should judge equitably and take into consideration the disadvantaged social position that most often brings people to cause crimes.

In the place of measurable retribution Schwartz suggests forgiveness in the sense of overcoming resentment. All along Shakespeare's production revenge is seen as sinful and suspect: it generates more errors and it does not redress justice. Shakespeare rather purports forgiveness as a harmonizing factor, forgiveness connected to the recovery of love.

Schwartz's book, while speaking of Renaissance society and of how Shakespeare envisages the possibilities of justice, also speaks for the contemporary world: it offers a possible solution to the difficulty of harmonizing justice in our diasporic cultural European situation. Also my own longstanding studies both on postmodernism and on the Renaissance have brought me to compare the two periods and to observe that the Renaissance has strong seeds of anticipation of what was to reach its climax in the late twentieth century.[5]

Rather than applying a rigorous legal code of behaviour or the economy of punishment and revenge, Schwartz fosters forgiveness and mutual understanding as ways to solve the strictures of our times. Schwartz's volume is very much in trend with contemporary analyses of Shakespeare's Biblical perspectives[6] and stresses the idea that justice to be such must be connected to love. We are back in

4 Daniela Carpi, "Contracts in Literature: from Doctor Faustus to Vampires," in *Comparative Contract Law*, ed. Pier Giuseppe Monateri (Celtenham, UK: Edward Elgar, 2017), 322–360, 322.

5 Daniela Carpi, "Renaissance into Postmodernism: Anticipations of Legal Unrest," in *Liminal Discourses. Sublime Tensions in Law and Literature*, eds. Daniela Carpi and Jeanne Gaakeer (Berlin and Boston: De Gruyter, 2013), 177–189.

6 Piero Boitani, *The Gospel According to Shakespeare* (Paris: University of Notre Dame Press, 2014); Sarah Beckwith, *Shakespeare and the Grammar of Forgiveness* (New York: Cornell University Press, 2011).

the debate between law and equity, from a more religious perspective. In fact her reasoning finds its focal point in some passages from the Bible which she takes as examples for Shakespeare's view of justice.

Also Gary Watt's latest volume *Shakespeare's Acts of Will*[7] analyses Shakespeare from a legal perspective and offers the opportunity for a reflection on the word "will." The term "will" in the volume has many valences: it plays ironically with Shakespeare's name itself, it implies testaments and heritages, it means will-power, performing will, the actor's and the playwright's will.

At the very opening of the book Watt presents two very interesting assumptions for a scholar of law and literature: that the book is concerned with cultural practices, and specifically the cultural practices that connect theatre and law to the wider world, that is law as creative practice. This sounds strange to outsiders of the juridical field that have always considered law as a hard, dreary practice, unimaginative and empirical. The law can also be connected to fairy tales, because it is rooted in "magic words," formulas, rhetoric. So law "spins a good yarn."[8] If in the theatre language is a sort of magic, transforming a linguistic reality into a material body essence (the actor's physical presence), in law operative words such as "I agree," "I declare," "I swear" transform a person into somebody else, they create a parallel and virtual world. In the same way a legal testament remains *in potentia* until its testator dies. Its action takes place only *in absentia* of the person who wrote it. It is a presence/absence, where word and action are at variance. Both situations (performance and will) are based on the power of words to make things happen: words are operative.

These two opening assertions spread out the field of law, and connect Watt's book to two very important latest trends in the law-and-literature field: law as culture, and law as fable. In particular, as far as the latter is concerned, we must consider Derrida's argument that:

> What is fabulous in the fable does not only depend on its linguistic nature, on the fact that the fable is made up of words. The fabulous also engages act, gesture, action [...] in organizing, disposing discourse in such a way as to recount, to put living beings on stage, to accredit the interpretation of a narrative, to faire savoir, to make knowledge, to make performatively, to operate knowledge.[9]

Marett Leiboff, in her turn, stresses the causative and operative capacity of law:

7 Gary Watt, *Shakespeare's Acts of Will* (London: Bloosmbury, 2016).

8 Watt, *Shakespeare's Acts of Will*, 3.

9 Jacques Derrida, *The Beast and the Sovereign*, Volume I, eds. Michel Lisse, Marie-Louise Mallet and Ginette Michaud, trans. Geoffrey Bennington (Chicago: University of Chicago Press, 2009), 35–36.

> Words do not act on their own, nor does law. Law's actors inevitably are involved in "making to know," but law's practice is such that it denies the possibility that law, with its techniques grounded in the assumptions that rationality and reason immunize law's actors from fabling, might result in "making like knowledge."[10]

What is very innovative, considering the time of the Renaissance, is the fact that Shakespeare invites the audience to speculate on whether affairs of state might be better handled by common folk. This idea is very unsettling in a period dominated by the concept of absolute monarchy.

According to Watt, the most testamentary play in all of Shakespeare's production is *As You Like It.* Here the concept of will is at its widest perspective: it means both governing will and performance as communal approbation; it is testamentary fashion and personal will. In *The Merchant of Venice*, the stubborn will of a dead father, which requires a certain performance, clashes against the will of a living daughter; in *As You Like It* the "letter" of a father's will appointing his eldest son Oliver as his hierarchical heir opposes itself to the natural rights of a son, Orlando, who better embodies the "spirit" of the will.

Moreover, in other plays, such as *King Lear* and *The Merchant of Venice*, we have cases which we can define as living will *ante litteram*. Lear subverts the inheritance laws and custom in the division of his reign among the three daughters in the same way as Shylock embodies a stubborn will that he tries to impose on others (the Jewish rites that Jessica should respect and the written word that he divinizes): he is finally baffled by a more modern play of wills during the trial.

The focal idea of Paul Raffield's volume *The Art of Law* in Shakespeare[11] is that during the first Jacobean period law and the theatre mutually influenced each other, the theatre taking from law the courtroom perspective, but the law taking from theatre its rhetorical devices. Both forms are linked through rhetoric. Raffield's main aim in this volume is to demonstrate a closer interest for the ruler's persona in the Jacobean period than in the Elizabethan one. Both James' I *Basilicon Doron* (1599) and his *The Trew Law of Free Monarchies* (1598) triggered a widespread interest for the problem of kingship and for the relation between the crown and common law. The crown was presented to the public as a form of theatre (see Elizabeth's speech and James I's speech to both Houses of Parliament in March 1610). Raffield speaks of a "correlation between the Jacobean

10 Marett Leiboff, Introductory chapter to *Fables of the Law*, eds. Daniela Carpi and Marett Leiboff (Berlin and Boston: DeGruyter, 2016), 33–46, 38.

11 Paul Raffield, *The Art of Law in Shakespeare* (Oxford and Portland: Bloomsbury, Hart, 2017).

masque and the juridical processes of English law"[12] through the shared theme of divine justice.

Raffield explores how classical rhetorical techniques are influential to the development of juridical procedure. He mentions the recourse to juridical fables to teach young lawyers ethics and the use of narrative. Law and narration were therefore strictly connected as far back as the Renaissance. Legal education in the early Inns of Court was provided by the study of the art of rhetoric and ethics, which helped lawyers develop their craft. However in the course of the Renaissance lawyers passed from the awareness of having a sacerdotal role (they thought they were Ministerial Officers) to the fall into the sin of pride and avarice. This is why lawyers in the plays of the period were very often made fun of. They were presented as torn between moral law and individual desire. They were also accused of lack of learning. We have many instances of such accusations in the Jacobean plays: for instance from *The White Devil* by John Webster we derive a sense of the law as a mischievous tool in the hands of clever manipulators. *The English Lawyer* by Edward Ravenscroft presents an unethical use of forensic eloquence and lawyers are frequently accused of using a nonsensical law-Latin jargon. Also in Shakespeare's *Love's Labour's Lost* we have an example of parody of forensic obscure language.

In 1534 with the Act of Supremacy English jurisprudence got independent from Rome and the Justinian code, thus setting the foundations of a secularized English jurisprudence. In this way the lawyer from being a *sacerdos* is transformed into a lawless being. The sacred aspect of the law was demonstrated also by what was customary in the Halls of the Inns of Court: the common consumption of food as a sacred act of communion, as a metaphor for the eating of the holy wafer. But rapidly the law fell under the harsh criticism of satire: Thomas Nashe in *The Isle of Dogs* in fact connects the practice of law with the powers of evil. The lawyer is dehumanized by Nashe and reduced to a malevolent monster.

Raffield also speaks of treason and regicide. If for Aristotle, whose influence is all pervading in the period, the ideal state was rooted in *amicitia* and concord, the act of treason was a betrayal of the state and of love: it is an act of infidelity against the spiritual body of the monarch.

Many plays by Shakespeare present trial scenes, which has a metatheatrical meaning, in that plays and trials share a common spectacular element and a dramatic engagement. Moreover the act of transcribing the law and the legal precedent correspond to the assimilation of food for the body's nourishment (the

12 Raffield, *The Art of Law in Shakespeare*, 12.

king's body, in this case). We have horticultural metaphors: if through grafting nature is transformed into art, so the political succession of James I to queen Elizabeth is often described in paintings as a climbing rose stemming out of two conjoined hands: a thistle is grafted onto a rose rootstock. There is a subtle correlation between law and horticulture: gardening and the law have a common matrix.

Kevin Curran's volume *Shakespeare and Judgment*[13] adds another "and" to the many works comparing Shakespeare to other fields of study. It can be considered to be the first thorough analysis of how judgment gives form to Shakespeare's plays and how Shakespeare's representation of judgment in its turn helps the common people of the time understand how judgment works. The first aspect of judgment that is taken into consideration pertains to reason: it is a rhetorical skill that has to do with invention. Invention triggers ideas and judgment orders them. The volume also considers judgment as pertaining to law courts, hence its connection to classical rules of oratory and the capacity to follow certain rules of expression. This last perspective on judgment is contrasted to the religious one: only the Church can judge according to moral dicta.

Curran mentions the many characteristics a good judge should be endowed with, above all modesty and respect for legal doctrine. But judgment to be sound must be based also on a communal sharing with others, as Hannah Arendt affirms: she connects judgment with collective perception, therefore the term has also a political connotation.

"There can be no account of judgment that does not make reference both to subjectivity and to the milieu of ideality in which it operates."[14] The various chapters in the volume illustrate the possible perspectives on judgment that Shakespeare's texts purport. Virginia Lee Strain[15], for instance, considers *Measure for Measure* through the lens of the judge's judgment of Barnardine: what the judge strives to obtain is an ideal justice and not the mere rigorous application of punitive law. In particular Strain speaks of preventive justice, which is a new context in which to evaluate Shakespeare's magistrates.

---

13 Kevin Curran ed., *Shakespeare and Judgment* (Edinburgh: Edinburgh University Press, 2017).

14 Vivasvan Soni, "Believing in Ghosts, in Part: Judgment and Indecision in *Hamlet*," in *Shakespeare and Judgment*, ed. Curran, 45–70, 56.

15 Virginia Lee Strain, "Preventive Justice in *Measure for Measure*," in *Shakespeare and Judgment*, ed. Curran, 21–45.

On the same play we have the interpretation of Carolyn Sale[16], who, on the contrary, stresses the fact that this play may be set in a civil law jurisdiction that questions to whom judgment pertains: to the judge or to the commons? Sale analyses the concerns with the jurisprudence of the period that the play demonstrates side by side with its effects on the present time. Paul Yachnin[17] in his turn takes into consideration *Measure for Measure*. At the opening of the play Shakespeare opposes law to justice: Isabella considers that the death penalty is too severe for the sin of having begotten one's betrothed lover with child. When Isabella places justice with God and the law with human beings she opens a chasm between law and justice. However towards the end of the play she mixes once more law with justice: law must necessarily produce a just treatment. Finally, mercy is showered on everyone creating a big feast where everybody is pardoned. Even in this case, as other critics have observed, Shakespeare appears not to believe in the well-functioning of the juridical system. However the play develops a critical representation of three kinds of law: the law of sovereign will, the law of kind, and the law of judgment. The first one is at the basis of public and private life and rests in the monarch. The law of kind has to do with our humanness and with natural feelings. The third one, the law of judgment, is connected to active public life and is subjected to change and to precedent. Shakespeare in his plays tries to cultivate popular judgment thus to educate people to law.

In order to discuss his own new view of what sort of judgment is called into question, Curran has recourse to Hannah Arendt and her view of judgment as linked to responsibility and freedom. "This has the effect of lifting Prospero's epilogue out of the historically specific world of Renaissance drama and rhetorical theory and reframing it in terms of the ethical dynamics of participatory politics."[18] The audience is expected to judge, in a real and active participation with the action. Once more the modernity of Shakespeare's perspective extends the message of his play to the contemporary world, where we as citizens are constantly called to judge and evaluate.

---

16 Carolyn Sale, " 'Practis[ing] judgment with the disposition of natures': *Measure for Measure*, the 'Discoursive' Common Law, and the 'Open Court' of the Theater," in *Shakespeare and Judgment*, ed. Curran, 115–138, 115.

17 Paul Yachnin, "The Laws of *Measure for Measure*," in *Shakespeare and Judgment*, ed. Curran, 139–156, 139.

18 Kevin Curran, "Prospero's Plea: Judgment, Invention, and Political Form in *The Tempest*," in *Shakespeare and Judgment*, ed. Curran, 168. See Hannah Arendt, "Personal Responsibility Under Dictatorship," in Responsibility and Judgment, ed. Jerome Kohn (New York: Random House, 2003), 17–48, 18.

Quentin Skinner's volume *Forensic Shakespeare*[19] takes into consideration a series of Shakespeare's plays produced between 1594 and 1605 where his involvement with the technicalities of forensic language is particularly evident. He stresses the frequent use in certain plays of the terms "foul" and "honest," which were frequent rhetorical devices in forensic language. Considering the five principles that Cicero enlists in his *Ars Rhetorica*, "inventio," "dispositio," "elocutio," "pronuntiatio," "memoria," Skinner stresses the place of "inventio" and "dispositio" in the construction of judicial arguments which Shakespeare re-echoes in his plays. Many of his plots are based on judicial controversiae. Skinner objects to most of the critical production on the legal aspects of Shakespeare that, in his opinion, tend to exaggerate Shakespeare's legal competence. On the contrary Skinner asserts that if we wish to explain Shakespeare's particular vocabulary we should rather turn to the rhetorical sources of the scenes. As we have seen, also Raffield revises this concept of Shakespeare's rhetorical skill.

Another interesting perspective that was highlighted by a very recent volume is the performing body: in the Renaissance "the body becomes the focus of the social, legal and cultural imagination and the privileged metaphor for specific cultural discourses and political practices."[20] The body has the function of defining one's identity as distinct from the Other. It also marks the juridical constitution of authority. This legal perspective is necessarily intertwined with visuality, because authority very much leans on its spectacularization. These discourses are strictly connected to the latest studies on law and the image, so deeply influenced by Richard Sherwin's recent production[21], but are also in the trend of performance studies. The "volume demonstrates how the body is positioned centre-stage in the Elizabethan and Jacobean period as the ideological focus of the articulation of power and, at the same time, as a repertoire of infinite (cultural and historical) possibilities." [22]

At the basis of Zurcher's volume *Shakespeare and the Law*[23] is the by-now obvious assessment that the two fields of law and literature are connected through interpretation. The law offered Shakespeare not only a tool for interpre-

---

19 Quentin Skinner, *Forensic Shakespeare* (Oxford: Oxford University Press, 2014).

20 Sidia Fiorato, "Performances, Regulations and Negotiations of the Renaissance Body. Legal and Social Perspectives," in *Performing the Renaissance Body*, eds. Sidia Fiorato and John Drakakis (Berlin and Boston: De Gruyter,2016), 1–26, 11.

21 Richard Sherwin, *When Law Goes Pop* (Chicago and London: The University of Chicago Press, 2000); Richard Sherwin, *Visualizing Law in the Age of the Digital Baroque: Arabesques and Entanglements* (New York: Routledge, 2012).

22 Fiorato, "Performances, Regulations and Negotiations of the Renaissance Body," 36.

23 Andrew Zurcher, *Shakespeare and the Law* (London: Methuen, 2010).

tation, but also an apt language through which to give voice to his insights. This volume stems from the question of what was it that so attracted Shakespeare to legal ideas. "The law offered Shakespeare not just an analogy for the interpretative opportunities and perils facing his own literary art, but a rich and apt language in which to posit and test these insights."[24] Very often in his plays he stresses the interactions between personal interests and legal processes.

François Ost's *Shakespeare. La comédie de la loi*[25] aims at assessing the legal innuendos of Shakespeare's plays. Shakespeare can be considered a major source for our contemporary juridical conscience. As a matter of fact, Ost uses the term "comedy" in his title not to suggest a limitation to his analysis of Shakespeare's comedies, but in the Latin sense of *comoedia* as the whole of human actions. From the very start, Ost stresses the fact that there is a deep interchange between theatre and society in the Renaissance, in that trials have very strong theatrical connotations, being based on ritual and performance. If Greenblatt theorizes about the exchange or negotiation between society and theatre, this definition can also be applied to the interplay between law and Shakespearean theatre.

The Renaissance is characterized by great economic changes, with a merchant class rapidly emerging against a land-owing class, a lurking dissent against absolute monarchy, and the antagonistic force of Puritan individualism resisting Parliament. All this brings about a debate on sovereignty and its legitimacy and on the contraposition between law and equity.[26]

Daniela Carpi has extensively written on some legal perspectives in the Shakespearean texts: from the problems concerning equity and law in *The Merchant of Venice* and *Measure for Measure*[27] to accusations of defeating of defective mind in *Othello*[28]; from *Shakespeare and the Law*[29] to power and legitimacy in *King Lear, King John, Julius Caesar*[30]; from the importance of a name in *Romeo*

---

24 Zurcher, *Shakespeare and the Law*, 3.

25 François Ost, *Shakespeare. La comédie de la loi* (Paris: Michalon, 2012).

26 Daniela Carpi, "Review of François Ost, *Shakespeare. La comédie de la loi*," *Pólemos* 7.1 (2013): 143–148.

27 Daniela Carpi, "Law, Discretion, Equity in *The Merchant of Venice* and *Measure for Measure*," *Cardozo Law Review* 26.6 (2005): 2317–2329.

28 Daniela Carpi, "Law and Aesthetics in Othello," in *Le Cabinet du Curieux. Culture, Savoirs, Religion de l'Antiquité à l'Ancien Régime*, Mélanges en l'honneur de Jean-Paul Pittion, eds. Witold Konstanty Pietrzak and Magdalena Koźluk (Paris: Classiques Garnier, 2013), 79–90.

29 Daniela Carpi ed. *Shakespeare and the Law* (Ravenna: Longo, 2003).

30 Daniela Carpi, "Power and Legitimacy in *King Lear, King John, Julius Caesar*," *Pólemos 10.2* (2010): 85–98

and Juliet[31] to the sacralization/de-sacralization of Caesar's body in *Julius Caesar.*[32]

The rich spectrum of ideas presented by all these volumes demonstrates how fertile the comparative studies on Shakespeare and the law still are and how the Shakespearean texts can still speak to the contemporary legal mind, highlighting fruitful connections between the Renaissance period and the contemporary one.

These connections are drawn together by the innovative perspectives that interdisciplinary and multidisciplinary studies offer in this volume, which broadens the fertile fields of investigation of both the Shakespeare &s and of the Law &s, by interfacing with original aspects of culture. The intersections with meta-criticism, diaspora studies, the body, and the concept of authority, create a multifaceted critical prism whose refractions extend to several areas of knowledge, highlighting how, despite the abundance of literature on the matter, much more can be looked at when it comes to Shakespeare and the Law. If Literature is emotion, Law is in-motion, and it is in virtue of the ever-changing essence of the Law itself that the grandeur of Shakespearean works is to be inquired, for their contemporary value, made clear by diachronic analysis, is not only crucial for a deeper understanding of Early-Modern culture, but becomes essential for an appreciation of the contemporary Self.

---

31 Daniela Carpi, "*Romeo and Juliet:* The Importance of a Name," *Pólemos* 9.1 (2015): 37–50.
32 Daniela Carpi, "Sacralization/De-sacralization of Caesar's Body in Shakespeare's *Julius Caesar,*" *Pólemos* 9.2 (2015): 281–294.

François Ost

As You Law It...: Of Certain Objects and Functions of Ambiguity in Shakespearean Theatre

As you law it... the wordplay inspired by the play *As You Like It* gives a clear access key to Shakespearean law, yet it is digging an abyss beneath its certainties at the same time. As Leiboff notes in her contribution to this volume, a series of previously unseen questions are immediately heard: *can law be liked, what is law like, wat [sic] is like law?* And furthermore: a law for all seasons? A law for each one? Justice on this side of the Pyrenees, injustice on the other? The present collection delivers a rich harvest of the ambiguities which characterise the Shakespearean theatre of the law.

The modern critic, fascinated by this multifaceted kaleidoscope, agrees at least on one point: Shakespeare is elusive. A.D. Nuttall does not hesitate to maintain that on all the essential questions he presents we will never know his definitive point of view.[1] It is as if his mind is never at peace: he scarcely develops one point of view to then contradict it in the next scene. Therefore, we can easily find quotations for and against any given thesis on legal or political problems of some importance. This is disconcerting, without a doubt; yet at least, as J. B White points out, the world is embraced in all its aspects, and the first advantage of this is that we will suspend our hasty judgments and take time to consider the whole scene, beyond the soliloquy and then also beyond the whole play and even the work in its entirety.[2] It is the world and its humanity which Shakespeare makes a spectacle of, and taking only one character or one quote would be like taking the wrong end of a telescope. This ambiguity requires an active and interpretative engagement from the reader – and that is a second benefit. Everyone, in their own time, is led to choose who to support, and soon encounters cruel contradictions in the Shakespearean Hall of Mirrors: if he believed, for example, in the superiority of Christian mercy over formal justice, the story which follows soon instils doubt on the soundness of his interpretation. The perplexity reignites our curiosity, reopens the interpretation game and refines our judgement.

---

translated by Daniela Carpi, Raffaele Cutolo, Kirstie Gifford

1 Anthony Nuttall, *Shakespeare the Thinker* (New Haven and London: Yale University Press, 2007), 1.

2 James Boyd White, *Living Speech* (Princeton and Oxford: Princeton University Press, 2006).

https://doi.org/10.1515/9783110591514-002

And, when the game is interrupted, and the reader finally decides in favour of this or that conclusion, Shakespeare will be, once again, the lucid revelator and the acid test, to the clashing ideologies of his time.

It remains to be seen whether one can ask one's self where this genius of doublespeak, this consummate art of ambiguity comes from. There are three reasons for this, ranked here in order of importance. In certain instances, at least, doublespeak acts simply as a prudent political reflex at a time when censorship was not a theoretical threat, and when taking a position, notably a religious one, could easily send authors to the Tower of London. We remember, in this regard, the persecution which some of Shakespeare's friends and close relations suffered from being suspected of keeping to Catholic practices. In the Catholic world, secrets were a second nature and, from this point of view, it was very shrewd to convince the poet of this or that allegiance. However, this first reason is put forward here only hypothetically.

A second, clearly more solid, reason is found in the critical spirit of the poet. As a witness to the violent ideological, social, political, dynastic controversies of his time, with their cortege of violence, betrayal and cowardice, Shakespeare took a critical distance, and not only for prudent strategic motives. He learned to discern the reality behind the deceptive game of appearances, he knew how to decode the most edifying or flattering remarks and, in doing so, he educates his audience, playing the role of "teacher" of the people, that who teaches men the game of "passions at the foundation cities".

Finally, and this third motive is really decisive, ambiguity is a theatre resource *par excellence*, and Shakespeare is a master in this art. As he is fascinated by themes of duality, of twinship (how many twins are in this work!), of brotherhood (real and false brothers, real and false friends), he also becomes a virtuoso of the false bottoms of all the theses defended by his characters. And if the double fails, it is the hero who doubles himself, and carries these flaws and contradictions within himself: Hamlet is the model for this, but the theme of divided heroes spans across his works. It is no coincidence that the image of "two bodies of the law" haunts his work: the truth of the monarch lies in the gap between the two, as it probably does in each of us, complex enough, human enough, to recognise "oneself as another" (soi-même comme un autre").

Shakespeare does not expose these double-sided truths; he performs them in theatrical performance, he implements them, demonstrating by action and thus bringing them to life in its complexity, but also its incessant metamorphosis. Moreover, it is this ambiguity, which Shakespeare does not ignore for an instant, that equally characterises his audience. He rejoices in allowing two truths to be heard at the same time: "we can say each time that he puts pen to paper, he writes two plays in one" comments René Girard.[3] In the stalls, he serves the audience an intrigue which seems to consolidate all his prejudices; but for those who develop a finer ear, he distills a music which, like the charms of *A Midsummer Night's Dream*, will soon dissolve these heavy certainties. Hamlet says as much to the comedians that come to play at Elsinore: "though it make the unskilful / laugh, cannot but make the judicious grieve; the / censure of the which one must in your allowance / o'erweigh a whole theatre of others" (3.2.26–29).[4]

It will be these ambiguities, double dealings, deceptions, transformations, metamorphoses and shifting of all kinds which I propose to follow in the remainder of this brief introduction. To make an exhaustive list, or claiming to say the definitive meaning would be an exercise in vanity, like drying the sea – *Shakespeare, the ocean man,* Hugo said; at least, I can attempt to raise several themes from the contributions which follow, at the same time proposing several hypotheses as to the functions they fulfil. *King John,* one of Shakespeare's first plays, here analysed by D. Carpi, brings us to the Hall of Mirrors: we are shown all the aspects of an authority led astray, at the same time as speech invalidates itself in the labyrinths of lies and falsehoods. A throne contested between rival powers, alliances which are made and unmade in the will of interests, a people assisting in the play of this comedy of power and determining themselves by the will of success of one or another, of bastards defying the legitimate order of the world... all these ingredients of political theatre are already there, based on the shift in meaning and the disqualification of words, which denounces a chasm between the said and the unsaid. Constance – well named – denounces this corruption of words which expresses the duplicity of souls and the denaturation of authority: "Faith itself to hollow falsehood change" (3.1.21); all is counterfeit, all is nothing but false money, from the moment the Prince who issues money in his own image makes a trade of his speech and his high office. When there is nothing any longer to make it possible to distinguish right from wrong, rhetorical tricks quickly take away convictions and values in a significant shift that is as frightening as it is corrupting. As D. Carpi notes, from that point on, a gulf grows wider between signifying and signified royal authority; the two bodies of the king are broken, as will often be the case thereafter – the sacred and time-

3 René Girard, *Shakespeare. Les feux de l'envie*, trans. B. Vincent (Paris: Grasset, 1990), 13. In Girard's opinion, all first readings are sacrificial, while critical readings are mimetic (each of them able to decode the logics of the scapegoat.)

4 And a little lower down: "And let those that play your clowns speak no more than is set down for them; for there be of them that will themselves laugh, to set on some quantity of barren spectators to laugh too; though, in the mean time, some necessary question of the play be then to be considered" (3.2.39–44).

less (the signified) is no longer found rooted in living kings (the signifying), which destroys power, and, above all, sells off its transcendence in a business of influence which will soon carry them away.

The body – the human body (embryo, child, adult, corpse), the political body, the double body of the king – is a subject *par excellence* of the double dealing of ambiguity. *Richard III*, the monstrous King who illustrates all of the political malfunctions of his time, is the subject of two penetrating studies here, one by C. Battisti and one by S. Fiorato. We know that disability is a social construction, and that each culture develops a different interpretation of it, depending on the place that it intends to reserve for these physical variations within itself. The Elizabethan Renaissance thought of this difference in terms of deformation and monstrosity, which it gladly made shows of on temporary fairground stages. Richard, misshapen and hunchbacked, does not make a mystery of his monstrosity. But in exhibiting it as a challenge to the world, he understands how to twist the astonishment that he arouses to his own profit. He hams up his claimed monstrosity, distorts it, and makes a trophy of it, which will be embellished by ten or twenty tailors and which will be reflected in mirrors that he calls for throughout the play. This deformed natural body which he plays upon, then operates as the instrument of his approbation of the political body that he covets, explains C. Battisti. He, the circus freak, the exception that we fear and are fascinated by, will be the in-action symbol of a Great Britain destined to be in a state of exception. The permanent malfunction of the institutions – the usurping of the throne, assassination carried out as a ruling behaviour, rape passed on as a genealogical law, can openly be read as a spectacularisation of royal monstrosity. In this way, Richard will automatically self-fashion himself through his rhetoric ability and his total lack of scruples, as if he had to take vengeance on the whole world. S. Fiorato has fascinating words to say on the role which the unhappy Queen Anne plays in this story. Seduced right in the middle of the funeral procession for her husband, killed on the orders of Richard himself, she becomes, in defending her *body*, the instrument of this monstrous design. Through her, Richard fashions himself the royal genealogy which was denied to him. In spite of herself, she will uncover a second Ricardian body, monstrous counterfeit of regular genealogy and legitimate authority. Anticipating the manner of national rape which she will soon be subject to, she curses Richard's offspring in advance: "If ever he have a child, abortive be it" (1.2.21).

The figure of the other, *l'autre*, whose most common expression is the stranger, represents an ambiguous favoured theme in Shakespeare's works. And with it, the thorny question of treatment that us, *les mêmes*, that is to say the dominants, will reserve to him. One may well think of *Othello*, of course, but above all of *The Merchant of Venice* which is the subject of two sharp studies here. H.

Antor rightly points out that, far from reducing the play to an antisemitic manifesto, as one often does, we are in the presence of a *problem play:* comedy for the Venetian clan, tragedy for the Shylock the Jew. While it is true that the play does not lack in antisemitic clichés (the Jew as cannibal, the Jew as rabid dog, the Jew as the figure of the Devil), we also remember the magnificent soliloquy in which the ostracised money lender reminds the arrogant Venetians (who invented the term *ghetto*) of the shared humanity of Christians and Jew. All of them have a nose, eyes and ears and all of them are tempted to avenge the offence that was made to them. But this, as we well know, will not render justice to the money lender – Venice will know how to turn this gamble to its advantage and will oppose this creditor who claims to hold on to the letter of his bond, and the absurdity of the logic of his literalism: the pound of flesh, yes, but not a drop of blood. The victors will even return the weight of the debt against the unhappy money lender, robbing him of his goods and forcing him into a conversion which annihilates his racial difference. Moreover, he has the luxury of a lesson in equity taught by Portia under false identity who, cloaked with the generosity of Christian mercy, is faced by the legal threat of the avaricious Jew. We can see what a corrupting role ambiguity plays here, as everything sounds false in this lesson of equity: from the disguising of Portia (who passes herself off as the spokesperson for a wise juris consult) to the legal vengeance of Antonio, the glorious shipowner who, with the blessing of the *doge,* destroys the very identity of his adversary by using the pseudo-literality of the interpretation given to the famous clause in the bond. Equity becomes corrupted in this sham trial, against a playful and triumphant Venice which sometimes allows itself to enjoy the thrill of loss, before the party resumes at Belmont and Shylock returns to his ghetto.

But the lesson is not forgotten, and it is J. Gaakeer's merit to follows its distant but still virulent echoes in German legal doctrine of the end of the nineteenth century. All starts with a footnote in R. Ihering's major work *The Struggle for Law* (1872): the great legal theoretician, who purports a law free of formal constraints and open to social interests, evokes the character of Shylock (alongside that of M. Kohlhaas, Von Kleist's rebel in the eponymous story) as a subject whose rights have been violated and who, in claiming his own law, fights for the integrity of the Law. Ihering makes it very clear that in his eyes the penal clause was null and void, as it contravenes good moral standards; but, he adds, as its validity is recognised by all, it was unjust to deprive Shylock of his profit. "Chicanery" he adds "remains chicanery, even while it uses the name of humanity". The controversy was widespread and a number of authors were against the tolerant and courageous reading given by Ihering. According to them, a certain Josef Kohler congratulates Portia, a creative judge (?) *[sic],* who, with good reason, does not hesitate to redress a bad law when necessary. By claiming to belong to the "free law" movement, Kohler thus aims at enhancing the judge's initiatives in a text (1883) whose anti-Semitic hints proclaim the drift to come. But the debate between justice and equity, its ambiguity and double dealing, will undoubtedly never cease, and neither will the tensions between the Self and the Other. Even at the end of the twentieth century, the controversy reappeared in the production of two major current American "law and literature" authors: Richard Weisberg and Richard Posner.

Measure for Measure, here studied by F. Ost and alluded to by F. Sgubbi, is another *problem play* applied this time to penal law and therefore to the treatment of crime. Games of law and justice take the dramatic form of the sanction (sometimes capital), itself confronted by two alternatives, as radical as they are opposing: private vengeance or forgiveness. At the same time, the figure of the other becomes here one of evil and a criminal – a delinquent who, Shakespeare suggests to the advantage of a new ambiguity, could well be a part of the subject itself; if "I, at least sometimes, am an other," is one not also sometimes a little criminal? It is the masterful lesson that the Duke of an imaginary Vienna will inflict; for a time, he steps away from power to the benefit of the (too) virtuous Angelo (who plays the angel...) – who will not rest until he has restored capital punishment for the crime of fornication. But while he, abusing his own power, proposes "the abhorrent market" to the sister of the first victim of this edict (her virtue for the salvation of her brother), the duplicity of the character, soon confused by the Duke, appears in front of everyone's eyes. But the lesson is general; in the meantime we shall have understood that desire subverts the law, and, above all, that the law is made for the most rigorous (Isabella, the cold novice who, when courted, does not depart from this truth). Also, wisdom recommends applying the law in moderation – and, above all, penal law. The measure of the law, subject of the play, is regulated more by forgiveness than by vengeance – the affair is not solely inspired by comedy, but more by a life logic which ends up dragging everything right into the cold bitterness of death. An enormous burst of laughter and a domino of marriages is the moral of this story, which reminds us that in order to throw the first stone, one must have never sinned. Here, we see the game of ambiguity, omnipresent in the play, whose multiple disguises, substitutions and double-dealings exerts an essential heuristic function: it invites the spectator to take the place of the other, which, all considered, is the basis of an ethical position and, according to H. Arendt, the first condition in the operation of judgement.

The study, as referenced as it is profound, that P. Raffield gives to *The Comedy of Errors* confirms this lesson, with a radicalness that borders on metaphysics. It is impossible to summarise this play based on confusion, and whose first performance, during a memorable evening of revelry at Gray's Inn on the

28th December 1594, turned the telling of this story about several pairs of twins who are lost and found into a general mayhem. And yet: migrants whose boat sinks in the Mediterranean, who finally are found in Ephesus, a town dedicated to business and profit which does not hesitate in throwing them back into the sea – is that not immediately reminiscent of something else? A father of an exiled migrant family, powerless in this hostile environment, who only has a few hours to gather the total ransom which would allow him to escape the death penalty – does that say nothing to us? History repeating itself: Cain and Abel, the enemy brothers dedicated by fate to two different destinies are here Antipholus of Ephesus and his twin brother Antipholus of Syracuse. Will history repeat itself, with its share of exclusions and murders? Here ambiguity is pushed to the extreme – "gém ellité oblige": we can discuss reversibility and transitivity at the same time. And yet what is exchanged between these two twins whom life has separated to the point of setting one against the other? Shakespeare again poses the question "if" – and if it were you? If you were the immigrant seeking asylum, where would you wish to rest your head? Once again the talisman operates: the benevolent duke will pay the father's ransom, and Syracuse's son will fall into the arms of Ephesus's brother. Metaphysics, should I say? Without a doubt, as soon as we know – didn't we notice? – these brothers are called Antipholus, literally the opposite of a friend. One, the lost brother, looking for his identity, lost in a foreign land. The other brother full of hatred, carrier of discord and withdrawn into himself. Like the two divided pieces of the *sun-bolon*. Divided, then eventually reunited. As the chain of gold that Antipholus is looking for for his wife, so the social link is renewed. Brotherhood restored the invisible link that assures agreement between cities, and which Plato said was more essential than the law, which is only the result of it. Once again, life and the symbolic energy that supports it are revealed to be the strongest.

The fact remains that ambiguity does not always have a positive connotation. Sometimes, quite simply, it conveys the inevitable uncertainty of real historical changes: certain forms are therefore consigned to the pages of history, while others bear new uncertain beginnings. The passage from the Republic to the Empire in Rome is an example of this; Shakespearean times, marked by the collapse of the codes of honour from the Middle Ages (the degree), the rise of absolute monarchy, simultaneous with the progress of bourgeois individualism and puritan "rigourism," are another. The play, *Julius Caesar*, commented on here by C. Pelloso, illustrates this painful transition effectively. Pelloso asks the following question: ultimately, do Brutus and the conspirators operate as vulgar murderers ("butchers", as Shakespeare would say) or virtuous sacrificers? The questions must be dealt with according to the Roman concept of *ius sacrum* – and the author notes that in view of this ancient right, whoever was guilty of sacrilege became *proprietas deorum*, there was nothing more that anyone could do for them, and those who lay a hand on that *homo* became *sacer* (literally separated from the community, property of the Gods), benefitting from total impunity. Hence the question: did Caesar fall under the blame of accusation *sacer esto?* Could he have, in flouting the institutions of the Republic, offended the Gods (*adfectatio regni* crime). Doubtless, he refused the crown that was offered to him but, by gathering all the powers to his person, in crossing the invisible border, as Lord Protector of the city (the *pomerium* – here the Rubicon) did he not attempt a serious attack on the institutions? The conspirators sincerely believed so, and considered themselves necessary sacrificers. The Roman Senate put an end to the matter differently, in granting an official funeral to Caesar and treating the conspirators as murderers – while according them impunity, however. This clumsy compromise reflects the limits of ambiguity: far from being meaningful, it expresses the limits of the dialectic and the pure and simple wreckage of a certain form of social bond.

Many other aspects of ambiguity receive an original perspective in this present volume. G. Ben-Nun, specialist in diplomatic history, takes advantage of the play *Henry V*, which, as we know, relates the sombre negotiations between the French and English courts regarding English lands in France (a recurring theme in Shakespeare's historical plays) to underline how the rights of the people (law of nations), so close to brute force, lend themselves to clever manipulation, while the affairs of State only prosper under the shadow of secrecy. These are the famous *arcana imperii* – the state secrets, the perfume of suffering, which surround the abject works of power veiled in smoke. Shakespeare could not fail to be sensitive to it, surely he knew about the proliferation of spies under Elizabeth and the mystical incantations of royalty on the Divine Right Kings under James I. When at the service of absolute power, ambiguity ceases to function and no longer reveals anything.

On the other hand, G. Watt endeavours to do justice, with an attentive ear, to the thousand effects of meaning suggested by the vocalisation of Shakespearean poetry. Before it was a read text, this poetry was recited and heard – the finest ears perceiving there several strategies, including that of *fractional inference*, both concealing and revealing a central word which illuminates a whole scene with its meaning. A practitioner of law would be wrong to neglect these tricks of the trade – is not the law first and foremost an attentive listening to voices who try to make themselves heard in court? In the French language, is the sitting of the court not referred to as the "*audience*" [hearing]? And is the most fundamental principle of law in action not that of the right to a fair hearing: *audi et alteram partem?*

We shall conclude this very brief evocation of the rich contents of this volume, by mentioning the contribution that M. Leiboff gives to *A Midsummer Night's Dream*, the most ambiguous of all the plays in the corpus. The author returns to our starting point: as you like/law it, and engages in a vigorous plea in favour of ambiguity, here envisaged under its imaginative and socially emancipatory side. In her line of fire: all the conservative dogmatisms and withdrawals, like those which finally shatter in the *Dream*. Going back to Chancellor Bacon, contemporary of Shakespeare, the author proceeds to an attentive rereading of *Novum Organon* (1620) and there discovers a new critique in the regulation of theatrical idols. In a very Platonian vein, Bacon shreds the distortions of reality and dressing-ups of reality produced by theatrical tricks – those, he writes, lead to *sciences as one would*. But, as he wrote this in Latin, others translate it as *sciences as you like it*. This, then, is the nature of the offence: imagination leads to departure from truth. We know where this doctrine led the Chancellor in his function as a lawyer: to the punctilious attachment to the letter of the law, firmly assured in his analytic formalism. Didn't Bacon write, seventeen years earlier "it is not good to stay too long in the theatre," inviting his readers to go "to the judicial place or palace of the mind"? M. Leiboff explains that Bacon's lesson was only too well understood by Australian officials and government lawyers of the regime, with things starting to move in the 1980s. Imagination is liberated progressively, political discourse is emancipated from the motherland, while the islanders rediscovered the aborigines who had preceded them on the land, as well as the historical injustices that they were victim to. Therefore, in liberating all the virtues created by an imaginative thought, indexed by the *as you like/law it*, Australian judges were authorised to rewrite history in view of liberating the future – these are the famous *Mabo* High Court decisions (1988 and 1992), known worldwide, which finally gave identity and justice to the natives. In this "Australian Night's Dream," the law renews itself with the force of theatrical imagination. Yes, another world is possible, said Shakespeare, and it is up to you – as you like it.

Part One **The Body Politic and Power Politics**

Daniela Carpi

King John or the Proliferation of the Word of Authority

If up to a few years ago the Elizabethan period was nostalgically studied according to founding orthodox ideologies, such as "the great chain of being" and the "Elizabethan world picture," such a myth of the Arcadian and pastoral past has been dismantled, bringing to the surface symptoms of unrest and anticipations of the many contemporary crises in society.

One of the many tragic dimensions arises "in the displacement of meaning, in the disturbance within the present of 'another' time [...] that, in consequence, is always in some way historical, pivoted upon a crisis of times and so of models."[1]

> The word acquires a cultural mobility of necessary signification for the integration of literature within history and within cultural politics. Such an integration is realized both as a dynamic interaction and as a potentiality of pragmatic intervention of language upon the extra-textual reality.[2]

According to such statements, *King John* becomes the emblem of the search for "the infinite potentialities of dissent inscribed in Shakespearean language, which can be re-inscribed into our daily praxis of social and political conflicts."[3] The tragic element in *King John* is constituted by the recession of the concepts of obedience and loyalty, undermined by the inadequacy of power; and it is represented by the gap between a divine and mythic concept of authority and its application to the historical context, to the quarrel between the two sovereigns.

> The starting position of King John resembles that of Richard III: no legitimate supremacy can be established in a politically volatile period. The cause of the difficulty in this case is a loophole in the regulation defining royal succession.[4]

1 Alessandro Serpieri, "Shakespeare: la storia, le storie," in *L'altro Shakespeare. Critica, Storia, Ideologia*, ed. Alessandra Marzola (Milano, Guerini, 1992), 15–28. [My translation]

2 Alessandra Marzola, "Introduzione," in *L'altro Shakespeare* [My translation.] See also Kiernan Ryan, *Shakespeare* (Brighton: Harvester, 1989).

3 Marzola, "Introduzione" [My translation].

4 Björn Quiring, *Shakespeare's Curse. The Aporias of Ritual Exclusion in Early Modern Royal Drama* (London and New York: Routledge, 2014), 142.

https://doi.org/10.1515/9783110591514-003

From the opening lines the theme of the desecration of the term "majesty" is introduced:

> Chatillon: [...] the borrowed majesty, of England here.
> Elinor: A strange beginning: borrowed majesty![5] (1.1.4–5)

However, the focal point for our analysis is constituted by the dialogue between Constance and Salisbury in Act III, scene I: this is the moment in which Constance is informed of the previous alliance between the two kings, an alliance that makes the promises of help of her brother, king Philip, useless. The "divine" social order represented by the monarchy is unveiled as human/too human, as an artificial and fictional construction (from "majesty" to "counterfeit," from "faith" to "falsehood change"), disclosing an anxiety that becomes a linguistic anxiety, making evident its partial and purely signifying nature. An extremely modern way to place us in front of and within language is thus demonstrated in order to unveil the play's ambiguous and multi-layered structure.

The play upon contrasting words ("form/formless," "order/orderless"), used as a counterpoint to the rapid changing of alliances within the text, is a frequent rhetorical device employed by Shakespeare (bear in mind also the famous "fair is foul and foul is fair" in *Macbeth*), and it underlines the semantic multi-valences of words and of actions in a context of political corruption. The linguistic confusion, which is also a theological interrogation, indicates a previously existing moral confusion.

Constance represents the "resistance to theory" or the resistance to topical concepts of "policy," majesty and honour. The juxtaposition between "seeming" and "being" expressed by Hamlet occupies a considerable part here too. Constance's duty is to unveil the other side of the public message, diametrically opposing meaning to meaning.

All the discourse directed to Salisbury is in fact played upon the contrast between "word" and "sign:" the word is "misspoke" and "misheard," it is a "vain breath" which causes a lack of faith. "Believe me, I do not believe thee:" the essence of the word (the idea of "truth") becomes "false," transforming the concepts of "truth" into "seeming" and of "falsehood" into "being." The epistemological stability of medieval knowledge is made redundant by the use of a rhetoric where the trope of irony and the trope of the unutterability of meaning prevail. After all, the "nostalgia for the lost unity, the univocal correspondence between words and things is the aspiration for the imaginary, a desire to return

5 William Shakespeare, *King John*, in *Complete Works*, eds. Jonathan Bate and Eric Rasmussen (Houndmills: Macmillan 2007), 772–828. Further references in the text.

to simplicity and certainty in a world that comes before symbolic difference, a world that is without visible power, since power itself is a relation of difference."[6]

If "humanism can be defined in the first instance as a rhetorical practice that resists theory conceived of as an epistemological project,"[7] Constance's verbal confutation is used precisely to underline the concept of linguistic imprecision. Such a subversion of "policy" through the dilation of verbal sense corresponds to the general humanistic attitude of the Scholastic critics as a formulation of universal principles, and it corresponds to the emergence of rhetoric in its aspect of attention to the linguistic dimension of communication.

The word thus becomes epistemologically unstable. Constance is the figure of the humanist who undermines the stability of language and, at the same time, attempts to resist such an instability. The word is divorced from its practical application, creating a semantic gap: "signs" (gestures, actions) vs. "words".

> It is not so, thou hast misspoke, misheard,
> Be well advised, tell o'er thy tale again.
> It cannot be, thou dost but say 'tis so.
> I trust I may not trust thee, for thy word
> Is but the vain breath of a common man:
> Believe me, I do not believe thee, man,
> I have a king's oath to the contrary.
> [...]
> Be these sad signs confirmers of thy words?
> Then speak again, not all thy former tale,
> But this one word, whether thy tale be true. (3.1.4–26)

This juxtaposition occurs also between the "tale," that is, an account, narration, or linguistic articulation, and the "word." Within this structural binary opposition an even more hidden subversion is situated, since it is realized within the meaning itself of "word" that from time to time represents the meaning of true or false.

Constance repeatedly exhorts Salisbury to make his "word" and "truth" coincide, but the truth, the real essence of the term, cannot be attained since it slides once again to the level of "false," making any attempt to attain a stable and founding meaning redundant.

6 Catherine Belsey, "Creare storie ora ed allora: da *Riccardo II* a *Enrico V*" in *L'altro Shakespeare*, ed. Marzola, 129–155, 130 [My translation].

7 Victoria Khan, "Humanism and the Resistance to Theory" in *Literary Theory. Renaissance Texts*, eds. David Quint and Patricia Parker (Baltimore and London: The Johns Hopkins University Press, 1986), 373–396, 382.

Another element, emerging from this incessant alternation between the levels of linguistic truth and falsehood, is the narrative, or the "tale." The tale is a necessarily artificial organization of the "word" and consequently it puts an emphasis on fictionality: the tale implies a narrator's awareness of both the resistance of language to signify and of the resistance of the listener to the "suspension of disbelief." In such a way the principle of counterfeit, and consequently Constance's exhortation to make the "tale" "true," is transformed into a contradiction in terms and an exhortation to an impossible mimesis. Following Aristotle's dialectic, it can be maintained that the *téchné*, or productive knowledge, aware of the application of rhetorical artifice, clashes against the *theoria*, or speculation, the *mise en abîme* of meaning through rhetoric itself. The movement is from social consensus (adherence to the "policy" dictates and to the sovereign's decisions) to epistemological menace (the redundancy of the sovereign's orders through dialectic/rhetorical subversion). The use of irony becomes an exemplary practice to unveil the epistemological/ethical multi-valence of meaning.

Just as Constance questions the official meaning of the message, controverting term with term, in the same way the two opposing struggles for royalty lead to a vacancy in power and to a suspension of loyalty and adherence. Constance does nothing but give voice to this ambiguity of power that is affirmed and denied at the same time. We are witnesses to a reaction of discomfort towards authority, which is *in primis* expressed as linguistic anxiety. In an "out of joint" world, where the univocal power of authority is broken, causing loyalty problems in the subjects (which king to believe in?), "strength and signification" are separated so that the separation itself (between sign and meaning) becomes the linguistic condition *par excellence:* the new strength of language lies precisely in its non-signification. The form (the dilation of meaning and carnivalesque, desecrating play) is opposed to the (theological and signifying) strength of linguistic articulation.

We witness the melancholic pathos of speech that turns on its own axis searching for a missing referent, attaining in this way a neutralization of meaning through form. The message (*energeia*) of power is in fact neutralized by a linguistic invasion, by a deconstructing play, which undermines the very basis of its own significance, becoming a historical-metaphysical menace to its own foundations. As soon as the sacred concept of royalty is annihilated by the conflict between the two opposing kinds of legality, a subverting element, here mainly expressed as linguistic subversion, insinuates itself into the gap in power. A "Holy day" is transformed into a "wicked day, day of shame," "war" is mutated into "peace" and vice versa, and "little valiant" into "great villainy:" everything is "painted" and "counterfeit" so that at the end we have a total coalescence of opposites: "odoriferous stench" and "sound rottenness." In such diametrical oppositions signification lingers in a linguistic void of the absence of the referent, of a methodical menace that is a denunciation of the frailty of meaning and of the relation between signifier and signified. The linguistic confusion points to a previous moral confusion and is a theological interrogation. It is a bombastic use of the word based upon the rhetoric that is a symptom of the *ad infinitum* openness of significance, a symptom of the anarchy of the message once it is freed from the *imprimatur* of power.

Constance's linguistic anxiety mirrors the perplexity of the citizens: "the split between legitimacy and actual power was always a potential malfunction in the developing Absolutist State."[8] In other words, the struggle between the two legitimacies questions the concept of legitimacy itself, overtly opposing it to the rights of those who can take and maintain power. In practice we are dealing with a crisis of authority that becomes absence and obsession with the divine sign of royalty, mutating into a problematic sign, a desperate symbol of the end of theological optimism that does not express the universe any longer but rather shows it as separate and insecure. In this way the subjects fill the gap in power and claim the right to argue about the principle of loyalty, and to discuss and to theorize on the formation of regal power. "In *King John* and *Richard II* Shakespeare invites us to question the capacity of individual will to determine the destination of the crown and of other landed estates," asserts Watt in his *Shakespeare's Acts of Will.*[9]

> Citizen: He that proves the king,
> To him will we prove loyal. Till that time
> Have we rammed up our gates against the world. (2.1.270–273).

"The conflict before the walls of Angiers is between traditional lineal succession and individual will, but the subject matter of the issue between King Philip and King John concerns nothing less than the proper descent of the English crown."[10] The citizens take active part in this contest, and are not mere bystanders. The result is the passage of authority from monarch to commoners.

The loyalty of the citizens is put up for auction and offered to the best bidder: "One must prove greatest: while they weigh so even, / We hold our town for

8 Alan Sinfield, "*Macbeth:* History, Ideology and Intellectuals," in *New Historicism and Renaissance Drama*, eds. Richard Wilson and Richard Dutton (London and New York: Longman, 1992), 63–77, 68.

9 Gary Watt, *Shakespeares's Acts of Will: Law, Testament and Property* (London and New York: Bloomsbury, 2016), 63.

10 Watt, *Shakespeares's Acts of Will*, 65.

neither; yet for both" (2.1.332–333). This is a declaration of the decline of a universe based on the oral (or implied) transmission of principles and the emergence of the written code: bear in mind how the generational betrayal of the concept of monarchy by divine right changes into the necessity of written pacts, even to sell one's own soul as in *Doctor Faustus*. The word, becoming mad, affirming and negating itself, mirrors the collapse of the medieval principles of loyalty and honour, causing a new bourgeois and mercantile mentality to emerge, where everything is traded, even loyalty. The evolution from tradition to a new mercantile perspective is made evident for instance in *Richard II*, where the action of Richard's giving and Bolingbroke's taking the crown looks as if they were shaking hands upon a bargain.

Therefore the point where the citizens themselves decree the canon of the behaviour of kings is reached, and the citizens offer the two kings the possibility of a "friendly treaty": the youths of both families should be united in marriage, thus returning to a unitary regal concept. The principles of loyalty and of the sacredness of royalty are submerged by the flow of words of the Citizen, who with his logorrhea decrees the finiteness of a theological meaning, relegated to mere historicity:

> Here's a large mouth indeed,
> That spits forth death and mountains, rocks and seas[...]
> What cannoneer begot this lusty blood?
> He speaks plain cannot fire, and smoke and bounce,
> He gives the bastinado with his tongue.
> Our ears are cudgelled – not a word of his
> But buffets better that a fist of France:
> Zounds I was never so bethumped with words (2.1.458–468).

This accusation of logorrhea sounds even more paradoxical by being pronounced precisely by the Bastard who is not characterized by linguistic economy either. In fact, the Bastard, like Constance, is also a real "corruptor of words" who, thanks to his "abundance of superfluous breath", causes the "break[ing] off of your conference" (2.1.147–150), that is, the dialogue between Austria, King Philip and King John; in this case, once again, the flow of words makes the dignity of authority redundant.

A hierarchical universe in defection receives the *coup de grâce* of rhetoric which, using the ironic juxtaposition between "grandam" and "mother," causes a parallel universe made of words to emerge, words that are independent from the socio-political referent. What was a dynastic struggle is transformed into a war of paradoxical "wit," underlining a purely logocentric dimension. We are thrown into an upside-down world, in a "plagued bedlam" of inflated words.

Similarly, Constance mainly recurs to the reiteration of terms such as "plague," "will" and "grandam" to create a thick verbal fog ("Words folded up in smoke," "ill-tuned repetitions" – 2.1.229,198), which envelops, as in a torpor, precisely this meaning of royalty. The monarchy, or authority, is thus degraded to a theory to be demonstrated: "K. John: Acknowledge then the king [...] /Citizen: That we cannot: but he that proves the king/ To him will we prove loyal" (2.1.268–270). Royalty is transformed into "performance," "scenes" and "acts," and the citizens become spectators to this performance: it is up to the king to convince his subjects regarding his legitimacy and in this way the stress is moved from a concept of unconditioned loyalty to a concept of loyalty to be won.

> By heaven, these scroyles of Angiers flout
> You kings and stand securely on their battlements,
> As in a theatre, whence they gape and point
> At your industrious scenes and acts of death. (2.1.373–377)

The meta-theatrical opening, which characterizes almost all of Shakespeare's works, here underlines the critical and detached, scornful and derisory, attitude through which authority is observed, and this marks the decline of total adherence and the emergence of mutiny. Authority is degraded to a mere term that has to fight for its own referent and becomes an alternative.

Such a fragmentation is brought to light precisely by the choice between the two different monarchies and it is offered to citizens, freeing them from the necessity of loyalty: the imbalance of the preference ends up subverting a system of objective relations, a relational configuration that thus becomes a methodological decision, giving rise to a critical and disenchanted reading of the ontological aims of royalty itself and to a reflection on the concept of authority as a theoretical norm. The citizens are transformed into readers of a text, of a "play" or "script" of war action that is written "with purple hands/ Dyed in the dying slaughter of their foes" (2.1.322–323).

Therefore, the acts of the kings are converted into narration, fictionalisation, theatrical action, *reductio ad absurdum* and phono-logocentrism devoid of morphological correlation. This intrinsic harmony, founded upon the social hierarchical structure of Tillyardean memory, paradoxically turns out to be an artificial construction that by then lacked consensus; as in any form of narration, if the listener, or the consenting spectator is missing, the word falls into a void and it cannot fulfil its duty as the creator of the message. Bear in mind the necessity of the listener in the accomplishment of the cathartic aims in *The Rhyme of the Ancient Mariner*, and in Prospero's exhortations in *The Tempest* to Miranda to listen to his tale. Therefore in *King John* the concept of royalty is put into question precisely because of the continuous verbal dilation that is used and because of the fact that the subjects do not passively listen to the tale of authority any longer, but rather they wake up from such an almost hypnotic form of adherence to power in order to question its auraticity.

"Monarchy" is degraded into an assumption to be demonstrated, it causes the founding skeleton of its own structure to emerge, and this becomes an object of investigation and interrogation. The split between the signified (the sacred meaning of the term) and the signifier (the *personae* of the two kings) leaves a power vacuum into which the common man insinuates himself: so it is the Bastard that governs the kings, who clearly demonstrate a decision making inability.

> Your royal presences be ruled by me. (2.1.378)

> O prudent discipline! From north to south!
> Austria and France shoot each other's mouth.
> I'll stir them to it. (2.1.413–417)

The gap in power is manifested in a linguistic subversion that is the cause of a free fall into the abyss of non-significance, but also an effect. What emerges from this is an inversion of political and verbal strength: now the subjects apply the "policy" and express authority. Now the subjects, in a total subversion of roles, administer demiurgic linguistic power. The authority principle has become a metaphorical play, a deferral between sender and receiver in a confusion of models that relativizes meaning. The "word" is still powerful but it is a "tale," the social and organic structure that came to a crisis.

The power of the word is set against the power of authority and the Bastard's statements ("Here's a large mouth indeed") mentioned above describe precisely the image of authority/legitimacy besieged and attacked by the word. Language here represents a physical element and a means of aggression: subversion has its origin in the "cannonade" of the word. The power of the word is also epitomized by the various curses that run through the play. Basically the term "curse" indicates a reaction to a transgression. Dating back to the Bible, the curse indicated either an act of punishment by God or an appeal to God's justice. The curse implies a juridical order which has in some way been violated and which must be restored through the curse. In this perspective, the curse has a transcendental value: it is established as strictly connected to law, which it presupposes and determines at the same time. Basically the term indicates a reaction to a transgression.

Like the avenger, the curser appears to act in God's name: he acts as God's mouthpiece to reaffirm the law but, at the same time, he becomes blemished by the utterance. The curser shows his power in the utterance but is endangered by it: power and impotence are mixed in the act of cursing, because the curse follows a ritual but it also marks a state of exception. Therefore the curse is an ambiguous act that is an exception on one hand, but is ritualized on the other hand, thus becoming a political act. Correctly, Quiring asserts that the curse can be set as a borderline: it is an individual act that operates onto a body politic.

The double register, legal and linguistic, clashes against the dramatic agon in a process of affirmation/negation of legitimacy/authority, in a disrupting disquisition on the right to power. An already unstable universe of royalty (as it results from the first part of the text where the decision making ability is seen as falling to the subjects) is checked due to "perjury." The king's betrayal of the word is transformed into "original sin" which infringes the edenic world of legality and transforms it into "counterfeit," "painted peace," "forsworn:" "All things begun come to ill end" (3.1.94).

Actually the tear in the fabric of authority is transformed into the collapse of a whole linguistic universe that becomes its own opposite: from reality to "falsehood," from "majesty" to "counterfeit," from "peace" to "war." In this way the linguistic subversion mirrors the hierarchical chaos into which society fell because of the sin of "perjury" committed by the king. The missing word makes the canon explode, and it becomes an abyss of non-significance in which respect for authority collapses and makes the pact stipulated between the monarch and the subjects redundant, opening a chasm that becomes a linguistic chasm. Here Constance's verbal violence gives voice precisely to this dissent within legitimacy and seems particularly subversive exactly because it is the woman, the "other" *par excellence*, who expresses it. Such is the case that her irreverent jest to the king, "And hang a calf's skin on those recreant limbs" (3.1.129), is recalled by the Bastard more than once, and by the "fool", the other discordant element, who is always speaking from the margins of society. If the woman and the "fool" normally share a peripheral and marginal position within Elizabethan texts and what would otherwise constitute high treason is here permitted to them, in this text they are the spokesmen of an uneasiness that is recalled and amplified also by the subjects and which consequently constitutes an overt element of subversion recurring in the text.

Such a critical and reflexive awareness offers an insight into the operations of power and it also becomes an insight into the changeable aspects of history. The sacredness of royal power is connected to the time of immortality: it is a perpetuation in time by legitimate heredity until the achievement of mythical time. Bear in mind the attempt to make the day of the alliance between the two kings sacred:

> [...] this blessed day
> Ever in France shall be kept festival:
> To solemnize this day, the glorious sun
> Stays in his course and plays the alchemist,
> Turning with splendour of his precious eye
> The meagre cloddy earth to glittering gold. (3.1.75–81)

The allusion is to the stopping of the sun on its course and to the fixity of the solemnity of that moment. But the "day", here meant as the eternal day of the present, is transformed into mortality and oppression because of the sin of "perjury" committed by the king. The cosmic upheaval caused by the violation of the word also involves the passage of time, which is mutated into thanatoic time:

> A wicked day, and not a holy day!
> [...] return this day out of the week,
> This day of shame, oppression, perjury.
> [...] This day, all things begun come to ill end. (3.1.83–96)

The passage is from a concept of a Golden Age to a biblical hell of damnation and of loss. The royal perjury rendered the concept of "majesty" a "counterfeit," a shadow ("resembling majesty"), also subverting the semantic value of terms such as "war" and "peace."

Constance's words, along with the Bastard's, are Dionysian leaps in the antiform, into desecration and into opposition, and they rebel against the Apollonian structure required by authority: it is a matter of the primordial urge towards the codification of meaning within the law. But the obedience to the law ceases precisely when the legal pact is not accomplished by authority itself. We are in a total travail, in danger of interrogation. The agonistic dimension becomes a rhetorical dimension, inside and outside sense itself, in a continuous negation of the words of authority that are formed into a banished object, into something other than the self. The language of subversion presupposes, however, a primitive adherence to the principle of authority.

The interweaving of given and withdrawn words creates a tangle of oaths and perjuries that, in the impossibility itself of the concept of loyalty, are both loyal to one side and necessarily disloyal to another side. Pandulph's speech in Act III, scene I, in fact, plays completely upon the ambivalence of the terms "swear/forsworn," semantically tied to "faith" and "oath." The whole speech is posited in an absolute dilation *ad infinitum* of a few key words, which keep legality and authority together.

Such a making and unmaking of meaning brings about cosmic chaos, almost Armageddon: "The sun overcast with blood" (3.1.327); "This day grows / wondrous hot,/ Some airy devil hovers in the sky,/ And pours down mischief" (3.2.1–4). We witness nature's rebellion against the reiterated violation of a hierarchical order that reminds us of the unnatural phenomena scattered throughout *Macbeth* and the various (metaphorical and non metaphorical) tempests of Shakespearean works: everything indicates a rupture and a dismemberment of the social corpus (here represented by Blanch, who first becomes Lewis's wife, and is then torn between the husband's and the uncle's factions). Such a rupture in authority, however, has an ominous influence on social harmony: "Whoever wins, on that side shall I lose" (3.1.335).

The wavering of authority requires continuous confirmations and here King John's second coronation demonstrates the uncertainty of the sovereign: the whole text of *King John* is permeated precisely by the problem of "guard[ing] a title" (4.2.10). Authority needs the allegiance of the subjects since the concept exists only as long as there is a concordance of meaning: the convergence of meaning between *destinateur* and *destinataire* creates a harmonious circle where the hierarchy is located. The interruption in the convergence provokes a language without support, an articulation in a syntax of reason opposed to a syntax of authority: such an interruption provokes the questioning of a metaphysical principle that is foundational against a metaphorical pathos.

The linguistic juxtaposition reveals an even wider lack of centre in the text. As John Blanpied correctly observes: "The effect is of dissipated strength[...] It is a play in which nothing seems to take root [...] Split of the power centre [...]"[11] The loss of a stable centre in the "play" is rendered also through the images of dismemberment: bear in mind Blanch's words:"They whirl asunder and dismember me"(3.1.326). The clash is between two, paradoxically inverted, models of history: Constance and the Bastard seem to be connected to a classical view of authority, conferred with legitimacy by divine and hereditary right founded upon concepts of honour and respect to the given word, whereas King John symbolizes the "new rationalistic and sceptical laicism" that is typical of the "new bourgeois civilization and of the new science," founded upon the principle of "commodity."[12]

In a reading that pivots on the concept of power, "resistance could be seen as otherness that defines power in that it differentiates from it and that, there-

11 John W. Blanpied, "Stalking Strong Possession in *King John*," in *William Shakespeare: Histories and Poems*, ed. Harold Bloom (New York, Chelsea House, 1986), 98–119, 98.
12 James L. Calderwood, "Commodity and Honour in *King John*," in *Shakespeare: The Histories*, ed. Eugene M. Waith (Englewood Cliff: Prentice Hall, 1965), 341–356.

fore, guarantees its existence."[13] "In order to give justice to the complexity of both power and the Shakespearean theatre, a theory of textuality, taking into consideration the meaning of the terms difference and deferral, is necessary,"[14] but in the world of Shakespearean historical plays, as Belsey also correctly observes, we cannot really talk about "difference," since such a concept would imply the existence of metaphysical certainty, of a univocal concept of power that such historical plays do not really portray, since they narrate the endless alternation of such royal absolutisms so as to question dynastic legitimacy itself. Thus, using a definition by Derrida, in my opinion we should talk about *différance* which reasserts an endless uncertainty. Constance's rebellion and the subverting-commenting function of the Bastard are precisely the linguistic outcome of royalty, the linguistic invasion of a universal/theological concept of power where the sense of absolute is lost in order to make it a centre of a system of differences.

"The absence of a transcendental signified extends the domain and the play of signification infinitely."[15] We are dealing with a decentering that leads to a rethinking of the structurality of power itself. A metaphysics founded upon principles of interpretation and sign substitutes a previous metaphysics based upon concepts of Being and Truth. Royalty is reduced to "sign" and leaves the field of its own privileged signification.

13 Belsey, "Creare storie ora ed allora," 136. [My translation]
14 Belsey, "Creare storie ora ed allora," 145. [My translation]
15 Jacques Derrida, *Writing and Difference* [1967] (London: Routledge, 1997), 280.

Chiara Battisti

Richard the Freak: The Dis-ability to Show Power

1 *Disability Studies:* the theoretical approach[1]

> In mythology it is a universal characteristic of men born from the Earth that at the moment they emerge from the depth they either cannot walk or they walk clumsily.[2]

Claude Levi-Strauss' words – which evoke the image of fascinating one legged creatures, of heroes struggling to walk upright, of crippled gods, and of limping gaits – emphasize how disability and body's anomalies are not only biological, social, and cultural conditions, which exist in every historical time. Indeed, within Western culture, they take on a founding and representative function of the complex relationship of human beings to Earth, thus becoming important archetypes for the self-representation of the body. The totality of cultural activities establishing links between disability inscribed in the bodies and their social construction is evident; yet any form of impairment and especially its social codification as disability has been for a long time excluded from traditional fields of knowledge. This exclusion has caused a vacuum that is at the same

---

1 Cf. Lennard J. Davis, *Bending Over Backwards (*New York and London: New York University Press, 2002); Lennard J. Davis, *Enforcing Normalcy: Disability, Deafness and the Body* (London and New York: Verso, 1995); Lennard J. Davis ed., *The Disability Studies Reader* (New York: Routledge, 1997); Roberto Medeghini ed., *Norma e normalità nei Disability Studies: Riflessioni e analisi critica per ripensare la disabilità* (Trento: Erickson, 2015); Alice Hall, *Literature and Disability* (New York and London: Routledge, 2015); David Mitchell, Sharon L. Snyder, *Narrative Prosthesis: Disability and the Dependencies of Discourse (*Ann Arbor: University of Michigan Press, 2000); David Mitchell, Sharon L. Snyder, *Cultural Locations of Disability* (Chicago: University of Chicago Press, 2006); Mike Oliver, *The Politics of Disablement* (London: Macmillan, 1990); Mike Oliver, *Understanding Disability, from Theory to Practice* (London: Macmillan, 1996); Tobin Sieber, *Disability Theory* (Michigan; University of Michigan Press, 2008); Matteo Schianchi, *Storia della disabilità* (Roma: Carocci, 2013); Matteo Schianchi, *Disabilità* (Milano: Bruno Mondadori, 2013); Ato Quayson, *Aesthetic Nervousness* (New York: Columbia University Press, 2007); Henri-Jacques Stiker, *A History of Disability.* (Ann Arbor: University of Michigan Press, 1999); David M. Turner, Kevin Stagg, *Social Histories of Disability and Deformity: Bodies, Images and Experiences* (New York: Routledge, 2006).

2 Claude Lévi-Strauss, *Structural Anthropology* (New York: Basic Books, 1963), 215.

https://doi.org/10.1515/9783110591514-004

time "a mirror of the socio-cultural taboo represented [...] by disability and a contribution to the reproduction of marginalization."[3]

Therefore, if the persistence of an ancestral prejudice towards disability is ascribable to the cultural irrelevance willingly given to this matter – indirectly exposed by this scholarly neglect – an important role in perpetrating the logic of denial and of stigmatizing silence may also be attributed to the difficult comprehension of a term, such as "disability," "that did not exist in the past,"[4] a term whose meaning is muddled and ambiguous also in the present time. In fact, "[i]t is not immediately clear whether it is an expression identifying a specific disability or the person affected by that disability or the social position of the handicapped person. Often the meanings are obscure and confusing."[5] Recent researches in the field of disability studies have contributed to a partial solution of this conceptual incomprehension and to the codification of its problematic features. These studies cast an explicatory light on the phenomenon of disability. They developed along the line of cultural politics upheld by the initiative of people subjected to various forms of exclusion and marginalization; this field of research has analysed the complexity – often rejected by simplistically arbitrary interpretations – which characterizes the concept of disability by relating such a concept to a biological condition, but also by revealing the social pressure through which the person differing from the norm is designated as disabled.

Disability studies, grown out of the cultural studies established in Great Britain in the Seventies of the twentieth century, have progressively consolidated acquiring the status of an academic discipline thanks to the work of British scholars such as Mike Oliver and Vic Finkelstein. In the 1980s these analytical studies began to be recognized as a new, stimulating, and critical approach by the Anglo-Saxon world, the United States, Australia, Northern Europe, and France. Although presented under one label, disability studies appear as a diversified research field that can hardly be brought back to a sole unifying theory, as its definition seems instead to suggest. The diversification of approach can also be traced back to and determined by the programmatic will of the movement to modify the cultural paradigm through which the concept of disability is interpreted, using a research that involves a variety of disciplinary fields, such as, for instance, sociology, law, philosophy, and psychology.

---

3 Schianchi, *Storia della Disabilità*, 14. [My translation.]
4 Schianchi, *Storia della Disabilità*, 17. [My translation.]
5 Schianchi, *Storia della Disabilità*, 4. [My translation.]

Disability studies analyse the society within which the disabled person lives, they critically challenge a functionalist medical paradigm that has suggested conceptualizations regarding disability and deficiency considered as individual elements based on the *causal* link between impairment and disability. From the perception of disability studies, disability can no longer be conceived as a deviation from normality, nor can the social experience of the disabled person be considered without taking into account the contextual factors provoking the exclusion. In such a critical scrutiny, the distinction between impairment and disability is founding. As stressed by Leonard Davis, an important spokesperson for this critical movement, a physical deficiency implies a biological, cognitive, sensorial or psychological difference, whereas disability is the result of a negative social reaction to such a difference.

> An impairment involves a loss [...] of sight, hearing, mobility, mental ability, and so on. But an impairment only becomes disability when the ambient society creates an environment with barriers- affective, sensory, cognitive, or architectural.[6]

Impairment is a real and physical condition, whereas disability is a social and political construction. The very concept of normality is a cultural construct: "the problem is not the person with disabilities; the problem is the way normalcy is constructed to create the "problem" of the disabled body."[7] The critical charge against the medical model of the approach to disability can therefore be attributed to the assumption, supported and promoted by such an approach, that sickness is a form of deviance, a disturbance to the social order, and that disability is an "abnormal" or "unnatural' condition in contrast with the normality of other people. According to the medical template, the integration of disabled people in society therefore envisages a process of rehabilitation and normalization.[8]

The social model[9] constituting the theoretical framework of disability studies challenges the medical approach[10] in opposing the construction of disability

---

6 Lennard J. Davis, "Constructing Normalcy: the Bell Curve, the Novel, and the Invention of the Disabled Body in Nineteenth Century," in *The Disability Studies Reader*, ed. Lennard J. Davis (New York: Routledge, 2006), 17.

7 Lennard J. Davis, "Introduction: Normality, Power, and Culture," in *The Disability Studies Reader*, ed. Lennard J. Davis (New York: Routledge, 2006), 9.

8 Cf. Talcott Parsons, *The Social System* (New York and London: Routledge, 1951).

9 Oliver, *The Politics of Disablement*.

10 Although critically opposing the medical model, the social model acknowledges the contribution that medical science has brought and can still bring to the improvement of the lifestyle of disabled persons. What is criticized in this model is, rather, the gaze cast on the individual, considered as an unfortunate subject. Mike Oliver, precisely in order to avoid inaccurate critical al-

as an individual phenomenon; instead, it chooses to identify those factors that "disable" the human being (the appropriate term being "disablement"). The effort not to focus on the biological condition supported by the social model does not mean, however, forgetting the individual his/her pathological condition, but rather concentrating on issues to be shared by a subjective collectivity and therefore likely to be used in political struggles. The supporters of disability's social model actually expose the society's tendency to isolate the disabled person, underscoring instead the importance of cohesion in sharing ideals and objectives.

> It is society which disables physically impaired people. Disability is something imposed on top of our impairments by the way we are unnecessarily isolated and excluded from participation in society. Disabled people are therefore an oppressed group in society.[11]

The study of disability's social stigma does not involve only its medical, legal, and sociological aspect, but also the humanistic one, namely, the representation of disability in historical, literary, and artistic perspective[12]. The analysis of disability within the context of humanistic research answers to and is in correspondence with the programmatic objectives of the social model because it constitutes in itself "a way of resisting the idea that disability is a personal tragedy or a pathologised medical issue."[13] Far from dealing with the silence and the absence of disabled beings as found in political and social life, literary texts return very frequently and with different perspectives to the theme of disability that becomes, in turn, an effective metaphor for social anxiety, or the "fulcrum or pivot out of which various discursive details emerge, gain salience, and ultimately undergo transformation,"[14] taking on "a defamiliarizing effect on the basic categories of identity and of literary criticism."[15] As for the latter aspect, Tobin Sieber in his *Disability Theories* strongly argues for a link between instability, disability, and identity; he calls attention to how "the presence of disability creates a different picture of identity – one less stable than identities associated with gender, race, sexuality, nation, and class – and therefore presenting the opportunity

---

lusions about the work of professionals and to medical contributions, prefers using the concept of "individual model" of disability and model of social oppression.

11 Michael Oliver, *Understanding Disability, from Theory to Practice* (London: Palgrave Macmillan, 1996), 22.

12 Catherine J. Kudlick, "Disability History: Why We Need Another 'Other'," *American Historical Review* 108 (June 2003): 763–793. http://www.historycooperative.org/journals/ahr/108.3/kudlick.html (last access July 20, 2016).

13 Hall, *Literature and Disability.*

14 Quayson, *Aesthetic Nervousness*, 34.

15 Hall, *Literature and Disability*, 39.

to rethink how human identity works."[16] Understanding and analysing the cultural and literary representation through the critical lens of disability studies implies bringing into play alternative readings concerning concepts of culture and power by analysing, first of all, the notion of norm.

Having clarified the critical potential of applying the approach of disability studies to literary research, it is however necessary to state a methodological caveat. Actually, such an analysis entails a contemporary conceptual and terminological projection on a time when disability was not a codified concept as it now is:

> From a methodological viewpoint it is [...] necessary to keep in mind that the very concept of disability through time is not unequivocal. It is conceptually wrong to project onto the past our present perceptions, especially in epochs preceding the previous century, when the health conditions of the total population were much more precarious.[17]

Contemporary criticism acknowledges the necessity of a historical sensibility that goes along with the application of theories and of contemporary concepts to the literature of the past. However, it is also appropriate to consider Lois Bragg's belief that disability was defined and redefined in the course of years and centuries.[18] In his *Oedipus Borealis: The Aberrant Body in Old Icelandic Myth and Saga*, Bragg highlights that in the course of the centuries different attitudes have emerged on the theme of disability, as well as different definitions of a concept at any rate always present in intellectual evaluations, in collective consciousness, and in every epoch linked to the reflection on deficiency and disability.

Recent critical studies[19] emphasize, however, how the social process of the definition of "disabled" people has become institutionalized with the progress of industrialization and through practices and formal debates dating back to the end of the eighteenth century and nineteenth century. Proponents of English Historical Materialism,[20] (with particular reference to Antonio Gramsci's categories, for what concerns the work of Vic Finkelstein, Mike Oliver, and Colin Barnes) have called attention to the role of industrial capitalism and the resulting development of the production sector based on assumptions of skillfulness;

---

16 Sieber, *Disability Theory*, 5.

17 Schianchi, *Storia della disabilità*, 35.

18 Lois Bragg, *Oedipus Borealis: The Aberrant Body in Old Icelandic Myth and Saga* (Madison, NJ: Fairleigh Dickinson University Press, 2004), 167.

19 Stiker, *A History of Disability*; Schianchi, *Storia della disabilità*; Turner, Stagg, *Social Histories of Disability and Deformity: Bodies, Images and Experiences.*

20 Anne Borsay, *Disability and Social Policy in Britain since 1750*, (London: Palgrave, 2005); Brendan Gleeson, *Geographies of Disability* (London and New York: Routledge, 1999).

these factors have relegated disabled persons to a position of marginality and dependency that has found its codification in the discourse on "normality." In support of such a position, Leonard Davis, for example, reminds us that in English the term "normal" – whose ambiguous link with the noun "norm" is more than obvious – with the meaning of "constituting, conforming to, not deviating, or different from, the common type or standard, regular, usual" entered the common language around 1840.[21] Similarly, the term "norm" in its contemporary meaning was included in dictionaries since 1855.

2 English Renaissance and disability

If it is only in the last part of the eighteenth century and during the nineteenth, that "the systematized, divided structure of normal and abnormal bodies [...is] institutionalized, treated, and made into a semiology of metonymic meanings,"[22] the obvious question is how debates concerning non-normative identities were conducted during the Renaissance. This is the historical period when William Shakespeare wrote *Richard III* (1591–1592), the last of his four dramatic works dedicated to English history.

According to Allison Hobgood and David Houston Wood, a "notion of early modern disability is not anachronistic because human variation, though conceived of and responded to diversely, has always existed."[23] The text quoted above takes on and restates Bragg's conviction, cited earlier, that disability is an identity category present in every epoch and understood to designate the "human variation." Even if the lemma was not yet present in the dictionary, the concept of disability existed. It evoked different images, taking on different meanings when applied to sixteenth- and seventeenth-century England because such a concept was strongly influenced by the scientific and cultural episteme of the time. From this perspective David Turner and Kevin Stagg in *Social Histories of Disability and Deformity* call attention to the fact that "in the early modern period the concept of disability was subsumed under other categories, notably deformity and monstrosity."[24] Furthermore, many critics highlight that such a topic can be connected to concepts derived from classic aesthetics, to the Medieval

21 Davis, *Enforcing Normalcy: Disability, Deafness and the Body*, 24, chapter 2, passim.
22 Davis, *Bending over Backwards: Disability, Dismodernism, and Other Difficult Positions*, 66.
23 Allison Hobgood, David Houston Wood, "Introduction: Disabled Shakespeare," *Disability Studies Quarterly* 29.4 (Fall 2009), available at http://dsq-sds.org/article/view/991/1183 (last access June 14, 2017).
24 Turner, Stagg, *Social Histories of Disability and Deformity*, 4.

concept of the marvellous, and to elements of medical pathology linked to the theory of humours.

The Renaissance is a period of deep epistemic fractures during which the conflict between the new science (represented in works by Copernicus, Galileo, Vesalius, Bacon...) and the authority of ancient texts produces the very notion of modernity. The corporeal entity of the modern self comes to define itself in a lively arena, a locus of encounter and clash for an ideal body and a monstrous body, a humoral Hippocratic body, an iconic body, a body rich in symbols to be interpreted by studying the manuscripts of the great classic physicians, an astrological body and a body placed at the intersection of microcosm and macrocosm, a cross reference between plants, minerals, animals, stars, and planets. Furthermore, many critics underscore that such a topic can be connected to concepts derived from classic aesthetics to the Medieval concept of the marvellous, and to elements of medical pathology linked to the theory of humours. Such a system, culturally structured by sometime contradictory cross-references, gives to the Renaissance body a "strangeness" attributable precisely to the "survival of older conventions of representation alongside newer fashions."[25]

During this time there still is the notion of the classical concept of "ideal beauty" which, from a visual point of view, presupposes a body formed by the best anatomical parts of various individuals. No one embodies in himself/herself ideal beauty because the later is indissolubly connected with the divine. If the mythopoeic and divine body is unattainable by any human being, in a culture focalized on the image of the ideal body all the members of a population are not endowed with an ideal body and "there is no social pressure [...] that populations have bodies that conform to the ideal."[26] The counterpoint to the distance from the normality of ideal beauty is the awkward and grotesque distance from any canon of beauty: the monster.

The concept of monstrosity grows out of a social construct through which a being is perceived according to a deceptive norm; in Renaissance modernity, the monster contextualizes the relationship between disability, deformity and physical defects. However, it is important to point out that the two categories, deformity and monstrosity, are not completely equivalent. The former refers to ugliness or to physical conditions – such as, for instance, misshapen or crippled limbs that could cause functional damages. It is a concept bearing a social stigma, although accepted by civil or canonic law.

---

25 *Renaissance Bodies: The Human Figure in English culture c. 1540–1660*, eds. Lucy Gent, Nigel Llewellyn (London: Reaktion Books, 1995).

26 Lennard Davis, "Introduction: Normality, Power and Culture," in The *Disability Studies Reader*, ed. Lennard J. Davis (New York: Routledge, 2006), 2.

The latter, monstrosity, includes congenital defects, believed to be caused by either excess or deficiency of the semen ejaculated during conception. In addition, monsters constitute significant social metaphors allowing for the conceptualization of characteristics that could actually refer to disability, but they could also address a critique of the political, social, and moral system (in fact, monstrous births were considered as bearers of messages addressed to holders of political, religious or moral power).

The impact of the idea of monstrosity is broadened by its being an absolute concept that forces the law to question its own rules in the institution of socially inclusive and exclusive hierarchies:

> Within the traits that make a body monstrous – that is, frightening or ugly, abnormal or disgusting – we may read the difference between an other and a self, a pervert and a normal person, a foreigner and a native.[27]

The analysis of the dramatically monstrous body, representing a symptomatic complexity of fears, brings about a reflection on human variability and on a modern and pre-modern subjectivity, making Renaissance representation of the abnormal body an instrument for re-reading and re-interpreting a historically distant cultural imagination of disability: "Renaissance cultural representations of non-standard bodies might provide new models for theorizing disability that are simultaneously more inclusive and specific than those currently available."[28] Within the complex Renaissance episteme, the ideal and the monstrous body are juxtaposed to the humoral body. The medical paradigm of the four humours is of great importance also for the Renaissance discourse about disability because the very notion of pre-modern and Renaissance individuality can be constructed as a historicized inquiry about the body's variations and differences. The fundamental concept of material incarnation, as conceived within the theory of humors (a mixing of the four main humours: choleric, sanguine, melancholic, and phlegmatic), is implicitly based on imperfection: excesses or deficiencies of humoral components create bodily differences of temperament. This consideration introduces the allusion to an initial definition of disability as excess or deficiency with respect to, in the specific case of the theory of humours, an even means of equilibrium and proportion. At the same time, however, the representative transformism of the humoral selves in Renaissance works shows the precarious-

27 Judith Halberstam, *Skin Shows: Gothic Horror and the Technology of Monsters* (Durham: Duke University Press, 2000), 8.
28 Hobgood, Houston Wood, "Introduction: Disabled Shakespeare."

ness of the matter of which pre-modern identity is composed, thus making pre-modern categories of disability much more unstable than the present ones.

In its use of vocabulary related to the ideal, the monstrous, the misshapen, and the humours, the philosophical and cultural representation of disability reveals how in the Renaissance a disabled identity may be considered both as a complex negotiation of the discourse on deformity and monstrosity, and also as a perception of identity as fluid matter in continuous negotiation and, as such, remarkably contemporary.

However, the Renaissance period is also characterized by an important epistemological leap[29] from the theory of humours, according to which the self is conceived as a "semi-permeable irrigated container in which humours moved sluggishly"[30], to the successive Cartesian philosophy, where the self is perceived as "a static, solid container, only barely breached, autonomous in principle from culture and environment, tampered only with diseases and experts."[31] What happens, therefore, is an epochal transformation of identity categories with a transfer from a "humoral" self in constant connection and dialogue with its environment to a self characterized by a marked dualism and essentially isolated from the environment. It is precisely the liminality of Renaissance writing, the act of writing at the threshold of this epistemological transformation, that makes the representation of disability in Renaissance works so challenging and so far from contemporary perspective and yet sometimes so close to and precursory of themes present in our own time:

> early modern English authors portray stigmatized illness, disease, and deformity- in a word, disability- by conceiving of it in ways that can simultaneously appear either entirely alien to current Western (that is, Cartesian) ways of thinking or, on the contrary, as utterly and even painfully familiar.[32]

---

29 Cf. in particular Gail Kern Paster, *The Body Embarassed: Drama and the Discipline of Shame in Early Modern England* (Ithaca, NY: Cornell University Press, 1993); Gail Kern Paster, *Humoring the Body: Emotions and the Shakespearean Stage* (Chicago: University of Chicago Press, 2004); John Sutton, *Philosophy and Memory Traces: Descartes to Connectionism* (Cambridge: Cambridge University Press, 1998).

30 Paster, *The Body Embarrassed: Drama and the Discipline of Shame in Early Modern England*, 8.

31 Sutton, *Philosophy and Memory Traces: Descartes to Connectionism*, 41.

32 Allison P. Hobgood, David Houston Wood "Introduction. Ethical Staring: Disabling the English Renaissance" in *Recovering Disability in Early Modern England*, eds. Hobgood, Houston Wood, 13.

3 Richard III and disability

Richard III has often been read and interpreted through the analysis of his body, which has been connected to the stormy fractures that developed within English history. Thus, Richard is a monstrous political figure who usurps the throne, an emblematic witness of the Renaissance creed according to which there is continuity between inner morality and exterior appearance. Richard's deformity embodies and represents all that is wrong in Richard, in England, and in the cosmos, in the attempt to condensate a wider and deeper disorder in the visible body of a single person.

Michael Torrey[33], for instance, analyses Richard's deformity through the critical perspective of physiognomy, attributing the peculiar success of Richard's politics to the complex and ambivalent approach to deformity in the Renaissance. Mark Thornton Burnett[34] too connects Richard's political ambivalence to the concept of monstrosity, underscoring how the King's incompleteness, his "unfinished state" may be an effective and sinister image of the succession crisis that might have happened at the end of Elizabeth I's reign. Linda Charnes as well emphasizes that "Shakespeare's audience would immediately have recognized Richard's physical deformity and moral depravity as a synecdoche for the state," since in pre-modern England "the body was one signifier in an elaborate network of signification in which God's signature could be read in the physical world."[35] In the play there are in fact numerous references to the anomaly of political transactions and to the deep connection of such an anomaly with Richard's deformity. An emblematic example can be found in the bitter words of Anne Neville's grief for the death of Henry VI:

> Foul devil, for God's sake, hence, and trouble us not;
> For thou hast made the happy earth thy hell
> Fill'd it with cursing cries and deep exclaims.
> If thou delight to view thy heinous deeds,
> Behold this pattern of thy butcheries
> O, gentlemen, see, see! Dead Henry's wounds
> Open their congeal'd mouths and bleed afresh!

---

33 Michael Torrey, "The Plain Devil and Dissembling Looks: Ambivalent Physiognomy and Shakespeare's *Richard III*", *English Literary Renaissance* 30.2 (2000): 123–153.
34 Mark Thornton Burnett, "'Monsters' and 'Molas': Body Politics in *Richard III*" in Mark Thornton Burnett *Constructing 'monsters' in Shakespearean drama and early modern culture* (Houndmills, Basingstoke, Hampshire: Palgrave, 2002).
35 Linda Charnes, *Notorious Identity: Materializing the Subject in Shakespeare* (Cambridge: Harvard University Press, 1993), 30, 22.

> Blush, Blush, thou lump of foul deformity;
> For 'tis thy presence that exhales this blood
> From cold and empty veins, where no blood dwells;
> Thy deed, inhuman and unnatural,
> Provokes this deluge most unnatural.(1. 2. 51–62)

In the critical stance mentioned above it is obvious that "the use of deformity as master metaphor for social ill serves to suppress the personal and social implication of disability."[36] Considering Richard as a liminal figure, "a Renaissance version of late medieval attitudes toward deformity"[37] helps understanding the negativity attributed in the play to his body, to a physicality that is a sign indicating, showing, announcing, and predicting. The critical approach of disability studies allows instead for the analysis of *Richard III* as a work about the power of the disabled body. With an anticipatory awareness that bodily experiences and physical illnesses are constructed and mediated by culture and society, Richard takes advantage of the language of deformity to describe his physicality, playing with the plurality of meanings of his deformity, thus morphing it into a technology of power.

From this perspective, the famous lines "My conscience hath a thousand several tongues/ And every tongue brings in a several tale" (5.3.205–207), beside describing conscience as a great political force, could pre-announce a prism of interpretative possibilities. In fact, such words could contribute to trace the image of Richard himself as a creature with multiple performances of his identity and physicality, thus becoming also a metaphoric allusion to the interpretative plurality of the idea of disability in the work itself; such a plurality may refer to the above mentioned coexistence of different epistemological approaches about the body.

Richard literally places his body on the stage sometimes to emphasize and sometimes to minimize his physical difference. His physical impairment is always present, but Richard consciously plays with the cultural construction of disability: he transforms his body into a dynamic entity that not only opposes and refuses the script assigned to him, but also uses such a script to his own advantage. Let us consider now some examples of these multiple performances that offer a post-modern possibility "of a mutable self, of a fluidity of subjectivity."[38]

---

36 Turner, Stagg, *Social Histories of Disability and Deformity*, 9.

37 Mitchell, Snyder, *Narrative Prosthesis: Disability and the Dependencies of Discourse*, 102.

38 Annette Kuhn, "Sexual Disguise and Cinema," in *The Power of the Image: Essays on Representation and Sexuality* (Boston: Routledge and Kegan Paul, 1985), 52.

We may ponder first on the stunning verbal power of the first monologue when Richard appears on the stage walking with enraged deformity and looking at the audience straight in the eye:

> Now is the winter of our discontent
> Made glorious summer by this son of York,
> And all the clouds that loured upon our house
> In the deep bosom of the ocean buried.
> Now are our brows bound with victorious wreaths,
> Our bruisèd arms hung up for monuments,
> Our stern alarums changed to merry meetings,
> Our dreadful marches to delightful measures.
> Grim-visaged war hath smoothed his wrinkled front;
> And now, instead of mounting barbèd steeds
> To fright the souls of fearful adversaries,
> He capers nimbly in a lady's chamber
> To the lascivious pleasing of a lute.
> But I, that am not shaped for sportive tricks,
> Nor made to court an amorous looking glass;
> I, that am rudely stamped and want love's majesty
> To strut before a wanton ambling nymph;
> I, that am curtailed of this fair proportion,
> Cheated of feature by dissembling nature,
> Deformed, unfinished, sent before my time
> Into this breathing world, scarce half made up (1.1.1–23)

Richard's description of his own physical aspect emphasizes the conscious manipulation of his physicality, underscoring the dramatic qualities of a body capable of taking on different nuances and appearances in order to answer the aims and needs of a manipulating "I."

Let us examine now the words Richard used in his opening monolog: "curtailed of this fair proportion," "cheated of feature," "deformed, unfinished, sent before my time," "scarce half made up". These words, left to resound in the spectators' ears, blend and mingle together, evoking the words with which freak shows' presenters invite the public to stop and admire the fun fair phenomenon on display: "Step up and see the bearded lady, the single skeleton with two heads, the baby with one eye-socket and no nose!," and again "Step right up...see the most astonishing aggregation of human marvels and monstrosities gathered together in one edifice."[39]

39 Felix Isman, *Weber and Fields. Their Tribulations, Triumphs and Their Associates* (New York: Boni and Liveright, 1924).

As noted by many critics, the Shakespearean public was familiar with phenomena of representation of diversity – "by the sixteenth century [...] representations of monstrous bodies, rather than the physical bodies themselves, circulated freely within and beyond Europe in the print culture that witnessed an explosion in the early modern period,"[40] – as well as with phenomena of representation of diversity as a spectacle.

Showing anomalous persons for the sake of spectacle is not a practice limited to caravans and fair grounds in the eighteenth and nineteenth centuries, but was already popular in Shakespeare's time. The custom of the time to exhibit abnormal bodies in taverns or at crossroads became official in the nineteenth century with freak shows:

> the early itinerant monster-mongers who exhibited human oddities in taverns and the slightly more respectable performances in rented halls evolved in the mid-nineteenth century into institutionalized, permanent exhibitions of freaks in dime museums and later in circus sideshows, fairs, and amusement park midways.[41]

Therefore, the present interpretative hypothesis presumes that the opening soliloquy should conjure a figure with unusual shape and diversified perspective: the freak[42]. Such a figure must be understood in the context of a historical period characterized, as underscored earlier, by the simultaneous presence of cultural and philosophical beliefs, often diverging for what concerns the definition of the dis-abled body. If in Shakespeare's work there is no invitation to stop

---

40 Nadja Durbach, *Spectacle of Deformity: Freak Shows and Modern British Culture*, (Berkeley and Los Angeles: University of California Press, 2010), 2.

41 Rosemarie Garland Thomson, "Introduction: From Wonder to Error. A Genealogy of Freak Discourse In Modernity," in *Freakery: Cultural Spectacles of the Extraordinary Body*, ed. Rosemarie Garland Thomson (New York and London: New York University Press, 1996), 4–5.

42 Cf. Rachel Adams, *Sideshow U.S.A: Freaks and the American Cultural Imagination* (Chicago: Chicago University Press; 2001); Robert Bogdan, *Freak Show: Presenting Human Oddities for Amusement and Profit* (Chicago and London: University of Chicago Press, 1988); Lorraine Daston, Katharine Parks, *Wonders and the Order of Nature, 1150–1750* (New York: Zone Books, 1998); Katherine Dunn, *Geek Love* (London: Abacus, 2002); Sarah Hall, *The Electric Michelangelo* (London: Faber and Faber, 2003); Armand Marie Leroi, *Mutants: On the Form, Varieties and Errors of the Human Body* (London: HarperCollins, 2003); Michael Mitchell, *Monsters: Human Freaks in America's Gilded Age: The Photographs of Chas Eisenmann* (Ontario: ECW Press, 2002); Margrit Shildrick, *Embodying the Monster: Encounters With the Vulnerable Self* (London; Thousand Oaks California Sage, 2002); Rosemary Garland Thomson ed., *Freakery: Cultural Spectacles of the Extraordinary Body* (New York: NYU Press, 1996); Rosemarie Garland Thomson, *Extraordinary Bodies: Figuring Physical Disability in American Culture and Literature* (New York: Columbia University Press, 1997).

and look since Richard addresses an already present, real, and imaginary audience, the voice and the words, in an astute intertwining of images and symbols, are apt to communicate – in the theater work as well as in the freak shows – a public identity for the exhibited person that may arouse interest and curiosity among the audience.

With his being and his words, Richard insinuates himself, by deconstructing it, into the clear distinction, even in his own time, between the "monster-monger" evoked in the passage quoted above – the lucid and rational itinerant monster-monger – and the exhibited "human oddity," namely, the person morphed into an object of gazing. First spectator of himself, pleased with but also amazed by his histrionic interpretations, Richard is the actor and his public, the scene to be filmed and the camera framing it, it is the thought taking action at the very moment in which the thought is formulated.

Anticipating the contemporary politics of transgression, Richard manipulates the watchful and idiomatic mechanism of the freak performance, making himself both uttering "subject" and "object" exhibited in the performance. In so doing, he destroys the rigidity of certainty and the clear line of distinction between able and un-able, rational and irrational, man and animal.

The proposed reading perspective, focalized on the figure of the freak and on the role of the freak show, may be considered problematic from the viewpoint of disability studies. If the freak show is considered as a spectacle focused on the disabled person, such a spectacle has the function of structuring and codifying normality by contrasting it with the abnormality of the exhibited body; in this case, it is necessary to protect the disabled person from being exploited by a cultural fetishism legitimating a compulsive necessity to define and control physical differences. However, the dialogue between disability, cultural, and performance studies, has recently led numerous critics to reconsider the freak show, underscoring its value as a "site for contesting some of the cultural logics it enacts."[43] For example, Robert Bogdan calls attention to the fact that scholars and activists connected with the disability world, in their desire to protect disabled persons from being exploited, have mistakenly underestimated the degree of independence and freedom granted by freak shows to such persons.[44]

First of all, it is possible to consider the freak performance staged by Richard as an early example of independent control of his narrative – or of an attempt to control it; such an attempt morphs his crippled body into a readable and deci-

43 Bree Hadley, "Mobilising the Monster: Modern Disabled Performers' Manipulation of the Freakshow" *M/C Journal* 11.3 (2008), available at http://journal.media-culture.org.au/index.php/mcjournal/article/viewArticle/47 (last access June 20, 2016).

44 Bogdan, *Freak Show: Presenting Human Oddities for Amusement and Profit*, 280–281.

pherable text. Since Richard's experience of himself is inseparable from his reading of his body's signs as a signifying text, Richard tries to take control of the social construction and manipulation of the body as signifier. Instead of negating his disability or depriving it of its expressive ability, Richard uses it, moulds it, exacerbates it, makes it "freak," morphing it into an instrument of power and validation of disability. In so doing, Richard puts into question the power logics that, in the course of the centuries, have brought about the conviction that disabled people are incapable of making sense of their experiences, thus depriving them of voice and communication. "The cultural representation of disability," as Thomas Couser argues, "has functioned at the expense of disabled people, in part because they have rarely controlled their own images."[45]

The play's tragic conclusion, as it will be argued later, invalidates Richard's power performance. Even if ineffective, Richard's attempt reminds the reader, especially the informed contemporary reader, that the body is always "labelled as" something else in representational economies; [...] "*labelled as* identifies metaphorically the space between the materiality of the body and the materializing of cultural difference."[46] In fact, labelling the body as disabled or unnatural transcends its mere physicality and makes visible the sphere of cultural practices that historically defines such a physicality. In an intelligent and anticipatory appropriation of the figures, symbols, and stage setting of the freak shows, Richard's disability performance begins to deconstruct the mechanism that supports and legitimizes these cultural practices, thus compelling readers and spectators to question their own complicity in the construction and definition of the freak. At any rate, the freak's performance defines itself as destabilizing because it complicates and explodes the space between signifier and signified, showing and demonstrating that the freak is a cultural construction.

From such a perspective, it should be noted that Richard begins his first monologue with an imperious "Now," a word repeated twice in the subsequent lines. Richard's preoccupation with time and the cyclic emphasis with which the word "now" is repeated, seem to nod at the "natural" rhythms of life and things, underscoring how such rhythms define also the social normative paradigms of actions and body conduct. The subsequent description of himself as different, as excluded from these natural rhythms, becomes a way to assert and justify his inadequacy in respecting such norms. But there is more: by offering his

45 Thomas Couser, "Disability, Life Narrative and Representation" in *The Disability Studies Reader*, ed. Lennard J. Davis (New York: Routledge, 2006), 399.

46 Charmaine Eddy "Material difference and the supplementary body in Alice Walker's *The Color Purple*" in *Body Matters*, eds. Avril Homer and Angela Keane (Manchester: Manchester University Press, 2000), 100.

own body as a deforming mirror that does not reflect the reality it represents, Richard challenges the personal "I" and the extended "I" of the audience by bringing back his being a freak, and therefore his exclusion from natural rhythms, to the mere order and ontological level of the narrative. Thus, identity is just an endless play of mirrors in a circus-like spectacle. The freak body is not only exhibited, but it is also staged as an unstable and destabilizing product of the dynamic relationship between performer, audience, and theatrical space.[47]

The stage setting, the deliberate emphasis on alterity, and the relationship between freak and audience (elements that, according to David Hevey, are part of what he defines as "process of enfreakment,"[48]) transform the "freak of nature," namely the person born with congenital or genetic malformations, into "freak of culture" that representational practices and socio-cultural processes try to silence, to turn away from the norm.

Ever since Shakespeare's time, the freak has constituted the re-elaboration in ludic form of the exclusion and stigmatization of disability, and the freak body is precisely the locus of metamorphosis and transformation. The cultural and physical volatility of the freak body – the refusal ingrained in the body to adhere to a natural order that, in turn, ratifies a social order – makes it socially and politically disruptive.

These considerations suggest a further interpretation of Richard's power performance that could be connected to the basic theme of the state of exception, as argued by Rebecca Lemmon in her "Tyranny and the State of Exception in Shakespeare's *Richard III*."[49] So far we have highlighted the extent to which Renaissance performance practices labelled Richard's presence as transgression of natural limits, transgression of classifications, and transgression of the social system of reference. It has also been emphasized how Richard's freak performance has embraced the volatile opportunities offered by his deformity "for raising important questions about the naturalization of concepts of 'normal' and 'abnormal'."[50] However, it should be noted that Richard's freak performance literally stages political and legal effects connected with Richard's (bodily) state of exception.

---

47 Elizabeth Stephens, "Cultural Fixations of the Freak Body: Coney Island and the Postmodern Sideshow," *Continuum: Journal of Media and Cultural Studies* 20.4 (2006): 485–498, 486.
48 David Hevey, *The Creatures that Time Forgot: the Photography and Disability Imager*, (New York and London, Routledge, 1992), 53.
49 Rebecca Lemmon, "Tyranny and the State of Exception in Shakespeare's Richard III" in *Richard III a Critical Reader*, ed. Annaliese Connolly (London, New York: Bloomsbury Arden, 2013).
50 Michael Chemers *Staging Stigma* (New York: Palgrave Macmillan, 2008), 5.

In many lines throughout the work Richard's body is discussed and stigmatized by the other characters: Anne and Elisabeth deride Richard describing him as "diffused infection of a man," "hedgehog," "bottled spider," and "foul bunch-backed toad," all expressions recalling anomalous and inhuman bodies. However, Richard's real monstrosity – a category that at that time, as noted earlier, differed from infirmity or deformity – is codified by Margaret's words:

> Thou that wast sealed in thy nativity
> The Slave of Nature and the son of hell;
> Thou slander of thy heavy mother's womb,
> Thou loathed issue of thy father's loins (1.3.228–231)

Margaret seems to draw her imagery from the vocabulary and the categories introduced by erudite treatises[51] about monsters in Shakespeare's time. The monster is such by birth ("wast sealed in thy nativity") and his different physical shape is the result of an erroneous mixing of the male and female semen (evoked in the text by "heavy mother's womb" and "thy father's loins") or by the inadequate reproductive strength of the male semen or by the negative influence of the female menses. If Richard is a monster, he represents not only an infraction to nature's order, but also, as Michel Foucault argues, a juridical enigma. For civil, religious, and canonic law, monstrosity, in difference from infirmity:

> is the kind of natural irregularity that calls law into question and disables it. Law must either question its own foundations, or its practice, or fall silent, or abdicate, or appeal to another reference system, or again invent a casuistry. Essentially the monster is casuistry that is necessarily casuistry introduced into law by the confusion of nature.[52]

However, the monster, aware of being "a legal labyrinth, a violation of and an obstacle to the law, both transgression and undecidability at the level of the law"[53] passively awaits to be normalized; the freak's exemplary quirkiness, purposely staged by Richard, reveals how the normative social system describes as innate an identity which is, instead, imposed:

---

51 Jakob Rueff, *De conceptu et generatione hominis* (1554); Conradus Lycosthene, *Prodigiorum ac ostentorum chronicon* (1557); Lievin Lemnes, *Occulta naturae miracula* (1559); Gerolamo Cardano, *De rerum varietate* (1557); Ambroise Parè, *Des monstres et prodiges* (1573).
52 Michel Foucault, *Abnormal: Lectures at the Collège de France, 1974-1975*, trans. Graham Burchell, English series, ed. Arnold I. Davidson (New York: Picador, 2003), 64.
53 Foucault, *Abnormal*, 65.

> Freaks are above all products of perception: they are the consequence of a comparative relationship in which those who control the social discourse and the means of representation recruit the seeming truth of the body to claim the center for themselves and banish others to margins.[54]

Richard decides to create a new center that, considering his diversity, is necessarily ex-centric, therefore distant from the normative center. For example, when the dying king Edward IV tries to secure peace in his kingdom, Richard turns his misshapen body into sign and exhibition of his exceptional status:

> Because I cannot flatter and look fair,
> Smile in men's faces, smooth, deceive and cog,
> Duck with French nods and apish courtesy,
> I must be held a rancorous enemy. (1.3.47–50)

Richard describes himself as "physically" predestined to break the rules of decorum in order to uphold an "ex-centric" truth; in fact, his very body seems to keep him away from social normative attire. He stresses the congruence between his person and his appearance: his body becomes an authentic and reliable text because his deformity prevents Richard from building himself according to the parameters of a normality that actually does not belong to him.

In the specific case, his physical difference implies and presupposes a different behaviour, marked by an integrity that is not present in the court environment characterized, instead, by fictitious and illusory "apish courtesy." Richard's objection "I cannot [...] look fair" baffle the gazing subject and the object of such a gaze, wilfully invalidating the spectators' perspective. In fact, Richard induces his audience to see what he wants of his body and he has such a power that the viewers must, partially at least, accept his description of reality.

In the course of the play, this freak and ex-centric Richard interrupts and deconstructs the ceremonies[55] connected to rites of passage (from funereal mourning, to specific funeral rites, to marriage), and "deforms" the juridical institutions linked to succession and inheritance. With Hastings' execution, he goes as far as suspending the "form of law" in name of his own security and that of the state ("The peace of England").

---

54 Thomson, *Extraordinary Bodies: Figuring Physical Disability in American Culture and Literature*, 62.

55 William Carroll, "'The Form of Law': Ritual and Succession in *Richard III*" in *True Rites and Maimed Rites: Ritual and Anti- Ritual in Shakespeare and His Age*, eds. Linda Woodbridge, Edward Berry (Urbana: University of Illinois Press, 1992): 203–219.

> Richard: "What? Think you we are Turks or infedels?
> Or that we would, against the form of law,
> Proceed thus rashly in the villain's death,
> But that the extreme peril of the case,
> The peace of England, and our persons' safety,
> Enforced us to this execution? (3.5.41–46).

The simultaneous suspension of the law and its affirmation is a true narrative representation of the concept of "state of exception." From a theoretical viewpoint, the state of exception is that figure of the order suppressed and constantly broken in which "the normative aspect of law can thus be obliterated and contradicted with impunity by a governmental violence," thus producing a permanent state of emergency. And yet, although generating "a juridical vacuum," the state of exception "still claims to be applying the law."[56]. Within this state, the practice of pure violence unleashed by law enforces the *fictio juris* according to which it is always the law that can impose order. Therefore, if the state of exception appears as "the legal form of what cannot have legal form,"[57] Richard represents a strong form of the state of exception "drawing on physical and political distortion of form."[58] The source of Richard's charisma and political power derives precisely from his not having legal form, from his exceptional status as a "monster" that denounces and rescinds normative limits, thus offering him physical, political and even epistemological freedom.[59] If the orderly body, the able body is the normative result of the state of law, the (dis)orderly body, the (dis) abled body can only be connected to the state of exception where the volatile force of Richard's freak performance allows for a process of re-definition of social identity. In such a process, the tyranny of the normal and the normative is openly denounced.

In this perspective let us consider Richmond's ascent to the throne. It is characterized by the same violations of legal precepts that marked Richard's:

> Both seek the hand of Elizabeth; both usurp the crown from a ruling prince; both dream of their own exceptionalism the night before the battle [...]; and both deploy nationalist rhetoric based in emotion and instinct, rather than law and reason.[60]

---

56 Giorgio Agamben, *State of Exception. Homo sacer, II, I*, (Chicago and London: The University of Chicago Press, 2005), 87.

57 Agamben, *State of Exception*, 1.

58 Lemmon, "Tyranny and the State of Exception in Shakespeare's *Richard III*," 127.

59 Katherine Schaap Williams, "Enabling Richard: The Rhetoric of Disability in *Richard III*," *Disability Studies Quarterly*, 29.4 (2009), available at http://dsq-sds.org/article/view/997 (last access June 30, 2016).

60 Lemmon "Tyranny and the State of Exception in Shakespeare's *Richard III*," 127.

The end of the play, however, justifies and glorifies Richmond's illegal rebellion because it aims at re-establishing the normative order in an England that "hath long been mad" (5.5.23), and, in so doing, it invalidates Richard's performance as a disabled person. This performance is defined as "mad" because Richard has put into question deeply rooted social, cultural, and legal paradigms. From the freak's political approach, the conventional ending insists on and shows how true tyranny is in fact normality.

Beside questioning the limits of legal legitimacy in the definition of the disabled body, out of historical necessity involving the period of the composition of Richard III, the last act reintroduces the fantasy of an "ideal" body in Richmond's character. This element invalidates Richard's power performance, suggesting the impossibility of upholding the strength of disability in a culture where ability is valued. On the eve of the battle of Bosworth, both Richmond and Richard appeal to St. George, the patron saint of England iconically connected with the dragon's killing. Let us now examine the two invocations: Richmond's words – "God, and Saint George, Richmond, and victory" (5.3.270) – with the explicit invocation to God, allude to a battle for a superior cause. Richard's words, "This and St. George to boot" become instead the verbal translation of his physical aspect, taking on twisted and contradictory traits. Richard evokes St. George, aware of the fact that the "able" normative system around him expects this conduct from a king and a leader. However, he later ambiguously urges his troops to be inspired and driven by the fury of the dragon, St. George's antagonist: "Our Ancient word of courage, fair Saint George,/ Inspire us with the spleen of fiery dragons." (5.3.349 – 350).

Like the national patron he invokes, Richmond frees England from a monstrous body that, like the dragon symbolizing it, "figurant, lui, la *Bête-en-nous*,-qu'il faut tuer, c'est-à-dire rejeter."[61]

In the fight between St. George and the dragon, Richmond is St. George from whom he draws physical strength kept in check by moral strength (thus coming close to the concept of the "ideal" body); with his twisted and crippled body, Richard is the dragon that must be killed, rejected in order to re-establish a clear line of distinction between able and disabled, normal and abnormal, monstrous and ideal. The discursive practices of hegemonic power linked to the definition

61 Jean Chevalier and Alain Gheerbrant, *Dictionnaire des symboles: Mythes, réves, coutume, gestes, formes, figures, couleurs, nombres* (Paris: Robert Laffont, 1982), 232.

of acceptability of bodies implies "the emptying (*kenosis*) of normalcy [...] through the purging of those beings that confuse, [and] are misrecognizable."[62]

Finally, Richard's performance, analysed from the freak point of view, leads to a discussion of Lindsay Dawn Row-Heyveld's interpretative hypothesis according to which "Richard, albeit genuinely impaired, enacts a performance of disability that clearly links him to the charity-hungry thieves of rogue literature and to the tradition of the counterfeiter on the early modern stage."[63] Row-Heyveld attributes Richard's rise to power to the "manipulation of his audiences' charitable impulses;" she reads into Shakespeare's work a warning to replace charity with suspicion "when dealing with people with disabilities, fraudulent or otherwise."[64]

The category of crippled beggars was well known in Shakespeare's time and was considered suspicious because crippled beggars hoped to arouse empathy and to get alms precisely for their obvious inability to work. Furthermore, frequent simulations of malformation had induced the state to introduce a distinction, from a legal point of view, between persons unable although willing to work ("the deserving poor"), who could enjoy the benefits of alms, and persons unwilling to work ("the undeserving poor").

An early definition of disability links such a condition to the inability to work, and therefore to the necessity of benefitting from alms. The fear of simulation, strengthened and validated by legal codification, appeared forcefully in every aspect of English Renaissance culture and found literary expression in popular ballads, a literary genre known as "rogue literature"[65] and in those shows that could be defined as "fraudulent disability plays,"[66]suitable to educate spectators to be suspicious and watchful in dispensing alms.

---

62 Fiona Kumari Campbell, "Refusing Able(ness): A Preliminary Conversation about Ableism," *M/C Journal* 11.3 (2008), available at http://journal.media-culture.org.au/index.php/mcjournal/article/viewArticle/46 (last access July 10, 2016).

63 Row-Heyveld, *Dissembling Disability: Performances of the Non-Standard Body in Early Modern England*, 163.

64 Row-Heyveld, *Dissembling Disability: Performances of the Non-Standard Body in Early Modern England*, 164.

65 Kathleen Poires, "The Intersection of Poor Laws and Literature in the Sixteenth Century: Fictional and Factual Categories" in *Framing Elizabethan Fictions: Contemporary Approaches to Early Modern Narrative Prose*, ed. Constance Caroline Relihan (Kent: Kent State University Press, 1996).

66 Among contemporary works that can be included in the genre of "fraudulent disability plays" or containing references to the theme of the fraudulent beggar, we should mention (in alphabetical order): Richard Brome, *The City Wit* (1629–30); Richard Brome, *A Jovial Crew, or The Merry Beggars* (1641); George Chapman, *The Blind Beggar of Alexandria* (1595–96); Thomas

The deceitful appeal to public or even government generosity, exposed in fraudulent disability plays, or the attempt at arousing empathic commiseration for the crippled beggars, is very different, however, from the logic of freak shows' artists who refused compassion as a mode of show, since "pity did not fit in with the world of amusement." [67]

Often freak artists did not consider themselves as disabled persons needing public pity, rather they tended "to construct themselves as skilled performers whose bodies allowed them to lead normal, if not extraordinary, lives, a fact that was clearly central to their public personae."[68] These words do not connect the size of the able body with conformity, expectations, social constructions, but with the ability to act using one's own disability or deficiency as "technology performance."

Once more the freak perspective allows for the dismantling of the dichotomy able/disabled with anticipatory reference to the new approaches toward disability that find their theoretical codification in Lennard Davis'*Bending over Backwards: Disability, Dismodernism, and Other Difficult Positions*. Davis presents the condition of disability as a fundamental and essential characteristic of the postmodern that he defines as dismodern, precisely because of this new conception. The awareness that all human beings in some way or at some moment of their lives are "wounded" or "maimed" leads Davis to state that "impairment is the rule, and normalcy is the fantasy."[69]

By availing himself of his deformity as power technology, Richard fits Davis' concept of dismodern subject. Considering Richard as a dismodern subject enables us to observe how, in different ways, all the bodies described in the play – from the king's dying body, to the nation as a metaphoric body, from the soldiers' wounded body to the wasted body of Margaret, Henry VI's widow – are unstable. Richard challenges the dichotomy able/disabled bodies showing how everybody starts with or reaches a condition of disability at a certain moment in life: in this way he rejects the narration of modernity that insists on the description of a sub-

---

Dekker, *The Honest Whore*, Part 1, (1604); Ben Jonson, *Every Man in His Humour* (1598); Ben Jonson, *Bartholomew Fair* (1614); Ben Jonson, *Volpone* (1605–06); Thomas Kyd, *The Spanish Tragedy* (1582–92); John Marston, *Antonio's Revenge* (1599); Thomas Middleton and William Rowley, *The Changeling* (1622); Thomas Middleton, *A Mad World, My Masters* (1605); Thomas Middleton and Thomas Dekker, *The Roaring Girl* (1607–10); James Shirley *The Constant Maid* (1640); William Shakespeare, *Hamlet*, (1599–1601); *Henry VI, Part 2* (1591); *King Lear* (1603–06); *Titus Andronicus* (1590–93); *The Winter's Tale* (1610–11); Cyril Tourneur, *The Atheist's Tragedy* (1601–04); Thomas Heywood, *The Rape of Lucrece* (1608); John Webster, *The White Devil* (1612).

67 Bogdan, *Freak Show: Presenting Human Oddities for Amusement and Profit*, 277.

68 Durbach, *Spectacle of Deformity: Freak Shows and Modern British Culture*, 20.

69 Davis, *Bending over Backwards: Disability, Dismodernism, and Other Difficult Positions*, 31.

ject with an able body whose complete independence suggests the possibility of perfection.

Thus Richard gives a provocative potential to the category of disability by revealing its aspect as that of an unstable category. With his emphasis on the multiple ways through which his body difference is negotiated within the text, he allows for the observation that these repeated performances, even in the case of a normatively able identity, "[are] bound to fail, as the ideal able-bodied identity can never, once and for all, be achieved."[70]

70 Robert McRuer, *Crip Theory, Cultural Signs of Queerness and Disability* (New York: New York University Press, 2006), 9.

Sidia Fiorato

Performance, Power, Politics: The Body as Stage in *Richard III*

In the Early Modern Period, the body is a "cultural text that is interpreted, inscribed with meaning – indeed *made* – within social relations."[1] Central to the period is the metaphor of the body politic, which is based on the analogy between the human body and the political order and which is expressed in the image of a harmoniously articulated body divided into different parts and functions, that correspond to the members or organs of the community which cooperate for the well being and balance of the whole. At a jurisprudential level, "Calvin's case" in Plowden's *Reports* incorporated the conception of the king's two bodies into substantive law as the representation of the ordered state: the body natural of the king was "subject to all Infirmities that come by Nature or accident [...] and to the like Defects that happen to the natural Bodies of other People."[2] The physical frailty of the body natural is transcended by the ethereality of the body politic, which cannot be seen nor handled, but is represented through the image of the lawful authority of the state in a presentification of its ontological conception.[3]

Within this context, the historical and Shakespearean figure of Richard III acquires a relevant meaning in the embodiment and articulation of such political metaphor. As a matter of fact, his disability, reported in the historical records but belied by recent findings, is invested with a political meaning: "Richard becomes the nation's fate turned flesh; and his contorted body seems to grow directly out of England's twisted fate during the Wars of the Roses. The body politic deformed by decades of civil war materializes in the monstrous body natural of

---

1 Rosemarie Garland-Thomson, *Extraordinary Bodies* (New York: Columbia University Press, 1997), 22.

2 Edmund Plowden, *Commentaries or Reports* (London: Brooke, 1816), 212a.

3 See Paul Raffield, *Images and Cultures of Law in Early Modern England: Justice and Political Power 158–1660* (New York, Cambridge University Press, 2004), 57–58, and Cristina Costantini, "Representing Law: Narrative Practices, Poetic Devices, Visual Signs and the Aesthetics of the Common Law Mind," in *Liminal Discourses. Subliminal Tensions in Law and Literature*, Daniela Carpi, Jeanne Gaakeer, eds. (Berlin: DeGruyter, 2013): 27–36. See also Plowden, *Commentaries or Reports*, 212a: "his body politic is a Body that cannot be seen or handled, consisting of Policy and Government, and constituted for the Direction of the People, and the management of the public weal."

https://doi.org/10.1515/9783110591514-005

the hunchback king and there finds its 'final physical manifestation'." [4] Underlying this image is the belief that a nation cannot function as a disharmonious and disabled body, therefore "Richard's death symbolically purges the nation of the evils of civil war."[5] Richard's corporeality comes to represent an interpretive framework for historical events, in particular a failed, misshaped former age (with the fall of the Plantagenets) and the consequent validation of the new one, with the advent of the Tudor Dynasty.

On a personal level, physical impairment determines the ascription of disability by society, whose created constructs prescribe meaning to difference. Already at the play's inception Richard recognizes his de-formity (his being misshaped, incomplete), but it is only in Act 1 Scene 3 that we learn the precise nature of his deformity, when Queen Margaret calls him a "poisonous hunchbacked toad" (1.3.246). Medieval belief held that such impairment would keep him "from participating in society's 'normal functions' of daily life."[6] However, Richard proves able to fulfill the functions of a royal, he wields power and is always responsible for his destiny, claiming agency and the assertion of his subjectivity. He thus disrupts his own disability by disrupting at the same time the view that posited it as foundational to his character. By the end of the text, his disability recedes into the background and Richard is restored in his military and bodily value, as he valiantly leads his troops into war, himself fighting into the battlefield.

However, Shakespeare's text was meant to be performed more than read, and performatively, disability is a stage presence. The theatre, "an art of body and an art grounded in body"[7] allows it to become a site of negotiation: "[a]lone among the elements that constitute the stage's semiotic field, the body is a sign that looks back."[8] Onstage, the body acquires multiple modalities of expression, it opens itself to play and display and at the same time enters the imaginative dimension of the audience: in this multimodal context, speech acts

---

4 Ralf Hertel, *Staging England in the Elizabethan History Play: Performing National Identity* [2014] (New York: Routledge, 2016), 106. With regard to this, see also John Jowett, "Introduction" to William Shakespeare, *Richard III* (Oxford: Oxford University Press, 2000), 356.

5 Hertel, *Staging England in the Elizabethan History Play*, 106.

6 Abigail Elizabeth Comber, "A Medieval King 'Disabled' by an Early Modern Construct: A Contextual Examination of Richard III," in *Disability in the Middle Ages. Reconsiderations and Reverberations*, ed. Joshua R. Eyler (London: Ashgate, 2010): 183–196, 191.

7 Simon Shepherd, *Theatre, Body, and Pleasure* (New York: Routledge, 2006), 7.

8 Stanton B. Garner, *Bodied Spaces: Phenomenology and Performance in Contemporary Drama* (Ithaca: Cornell University Press, 1994), 49. See also Sidia Fiorato "Performances, Regulations and Negotiations of the Renaissance Body. Legal and Social Perspectives," in *Performing the Renaissance Body*, eds. Sidia Fiorato, John Drakakis (Berlin: De Gruyter, 2016), 1–26.

prompt the audience's imaginative participation and involve them in the circulation of social energy implied by the construction of the individual character, through their auricular quality.[9]

The poetics of Elizabethan power was indivisibly linked to a poetics of the theatre:[10] "figurative art speaks directly to the visual sense, but poetry also appeals to the visual imagination by its capacity to conjure pictures into the minds of [...the] audience."[11] The subject thus opens himself to self-invention in social networks of established meanings and negotiations of power. In this way, Shakespeare manages to contrast a huge triumphal stage personality[12] with the rigid Tudor schema of interpretation based on retributive justice and the religious vision of disability as a sin. His Richard manages to gain control over the social perception and manipulation of bodily signifiers and proves able "to sublate his deformed body into the perfect body of the king."[13]

Richard III opens with a soliloquy of the homonymous protagonist, a unique instance in the Shakespearean canon, which signals its stage entrance. The stage instructions say: "Enter Richard, Duke of Gloucester, solus"; this powerfully posits Richard at the concrete and metaphorical centre of the representation. Such effect is amplified by the structure of the Elizabethan "thrust stage,"[14] which extends itself towards the audience, favouring in this way a privileged relationship of the character with the audience and empowering the value of his soliloquies and *asides*. Richard's stage entrance, "solus," master of the stage through the powerful verbal and physical expression of his personality, completely captures the attention of the audience, since his first words. As Garber asserts, "Shake-

---

9 A.R. Braunmüller, "The Arts of the Dramatist," in *The Cambridge Companion to English Renaissance Drama*, eds, A.R. Braunmüller, Michael Hattaway (Cambridge: Cambridge University Press, [1990] 2002): 53–90, 61.

10 See Stephen Greenblatt, "Invisible Bullets: Renaissance Authority and its Subversion, Henry IV and Henry V," in *Political Shakespeare: Essays in Cultural Materialism*, eds. Jonathan Dollimore, Alan Sinfield (Manchester: Manchester University press, 1994), 18–47, 44.

11 Paul Raffield, *Shakespeare's Imaginary Constitution. Late-Elizabethan Politics and the Theatre of Law* (Oxford and Portland: Hart, 2010), 1.

12 Arthur Percival Rossiter, "Angel with Horns: The Unity of Richard III," in Rossiter, *Angel with Horns: And Other Shakespeare Lectures* (London: Longmans, 1961), 1–22, 2.

13 Linda Charnes, *Notorious Identity. Materializing the Subject in Shakespeare* (Cambridge, London: Harvard University Press, 1993), 32.

14 The Thrust or apron stage is defined as follows: "This 'extension' to the normal proscenium stage enables the performance space to be prolonged into the auditorium while at the same time retaining the scenographic possibilities of the separate stage." (Christopher B. Balme, *Cambridge Introduction to Theatre Studies* (Cambridge: Cambridge University Press, 2008), Kindle Edition, ch. 3.)

speare's Richard is the creation of a powerful political as well as dramatic imagination."[15]

In the incipit, Richard laments the peace granted by Edward IV's reign as a time of "discontent," as it does not allow him the possibility to express his potentialities. As a matter of fact, he had previously distinguished himself by defending the English crown, as it is also reported in historical records and as later in the tragedy Buckingham will recall in the following terms: "your victories in Scotland, / Your discipline in war" (3.7.15–16).[16] The epic terms of the war images he employs underline how he does not feel he belongs to the new context of "merry meetings" and "delightful measures", as it is also indicated by the adversative with which he introduces himself: "But I [...]" (1.1.14). The terms he uses to refer to his own person focus on his physical disability, often indicated as an absence or incompleteness of form: "not shap'd," "rudely stamped," "curtail'd of this fair proportion" (where "fair" signifies physical perfection[17]), "cheated of feature," "deform'd, unfinish'd" (1.1.14,16,18,19,20). Richard appears, however, as striving to transcend such incompleteness precisely when he states that he can only "descant on my own deformity" (1.1.27); this musical metaphor underlines how Richard is celebrating his ability to "counterpoint and discourse upon a given theme,"[18] that is, his deformity, through a two-voice polyphonic improvisation. In an elegant metatheatrical play, he appears to be striving to bring his own incompleteness to completeness through role playing. This attunes with the meaning of performance as "acting through form", which is to say "by means of form,"[19] or, expanding Watt's definition, by articulating and negotiating forms.

Richard's words "Why I, In this weak piping time of peace,/ Have no delight to pass away the time, / Unless to spy my shadow in the sun" (1.1.24–26) underline his ineffable essence, which like a shadow does not possess clear and defined contours, but constantly varies according to his position with respect to

---

15 Marjorie Garber, *Shakespeare after All* (New York: Anchor Books, 2004), 132.

16 William Shakespeare, *Riccardo III* (Milano: Garzanti, 2010). All quotations in the text will be taken from this edition.

17 See Mark Thornton Burnett, *Constructing "Monsters" in Shakespearean Drama and Early Modern Culture* (Houndmills: Palgrave Macmillan, 2002), 90.

18 Marie-Hélène Besnaut, Michel Bitot, "Historical Legacy and Fiction: The Poetical Reinvention of King Richard III," in *The Cambridge Companion to Shakespeare's History Plays*, ed. Michael Hattaway (Cambridge: Cambridge University Press, 2002), 106–125, 106. See also Christopher R. Wilson, Michela Calore, eds., *Music in Shakespeare: A Dictionary* (London: Bloomsbury, 2014): in the sixteenth century, "descant" referred both to a kind of vocal counterpoint, and to a method of improvisation in song; the term originally (in the twelfth century) indicated a two-voice polyphonic improvisation.

19 Gary Watt, *Shakespeare's Acts of Will* (London: Bloomsbury, 2016), 165.

the sun (and therefore maintaining the initial pun of power itself) and, at the same time, of the observer. Richard willingly identifies with the body of the actor and exploits its protean qualities and its continuous change[20], as well as the potentialities of multiple roles, which he actualizes through his rhetorical ability with performative speech acts. When he asserts: "I am determined to prove a villain" (1.1.30) he in fact ascends to a theatrical dimension which is fully realized through the kinaesthetic energy of his stage presence and his mastering of the visual and hearing space of the audience; Richard's image as master performer becomes the structural principle of the dramatic action and goes back to the meaning itself of the word "theatre," which comes from the Greek *theatron*, that is, "a place for looking. [...] a place as well as [...] a particular form of sense perception."[21] This characteristic intertwines with the period's awareness of self-fashioning, that is, "the fashioning of human identity as a manipulable artful process,"[22] and involves also speech and an attitude of hearing on the part of the audience.

The audience is privy to Richard's intents from their planning stage and subsequently during the development of the events through Richard's numerous asides. As a matter of fact, he "shares his wicked plots with the audience before stepping back into the frame of representation to execute them upon the other characters, and then returns to the platea to gloat about the efficacy of his performance."[23] Richard performs the function of chorus, author, director, and main character of the play. He continuously breaks the fourth wall, proving himself able to catch the attention of the audience in a sort of dramatic monologue *ante litteram*, through which the audience is transported into his mind, where they learn about his intentions and understand them in a subtle *Verfremdungseffekt*. This is superbly rendered in the opening soliloquy performed by Jonjo O'Neill in the 2012 Royal Shakespeare Company's staging of the play. Richard enters the scene solus and delivers his speech in ironic tones which enhance its metatheatrical dimension. The effect is rendered disturbing by his almost entering the camera with his face and offering a close up of his eyes and his tricky expression. O'Neill manages to reach the effect of his Richard condemning the

20 As he had affirmed in *3 Henry VI*, "I can change shapes with Proteus for advantages" (3.3.192).

21 Christopher B. Balme, *The Cambridge Introduction to Theatre Studies* (Cambridge: Cambridge University Press, 2008), Kindle Edition, Introduction: Theatre and Theatre Studies.

22 Stephen Greenblatt, *Renaissance Self-Fashioning. From More to Shakespeare* (Chicago and London: The University of Chicago Press, 1980), 2.

23 Gina Bloom, *Voice in Motion: Staging Gender, Shaping Sound in Early Modern England* (Philadelphia: University of Pennsylvania Press, 2013), 111.

whole context of his parable as the real masquerade by projecting his own conscious performance. His determination emerges when after the first part of the soliloquy he seems to abandon the stage (which would have created an impression of abandoning the social scene, a self-emargination on the borders of society) but then he goes back precisely on the line starting with "But I". In this way, he conquers both the stage and the attention of the audience and will hold it for the whole play. Actually, in this metatheatrical structure, built by the character himself, the audience tend to suspend their moral judgment to follow the tragic aspect of a fascinating individual who embodies the *libido dominandi:* "the line separating spectator from player is stretched so thin that the demarcation becomes precarious as Richard seduces us along with his other victims."[24] The object of the larger performance is in fact the control of the audience, of us, as Jowett underlines.[25]

We assist therefore to a fusion between the *outer frame*, that is, the "'cultural construct' that involves the production of the theatrical event" and the *inner frame*, that is, the theatrical performance itself, "the spectator's experience of [the] fictional stage world."[26] The external representation, the "outer play", that is the communication between Richard and the audience, is made aware of the shift with respect to the "inner play," that is the Shakespearean text; in such metatheatrical context, a "circulation of social energy" takes place, which demystifies the concept of sovereignty, underlining its characteristics of performance and preparing the audience's attention for Richard's performative strategy. Dissembling Richard, a self-willing actor on the political scene, scripts and enacts (actually, en-acts) his bloody (and bodily) path to power[27], in a performative self-construction.

24 Waldo F. McNeir, "The Masks of Richard the Third," *Studies in English Literature 1500–1900*, 11.2 (1971): 167–186, 174.

25 John Jowett, "Introduction" to William Shakespeare, *The Tragedy of Richard III* (Oxford: Oxford University Press, 2000), 1-142, 32.

26 Susan Bennet, *Theatre Audiences. A Theory of Reproduction and Reception* (London: Routledge, [1990], 1997 (2nd edition)), 1.

27 See A. J. Boyle, ed., *Tragic Seneca: An Essay in the Theatrical Tradition* (New York: Routledge, 1997), 195.

1 Richard and the appropriation of the *body politic*

In his first soliloquy, Richard communicates his past actions to the audience and sets the context for the following scenes: "Plots have I laid, inductions dangerous, / [...] drunken prophecies, libels and dreams" (1.1.32–33): he grounds the success of his plans on the counterposition between the nature of the king "true and just" and his own nature, which is "subtle, false and treacherous." (1.1.36,37) In this way, his metaphor of the mirror returns with new meanings; he had in fact defined himself as "no[t] made to court an amorous looking-glass" (1.1.15), but having to limit himself to "spy my shadow in the sun" (1.1.26). Such counterposition recalls the initial pun which identifies his kingly brother as "this son of York" (1.1.2), whose shining, however, for Richard does not symbolize peace but serves to illuminate the shadows of the current political situation. The mirror, besides symbolizing Richard's protean capacity for change and being part of his actor's persona[28], at the same time acts as a reflecting surface for the corrupted and distorted society which constitutes the context for Richard's action and which precisely for this reason he is able to exploit for his aims. Richard projects and displaces his deformity onto others[29] and he appears to do this metaphorically reflecting the image of society through his personal mirror.

After his encounter with Clarence, to whose arrest he contributed by spreading a false prophecy, Richard, once again solus on stage, shares his thoughts with the audience and confesses he is pursuing a "deep intent", a "secret close intent [... he] must reach unto" (1.1.149, 158–159), and for whose achievement he expresses his intention to marry Warwick's daughter, Lady Anne Neville. Such "secret intent" clearly delineates itself in the following scene, as his courtship of Anne becomes at the same time the expression of his ambition to the throne.

Anne enters the scene at the head of the funeral procession of King Henry VI[30] and stops its progress in order to express her lamentation[31]: "Set down,

28 See Marjorie Garber, *Shakespeare After All* [2005] (New York: Anchor Books, 2008), 136.
29 Marjorie Garber, *Shakespeare's Ghost Writers: Literature as Uncanny Causality* (New York and London: Methuen, 1987), 39.
30 According to historical records, Anne Neville was not present at Henry VI's funeral. (Cfr. Geoffrey Bullough, *Narrative and Dramatic Sources of Shakespeare* (London: Routledge and Kegan, 1962), 146.) For this reason, her presence in Shakespeare's text assumes a symbolical meaning.

set down your honourable load/ [...] Whilst I awhile obsequiously lament / Th'untimely fall of virtuous Lancaster [...] / Be it lawful that I invocate thy ghost / To hear the lamentations of poor Anne, / Wife to thy Edward to thy slaughtered son" (1.2. 1,3, 8–9). The scene soon transcends its own occasion. Anne's first words define the king as a "holy king" and his body as "Pale ashes of the House of Lancaster, / [...] blood remnant of that royal blood" (1.2.6–7). In this way, she powerfully calls the attention to the *body natural* of the dead king, and, implicitly, to the *body politic* connected to it.

The funeral ceremony had a social function "concerned with the public persona of the dead nobleman, rather than the burial of his private body. The church ceremony was about the transfer of his undying title, not taking leave of the dead."[32] At the moment of death, the *body politic* immediately in-vested the successor of the king, in whom it embodied itself, thus enacting an ideal continuity of kingship.[33] The funeral ritual can therefore be interpreted as the representation of the separation between the *body natural* (the body in the coffin) and the *body politic* (the effigy of the dead king) and, at the same time, of the preservation of the *body politic* itself, waiting for the ceremony of the presentation and official investiture of the king's successor. In the context of the Shakespearean work, the murder of the sovereign, of his *body natural*, provokes a political crisis caused by the anomaly in the transition of power, which puts under discussion the metaphysical continuity of the *body politic.*

In Act 1, Scene 2, the *body natural* becomes the theatre of the attempted appropriation of the *body politic* still connected to it. Anne's words underline her belonging to the Lancaster royal family in her position as wife of the now

---

31 In religious and literary tradition, the lamentation represented the expression of pain for the death of a person and as the semantic analysis of the word shows, it was characterized by a choral and theatrical dimension. See Daniela Carpi, "Caesar's Body in Shakespeare's *Julius Caesar:* Sacralization and de-Sacralization of Power," *Polemos*, 9.2 (2015): 281–294, 286. With regard to this, see also Katharine Goodland, "'Obsequious Laments': Mourning and Communal Memory in Shakespeare's *Richard III*," *Religion and the Arts* 7.1–2 (2002): 31–64, 31–44: Goodland underlines how in the same period of the Shakespearean text the Protestant church was distancing itself from the practice of "wailing the dead", considered as a "popish superstition" connected to the Catholic theorization of the Purgatory, while however it considered the pomp connaturated to the funeral ritual as functional to the representation and keeping of the social order.

32 Jennifer Woodward, *The Theatre of Death. The Ritual Management of Royal Funerals in Renaissance England 1570–1625* (Woodbridge: The Boydell Press, 1997), 35.

33 Cfr. Edmund Plowden, *Commentaries or Reports* (London: Brooke, 1816), 233a quoted in Ernts Kantorowicz, *The King's Two Bodies: A Study in Mediaeval Political Theology* (Princeton: Princeton University Press, 1997), 13: at the king's death "there is a separation of the two Bodies, and [...] the Body politic is transferred and conveyed over from the Body natural now dead, or now removed from the Dignity royal to another Body natural."

dead heir to the crown ("Wife to thy Edward") and seem to claim regency. Her appeal to the law ("Be it lawful that I invocate thy ghost" (1.2.8)) is grounded in her transgression of the "customary class and gender rules of heraldic funerals which held that mourners should be the same sex and near in degree to the deceased."[34] In her position as chief mourner she undermines the social hierarchy and undermines the legitimacy of the successor Edward.[35] Moreover, Anne pronounces her political lamentation in a civic space, in the streets of London, at the head of a military procession, as she is at the head of a group of halberds, thus putting under discussion also the traditional function of funeral procession which aimed at strengthening the *status quo*.

Richard interrupts the procession as well with the following words: "Stay, you that bear that corse, and set it down," "set down the corse" (1.2.33,36): in this way, the body of the dead king shifts to the centre of the action. The following dialogue configures itself as a struggle for the *body politic* of the king through his body natural.

Anne proves to be a cunning counterpoint to Richard in acknowledging and trying to exploit to her own advantage the theatricality connected to the funeral ritual and its performative dimension. In a metatheatrical shift, "Anne uses her onstage audience [and theatre audience] as witnesses for her appeal to justice."[36] The king's *body natural* becomes *body of evidence*, in particular the moment when, according to Renaissance belief, the victim's wounds bleed, pointing towards the presence of the murderer. Anne, therefore, tries to exploit this effect to accuse Richard of "deeds inhuman and unnatural" (1.2.60); she achieves her intent and she even obtains a confession on the part of Richard "I did kill King Henry", "'twas I that stabb'd young Edward" (1.2.183, 185). He also offers her the tool to exact her revenge "I lend thee this sharp-pointed sword" (1.2.178).

> Richard: Lo here I lend thee this sharp-pointed sword,
> Which if thou please to hide in this true breast,
> And let the soul forth that adoreth thee,
> I lay it naked to the deadly stroke,
> And humbly beg the death upon my knee. (1.2.178–182)

However, Anne stops and renounces her aims for two reasons. By inviting Anne to stab him, therefore by performing a metaphorical re-enactment of his own

---

34 Woodward, *The Theatre of Death*, 17.

35 Katharine Goodland, *Female Mourning in Medieval and Renaissance English Drama. From the Raising of Lazarus to King Lear* (Aldershot: Ashgate, 2005), 143.

36 Goodland, *Female Mourning*, 145.

crime, Richard tries to transfigure his own natural body into the body natural of the dead king, by likewise becoming "a punctured body, a signifying corpse."[37] Anne therefore stops not to sanction Richard as the king's successor. On the other hand, through his rhetorical power of fabulation, Richard disrupts the legal context she had created through her lamentation, and renders it a context of courtship by answering her accusations through terms of courtly love:

> Anne: Black night o'ershade thy day, and death thy life.
> Richard: Curse not thyself, fair creature; thou art both.
> Anne: I would I were, to be reveng'd on thee.
> Richard: It is a quarrell most unnatural,
> To be reveng'd on him that loveth thee.
> Anne: It is a quarrell just and reasonable
> To be reveng'd on him that kill'd my husband.
> Richard: He that bereft thee, lady, of thy husband,
> Did it to help thee to a better husband. (1.2.135–143)

This new context disrupts the legitimacy of revenge, subverting the position of the two speakers. Anne remains aware of Richard's true nature, as, after renouncing her revenge, she exhorts him to stand up in the following words: "Arise, dissembler; though I wish thy death / I will not be thy executioner" (1.2.188–189), and the scene concludes as follows:

> Anne: I would I knew thy heart.
> Richard: 'Tis figured in my tongue.
> Anne: I fear me both are false (1.2.196–198)

Finally, Anne surrenders the dead king's body to Richard when she complies to his request to "leave these sad designs / to him that has most cause to be a mourner" (1.2.214–215); in this way, Richard re-establishes the hierarchy of lamentation and acquires the symbolic position of the king's successor, "the prime mourner." Anne, therefore, by retreating from her position, actualizes a symbolic transfer of power: "the remains of the legitimate king embody the immortal ethos of the kingdom, which is now in Richard's power."[38]

The interruption of the funeral procession in 1.2 leaves the question of legitimate succession suspended, "the status of the *dignitas* unresolved and the state of the kingdom in turmoil."[39] Actually, in the course of the different phases of the

---

37 Thornton Burnett, *Constructing 'Monsters' in Shakespearean Drama*, 79.
38 Goodland, *Female Mourning*, 146.
39 Goodland, *Female Mourning*, 142.

funeral ritual, the stability of the kingdom becomes precarious, as the *dignitas* connaturated to the political and social body of the king is in a transitional status:

> this rite of passage progression is animated by a synchronic opposition between the immortal dignity (*dignitas*) of the kingship and the mortal remains of the king; an opposition that is radical at first, ambiguous during the procession, and resolved at burial.[40]

Richard deprives the body natural of the Plantagenet king of the solemn ceremony of the burial: he promises Anne to "solemnly inte[r] / at Chertsey Monastery this noble king" (1.2.218), but then he stop the alberds and directs them to Whitefriars while saying "I'll turn yon fellow in his grave" (1.2.265). In this way, Richard takes possession of the dead king's body politic and keeps it in a suspended state.

After his encounter with Anne, Richard celebrates the success of his plans in a new aside and underlines in particular how his performative ability can compensate and even overcome the "social lacks"[41] he had denounced in his opening soliloquy. His rhetorical ability becomes a form that substitutes the bodily form. He then goes back to the metaphor of the "looking glass": sure of Anne's favours although "misshapen" if compared to her dead husband who was "Fram'd in the prodigality of Nature" (1.2.255, 248), he seems to plan his own "self-fashioning" in order to acquire a "shape", that is, a *public persona:* "I'll be at charge for a looking glass, / And entertain a score or two of tailors / To study fashions to adorn my body" (260–262). However, such articulation of a form is not yet final, as soon after he asserts "Shine out, fair sun, till I have bought a glass, / That I may see my shadow as I pass" (267–268). Richard's visibility and his secret plans strengthen themselves, as from "*spy* my shadow", he shifts to "*see* my shadow." The "role-playing" has not ended. As he had previously asserted, the marriage with Anne serves a "deeper secret intent," that is, the acquisition of the crown. Through his union with Anne he inserts himself in a precise royal genealogy, through their common descent from the line of the Plantagenets (1.2.147). Moreover, as Quiring observes, Richard thus first unites "the white rose and the red" as Anne belonged to the Neville family, therefore to

---

40 Peter Metcalf, Richard Huntington, *Celebrations of Death. The Anthropology of Mortuary Ritual* (Cambridge: Cambridge University Press, 1991), 172, and cfr. 162–165.

41 Katherine Schaap Williams, "Enabling Richard: The Rhetoric of Disability in *Richard III*," *Disability Studies Quarterly* 29.4 (2009).

the House of Lancaster[42], thus demonstrating a political acumen which has remained mainly ignored by the critics.

Richard, however, proves to be the *dissembler* of Anne's final indictment when in the aside which follows the scene he asserts: "I'll have her but I will not keep her long" (1.2.234); his quick changes in attitude in relation to the political and social situation characterize him as a "consummate actor who delights self-consciously in his skill in whatever part he is playing; and he invites us to watch him and share his delight in his skill."[43]

2 Margaret and the *body politic*

Richard envelops his body with his rhetorical ability, thus creating powerful verbal constructions for which he at the same time acts as a prop and which sustain him to communicate precise intentions and prosecute his aims: "His rhetoric about his body inevitably leads to performing the kind of body he deems useful. […] the materiality of his form remains unclear until Richard [rhetorically] highlights his shape […] for specific purposes."[44] Richard (fore)grounds a "slippery view of the self as a role that is formed in moments of exchange and in response to particular circumstances."[45] For example, he rejects the accusations of court members about his future role as Protector of the royal heir as "dissentious rumors" (1.3.46) and disrupts their basis in his physical aspect which derives from the beliefs of the period, rendering instead his de-formity a symbol of his inability to dis-semble: "Because I cannot flatter and look fair /Smile in men's faces, smooth, deceive and cog, / Duck with French nods and apish courtesy, / I must be held a rancorous enemy." (1.3.47–50). By acting on visual strategies and the process of mirroring, Richard re-directs the focus on his misshapen body in a way which signifies "congruence between his person and his appearance; his deformity here "speaks" truth since it prevents him from [deceivingly] fashioning himself."[46] In this way, he reverses the animosity he is attributed, even anticipating the accusations and turning them instead against the queen and her family,

42 Bjön Quiring, *Shakespeare's Curse: The Aporias of Ritual Exclusion in Early Modern Royal Drama* (New York: Routledge, 2013), 38.
43 Charles W.R.D. Moseley, *A Guide to William Shakespeare Richard III* (Tirril: Humanities-Ebooks.co.uk, 2007), ch. 5.
44 Schaap Williams, "Enabling Richard."
45 Martine van Elk, "'Determined to prove a villain': Criticism, Pedagogy and *Richard III*," *College Literature* 34.4 (2007): 1–21.
46 Schaap Williams, "Enabling Richard."

that is, against the body politic itself. Actually, as Schaap underlines, the fact that Richard cannot "look fair" has a double meaning that can be attributed to Richard as object of the vision, but also as subject; the ambiguity of the expression perfectly inserts itself in his ironic portrait of the court, dominated by "apish courtesy" and "French nods."[47] Richard is the first to pronounce a curse against the courtiers "A plague upon you all!" (1.3.58) and to denounce their political schemes. The passage starts with Richard's strong counterposition to the group present on stage "They do me wrong" which reproduces in a certain sense the "But I" of the opening soliloquy; he interrupts their "comedy of pretenses to reveal the hollowness behind these feigned reconciliations"[48] and underlines "what you have been ere this, and what you are; / Withal, what I have been, and what I am" (1.3.132–133).

In 3.4, Richard brings this strategy to its extremes as he accuses the queen for his withered arm, thereby ascribing to the body politic the disability of his body natural, in a cunning reversal of terms of the common political thinking of the period:

> See how I am bewitched! Behold, mine arm
> Is like a blasted sapling wither'd up!
> And this is Edward's wife, that monstrous witch
> Consorted with that harlot, strumpet Shore
> That by their witchcraft thus have marked me. (3.4.67–72)

In 1.2 Margaret of Anjou enters the scene, wife of the dead king Henry VI Lancaster, killed by Richard.[49] As Richard himself underlines at the end of 3 Henry VI, "she lives to fill the world with words" (5.5.44)[50], and as a matter of fact the dispossessed and exiled queen is transfigured into a verbal dimension. Margaret seems to perform the role of Richard's counterpoint as she embodies ambition for power and the exploitation of its theatrical dimension: her power is based on her verbal ability for self-definition which allows her to define and sustain

---

47 See Schaap Williams, "Enabling Richard."

48 Garber, *Shakespeare After All*, 142.

49 According to historical records, the queen died in France in 1482, one year before Edward IV's death, therefore her function in the Shakespearean work assumes a special relevance. As a character that transcends the dimension of space and time, Margaret has been interpreted by critics as a prophetic voice for the future advent of the Tudor dynasty, in a similar role to the Senecan ghost and its presence in revenge tragedies. Her role, however, opens to other possible interpretations and functions.

50 See Naomi C. Liebler, Lisa Scancella Shea, "Shakespeare's Queen Margaret. Unruly or Unruled?," in *Henry VI: Critical Essays*, ed. Thomas Pendleton (New York: Routledge, 2001), 79–96, 92.

her role as queen, actually reduced to a void significant. This aspect represents a parallel with Richard who builds his ascent to power by exercising his rhetorical ability in the interpretation of the significant represented by his body: "Playing against Richard's assumption that he can control this world through his own will, his own language and his own protean skill as an actor is another kind of plot, whose spokesperson in this play is old Queen Margaret."[51]

Margaret significatively enters the scene in a political moment, during the discussion on royal succession:

> She is there and not there, a listener and then suddenly, shockingly, a participant, as if summoned into dramatic being by the circumstances that have brought these two Yorkists together, wrangling about the throne – a throne she feels should, in any case, be hers, as the widow of the dead king Henry VI and the mother of the slain Edward, prince of Wales.[52]

For this reason, her words can be considered as a sort of funeral lamentation for the lost *body politic* ("I am Queen [...] by you deposed," 1.3.161,162) which acts as a counterpoint to and disrupts Anne's lamentation and Richard's strategy.

As a matter of fact, Richard constantly appears as striving to contain her monologues, as he implicitly acknowledges her as his counterpart and main adversary. In particular, they both appear as striving to codify Richard's extra-ordinary dimension, his exception, his being a *homo sacer*, albeit from different perspectives. Margaret, by transcending spatio-temporal boundaries, as a liminal being between two worlds, invests Richard with her past role of sacrificial victim for the peace of the kingdom. As Liebler and Scancella Shea underline, Margaret's banishment from England had annulled the value of the ritual due to her French origins, and therefore non effectively part of English society.[53] Her curse therefore invests Richard of the role of *pharmakon*, at the same time cause and cure of social evils, due to his physical deformity, both in 1.3 and in the subsequent 4.4.151. In this scene, to Margaret's curse, which aims at removing guilt from the deposition and killing of the king, he manages only to answer through the physical presence of his royal body, "the Lord's anointed."

Richard, on the other hand, presents his exception by embracing his deformity not as a limitation but as physical and political liberty. The malleability of his body, his exception, allows him to embody multiple roles and avoid in this way

---

51 Garber, *Shakespeare After All*, 147.

52 Garber, *Shakespeare After All*, 147.

53 See Naomi C. Liebler, Lisa Scancella Shea, "Shakespeare's Queen Margaret. Unruly or Unruled?," in *Henry VI: Critical Essays*, ed. Thomas Pendleton (New York: Routledge, 2001), 79–96, 92.

normative requirements: "Richard's distorted physical form runs in tandem with [...] his distortion of other forms, be they moral, political and legal."[54] He therefore emerges as a charismatic figure who manages to undermine the juridico-political order and, by exploiting a situation of political exception, to conquer the control of the state.[55] In 4.4 however, Richard's predominance as "master performer" is harshly attacked and as a result, his attempt at convincing queen Elisabeth to consent to his marriage with her daughter remains suspended. Elizabeth manages to pierce the involuted outer shape of his role-playing annulling any further development and theatrical effect. Upon his asking a way to court her daughter, she replies he has to confess his crimes against her family: "There is no other way – / Unless thou couldst put on some other shape, / and not be Richard, that hath done all this" (4.4.285–287), and concludes with a final metatheatrical indictment "Thy self is self-misus'd" (4.4.377). She finally induces him to curse himself and this last curse will become effective: "Death, desolation, ruin and decay" (4.4.409). In this way, Richard self-proclaims himself *homo sacer* and starts the process of events which will determine his fall: "The self destroys the self [...and] The actor is taken in by his own skill."[56] In the conclusion of the scene, for the first time Richard does not manage to separate himself from his role in the plot in order to communicate with the audience; actually his last aside is a sole verse which misinterprets the woman's intentions and does not allude to future plans: "Relenting fool, and shallow, changing woman!"(4.4.431).[57]

3 Richard and the generation of the *body politic*

Richard attempts to control the body politic as well as any possibility of its embodiment by killing all the heir in the royal lineage: his brother Clarence, his

54 Rebecca Lemon, "New Directions: Tyranny and State of Exception in Shakespeare's *Richard III*," in *Richard III. A Critical Reader*, ed. Annaliese Connolly (London: Bloomsbury Arden, 2013), Kindle Edition, ch. 5 .

55 Lemon, "New Directions," ch. 5

56 Moseley, *A Guide to William Shakespeare Richard III*, ch. 6. See also Quiring, *Shakespeare's Curse*, 4: "One can describe the curse as marking a borderline, as inscribing the difference between an inside and an outside onto both the body politic and the individual subject. But the 'outside' a curse delimits is in fact not an extraterritorial place. Due to the curse's paradoxical structure, the outside takes the form of an 'interiorized outside' which in Richard's case leads to a scission of the two parts."

57 Cfr. Bill Overton, "Play of the King? "King Richard III" and Richard," *Critical Survey* 1.1 (1989): 3–9, 5–6.

brother Edward's sons. He likewise strives to control the body politic's new generation, as it is shown through his relationship with women. The woman's pregnant body becomes a literalization of two bodies, the keeper of the figurative king's two bodies.[58] In planning his marriage, Richard is thinking about grounding his own genealogy, a Ricardian issue, through the potential repository of the former body politics, which he therefore deems to actualize. Anne, however, rejects such intentions by reversing the mirror upon Richard and cursing him with self generation, notwithstanding the implications for herself. In this way, she condemns herself to become the body natural which will contain a second Ricardian body natural, and engender a monstrous body politic: Anne "poses an unsettling threat to Richard's construction of a strategic self."[59]

> Anne: If ever he have child, abortive be it:
> Prodigious, and untimely brought to light,
> Whose ugly and unnatural aspect
> May fright the hopeful mother at the view (1.2.21–24)

In the case of Elizabeth's daughter, Richard plans of making her an instrument for his own line, to generate his own body politic, by regenerating the previous one, once again in a monstrous birth performed through generational role playing:

> Richard: If I have killed the issue of your womb,
> [...] I will beget
> Mine issue of your blood upon your daughter (4.4.296–298)
> Elizabeth: Yet thou dids't kill my children
> Richard:But in your daughter's womb I bury them,
> Where, in that nest of spicery, they will breed
> Selves of themselves, to your recomforture. (4.4.422–425)

In this way, Richard on the one hand seems to appropriate the dead body politics in order to beget his own; on the other hand, he tries to control the body natural of the royal spouse for a monstrous self-perpetuation. As Thornton-Burnett suggests, the king maintains his indivisibility by generating facsimiles of himself, "avoiding the imprint of women only by using the womb as a temporary

---

58 See Sid Ray, *Mother Queens and Princely Sons: Rogue Madonnas in the Age of Shakespeare* (New York: Palgrave Macmillan, 2012), 71. See also François Ost, *Shakespeare. La Comedie de la Loi* (Paris: Michalon Éditions, 2012), 199.
59 Thornton-Burnett, *Constructing 'Monsters' in Shakespearean Drama and Early Modern Culture*, 76.

home for the next Ricardian generation,"[60] a disposable body natural. He actually comes to transfigure himself into the body of a pregnant woman by reversing Margaret's monstrous description of his disability as "bottled spider" and "bunch-back'd toad" (1.3.242, 246). In this case his distorting mirror refracts his image and transfigures it.

This strategy is perfectly illustrated by Cumberbatch's interpretation of Richard in *The Hollow Crown:* as a matter of fact he performs the opening soliloquy shirtless, thus creating a visual impact of the character's deformity. He then proceeds to dress himself while continuing his speech thereby staging his entrance into character.[61] The following scenes show how he struggles to fit into clothes (we see the arms of his jacket hanging by his sides) until he starts to in-vest himself of the body politic, reaching the extreme of investing himself of the womb of the body natural generating the body politic itself, as it has been illustrated above.

Richard acts as a centripetal force, moving from the inner core of London and trying to engulf everything and everybody that surrounds him. In *The Hollow Crown*, Richard moves very quickly through the corridors of the palaces of power, his hunchbacked position suggesting its disruptive force; this physical attitude symbolizes the political energeia of his hybris, which absorbs also the body natural of his future queen. By rendering the body the interpretative framework of the historical events as well as the tool for their expression, the Shakespearean text does not merely describe history but en-acts it. Richard becomes thus a metaphor for the theatre itself which does not limit itself to describe from an external position the historical processes, but "is inscribed into these processes and performs them."[62]

4 *Body politic* and self-fashioning

In the course of the text, the different characters are introduced according to the role orchestrated for them by Richard, who therefore "fashions" them through his verbal ability and renders them a reflection on the surface of his own mirror,

60 Thornton-Burnett, *Constructing 'Monsters' in Shakespearean Drama and Early Modern Culture*, 75.

61 See Michael Billington, "Benedict Cumberbatch proves a superb villain in *The Hollow Crown's* Richard III," *The Guardian*, March 21, 2016, https://www.theguardian.com/stage/theatreblog/2016/may/21/benedict-cumberbatch-the-hollow-crown-richard-iii (last access November 6, 2016)

62 Quiring, *Shakespeare's Curse*, 119.

a tool connaturated to each one of his actions which encloses their consequences and subjects them to an alienating effect through his reflection. As a matter of fact, he expresses his conspiracy in the following terms: "Shine out, fair sun, till I have bought a glass, / That I may see my shadow as I pass" (1.2.267–268).

Buckingham seems literally to become embodied and come from the liminal space of the mirror, a "shadow" that takes form in the moment of Richard's ascent to power, when the latter realizes that Buckingham shares his plans and identifies him as his double: "My other self, my counsel's consistory, / My oracle, my prophet, my dear cousin: / I, as a child, will go by thy direction" (2.3.151–153). It is as if Richard's performative tension embodied itself in another character who from this moment onwards takes the initiative and determines his ascent to power in bodily terms which reproduce those used by Richard himself. In 3.1. 199–200, Richard exhorts Buckingham to give form to their complots, and, as a matter of fact, Buckingham "re-shapes" Richard's body in his discourses to support his claim to the throne and builds his legitimacy in his report of his speech to the citizens of London: "I did infer your lineaments, / Being the right idea of your father / Both in your form and nobleness of mind" (3.7.12–14). In this way, as Schapp underlines, Richard's form has been "straightened" in a fashioning of the *body politic* which "fashions" the *body natural* investing it of himself. We can see here the achievement of what Richard had purported in 1.2.260–262, that is, "I'll be at charges for a looking-glass, / And entertain a score or two of tailors/ To study fashions to adorn my body"(1.2.260–262). Such adornment is realized by Buckingham, who, in particular, inverts the terms of the interpretation of Richard's body and transposes its characteristics upon the whole country (thus creating also a deep identification between the country and the future king): "The noble isle doth want her proper limbs" (3.7.124), presenting at the same time Richard as the remedy for such lack.[63]

Although he had previously celebrated his own histrionic qualities, asserting "I'll play the orator" (3.5.4), Buckingham does not succeed in his intent, as it is testified by the repeated allusions to the absence of the public vocal legitimation on the part of the population: "The citizens [...] say not a word" (3.7.3), "they spake not a word" (3.7.24), which provokes Richard's impatience: "Would they not speak!" (3.7.42) For the first time, he has to face the failure of his typical procedure through the imposition of a role to the other actors included in his stag-

63 Charnes points out that Richard uses his bodily distinctiveness to engineer a substitution of his deformed body for the imaginary king's body: "Gaining the crown will enable him to effect a kind of trade in which he imagines that he exchanges his misshapen half made-up body for the King's body and its divine perfection" (Linda Charnes, *Notorious Identity. Materializing the Subject in Shakespeare* (Cambridge: Harvard University Press, 1993), 32).

ing of the events. The audience does not respond to Buckingham's rhetorical prompts and he has therefore to transfigure their reactions and transform a minimal expression of assent into a "general applause and cheerful shout" (3.7.39), only to exit then the scene to avoid a possible continuation of the verbal exchange and lose the weak result he managed to obtain. In the imminence of the Mayor's arrival for the sanctioning of the succession, Buckingham organizes a second *mise en scène*, that is, the representation of the *body politic*, the metaphysical and religious dimension of the divinity that embodies itself in Richard "look you get a prayer book in your hand, / And stand between two churchmen, good my lord" (3.7.46–47); in this occasion Buckingham indicates his total identification with Richard when he defines his intentions in the following terms "I'll build a holy descant" (3.7.48). From "descant on my own deformity," we pass therefore to a "descant" which takes into consideration the rituality connaturated to royal succession in order to distort its metaphysical dimension and render it instrumental for its own purposes. Richard is therefore framed in a role in which his rhetorical abilities cannot emerge, as instead do his attributes of "virtuous Prince", "holy and devout religious m[a]n" (3.7.77, 91). The tableaux which is presented by Buckingham in metatheatrical terms posits the two religious men as "Two props of virtue for a Christian Prince / To stay him from the fall of vanity; / And see, a book a prayer in his hand – / True ornaments to know a holy man. Famous Plantagenet, most gracious Prince, / Lend favourable ear to our requests [...] take to your royal self / This proffer'd benefit of dignity" (3.7.95–100, 194–195). With these terms, Buckingham seems to bring to completion the ceremony of royal succession through the transfer of the *dignitas* connaturated to the role of the sovereign, which had been interrupted through the interruption of the funeral progress of king Henry IV in 1.2. Actually, the stage instructions recite "Enter Richard aloft": the vertical architectural plane of the stage symbolizes the hierarchical order of tradition[64] which is now visually endorsed by Richard in Buckingham's staging.

It is always Buckingham who sanctions Richard's role through a performative speech act by acclaiming him in the following terms "Then I salute you with this royal title: / Long live Richard, England's worthy King!" (3.7.238–239). Immediately afterwards, Buckingham proceeds to organize the coronation for the next day; however, such ceremony is not performed on stage, but transfigured and performed only by Richard and Buckingham. Richard's role-playing seems to implode the very same moment in which it should have been most un-

64 See Watt, *Shakespeare's Acts of Will*, 40.

derlined, that is, the coronation moment[65], the sanctioning of the investiture of the *body politic.* Richard transcends the metaphysical sacrality of the moment, through a *mise en scène* of his own ascent to the throne through the help (real and metaphorical) of the sole Buckingham.

> Enter Richard, in pomp, crowned; [...]
> Richard "Stand all apart. Cousin of Buckingham [...] Give me thy hand"
> Here he ascendeth the throne. [...]
> "Thus high, by thy advice / And thy assistance is King Richard seated." (4.2.1–4)[66]

The moment he becomes king, Richard seems to lose his rhetorical ability and his control on the events, thus proving that "an artifice is created, not a solid political reality" and he proves himself "not able to extend this web as a means of embracing the power of the kingdom".[67] As he asserts in 4.2.60–61: "I must be married to my brother's daughter, / Or else my kingdom stands on brittle *glass*" (emphasis added), that is, he has to try and give a concrete support to his construction reflected in the mirror. Such an attempt is enacted upon the news of Richmond's attack: Richard reacts by making appeal to the paraphernalia of his position and to the *dignitas* connected to his royal lineage: "Is the chair empty? Is the sword unsway'd? / Is the King dead? The empire unpossess'd? / What heir of York is there alive but we? / And who is England's King but great York's heir? [...]" (4.4.469–472). However, in a context in which the value of ritual has been disrupted by the vacancy of Richard's creative logos, such an attempt remains vane and the previous strategies become a counterpoint to his intentions. Even later he will make appeal to the dignity of his status: "the King's name is a tower of strength / Which they upon the adverse faction want" (5.3.12–13).

The disorder created in the state reflects itself in his personality; as he admits: "My mind is chang'd" (4.4.456). Such situation reaches a climax in the scene which precedes the battle of Bosworth, in which Richard's interior and exterior dimension intertwine and finally coexist. They materialize themselves in

65 Actually, Richard's coronation was historically significant as it was the first double coronation (with Queen Anne) since 1308. It is reported that he assembled an army of soldiers outside the gates of London, in order to avoid possible rebellions.
66 In *The Hollow Crown*, the interpolated coronation scene shows the protagonist enthroned and silent, looking straight at the camera, therefore at us, the audience, with a gaze full of irony, sneering upon the whole coronation pomp which underlines his own rhetorical success.
67 Richard P. Wheeler, "History, Character and Conscience in *Richard III*," *Comparative Drama* 5.4 (1971–72): 301–321, 310–311. Richard therefore is a forerunner of Prospero, a demiurge, who gives 'form' to himself and the world through words.

the scene of the appearance of the ghosts, psychological prompts that literally become embodied in an "in-between world that is the world of the stage."[68] In Richard's last performance, "the looking-glass is finally turned inward"[69] and we witness the realization of the curse that Richard had pronounced upon himself in 4.4.399: "Myself myself confound!" As a matter of fact, in this final scene he seems to disgregate into the multiplicities of his roles: "What do I fear? Myself? There's none else by; / Richard loves Richard, that is, I and I. / Is there a murderer here? No. Yes, I am! / Then fly. What, from myself? [...] / I am a villain – yet I lie, I am not! / Fool, of thyself speak well! Fool, do not flatter [...]" (5.3.183–193).

The morning of the battle we assist to a last powerful attempt at "self-engedering through a narcissistic embrace of self"[70], once more striving towards self-affirmation. Richard seems to return to his old role and encourages the troops demonstrating his military valour and encouraging his army in terms which recall the military images of the opening of the tragedy: "A thousand hearts are great within my bosom" (5.4.348). His last performance sees him as an embodiment of the hybris, as he manages to "enac[t] more wonders than a man, / Daring an opposite to every danger." (5.4.2) However, he is defeated by his opponent's different theatrical strategy, who enacts a parody of his royal role by investing five knights with his royal insigna: as Richard observes in his last lines, "I think there be six Richmonds in the field: / Five have I slain today instead of him. / A horse! A horse! My kingdom for a horse!" (5.5.9–13).

To Richmond remains to sanction his role through the symbolic transfer of the crown after Richard's death, which takes place on the battlefield through the words of Stanely: "Lo, here, this long-usurped royalty / From the dead temples of this bloody wretch / Have I pluck'd off to grace thy brows withal" (5.5.4–6). Once again, a distortion of the coronation ceremony. Richmond's first speech as a king sanctions Richard's deposition ("the bloody dog is dead", 5.5.2), thus bringing to completion the curse started by Margaret and passed through the Duchess and Elisabeth and climaxed in Richard's self-curse. Richard's body is carried off scene, reduced to an empty signifier, and seems to recede and return to the liminal space of the theatrical dimension:

---

68 Garber, *Shakespeare After All*, 156.

69 Garber, *Shakespeare After All*, 157.

70 John Jowett, "Introduction" to William Shakespeare, *Richard III*, ed. John Jowett (Oxford: Oxford University Press, 2000), 1–132, 69.

"The historical figure who ruled England dissolves into the theatrical figure who ruled the English stage."[71]

However, Richard's opponent is a rather flat character, a *rex ex machina*, so to speak.[72] The play presents the events and the contest for the crown exclusively from Richard's point of view, therefore, Richmond appears as a conqueror, an invader, bringing about yet another usurpation. Richmond's closing words ("Now civil wounds are stopped, peace lives again", 5.5.40) echo Richard's opening lines ("Now is the winter of our discontent made glorious summer by this son of York", 1.1.1–2). As Hertel observes, the circle closes, and although Richard is deposed, his initiatory speech, which has turned out to be mere rhetoric, is echoed by his successor's one.[73]

The filmic rendering of Richard III in the series *The Hollow Crown* perfectly conveys this final ambiguity, by presenting Henry VII enthroned after the solemn ceremony of his coronation, but closing on the battlefields, where the new body politic has been constituted. The final image from above showing the corpses of the dead soldiers spectrally reveals the components of Henry VII's body politic, the bodies which have brought it to life. Henry VII's royal dignity is undermined by an ominous shadow upon the final scene of peace, which ominously recalls "my shadow in the sun."

For this reason I would interpret Richard III as a notorious case, in the sense defined by Richard Sherwin, in his theorization of the relationship between law and the media. Actually, sixteenth-century theatres were the nearest equivalent to the modern mass media, and contributed to create a public opinion about political issues.[74] Notorious cases reveal deep social and cultural conflicts: they are

---

71 Bernard Spivak, *Shakespeare and the Allegory of Evil* (New York: Columbia University Press, 1972), 395.

72 Hertel, *Staging England in the Elizabethan History Play*, 109. Hertel also underlines the Unbestimmtheit of Richmond, whose character appeals to the audience's imagination in order to be brought to completion as a metaphor of the future Tudor dynasty. However, both characters' speeches to their armies were performed in the theatre, very probably addressing the audience. In this way, the power of Richard's speech would have affected their perceptions and thereby reenacted the political confusion of the Wars of the Roses (ibidem, 112). Actually, theatrical stagings of historical events had the effect of bringing the audience into the inner part of the mystery of state thus demystifying it. (See Margot Heinemann, "Political Drama," in the *Cambridge Companion to English Renaissance Drama*, eds. Braunmüller, Hattaway: 161–205, 177.) People were led to think about the staged political ideas and given aural images (at the same time pictorial and auditive) to think with.

73 Hertel, *Staging England in the Elizabethan History Play*, 114.

74 See Heinemann, "Political Drama," 167: As the author observes, "The opening up of secular political discussion and debate to anyone who could put a penny in the box was something quite new, and helped to transform the nature of politics."

"social dramas that take place on a field of embattled discourse where contested stories, metaphors, and character types vie for dominance in the culture at large."[75] This attunes also with the etymology of the word "tragedy," which comes from the Greek *tragoidia* or goat-play, and it implies the recognition that "the tragic hero is essentially another version of the sacrifice offered throughout known human history to appease an angry god – in other words, both to acknowledge and repress a contradiction in the culture's agreed way of perceiving reality."[76] Richard's case can be seen to embody a political anxiety about royal succession and is based in the collective legal imagination; his parable stages a competing world view to the official one, a competing nomos, which is at the basis of his personal legal framework. Richard has to be contained as it signifies the "outbreak of the uncanny in everyday life,"[77] but this perspective finally invests Richmond himself, as it has been argued above.

Recently, Richard has been restored his royal dignity through the belated burial of his body natural which took place on March 25 2015 at Leicester Cathedral. Through the solemn ceremony, Richard's body politic was finally restored in the temporal royal sequence, thus countering the play's effect of a suspension of time. As a matter of fact, according to some critics, "In the political discourse of Richard III, a straight 'lineal' progression of time awaits beyond the chronological unfolding of the play's narrative action, and premature births and untimely deaths are rhetorically figured as bodies moving at a different paces from the rest of the world."[78] The words of the officiating bishop, "Here, in a Cathedral, history meets the present, here eternity breaks into time" sanction the restoration of Richard into the linear development of English history, through the symbols of his royal position: the white rose of York and his name engraved in the coffin. The ceremony saw the participation of Prince Richard, Duke of Gloucester and descendant of the king, who manages an association devoted to preserve his memory, and Benedict Cumberbatch, his second cousin, 16 times removed, who also played in the role of Richard III in the series *The Hollow Crown*. In this stratification of history, the ceremony was concluded with the reading of a poem by Carol Ann Duffy. Once again, we have to imagine Richard appealing to the audience's hearing, and performatively asserting his identity:

---

75 Richard K. Sherwin, *When Law Goes Pop. The Vanishing Line between Law and Popular Culture* (Chicago and London: The University of Chicago Press, 2000), 74.

76 See Robert N. Watson, "Tragedy," in *The Cambridge Companion to English Renaissance Drama*, eds. Braumüller, Hattaway, 301–351, 307.

77 Sherwin, *When Law Goes Pop*, 76.

78 Jonathan Hsy, "Disability," in *The Cambridge Companion to the Body in Literature*, eds. David Hillman, Ulrika Maude (Cambridge: Cambridge University Press, 2015): 24–40, 37.

My bones, scripted in light, upon cold soil
A human Braille. My skull, scarred by a crown,
    Emptied of history. [...]
Grant me the carving of my name.

Gilad Ben-Nun

The Subjugation of International Law to Power Politics and Mystery of State (*Arcana Imperii*) in Shakespeare's *Henry V*

Foreword

As William Shakespeare's literary heritage enters its fourth century, the tendency to use passages from his *oeuvre* to denote certain perennial facets of human nature has also come of age. It is now well over a century since Sigmund Freud first made references to the Bard's work as he employed themes from the Shakespearean corpus and put them to use in his fields of enquiry, which were far removed from the literary, theatre-bound ones in which these works originated.[1] In addition to psychology, Shakespeare's works have also been used to elaborate on issues in the legal realm – most notably, those concerning the laws of war.[2] In this paper, I would like to follow this methodological pattern of using Shakespearean passages to document phenomena beyond the literary and theatrical realms in their strict sense. I opt to use Shakespeare as an aid to examine the conjuncture of secretive elements in statecraft (*Arcana Imperii*) and the tendency to abuse international law in the service of power politics. Both issues are strongly connected with absolutist regimes and modalities of governance, whose ethos stretches as far back as late antiquity and whose resurgence and influence were strongly felt during Shakespeare's time. In the conclusion, I examine the recent resurgence of strong, absolutist tendencies the world over (in Vladimir Putin's Russia or Viktor Orbán's Hungary), in light of Shakespeare's depiction of absolutism,

1 Norman N. Holland, "Freud on Shakespeare," *Proceedings of the Modern Literary Association* (PMLA) 75.3 (1960): 163–173. For a more detailed account and elaboration on themes from this article, see Holland's monograph, *Psychoanalysis and Shakespeare* (New York: McGraw-Hill, 1964). For a recent contribution in this direction, see: Henriette Michaud, "L'effet de Shakespeare dans l'œuvre de Freud," *Le Coq-hêron* no. 202 (2010/3): 55–60.

2 See, for example, the monographs by the former president of the International Criminal Tribunal for the former Yugoslavia (ICTY), Theodor Meron: *Henry's Wars and Shakespeare's Laws* (Oxford: The Clarendon Press, 1993) and *Bloody Constraint: War and Chivalry in Shakespeare* (Oxford: Oxford University Press, 1998).
For a recent contribution in this direction see: Paola Pugliatti, *Shakespeare and the Just War Tradition* (London: Routledge, 2016).

https://doi.org/10.1515/9783110591514-006

and ponder what this might mean vis-à-vis the nature of diplomacy in our day and age.

A word on method. As a diplomatic historian, whose primary works focus on the history of international law, I choose to treat Shakespeare's work first and foremost as *material historical evidence* pointing towards a certain *zeitgeist* of his time. This methodological approach has influenced my preference for *Henry V* over other works in Shakespeare's corpus that touch upon international law.[3] In contrast to *Julius Caesar* or even *King John*, in which the historical events portrayed were far removed from Shakespeare's time, those recorded in *Henry V* occurred less than two centuries prior to that play's performance. We know for certain that Shakespeare had access to several historical accounts concerning Henry's 1415 military campaigns in France, as well to his pre-war negotiations with the French king, Francois VI. Moreover, no other work by Shakespeare portrays *both* issues (*Arcana Imperii* and the manipulation of international law) in such an intertwined, dovetailed manner as do the relevant parts in *Henry V* (Act 1 Scene 2 and Act 2 Scene 4).

1 The manipulation of international law in Shakespeare

Tradition has it that, in 1599, *Henry V* was the first play to be performed on the stage of the newly opened, timber-built Globe theatre (later destroyed by fire in 1614).[4] It belongs to a string of historical plays that Shakespeare wrote during the last decade of the sixteenth century. It is a dramatized version of the historical events that led to the invasion of France by Henry V in 1415, through his successful military campaigns of 1416, up until his ultimate (albeit short-lived) unification of the crowns of France and England through marriage. The passages of the play that best portray both *Arcana Imperii* and international law occur in Act 1 Scene 2 (the discussion at Henry's privy council and the decision by the English king and his nobles to claim the throne of France) and Act 2 Scene 4 (when Henry's messenger – his uncle, the Duke of Exeter – delivers his ultimatum to the

---

3 Both themes – *Arcana Imperii* and international law – are treated by Shakespeare in *King John* and *Henry IV Part II. Julius Caesar*, and certainly *Richard III*, all have their ample doses of *Arcana Imperii*.

4 Hence, the play's famous reference to "this Woodden O, the very Caskes." Its first verified performance was in front of James I in 1605, at His Majesty's court.

French king, Francois VI, should the latter not relieve himself of the French crown in Henry's favour).

In the first of these scenes (1.2), Henry assembles his council of nobles to hear the learned arguments of the Archbishop of Canterbury as to why he indeed has the right to the French crown. A remarkable rendering of this scene, with an arresting cast of Shakespearean actors, can be observed in Kenneth Branagh's cinematic adaptation of Shakespeare's play.[5] Noting the perennial contest between Church and State, the king enquires, "where is my gracious lord of Canterbury," upon which the archbishop and the Bishop of Ely rush into the council chamber blessing the king, under the watchful eyes of the Duke of Exeter (masterfully played by the veteran British actor Brian Blessed), who is discontented due to their *retard*.[6] The king then requests the archbishop to explain to him and to the council whether he does indeed have a just claim to the throne of France:

> My learned Lord, we pray you to proceed,
> And iustly and religiously vnfold,
> Why the Law Salike, that they haue in France,
> Or should or should not barre vs in our Clayme:
> And God forbid, my deare and faithfull Lord,
> That you should fashion, wrest, or bow your reading,
> Or nicely charge your vnderstanding Soule,
> With opening Titles miscreate, whose right
> Sutes not in natiue colours with the truth:

In the subsequent passage, the king warns the archbishop of the consequences that his legal opinion will ultimately have should England go to war with France based on his legal interpretation:

> For God doth know, how many now in health,
> Shall drop their blood, in approbation
> Of what your reuerence shall incite vs to.
> Therefore take heed how you impawne our Person,
> How you awake our sleeping Sword of Warre;
> We charge you in the Name of God take heed:

5 Kenneth Branagh, *Shakespeare's King Henry V* (1989). All references here are to this film. In 1944, Laurence Olivier also made a screen adaptation of the play. His version is much more patriotic in its interpretation, having been made during World War II while Branagh's film enjoys a much higher degree of realism.

6 In the original Shakespearean text, Exeter explicitly mentions to the king that the Archbishop of Canterbury is not present, upon which Henry specifically sends for the archbishop, thus stressing further the issue of Church–State tensions.

> For neuer two such Kingdomes did contend,
> Without much fall of blood, whose guiltlesse drops
> Are euery one, a Woe, a sore Complaint,

Upon this request, the archbishop embarks on a long monologue filled with legal argumentation based upon the lineage of successions of the Kings of France dating back over a thousand years, coupled with geographic references to unfamiliar lands between Germany and France. The archbishop attempts to rebut the French legal line of argument; this precludes Henry's claim to the French throne based upon Salic law, which supposedly did not recognize the right of accession to the throne via female regal offspring. The archbishop then claims that the existing French royal line has consistently executed the right of legal accession to the throne via female lineages, and hence that Henry's claim, which is based on his direct ancestral link to Edward III, should be valid as well. During this elaborate presentation, the archbishop uses Latin phrases to cite legal sources, with geographical references to places most probably alien to most of the council members. Upon a signal from Exeter to make his final point, the archbishop cements his conclusion with the words "So, that as cleare as is the Summers Sunne," to which all the members of the council break out into laughter.

The king, obviously not understanding the bulk of legal argumentation set forth by the archbishop, asks for his final counsel: "May I with right and conscience make this claim?" to which the archbishop answers unequivocally, "The sinne vpon my head, dread Soueraigne." Once the archbishop had cast his judgment, Exeter and Westmorland take the floor and urge the king to take up the sword against France:

> Exeter: Your Brother Kings and Monarchs of the Earth
> Doe all expect, that you should rowse your selfe,
> As did the former Lyons of your Blood
>
> Westmorland: They know your Grace hath cause, and means, and might;
> So hath your Highnesse: neuer King of England
> Had Nobles richer, and more loyall Subiects,
> Whose hearts haue left their bodyes here in England,
> And lye pauillion'd in the fields of France.

While Westmorland reiterates to the king that the entire English nobility would provide the fighting forces required for such a military campaign, it is Exeter's argument that is most important here. Exeter speaks of the expectation by third-party powers – "Brother Kings and Monarchs of the Earth" – that Henry should make this claim, in order to conform to international diplomatic precedent and to avoid chaos within the international system, thus pressuring the king to uphold the diplomatic-legal code of his predecessors. The discussion ends with the Archbishop of Canterbury pledging to provide the king with the financial resources to execute this military endeavour, as he whispers in his ear:

> In ayde whereof, we of the Spiritualtie
> Will rayse your Highnesse such a mightie Summe,
> As neuer did the Clergie at one time
> Bring in to any of your Ancestors

And thus, the issue is resolved.

What can one infer from this depiction by Shakespeare of the legal discussions concerning England's international legal justification for her *Jus ad Bellum* call against France?[7] Moreover, what are the characteristics of the realm of international law according to this depiction? In short, how would the audience observing the play at the Globe theatre in 1599 have understood what international law actually was?

To begin with, international law seems, in Shakespeare's depiction, to comprise a very complicated legal field involving multiple layers of required knowledge (the legal codes of other countries, the geographies and intricate histories of those nations, and a multitude of foreign languages). This complexity contrasts starkly with the relative clarity with which Shakespeare chooses to treat other branches of law – for instance, the law of inheritance and its abuses (in *King Lear*) or the laws of debts and mortgages (in *The Merchant of Venice*). The intelligent and educated King Henry certainly does not understand whether he has or has not a claim to the throne of France. If one imagines Shakespeare's

7 The term *Jus ad Bellum*, coupled with the term *Jus in Bello*, has served as the bedrock of the laws of war since ancient Roman times. *Jus ad Bellum* refers to the laws of nations that provide the justification for going to war in the first place. Once conflict has commenced, humanitarian dictums require the execution of *Jus in Bello*, meaning the correct legal conduct *within* hostilities and armed conflict – most notably over the humane treatment of civilians (especially women and children); the accepted conduct towards prisoners of war; and refraining from deliberate, unnecessarily destructive policies (most notably "scorched-earth" tactics). For a good overview of *Jus ad Bellum* through the ages, see: Stephan Neff, *War and the Law of Nations* (Cambridge: Cambridge University Press, 2008): 7–68. On the specific influences of St. Augustine and St. Thomas Aquinas on the absolute requirement for a just cause for war in Christian theology (whose impact was crucial both on the historical figure of Henry V and, not least, on Shakespeare himself) prior to the "secularization of war" following the Thirty Years' War and the Treaty of Westphalia, see: Frederick H. Russell, *The Just War in the Middle Ages* (Cambridge: Cambridge University Press, 1975): 213–292.

own audience at the Globe, it too would most probably have been in a similar state of bewilderment to King Henry's character in the play, waiting patiently to hear the Archbishop of Canterbury's ultimate verdict as to the rightfulness of the English claim.

The contrast between international law and other branches of the law in Shakespeare deepens when one considers that the former (certainly in Shakespeare's time) actually lacked the most fundamental characteristic of law – namely, the presiding of role of the judge and his *ultima ratio*. In both *The Merchant of Venice* and *Measure for Measure*, the objectivity and conclusiveness of the judge's role is indispensable to the plot.[8] Yet it is precisely this lack of a final judicial authority in the engagements of nations that accounts for international law's heightened potential for abuse.

And there was indeed abuse of international law by Henry V. As the great medievalist E.F. Jacob noted in his authoritative historical study of the king, his claim to the throne of France between 1414 and 1416 was at best "a sham so as to disguise his preparations for war," and this aspect of English history was in all probability rather well known during Shakespeare's time.[9]

The understanding that international law was more prone to abuse than other fields of law was certainly not exclusive to Shakespeare. One succinct (yet powerful) example of this negative quality, from roughly the same period, appeared just over a century after Shakespeare's death. In 1724, the great French jurist Charles de Montesquieu – the father of modern constitutional law and the inventor of the doctrine of the State's separation of powers (between the executive, legislative and judiciary) – published his *Persian Letters* to great public acclaim. By this time, Montesquieu was a recognized legal authority, having served as the Lifetime President (*Président à Mortier*) of Bordeaux' Parlement Régional since 1716. His book features an exchange of letters between two fictitious Asian Muslim friends, one ("the Uzbek") residing in Paris and writing to the other, his younger friend "Rhedi" in Venice, about what appear to him to be the odd ways of the Europeans. This genre of writing, in which so-called "objective" outsiders unmask and expose unspoken negative truths about European societies, was well known in the late seventeenth and early eighteenth centuries. Concerning

8 Michael Jay Willson, "View of Justice in Shakespeare's the Merchant of Venice and Measure for Measure," *Notre Dame Law Review* 70.3 (1993): 695–726, 726.

9 Ernst. F. Jacob, *Henry V and the Invasion of France* (London: Hodder & Stoughton – English Universities Press, 1947), 5. Although published postwar, Jacob wrote this historical study during World War II and the German "Blitz" over London. He begins his introduction with an intriguing parallel between the D-Day landings on the shores of Normandy in June 1944 and Henry's disembarkation upon those same shores five centuries earlier.

international law and its manipulation, the Uzbek provides the following observations:

> International law is better understood in Europe than in Asia; and yet it must be said that the passions of princes, the patience of the people, and the flattery of authors, have corrupted all its principles.
>
> At the present time this law is a science which teaches princes to what length they may carry the violation of justice without injuring their own interests. What a design, Rhedi, to wish to harden the conscience by reducing iniquity to a system, by giving it rules, by settling its principles, and drawing inferences from it!
>
> [...] one would say, Rhedi, that there are two species of justice wholly different from each other: one which regulates the affairs of individuals, and rules in civil law; another which settles the differences arising between peoples, and tyrannizes over international law; as if international law were not itself a civil law, not indeed of a particular country, but of the world.[10]

2 "*Arcana Imperii*" in *Henry V*

The picture of the abuse of international law that emerges from Shakespeare's dramatization is immanently associated with competing quests for power by rulers, who, for the sake of that power, sidestep what ought to be "blind" and impartial tenets of justice. Yet this abuse of international law is not carried out in a cognitive limbo; rather, it demands varying degrees of darkness and sombre environments. The abuse of international justice is facilitated by an enabling political environment of concealment and secrecy: a *darkness* that runs counter to openly transparent, *enlightened*, moral and political environments. It is not for nothing that the age of "Enlightenment" also gave rise to the first fully-fledged "objective" envisioning of international legal systems. The most notable of these representative works include Emer de Vatell's *The Law of Nations* (1758) and Immanuel Kant's works *What is Enlightenment?*[11] and *The Metaphysics of Morals*

---

10 Charles de Montesquieu, *Persian Letters*, trans. John Davidson (London: George Routledge, 1899), Letter XCV (95): 217–218.

11 Kant's original German title, *Was ist Aufklärung?* implicitly retains within its etymology this idea of the *clarity* of the enlightened world that he wished to envisage, as opposed to the *obscurity* that he openly associated with the age of absolutism, which preceded his generation. The association of secrecy with darkness and obscurity, as opposed to transparency, light, and visual clarity has remained a feature of our world today, as in the workings of the most important NGO advocating governmental transparency and the fight against institutionalized state-based corruption, Transparency International. See www.transparency.org

(1797) – the latter known in its English translation as *The Philosophy of Law: An Exposition of the Fundamental Principles of Jurisprudence as the Science of Right.*

Darkness, in fact, plays a major role in *Henry V*, especially in Branagh's cinematographic interpretation of the scenes that evolve around international legal issues (1.2 and 2.4). In Act 1 Scene 2 (during the presentation by the Archbishop of Canterbury at Henry's privy council), the entire chamber is poorly lit, with the king walking into the scene backlit with his face blackened and only his silhouette visible to the spectator. In the second scene in which international legal issues are debated – during the delivery of the armed ultimatum by Exeter to Francois VI, the King of France – the French chamber is even darker, with Exeter walking from a bright foyer into the dimly lit chamber of the French king's council.

The spectator is immediately drawn into an emotional condition of fear – especially during the ultimatum scene (of whose thematic a separate discussion follows below). The frightening Duke of Exeter (brilliantly captured in Blessed's overbearingly huge stature) enters the dark chamber in full armour (plate mail over chainmail), sword at the ready, and delivers a chilling ultimatum of all-out war, along with a vile and gruesome threat of immense bloodshed. This obscenely violent content within its threatening, warlike context is contrasted with Exeter's soft-spoken tone of voice and his diplomatically polite speech. The episode becomes all the more frightening when Exeter and the French Dauphin politely exchange worrisome mutual insults. All this takes place right under the watchful eye of a deeply fearful and sombre French monarch (masterfully portrayed by that great Shakespearean actor Paul Scofield, who plays his part solely through a fantastic array of facial-expression acting which contrasts with his totally monotone delivery). This entire portrayal of statecraft – being undertaken in dark rooms, behind closed doors, in utter secrecy – is the very essence of the "Mystery of State" (*Arcana Imperii*) that Shakespeare was attempting to portray.

To what does this notion of *Arcana Imperii* pertain, and how does it connect to the manipulation and abuse of international law? Moreover, if *Arcana Imperii* is indeed what Shakespeare was pointing to here, where and how could he have come across it?

The term broadly refers to the existence of a secretive ethos, which underpins the entire realm of statecraft and policy making within a given political entity. *Arcana Imperii* not only condones the handling of state affairs behind closed doors and away from the public eye – it in fact advocates these conditions outright, as it stresses the dangers of populism and mob rule ("ochlocracy" is the Aristotelian term) when these make their way into the directing of international and state affairs. *Arcana Imperii* has always been intimately associated with autocratic, absolutist, and non-democratic or non-republican regimes. The German translation for the term – *Geheimpolitik* – immediately triggers acute, traumatic connotations of the *Geheime Staatspolizei* ("Secret State Police") of the Nazi regime, better known via its notorious acronym GESTAPO, and the later workings of its East German successor, the "Staatssicherheit," more widely recognized by its respective acronym: the STASI.

Yet the concept of *Arcana Imperii* and the very idea that statecraft inherently rests upon some sort of mysterious, secretive, non-explicable and even intuitive (that is, illogical) bedrock of ideas and practices have their origins in late antiquity. It was in fact Tacitus, in a famous passage from his *Annales*, who first made explicit use of the term.[12] While the idea carried forward through the Middle Ages, it was only in the early modern period, with the sixteenth- and early seventeenth-century rise in national consciousness in both the French and German-speaking intellectual-political milieus, that the term was revived with significant success. Arnold Clapmar in Prussia and, especially, the intellectual circle around Cardinal Richelieu in early seventeenth-century France developed *Arcana Imperii* as their-conduct-of-choice for both domestic and, particularly, international statecraft.[13] However, amidst the religious yet nakedly realistic political realities of the early modern era, Niccolò Machiavelli's lure, strong as it undoubtedly was, could not be easily called upon without exposing oneself to accusations of Christian heresy – especially given the pervasive, overbearing influence that the moralistic ethos of Thomism exerted upon matters of state. Yet Tacitus was an entirely different source. The Roman historian was compulsory reading in the political education of any learned man, let alone senior magistrate, anywhere in seventeenth-century Europe. What everybody knew about *Arcana Imperii* from Machiavelli's *Prince* but could not quote for fear of being charged with heresy was thus enabled, both discursively and politically, thanks to its sanctioning by Tacitus.

That *Arcana Imperii* was, by the 1630s, salient in Europe is well. However, Shakespeare had already put on *Henry V* in 1599, and it was certainly not the only one of his historical plays to include overt representations of the concept (the most obvious came in *Richard III* as early as 1592!). This means that Shake-

---

12 Tacitus, *Annales* 2:36: "that the proposal went deeper than this, and trespassed on the arcana of sovereignty" (*haud dubium erat eam sententiam altius penetrare et arcana imperii temptari*), translated by John Jackson in *Tacitus II* (Loeb Classical Library: London and New York, 1931). For a full explanation of the borrowing that early-modern writers took from Tacitus, see: Peter Donaldson, *Machiavelli and Mystery of State* (Cambridge: Cambridge University Press, 1988), viii, n. 3.

13 On Clampar, see: Richard Tuck, *Philosophy and Government 1572–1651: Ideas in Context* (Cambridge: Cambridge University Press, 1993), 124–126. See also: Donaldson, *Machiavelli*, 111–165. On Richelieu's dealings with *Arcana Imperii*, see: William F. Church, *Richelieu and Reason of State* (Princeton, NJ: Princeton University Press, 1972), 13–81.

speare must have come across *Arcana Imperii* in its acute form at an even earlier date – at the latest, some time in the 1580s. Conclusive proof as to where the Bard actually obtained his ideas for *Arcana Imperii* is beyond the scope of this paper; if this is at all possible (depending upon available existing sources, in terms of the methodological "burden of proof" required by historians to justify such a claim), this would merit a full-blown study in its own right. Rather, what I will try to do in the following pages is provide a *hypothesis* as to where Shakespeare *might* have taken some of these ideas from. I do this in the hope (and open-ended call) that other scholars will test this hypothesis of mine further, and see if it "holds water."

Arcana Imperii is intimately connected with the rise of the early modern European nation-state. The late sixteenth century was a crucial time, with two of the paradigmatic nation-states – Great Britain and France – actually coming into being. Germany and Italy did not come into their own before their unifications in the nineteenth century. Spain was more of an empire on the world seas than a confined nation-state, and as for the Hapsburg and Ottoman empires – these were relatively decentralized multiethnic entities. In the Europe of the late sixteenth and early seventeenth century, the rise of the State was embodied in these two countries: France and Great Britain (albeit only after the unification of the crowns of Scotland, England and Ireland under James I in 1603 – *after* the writing of *Henry V*). However, the most crystallized model of statehood – which encompassed *Arcana Imperii* in its most naked form, and which could have pressed itself upon Shakespeare's psyche as he began engaging with these ideas during the 1580s – must surely have been France. And it was France that first provided the world with that vital concept, the *conditio sine qua non* for any full statehood to come into being: sovereignty.[14]

In 1576, in his *Six Books of the Republic*, the French jurist Jean Bodin first formulated the concept of sovereignty as the non-divisible and exclusive control of all means of power over a people in a defined territory. Bodin wrote the *Six Books* in direct relation to the violent slaughter of the Huguenots in the 1572 St. Bartholomew's Day massacre, which he justified from a French royalist perspective given the Huguenots' perceived direct attack on the French crown and, conse-

14 For an important explanation as to why the State arose specifically in the late sixteenth and early seventeenth centuries – as an answer to the chaos of the wars of the Reformation, the Thirty Years' War, and as a result of the economic havoc that the expansion into the New World had wrought upon decentralized empire-economies in Europe – see: Theodore K. Rabb, *The Struggle for Stability in Early Modern Europe* (Oxford: Oxford University Press, 1976): 61–99.

quently, on the State.[15] The threat that the Huguenots posed to the French crown was more statutory than religious (after all, the French King Henry IV, who later issued the Edict of Nantes, was himself a Protestant). The strong and affluent Huguenot nobility, headed by Gaspard de Coligny, had requested noble prerogatives and a limitation of the Crown's sovereign powers in a similar manner to demands being voiced by the British nobility (which eventually resulted in the English Civil War and the beheading of one king, until parliamentary prerogatives were firmly cemented in 1689). The French crown's conceptual answer to the Huguenots' demand for a power-sharing arrangement (e.g. the limitation of the power of the crown in one way or another) was answered in Bodin's concept of sovereignty, which he saw as *ipso facto* indivisible and which he thus framed in his well-known Aristotelian syllogism as:

> Sovereign Authority is absolute
> The King of France is sovereign
> The King of France is absolute[16]

Many signals point to the possibility that Shakespeare was acquainted with Bodin's thought on sovereignty and statecraft. In 1581, the jurist accompanied Francois of Anjou to England; the French prince, who was wooing the young English Queen Elizabeth I, spent several months in London along with his entourage, to which Bodin belonged. We also have evidence that Bodin remained in contact, and on good terms, with Francis Walsingham, Queen Elizabeth's "spymaster," and that during these years Bodin also worked on a large treatise denouncing sorcery and witchcraft – yet another venture into alternative worlds of secrecy and darkness.

The events of August 1572, during the St. Bartholomew's Day massacre, probably had a certain influence upon Shakespeare. In 1593, Christopher Marlowe's play *Massacre at Paris* – which depicts the events surrounding the actions of the instigator of the killings, the Duke de Guise – was first performed.

Marlowe's influences on Shakespeare are common academic knowledge, and have been amply demonstrated. In fact, his literary impact on Shakespeare is virtually unquestionable when one considers the acute resemblances between

---

15 Julian H. Franklin, *Jean Bodin and the Rise of Absolutist Theory* (Cambridge: Cambridge University Press, 1973), Ch. 3: "The Shift to Absolutism": 41–69.

16 Franklin, *Jean Bodin*, 68. For a full exposition on the indivisible character of sovereignty, see Book I Ch. 8 of Bodin's *Six Books* in *Bodin: On Sovereignty – Cambridge Texts in the History of Political Thought*, ed. and trans. Julian H. Franklin (Cambridge: Cambridge University Press, 1992): 1–45.

Marlowe's *The Jew of Malta* and Shakespeare's *The Merchant of Venice* or the redemptive–punitive elements in *Macbeth* in comparison to Marlowe's *Doctor Faustus*, as well as similarities between Shakespeare's historical plays and Marlowe's *Edward II.* The two playwrights knew each other well and ample evidence points to Shakespeare's acquaintance with Marlowe's employment as a spy in the service of Walsingham – especially in connection with the character of the "English Agent" in *Massacre at Paris*, which in all probability was Marlowe's own self-portrayal of the spy that he indeed was.[17] If Marlowe was living a "life on the edge," which included considerable secretive elements that were connected to the Elizabethan court's real-life spy networks and a secretive state apparatus, the chances are that Shakespeare knew about (and probably tactfully kept a safe distance from) these secretive elements under the English crown.

In his *Massacre at Paris*, Marlowe was the first English dramaturge to provide a staged depiction of the events that led up to the St. Bartholomew's Day atrocities. The play roughly follows the sequence of events from the declaration of the forthcoming marriage of Henry of Navarre to Margaret of Valois, through the riots and killings in Paris up to the execution of the Duke de Guise. Throughout, the piece is dominated by Guise's character, who is portrayed as a classic Machiavellian, conniving political operator – albeit one who is totally committed to the preservation and protection of both the French crown and its Catholicism. The audience is struck by the extent to which Guise, the play's *bête noire*, is prepared to sacrifice his moral principles, and later even his life, for the sake of the monarchical Catholic French crown. Early in the play, as he enters for the very first time (Scene II), the duke provides the audience with a much-needed and rare insight into his true motivations for the sake of the protection of France:

> What glory is there in a common good,
> That hanges for every peasant to atchive?
> That like I best that flyes beyond my reach.
> Set me to scale the high Peramides,
> And thereon set the Diadem of Fraunce,
> Ile either rend it with my nayles to naught,
> Or mount the top with my aspiring winges,
> Although my downfall be the deepest hell.[18]

---

17 Richard Wilson, "Tragedy, Patronage and Power," in *The Cambridge Companion to Christopher Marlowe*, ed. Patrick Cheney (Cambridge: Cambridge University Press, 2004): 207–231, 207.
18 Christopher Marlowe, *Massacre at Paris* (1581), in *The Complete Works Of Christopher Marlowe* (Oxford: Clarendon Press 1987–1998), vol. 5. Scene II – last monologue before the scene's ending.

As for the personal, dubious attributes that Guise intends to employ to these ends, he leaves the audience with very little doubt about any moral scruples he might have had:

> For this, I wake, when others think I sleepe,
> For this, I waite, that scorn attendance else:
> For this, my quenchles thirst whereon I builde
> Hath often pleaded kindred to the King.
> For this, this head, this heart, this hand and sworde,
> Contrive, imagine and fully execute[19]

All this must be done through the inner dealings of secretive state matters, of which neither the peasants (to whom Guise eluded earlier) nor the nobility have any understanding:

> Matters of importe, aimed at by many,
> Yet understoode by none.[20]

3 The ultimate impact of *Arcana Imperii* upon Shakespeare – King James I

So much for the circumstantial influences that might have triggered Shakespeare's interests in *Arcana Imperii*. Yet beyond these arguable influences, which methodologically are suggestive at best, there remains the more immediate and direct effect that *Arcana Imperii* must have exerted upon Shakespeare due to his immediate and direct exposure to it – in the open and official proclamations of his king (and direct employer!), James I.

Thanks to Ernst Kantorowicz's pioneering enquiry into the ecclesiastical origins of monarchical justifications – later published in his renowned work, *The King's Two Bodies* – we are able to embed Shakespeare within his true, immediate political context.[21] In his "intellectual run-up" to this book, Kantorowicz published several important studies, within which he delved into various facets of monarchy. In one of these studies, published in 1957, the German-American historian claimed that the absolutism that began in the sixteenth century, and

19 Marlowe, *Massacre*, Scene II.
20 Marlowe, *Massacre*, Scene II.
21 Ernst H. Kantorowicz, *The King's Two Bodies: An Enquiry into Medieval Political Theology* (Princeton, NJ: Princeton University Press, 1960).

which reached its zenith in the seventeenth, in fact borrowed its authority and insignia from the ecclesiastical world of the Catholic Church.[22] While this claim ought to be revisited, given Tacitus' (that is, the non-Christian) historical precedence for medieval Christian theology, which would fault Kantorowicz's claim with a good measure of anachronism, the article itself is filled with first-class (and hitherto overlooked) early seventeenth-century absolutist sources that shed much new light upon *Arcana Imperii*. In 1610, King James I complained that "nothing is now unsearched into, neither the very highest mysteries of God-head nor the deepest mysteries that belong to the persons or state of King and Princes."[23] In 1616, James spoke of: "My Prerogative or mystery of State and of the mysterie of the King's power, and of the mysticall reverence, that belongs unto them."[24] Kantorowicz continues his quotations with one of the most representative examples of James I's attitude towards the British Parliament, the ultimate qualifier of regal power: the king "ordered the speaker of the House of Commons to acquaint that house with our pleasure that none therein shall presume to meddle with anything concerning our government or mysteries of State."[25]

James I ascended to the throne of England in 1603. We know for a fact that the first proven performance of *Henry V* (as opposed to the hearsay tradition that places its premiere at the Globe theatre in 1599) was at court – with the king as a member of its audience. James I's absolutist tendencies, as James VI of Scotland, were well known long before he acquired the English throne. While we do not have the words "mysteries of State" themselves in the play, Shakespeare's reference to *Arcana Imperii* is unmissable. When one considers the king before whom

22 Ernst H. Kantorowicz, "Mysteries of State: An Absolutist Concept and its Late Mediaeval Origins," *The Harvard Theological Review* 48.1 (January 1955): 65–91. Kantorowicz's central question – "How, by what channels and by what techniques, were the spiritual *arcana ecclesiae* transferred to the state [so] as to produce the new secular *arcana imperii* of absolutism (66) – already establishes as its meta-logical forgone conclusion that such a transfer from the spiritual to the temporal world indeed took place. This position by Kantorowicz is somewhat problematic given that he himself acknowledges (69, n.18) the origins of *Arcana Imperii* in the very same passage from Tacitus quoted here, above. I would argue that the mysterious elements of statehood need not necessarily have come only from the Christian spiritual world, as they existed full-well within the "real world" of northern European folk mythologies concerning statehood – most notably, in stories of the Knights of the Round Table, and even of Alexander of Macedon's mysterious ability to untie the Gordian knot (which, in itself, is a state-based mythological element already found in Homer). Subsequent scholars would do well to examine this alternative to Kantorowicz's origin of mystery.

23 Kantorowicz, "Mysteries of State," 68.

24 Kantorowicz, "Mysteries of State," n. 10.

25 Kantorowicz, "Mysteries of State," n. 11.

the play was first enacted; when one considers the well-known intellectual impact that Marlowe exerted upon Shakespeare; and when one merges Shakespeare's contemporary political context, of the bitter rivalry between European monarchs who demanded to be gods and who thus refused to accept any parliamentary limits upon their powers (be that in France with the Huguenots or in England with the "long and short" parliaments) we can grasp the full impression that *Arcana Imperii* probably had upon Shakespeare.

4 Conclusion: The return of *Arcana Imperii* and the end of democratic diplomacy

It is now time to revisit the topic with which I began this paper – namely, international law and its susceptibility to abuse, as portrayed by Shakespeare in *Henry V* – and to examine the intimate connections between *Arcana Imperii*, international law, and the realm of international diplomacy.

If time travel were possible, and one were to invite the signatories of the 1648 Treaty of Westphalia to visit the UN building in New York as the General Assembly was in its annual session (from September to December each year), with its habitual marathon of UN Security Council sessions, these guests would probably be appalled and disgusted by the publicity and openness with which diplomacy is exercised at the turn of the third millennium. While estimates vary as to exactly how many people were fully acquainted with the exact details inscribed into the Westphalian Treaties even at their most numerous these did not exceed several thousands of people the world over. And one must remember that we are talking about the treaties that ended the Thirty Years' War in Europe – a conflict that annihilated roughly a third of the population of the continent and its livelihoods.[26] Since the end of World War I, and especially since the creation of the UN after World War II, the world entered a new phase in the history of diplomacy – the age of "democratic diplomacy."[27] The hallmark of this new diplomacy is its subordination to public scrutiny, as the contents of and negotiations regarding international treaties, pacts, and diplo-

---

26 Several historians, foremost amongst them Chicago University's Michael Geyer, have subsequently argued that in proportional terms the impacts of the Thirty Years' War far exceeded the destruction and trauma caused by World War II.

27 Harold Nicolson, *Diplomacy*, 3rd edition (Oxford: Oxford University Press, 1963): 80–103.

matic alliances are known to electorates in democratically governed countries, and are subject to the latter's public control and questioning.[28]

To understand the stark difference between Shakespeare's time and our own, it would be sufficient to compare the manner in which a military ultimatum, the critical moment in any diplomatic engagement, was delivered in Shakespeare's time, under absolutism, with such a delivery in the age of democratic diplomacy. One can, in fact, compare the two visually by contrasting the ultimatum delivered by the Duke of Exeter to the French court in Branagh's cinematized version of *Henry V* with that delivered by Adlai Stevenson of the United States to Ambassador Valerian Zorin of the USSR at the publicly televized UN Security Council session of October 1962 on the subject of Cuba.[29] In 1416, the ultimatum was delivered in a dark and secretive chamber to a small group of men, the result of whose deliberations would "impawne," in Shakespeare's words, the life and well-being of their two nations. The 1962 ultimatum was delivered on public television and broadcast around the world. When Ambassador Zorin continued to attempt to mask his intentions concerning the placement of Soviet nuclear weapons in Cuba, around 100 miles off the coast of the United States and rebuked the American diplomat, declaring that he was not under prosecution in a US court room, Stevenson uttered the words that have since gone down in the pantheon of diplomatic conduct: "You are in the courtroom of world public opinion."

There is a message here for us all. In both cases, in the 1416 confrontation between England and France (so well portrayed by Shakespeare in *Henry V*) and during the Cuba Missile Crisis, two world powers experienced the acute presentation of an ultimatum before all-out war was intended to be waged upon them. For all the inherent differences of these two examples, one cannot deny the mitigating, indeed soothing, effect that public pressures (on both sides of the Iron Curtain, it should be added) played in preventing war in 1962. The de-

28 This change in the nature of diplomacy was evident to Harold Nicolson himself, who, just before his death in 1963, published his well-known essay "Diplomacy Then and Now" in *Foreign Affairs* (October 1961) (reprinted in Nicolson, *Diplomacy*, 244–262. Nicolson joined the British Foreign Office several months prior to the outbreak of World War I, and, as the youngest delegate at the British Embassy in Berlin at the time (as per diplomatic protocol), was chosen for the task of delivering Britain's declaration of war upon Germany in August 1914. He then served as the first secretary of the British delegation to the Versailles negotiations, and witnessed first-hand how public opinion swayed the diplomats there towards the cruel surrender terms imposed upon Germany in that treaty, which Nicolson himself criticized at the time.

29 For the ultimatum delivered by Exeter in Branagh's version of *Henry V*, see: www.youtube.com/watch?v=mKHihAPr2Rc&t=3s (last access February 3, 2017) For the speech by Adlai Stevenson at the UN Security Council, see: www.youtube.com/watch?v=xgR8NjNw__I (last access February 3, 2017)

mocratization of diplomacy – that is, the extrication of *Arcana Imperii* from statecraft under democratic regimes – has gone hand in hand with an enhancement of public accountability; with the rise of the ethos of human rights; and ultimately, as in the Cuba Missile Crisis, with belligerent leaders succumbing to a public opinion opposed to an unaccountable bloodletting. The involvement of democratic publics in diplomacy has also been a harbinger of the promotion of fairer and more transparent conduct with regard to international law – its development and usages.

With the recent rise – or rather resurfacing, for they have always festered beneath the visible surface – of absolutist tendencies in many of the world's regimes (as in Benjamin Netanyahu's Israel, Recep Tayyip Erdoğan's Turkey, Trump's US, and Viktor Orbán's Hungary) one can certainly anticipate a return to *Arcana Imperii*, and its corresponding tendency of abuse of international law in the service of narrow political objectives and at the expense of the well-being of publics at large. Shakespeare's archetypal depiction of these two traits provides an insight into the dangers of the world of diplomacy that were once, for a period during the twentieth century, held at bay, and whose re-emergence in the near future is unfortunately more probable.

Part Two **Ethnicity and Alterity**

Heinz Antor

Ethnicity, Alterity and the Law in Shakespeare's *The Merchant of Venice*

In his play *The Merchant of Venice*,[1] first performed in 1596 or 1597, William Shakespeare engages intensely with what it means to live in a multicultural environment in which encounters with otherness are part of everyday life and in which alterity can also lead to conflicts that need to be resolved peacefully through the workings of the law. This is not the only time the Elizabethan playwright negotiated the complications of racial and ethnic otherness, an earlier example being Shakespeare's depiction of blackness in *Titus Andronicus* (1589–92/1594) and the most famous later instance of course being his dramatization of the story of *Othello, The Moor of Venice* (1601). It is no coincidence that both his play about the Jewish moneylender and that about the black general have the same setting since Venice in Shakespeare's day was not only one of the leading political, military and economic powers in the Western world, but widely admired as a centre of culture and a potential point of reference, if not a model, for the negotiations of change in an England that was about to become an early capitalist and colonial superpower on the world stage.[2] But nowhere else in his works did Shakespeare link issues of otherness with those of justice and the law to such an extent as in *The Merchant of Venice*.

The first scene of the play immediately establishes the commercial context in which life in a trading nation with international economic relations has to be seen, with Antonio shown to be fretting, as Salarino surmises, about the success of his various enterprises and the fate of his diverse merchant ships at sea. The theme is continued with the arrival of Bassanio and his confession that he has spent too much money and will thus not be able to pay back his debts, including that owed to Antonio. Bassanio's plea for further credit from Antonio, who, since his argosies have not yet returned, is short of ready money himself, raises the issue of borrowing money from a third party. This economic initiation into the

---

1 William Shakespeare, *The Comical History of the Merchant of Venice, or Otherwise Called the Jew of Venice*, in *The Complete Works*, eds. Stanley Wells and Gary Taylor (Oxford: Oxford University Press, 1986), 479–508.

2 As Andrew Hadfield has stated, "perhaps the most significant reasons that Englishmen admired Venice were political. [...] for [...] Shakespeare, representing Venice was an [...] obvious means of thinking about the problems and opportunities of Elizabethan England"; Andrew Hadfield, "Shakespeare and Republican Venice," in *Visions of Venice in Shakespeare*, eds. Laura Tosi and Shaul Bassi (Farnham: Ashgate, 2011), 67–82, 67–68.

https://doi.org/10.1515/9783110591514-007

play enables the introduction of two of its main themes, i.e. the issue of gender in the love story between Bassanio and Portia that results from it as well as the topic of credit and usury through the linkage to Shylock, who is not only a merchant, but also a Jewish moneylender characterized by his ethnic alterity.[3]

Again, in the brief conversation between Portia and Nerissa that makes up the second scene of the play, we are not only made familiar with the ploy of the three caskets devised by Portia's father as a means of finding the right husband for his daughter, but this is also linked to the two main themes just mentioned. On the one hand, Portia's being bound to her father's method of choosing a husband for her raises the issue of patriarchal domination and arbitrariness[4] versus paternal wisdom and benevolence. But on the other hand, more indirectly, Portia's words also raise the issue of alterity since all her suitors, whom Nerissa enumerates one after the other, are foreigners come from afar to woo the fair lady from Belmont, and they are all of them – whether they come from Naples or the Palatinate, from France or England, Scotland, Germany or Morocco – rejected without fail or made fun of by Portia. Foreigners, it seems, simply are not up to par for Portia,[5] the only exception being Bassanio, whom she remembers favourably. It is doubtful, however, whether the gentleman from Venice is indeed perceived by Portia as a foreigner since Venice in this play is the geographic point of focalization and Belmont seems to be situated rather close to the Republic. The

3 Sàez also refers to the interlinkages between the various themes of the play when she states that "[l]ove is also related to law and justice and the world of commercial bonds." Rosa Sáez, "Religion, Law and Justice in *The Merchant of Venice, Los Intereses Creados* and *La Ciudad Alegre y Confiada,*" *Actas del congreso internacional de la Sociedad Espanola de Estudios Renacentistas Ingleses* (SEDERI), *Proceedings of the III International Conference of the Spanish Society for English Renaissance Studies* (Granada: SEDERI, 1992), 267–275, 273. Oldrieve similarly emphasizes the link between issues of gender and ethnicity when she points out that "[i]n *The Merchant of Venice* Shylock and Portia both represent marginalized groups, the one an ethnic and religious minority, and the other women."; Susan Oldrieve, "Marginalized Voices in *The Merchant of Venice,*" *Cardozo Studies in Law and Literature* 5.1 (1993): 87–105, 87.

4 Spinosa, for example, argues that Portia is "a devotress to the arbitrariness in male activity both of her father's casket game [...] and of the preposterous lies of men"; Charles Spinosa, "Shylock and Debt and Contract in *The Merchant of Venice,*" *Cardozo Studies in Law and Literature* 5.1 (1993): 65–85, 80. Oldrieve also emphasizes that "Portia's first appearance onstage [*sic*] show her struggling to balance her needs as an individual against the demands of the patriarchal society in which she lives."; Oldrieve, "Marginalized Voices," 88.

5 Ojeda Alba therefore points out that Portia's "racial prejudice is shown, for instance, when she talks about Morocco's black complexion [...]."; Ojeda Alba, "Justice and Injustice in *The Merchant of Venice,*" *Cuadernos de literatura inglesa y norteamericana* 9.1–2 (2006): 11–23, 21. Sáez also rejects interpretations that attribute an "apparent lack of racial prejudice" to Portia; Sáez, "Religion, Law and Justice," 270–271.

general impression created by Portia's comments on her wooers thus remains one of negativity and rejection of the culturally other.

In the scene that follows Shylock makes his first appearance, and significantly, in the stage directions he is referred to as "Shylock the Jew," which immediately opens up the possibility of re-introducing the theme of money-lending for interest since Christians were not supposed to engage in this kind of business so that it is because of Shylock's ethnic otherness that Bassanio and Antonio turn to him for financial help. This, however, also turns into an occasion on which the mutual resentment between Christians and Jews becomes palpable, primarily in Shylock's own words, for example in his negative reaction to Bassanio's invitation to dinner, which he refuses to accept on religious grounds:

> BASSANIO: If it please you to dine with us.
> SHYLOCK (*aside*): Yes, to smell pork, to eat of the habitation which your prophet the Nazarite conjured the devil into! I will buy with you, sell with you, talk with you, walk with you, and so following, but I will not eat with you, drink with you, nor pray with you. (1.3.30–35)

Shylock here points out that cultural alterity need not be an obstacle to economic transactions but is certainly a dividing factor when it comes to religiously determined everyday activities such as eating and worshipping. That this is not only motivated by Shylock's adherence to a different set of rules but by a deep-seated and religiously motivated hatred is expressed in his aside following the appearance of Antonio about whom he says:

> SHYLOCK (*aside*): How like a fawning publican he looks.
> I hate him for he is a Christian;
> But more, for that in low simplicity
> He lends out money gratis, and brings down
> The rate of usance here with us in Venice.
> If I can catch him once upon the hip
> I will feed fat the ancient grudge I bear him.
> He hates our sacred nation, and he rails,
> Even there where merchants most do congregate,
> On me, my bargains, and my well-won thrift –
> Which he calls interest. Cursèd be my tribe
> If I forgive him. (1.3.39–50)

The image of Shylock presented here is an ambiguous one[6] in as far as he is shown to be both hater and hated. He hates Antonio for religious and economic

6 Hamilton points out that many critics "have argued that the hallmark of *The Merchant of Ven-*

reasons, but he is also discriminated against as an interest-charging moneylender by the latter for the same reasons. To Shylock, the problems he has with Antonio are not only a personal matter between two economic rivals from different cultural backgrounds, but also a matter of collective identity. The individual grudge he bears Antonio within a collective frame of reference is turned by him into a duty towards his fellow Jews to harm his Venetian rival. Shylock's personal interest is thus justified by reference to a wider ethnic community, which allows him to use the alterity evinced by Antonio to harm him. The imagery used here by Shylock already points forward to what is to come in its references to feeding on Antonio to assuage his hatred of the other. Food here signifies the negativity of cultural difference, and the cannibalistic dimension of Shylock's thoughts not only characterizes him as a potential savage but also underlines his willingness to annihilate otherness by engorging it and thus transforming it into part of the self, i.e. into sameness. As a result, the audience can see that Shylock may be discriminated against by Antonio on the Rialto,[7] but the Jew is nevertheless depicted as the far less sympathetic character through the insight into the negativity of his thoughts provided by this aside.

This negative characterization of Shylock is continued in the dialogue that follows between him and Antonio, in which the latter's habit of never charging interest for lending money to others is once more cited in front of Shakespeare's Christian audience, and when Shylock tries to justify his diverging practice by telling a story about the biblical figure of Jacob, this is turned against him by Antonio in a mocking remark to Bassanio:

> ANTONIO: Mark you this, Bassanio?
> The devil can cite Scripture for his purpose.
> An evil soul producing holy witness
> Is like a villain with a smiling cheek,
> A goodly apple rotten at the heart.
> O, what a goodly outside falsehood hath! (1.3.96–101)

Even though many a Christian Elizabethan groundling may have shared Antonio's view of Shylock here and cast him in the role of Satan, an othering device we come across in *Othello* as well, just as in the case of the strategy of declaring

---

ice is 'ambiguity'."; Marci A. Hamilton, "The End of Law," *Cardozo Studies in Law and Literature* 5.1 (1993): 125–136, 125.

7 Oldrieve emphasizes the connection of racial and economic motives in Antonio's behavior towards Shylock: "his [i.e. Antonio's] berating Shylock would reflect not just anti-semitism, but an anti-semitism used to give the Christian an economic advantage." Oldrieve, "Marginalized Voices," 92.

the other to be a man-eating uncivilized cannibal, it is obvious that Antonio in his remarks does not take up Shylock's biblical example at all. Rather, he ignores the Jew's argument and instead vilifies his opponent by falling back on anti-semitic stereotypes, maligning the other in a way that takes for granted as a given Shylock's evil character. Consequently, it is only logical that this is followed by a complaint in which Shylock points out all the various humiliations Antonio has subjected him to, among which there figures yet another othering strategy Shakespeare also has his discriminating characters use in *Othello*, namely that of debasing the other to the subhuman status of an animal. To Antonio's calling him a "cut-throat dog" (1.3.110) and spitting at him, Shylock reacts with the question: "Should I not say/'Hath a dog money? Is it possible/A cur can lend three thousand ducats?'" (1.3.119–121), thus re-asserting himself as a human agent and launching an appeal to put oneself in his position in order to realize what it feels like to be othered and debased in such a way. This is a strategy Shylock will use again later in the play. Shakespeare, having provided his audience with food for engaging in the stereotypical white Christian mechanisms of anti-semitic discrimination, also provides us with the necessary material for a change of perspective, thus allowing us to put ourselves in Shylock's shoes and to see matters from his perspective.[8]

When Antonio ignores Shylock's argument and merely reacts with a repetition of his scathing remarks on the inappropriateness of charging interest when lending money, the Jew seemingly gives up his position and offers to lend money to Antonio without charging interest in order to at long last become his friend. However, the bond Shylock suggests, as we know, turns out to be anything but a token of friendship, and the wording chosen by Shylock when he suggests it with hindsight and in view of the Jew's earlier expressions of hatred as well as his determination to take revenge can only be read as an example of equivocation:

> SHYLOCK: This kindness will I show.
> Go with me to a notary, seal me there
> Your single bond, and, in a merry sport,
> If you repay me not on such a day,
> In such a place, such sum or sums as are
> Expressed in the condition, let the forfeit
> Be nominated for an equal pound

8 Gross notes that "[t]he seeds of sympathy are there [...] Shakespeare simply tried to imagine, within the confines of the plot, and within the limits that his culture set him, what it would be like to be a Jew." John Gross, *Shylock: A Legend and Its Legacy* (New York: Simon and Schuster, 1992), 349.

Of your fair flesh to be cut off and taken
In what part of your body pleaseth me. (1.3.142–150)

The "sport" suggested by Shylock, as we know, will turn out not to be so merry at all, and this act of equivocation can only be seen as a strategy chosen by the Jew to take revenge on white Christians in the person of Antonio, who is therefore referred to as "fair" here, the whole deal thus taking on the quality of an inter-racial undertaking. That what is depicted as an amicable offer on the surface is conflictual rather than friendly is underlined by the discussion that follows in which Antonio declares himself willing to accept the offer and says that "there is much kindness in the Jew" (1.3.152) – mind the ethnically generic reference to Shylock here again – while Bassanio counsels Antonio against accepting Shylock's suggestions and the latter reacts by accusing Christians of always suspecting others without justification. The first act thus ends with the tension between belief in the possibility of the other's melioration and forebodings based on the assumption of an incurably negative alterity of the non-white and presumably evil Jew:

ANTONIO: Hie thee, gentle Jew. [*Exit Shylock*]
The Hebrew will turn Christian; he grows kind.
BASSANIO: I like not fair terms and a villain's mind. (1.3.175–178)

Interestingly, Antonio's optimistic consideration of the possibility of Shylock changing his mores here is based yet again on the assumption of the latter's total assimilation to Christianity and the annihilation of his otherness, a notion Bassanio cannot bring himself to consider as feasible.

Act two opens by taking up the dominant theme of Act one again, in the first scene through the characterization of the Prince of Morocco as an exotic racial other, and in scene two by Lancelot's description of his master Shylock as a Jew and hence – from a Christian perspective – a fiend and a devil, thus perpetuating the anti-semitic stereotypes of the time. However, the negative categorization of the racially and ethnically other is transcended in Lancelot's hesitation as to whether his conscience would allow him to run away from his master, which raises the issue of whether a different set of rules can be applied to the other or whether the same norms should apply to all, a question that already foreshadows some of the problems of the trial scene later in the play. In Lancelot, however, it is his rejection of the other that wins over his qualms and makes him run away in spite of what his conscience tells him. He justifies his defection to Bassanio with his fear of infection, "for I am a Jew if I serve the Jew any longer" (2.2.107). As a reason for his change of allegiance he tells Bassanio that "you have the grace of God, sir, and he hath enough" (2.2.145 – 146), thus drawing a distinction between a good Christian and a materialist Jew in a rhetorical gesture that once more reconfirms negative stereotypes. As if this were not enough, the short third scene of Act two stages another defection from Shylock, this time by his daughter Jessica. She complains that "Our house is hell" (2.3.2), thus taking up the earlier negative categorization of the Jew as a devil, and she admits to her racial identity with her father but denies her cultural allegiance to him and his religion when she declares: "But though I am a daughter to his blood,/I am not to his manners" (2.3.18 – 19), a statement that is immediately followed by her decision to marry Lorenzo and convert to Christianity, thereby providing another example of the annihilation of Jewish otherness through assimilation to the white Christian norm. That this is to be seen as a crossing of a primarily racial borderline becomes clear in Lorenzo's reaction to Jessica's letter, which, he declares, is written in "a fair hand,/ And whiter than the paper it writ on/Is the fair hand that writ." (2.4.12 – 14) The greatest part of the remaining scenes in Act two is likewise devoted to the negative characterization of the non-white other, mainly in the shape of Shylock the Jew, ranging from the latter's declaration that he will "go in hate, to feed upon/The prodigal Christian" (2.5.14 – 15), which yet again has cannibalistic overtones, to Shylock's reprehensible confusion of priorities in his divided lament over both the theft of his money and the loss of his daughter:

> 'My daughter! O, my ducats! O, my daughter!
> Fled with a Christian! O, my Christian ducats!
> Justice! The law! My ducats and my daughter!
> [...]
> Stol'n by my daughter! Justice! Find the girl! (2.8.15 – 21)

Not only does Shylock discredit himself here by obviously mourning the loss of his money to the Christians at least as much if not more than the loss of his child,[9] but he also seeks redress by having recourse to the law which, apparently, seems to him to be the adequate means of re-establishing justice.

This is not only another early signpost towards the later trial scene, but it initiates a discourse on what is just in intercultural and interracial contexts of alterity, and it provides Shakespeare with the opportunity of allowing his audience insights into the perspective of the slighted Jew beyond the mere processes

---

9 Ojeda Alba also critically observes that in this passage Shylock "laments both the loss of his daughter and the loss of his ducats, mixing the two as if both paternal love and money were at the same level." Ojeda, "Justice and Injustice," 15.

of anti-semitic stigmatization that have by now been re-enacted so often. Nowhere does this become more apparent than in Shylocks famous soliloquy in the first scene of Act three where he tells Salarino that he will insist on taking Antonio's flesh if the latter fails to fulfil his bond, and be it only

> To bait fish withal. If it will feed nothing else it will feed my revenge. He hath disgraced me, and hindered me half a million; laughed at my losses, mocked at my gains, scourned my nation, thwarted my bargains, cooled my friends, heated mine enemies, and what's his reason? – I am a Jew. Hath not a Jew eyes? Hath not a Jew hands, organs, dimensions, senses, affections, passions; fed with the same food, hurt with the same weapons, subject to the same diseases, healed by the same means, warmed and cooled by the same winter and summer as a Christian is? If you prick us do we not bleed? If you tickle us do we not laugh? If you poison us do we not die? And if you wrong us shall we not revenge? If we are like you in the rest, we will resemble you in that. If a Jew wrong a Christian, what is his humility? Revenge. If a Christian wrong a Jew, what should his sufferance be by Christian example? Why, revenge. The villainy you teach me I will execute, and it shall go hard but I will better the instruction. (3.1.49–68)

This is an example of powerful rhetoric contributing to the audience momentarily identifying with a speaker who has been viewed critically so far – similar to other examples in Shakespeare's work, such as in *Macbeth*, to name but one other text. Shakespeare here manages to make his Christian audience see the Jew's point of view, and he gives Shylock strong arguments. The latter does not only complain about the slights and mistreatment he has suffered from Antonio in the past, but he also justifies his protest against these by referring in a very convincing and impressive way to a common humanity beyond the borderlines of race or ethnicity. Beyond the alterity of different nations and religions, he claims, there lies a fundamental sameness of, for example, Jews and Christians as human beings that constitutes a form of identity in the midst of alterity. He thus establishes an ethical claim as to the dignity and respect with which all human beings should be treated, irrespective of their origin or background, and this claim confers a certain dignity on the speaker of these lines.[10] However, unfortunately, Shylock is so embittered that he is not able to draw the conclusion of breaking through the nefarious cycle of negative othering. He goes wrong the moment he uses his argument of sameness as a justification for revenge, claiming that abuse and maltreatment need to be paid back in kind. Shylock's earlier wish for justice here degenerates into a perverted claim for the satisfaction of

---

10 This was seen differently by the well-known American actor Edwin Booth, who, in 1884, in a letter to the theatre critic William Winter, wrote that "I have searched in vain for the slightest hint of anything resembling dignity in the part [i.e. that of Shylock]"; Ojeda Alba, "Justice and Injustice," 11.

hateful feelings.[11] He rejects the option of silently suffering the wrongs committed by Christian Venetians and insists on re-establishing a balance by wronging Christians back in turn, a solution that places the principle of negative alterity above the notion of a common humanity. Not only does he lose again here much of the dignity he has gained through his earlier words on the sameness of all humans,[12] but he also characterizes the rejected option of silent suffering as "a Christian example," thus re-emphasizing the otherness of humans on different sides of racial and ethnic borderlines. Shylock's soliloquy characterizes him as a tragic character,[13] with his desire for revenge being the tragic flaw that causes the fall of a potentially dignified man. The audience has only been offered a short glimpse of a more positive side of Shylock, but not more.[14] In the ensuing exchange, therefore, the Jew is shown again as the greedy money-lender who would prefer to see his daughter dead rather than lose his money and his diamonds (3.1. 78–90), and Shakespeare reverts to the presentation of Shylock as an ugly character when he has him rejoice at the news of Antonio's loss of one of his argosies. The offended Jew's thirst for revenge smothers any pity and human fellow-feeling he might otherwise have evinced and his reprehensible side comes to the fore again: "I will have the heart of him if he forfeit, for were he out of Venice I can make what merchandise I will. Go, Tubal, and meet me at our synagogue. Go, good Tubal; at our synagogue, Tubal." (3.1.117–121) Shylock shows himself willing to sacrifice another's life to his economic interests, which is not only an unethical attitude here but one which, through the double mention of the synagogue at the end of this quotation, is marked as Jewish.

The stage is thus set for the trial scene in which Shylock will not only claim his pound of flesh but in which questions of justice and the law will be posed with reference to intercultural contexts of alterity. In preparation for the negotiation of such issues, however, at the end of Act 3.2, in which Bassanio chooses the right casket in Belmont and wins the hand of Portia, we also learn more about Shylock's further behaviour in Venice, which seems to spiral completely out of

11 This is why Rosa Sàez, referring back to an earlier reading by John Palmer, claims that "the speech is a rationalization of his [i.e. Shylock's] thirst for revenge, not the generally believed plea for human tolerance." However, we are not faced with two mutually exclusive alternatives here, but rather with two contradictory sides of one and the same character. Shylock's speech contains both aspects mentioned by Sàez; Sàez, "Religion, Law and Justice," 269.

12 Cf. Ojeda Alba, "Justice and Injustice," 15: "He loses the grandeur and dignity that he had."

13 Ojeda Alba also refers to him as such; Ojeda, "Justice and Injustice," 13.

14 This is sufficient, however, to explain "why criticism has seldom reached consensus when it comes to evaluating this character." Ojeda Alba, "Justice and Injustice," 12.

control with regard to his bond with Antonio. We learn that Shylock tries to instrumentalize justice and the law in order to quench his thirst for revenge. Salerio reports that

> He plies the Duke at morning and at night,
> And doth impeach the freedom of the state
> If they deny him justice. Twenty merchants,
> The Duke himself, and the magnificoes
> Of greatest port, have all persuaded with him,
> But none can drive him from the envious plea
> Of forfeiture, of justice, and his bond. (3.2. 275–281)

The audience know by now, however, that the notion of justice used by Shylock is a perverted one in as far as it is based merely on the notion of revenge and turned into a tool here for the satisfaction of his personal thirst for hurting Antonio back, although he claims that general issues of state are at stake. That things threaten to get out of proportion is made quite clear by what Jessica has to report about her father:

> When I was with him, I have heard him swear
> [...]
> That he would rather have Antonio's flesh
> Than twenty times the value of the sum
> That he did owe him; and I know, my lord,
> If law, authority, and power deny not,
> It will go hard with poor Antonio. (3.2.282–288)

The authority of the law here is invoked by Shylock's daughter as a necessary means of curbing her father's vengeful and disproportionate excess. But when Jessica refers to the law here, what she really means is the principle of equity because, viewed from a purely formalist point of view, Shylock's claim may be justified and lawful – Antonio is not able to fulfil his bond after all – while a resulting condemnation of Antonio in the terms specified by his bond with Shylock would appear to be excessive, disproportionate and unjust.[15] The demented

---

15 Maxine MacKay even reads the play as one "reflect[ing] clearly a conflict between the courts of law and of equity (chancery) in Elizabethan England"; Maxine MacKay, "*The Merchant of Venice*: a Reflection of the Early Conflict Between Courts of Law and Courts of Equity," *Shakespeare Quarterly* 15.4 (1964): 371–375, 371. For a survey of recent discussions of the role of equity in *The Merchant of Venice* see B.J. and Mary Sokol, "Shakespeare and the English Equity Jurisdiction: *The Merchant of Venice* and the two texts of *King Lear*," *The Review of English Studies* 50 (1999): 417–439. Stretton, referring to Shylock's claim to a pound of Antonio's flesh, points out that "the

craze for getting his own back again on Antonio created by Shylock's victimization as an ethnic other at the hands of the Venetian Christians has thus led to the creation of a legal and ethical problem and a potential crisis of legitimacy for the Venetian system of justice. The task to be faced now by the protagonists is how to find a way of leaving the law intact without producing a cruel, inequitable and unjust outcome in the confrontation between Antonio and Shylock.[16]

Act 3.3 further discredits the Jew because it shows the whole intransigence of his position. He tells the jailer: "Tell me not of mercy" (3.3.1), and in conversation with Antonio he reproduces the logic he already used in his famous soliloquy in Act 3.1., arguing that he will act according to the way in which he has been discursively constructed earlier: "Thou called'st me dog before thou hadst a cause,/ But since I am a dog, beware my fangs." (3.3.6–7) The discursive strategies of discrimination and of othering practised by the Christians now threaten to fall back upon them as a threat to the life of Antonio as one of Christian Venice's foremost representatives in this play. While Shylock cites his racial and ethnic victimization as the reason for his obstinate insistence on his bond with Antonio being followed to the letter and his refusal to listen to "Christian intercessors" (3.3.16) – mind the use of the adjective here, which stresses religious and cultural alterity – Antonio sees a primarily economic motivation in the Jew's behaviour who he claims wants to get rid of somebody who "oft delivered from his [i. e. Shylock's] forfeitures/Many that have at times made moan to me" (3.3.22–23).[17] He thus makes the Jew appear in an even more negative light and completely disregards the repeated slights and racial slurs suffered by Shylock. Rather, Antonio is aware of the plight he finds himself in because he realizes that the Duke cannot show mercy towards him in this case since this would jeopardize Venice's status as an open and cosmopolitan market-place in which the law is reliably ap-

---

metaphorical device of an unnecessarily harsh penalty fell on receptive ears in the 1590s, when bond forfeitures had been running high and litigants in equity courts regularly complained that the scale of penalties was excessive in comparison to the harm caused by default."; Tim Stretton, "Conditional Promises and Legal Instruments in *The Merchant of Venice*," in *Taking Exception to the Law: Materializing Injustice in early Modern English Literature*, eds. Donald Beecher, Travis Decook, Andrew Wallace, and Grant Williams (Toronto: University of Toronto Press, 2015): 71–99, 79.

16 As early as 1952 M.C. Bradbrook indirectly referred to the inequitable element in Shylock's position when he wrote that the latter "stands for the Law [...] for the legal system which, to be just to all in general, must only approximate to justice in particular cases."; Muriel C. Bradbrook, *Shakespeare and Elizabethan Poetry* (New York: Oxford University Press, 1952), 172.

17 Kornstein remarks that "restraint of trade may lurk behind much of the action in *The Merchant of Venice*. Shylock and Antonio are competitors [...]."; Daniel J. Kornstein, "Fie Upon Your Law!," *Cardozo Studies in Law and Literature* 5.1 (1993): 35–56, 40.

plied irrespective of the racial, ethnic or national background of the traders who use it:

> The Duke cannot deny the course of law,
> For the commodity that strangers have
> With us in Venice, if it be denied,
> Will much impeach the justice of the state,
> Since that the trade and profit of the city
> Consisteth of all nations. (3.3.26–31)

It is thus out of *raison d'état*[18] that Antonio resigns himself to losing a pound of flesh. At the end of the short prison scene in Act 3.3., therefore, an image of the Venetian merchant as a responsible and altruistic man is contrasted negatively with an image of Shylock as a spiteful, greedy and vengeful other who, in the blind pursuit of his economic advantage, appears as inhuman and unjust. The more understanding attitude towards Shylock potentially fostered by the Jew's great soliloquy here is made almost impossible again, and the play once more takes on a more anti-semitic tinge.[19]

In typically Shakespearean fashion, however, the text swerves back to a discussion of racial and ethnic othering as a strategy of discrimination in the scene between Lancelot and Jessica in Portia's garden in which Lorenzo worries about the negative effects of Jessica's family background on the girl: "Yes truly; for look you, the sins of the fathers are to be laid upon the children, [...] for truly I think you are damned" (3.5. 1–5).[20] Lancelot sees Jessica's only chance in the "hope that your father got you not, that you are not the Jew's daughter" (3.5.9–10), thus declaring being a bastard to be preferable to being a Jew. Jessica, in turn, replies that she "shall be saved by my husband. He hath made me a Christian." (3.5.17–18). The dividing line between different racial and ethnic groups here is left intact and shown to be very strong, the only chance of overcoming it being a complete change of identity through total assimilation. Once more, the annihila-

18 Cohen comments on Antonio's words as an example of "the close connection between common law and nascent capitalism"; Stephen A. Cohen, "'The Quality of Mercy': Law, Equity and Ideology in *The Merchant of Venice*," *Mosaic* 27.4 (1994): 35–54, 41.

19 This is one of the reasons why Isaac speaks about "the problem of the anti-Semitism implicit in Shakespeare's text."; Dan Isaac, "The Worth of a Jew's Eye: Reflections on the Talmud in *The Merchant of Venice*," *MAARAV: A Journal for the Study of the Northwest Semitic Languages and Literatures* 8 (1992): 349–374, 352.

20 Ojeda Alba correctly points out that "(w)hat Jessica does not understand is that in spite of her alliance to Christianity she will continue to be unaccepted, as is later demonstrated by the fact that she is still socially classified as an outsider (...)."; Ojeda, "Justice and Injustice," 18.

tion of the other is shown to be the prevalent model of thinking about alterity among the Venetian protagonists of the play. The notions of hybridity and tolerant openness are not taken into account in the binary patterns of the characters.[21]

Act four opens with a conversation between the Duke and Antonio which recapitulates the negative characterization of Shylock presented in the previous acts. Shylock is not mentioned by name, but rather referred to by the Duke as "A stony adversary, an inhuman wretch/Uncapable of pity, void and empty/ From any dram of mercy" (4.1.3–5). Lack of empathy is used here as a damning attribute that takes Shylock's othering so far as to put in doubt his very status as a human being, a strategy we also come across in Shylock being treated as a dog, as we have been told earlier, or, to use an example from another play, in Othello' being referred to as "an old black ram" (1.1.88).[22] When the Duke appeals to Shylock to show mercy to Antonio, he phrases this in such a way as to threaten the Jew with the stigmatization of a double othering:

> [...] touched with human gentleness and love,
> Forgive a moiety of the principal,
> Glancing an eye of pity on his losses,
> [...]
> And pluck commiseration of his state
> From brassy bosoms, and rough hearts of flint,
> From stubborn Turks and Tartars never trained
> To offices of tender courtesy,
> We all expect a gentle answer, Jew. (4.1.24–33)

The duke argues here that if Shylock does not show clemency, he will be considered to be worse than Venice's greatest enemies, the Turks, and more hard-hearted than the Tartars, who function here as the epitome of the exotic and inhuman other.[23] However, the gentle answer the Duke expects from the Jew to the latter would also be a gentile answer, i.e. one he does not find himself capable of producing. This is why, in his rejection of the Duke's plea, he refers back again to his

21 This kind of thinking in the divisive terms of racial othering is reinforced at the end of the scene when Lorenzo enters and – albeit in playful banter – accuses Lancelot of "the getting up of the Negro's belly" (3.5.36–37), an act of miscegenation that needs to be answered for "to the commonwealth" (3.5.35–36).

22 William Shakespeare, *The Tragedy of Othello, the Moor of Venice*, in *The Complete Works*, eds. Stanley Wells and Gary Taylor (Oxford: Oxford University Press, 1986), 925–964.

23 Cohen also points out that the Duke tells Shylock that if he does not show mercy, he will "remain more alien than even the Turks and Tartars in pursuing his suit"; Cohen, "The Quality of Mercy," 42.

religious identity: "by our holy Sabbath have I sworn/To have the due and forfeit of my bond." (4.1.35–36). In addition, Shylock underlines the threat a formal breach of law would constitute to Venice's status as an international marketplace, and he rejects any further negotiation of the matter by referring to his insistence on the pound of flesh as an arbitrary whim: "say it is my humour. Is it answered? [...] So can I give no reason, nor I will not,/ More than a lodged hate and a certain loathing/I bear Antonio" (4.1.42, 59–61). Communication has all but broken down by now, and the divisive mechanisms of racial and ethnic alterities fighting each other have taken over. Never does this get lost in the verbal altercations of this scene. When Antonio declares that it is useless to argue with Shylock, he refers to him as "the Jew" (4.1.69) and claims that immovable cruelty is lodged like a force of nature in "His Jewish heart" (4.1.79), thus attributing Shylock's inability to show mercy to his religion.[24]

When the Duke once more threatens Shylock by telling him that if he does not show mercy he can expect none, the Jew cleverly defends his position by insisting on strict adherence to the law and yet again pointing to the sameness between the actions of the Christian Venetians and his own:

> What judgement shall I dread, doing no wrong?
> You have among you many a purchased slave
> Which, like your asses and your dogs and mules,
> You use in abject and in slavish parts
> Because you bought them. Shall I say to you,
> "Let them be free, marry them to your heirs.
> [...]" You will answer
> "The slaves are ours." So do I answer you.
> The pound of flesh which I demand of him
> Is dearly bought. 'Tis mine, and I will have it. (4.1.88–99)

---

24 Sàez also refers to the religious dimension of different approaches to mercy and emphasizes that "Shylock follows a legalistic system imposed by his Old Testament Jehovah, while Antonio represents the New Testament, and almost re-enacts Christ."; Sàez, "Religion, Law and Justice," 274. Johnson also sees "the encounter between the two men [...] as the conflict between the law of the Old Testament or the letter of the law and grace of the New Testament or the spirit of the law."; Lonnell E. Johnson, "Shylock's Daniel: 'Justice more than thou desir'st'," *CLA Journal* 35.2 (1991): 353–366, 353. Majeske points out that Shylock is "punished severely, in harsh Old Testament form."; Andrew Majeske,"Striking a Deal: Portia's Trial Strategy in Shakespeare's *The Merchant of Venice*," in *Justice, Women, and Power in English Renaissance Drama*, eds. Andrew Majeske and Emily Detmer-Goebel (Madison: Fairleigh Dickinson University Press, 2009): 153–173, 164.

Shylock's argument is twofold here. On the one hand, he refers to the strict legality of his claim. In a purely formalistic sense, he has indeed done nothing wrong. But he is aware of the moral condemnation his insisting on the pound of flesh might produce, which is why, on the other hand, he comes up with the comparison between his behaviour and the slavery practised by the Christian Venetians, which both constitute the free use of property. In other words, he tries to reject the moral claims of the Christians as spurious in order to deconstruct their expectation of mercy from him and thus justify what his adversaries see as unjustifiable. And again, he constructs a wider context in which his individual case becomes a testing ground for the reliability and therefore the credibility of the law in Venice when he finishes with the following words: "If you deny me, fie upon your law:/There is no force in the decrees of Venice." (4.1.100 – 101)

When Gratiano makes one last attempt at softening Shylock, this proves to be unsuccessful and merely leads to further invective and negative othering of the Jew, in which Gratiano calls the latter an "inexorable dog" (4.1.128), "woolvish, bloody, starved, and ravenous" (4.1.137), thus placing the Jew yet again in the realm of animals and beasts and thereby denying Shylock's humanity. The Jew remains obstinate, however, and retreats once more into his formalist position by repeating: "I stand here for law" (4.1.141). Shakespeare has constructed the perfect and seemingly insoluble stalemate[25] here, then, with the formal claims of the law being opposed to considerations of equity and ethics in a situation in which the reputation of Venice as a reliable international marketplace governed by legal norms as well as questions of justice are at stake.[26] This is the perfect context for Portia's ploy in her role as Bellario's emissary to unfold its maximum effect.

The scene that ensues turns into a magnificent negotiation of issues of law, justice, ethics, equity and alterity. In her very first words to Shylock, Portia refers to his perceived otherness when she tells him: "Of a strange nature is the suit you follow,/Yet in such rule that the Venetian law/Cannot impugn you as you

---

25 Mackay in this context speaks of an "impasse"; Mackay,"Reflection of the Early Conflict," 373.

26 Cf. Kornstein who states that "[i]n essence, Shylock is saying [...] that a ruling in Antonio's favor will upset the entire reliability of commercial contracts in Venetian law, and discourage merchants and moneylenders from doing business in Venice."; Kornstein, "Fie Upon Your Law!," 43. Posner also points out that a decision denying Shylock's claim on the grounds of that claim being inequitable "would be an example of the operation of discretionary justice, of which aliens doing business with Venetians would be understandably mistrustful."; Richard A. Posner, "Law and Commerce in *The Merchant of Venice*," in *Shakespeare and the Law: A Conversation Among Disciplines and Professions*, eds. Brian Cormack and Martha C. Nussbaum (Chicago and London: The University of Chicago Press, 2013): 147–155, 152.

do proceed." (4.1..174–176) When Portia describes the Jew's claim as "strange" here, she does not only characterize it as highly unusual, but also as something that is alien to Christian Venetian customs so that yet again Shylock is positioned in the realm of the foreign, the unknown and the inacceptable.[27] After Antonio's admission that he cannot fulfil the bond, Portia produces her great soliloquy on mercy, which she characterizes as a divine attribute beyond the merely temporal power of rulers and lawgivers and therefore as something that should overrule the earthly justice produced by formal systems of law: "I have spoken thus much/To mitigate the justice of thy plea" (4.1.199–200), she says in an attempt to soften Shylock's insistence on blindly following the formal procedures of the law. When this proves unsuccessful, a second such attempt to escape what abstract law prescribes in the case at hand is started by Bassanio who not only offers to pay Antonio's debt "ten times o'er" (4.1.208) but also appeals to the Duke to overrule what the law prescribes, which he sees as "a little wrong" committed "To do a great right" (4.1.213). What the Venetians would need here is a court of Chancery and an equitable decision, but such an institution is not available in the context of the play, which is why Portia immediately contradicts Bassanio and points out that "It must not be. There is no power in Venice/Can alter a decree established./'Twill be recorded for a precedent,/And many an error by the same example/Will rush into the state. It cannot be." (4.2.215–219) The tension is thus heightened, and so is the suspense felt by the audience as to how the circle can be squared and the claims of the law may be overridden without lasting damage to Venice so that Antonio can be saved.

Shylock's rigidity and his refusal to exercise mercy and accept the offered payment of Antonio's debt by Bassanio despite his formally legal claims place him in the wrong in several respects. To begin with, he refuses to show the human empathy towards Antonio he himself implicitly demanded for himself in his great soliloquy "If you prick us, do we not bleed?" (Cf. 3.1. 49–68). Significantly, it is in this speech, in which he shows his more humane side, that he generates brief moments of sympathy in the audience, only to destroy them again through his vengeful attitude.[28] Rejecting Bassanio's offer of money also

27 And indeed, as Majeske puts it so aptly, "Portia is acting in the trial more as an advocate than as an impartial judge"; Andrew Majeske, "Striking a Deal," 153. Hamilton, refers to Antonio's claim as "an outlandish request."; Hamilton, "The End of Law," 129.

28 Greenstein aptly summarizes the speech's ambivalent nature: "His [i.e. Shylock's] oft-cited speech, 'Hath not a Jew eyes?', may be a humanistic appeal to the senses, but it equally appeals to the *lex talionis* (an eye for an eye) within the courtroom context and tale of revenge."; Michael Greenstein, "Breaking the Mosaic Code: Jewish Literature vs. the Law," *Mosaic* 27.3 (1994): 87–106, 89.

shows Shylock as a very narrow-minded and inflexible as well as literal-minded interpreter of the letter of the law, according to which Antonio himself must repay his debt rather than someone else. Moreover, in doing this, Shylock denies Antonio the possibility of borrowing the necessary money from Bassanio although he is a moneylender himself. This constitutes the Jew's revenge[29] for Antonio's criticism of his moneylending practice and thus is a product of the ethnic conflict that dominates the play. This is also documented by Shylock's claim that to show mercy would constitute an act of perjury, i. e. by a religious and therefore culturally determined argument, since "I have an oath in heaven." (4.1.225). The consequence, from Shylock's point of view, is quite clear and again due to the fundamental alterity he feels between himself and his Christian environment: "No, not for Venice." (4.1.227). Finally, the intransigent literal-mindedness with which Shylock reads the legal bond in a purely formalist and mechanistic way without any regard for wider considerations of appropriateness, proportionality, ethics, equity and justice prepares the ground for what is to follow, namely Portia's no less literal-minded interpretation of the bond[30] and its consequences for Shylock which potentially opens up the possibility of interpreting these as an instance of poetic justice.[31]

In the midst of a seemingly insoluble quandary in which Antonio's life almost seems lost, Bassanio rails against Shylock and refers to him as "this devil" (4.1.284) in a moment of ultimate moral othering that results from the apparent hopelessness of the situation. Gratiano similarly engages in yet another othering strategy by reviving the animal comparison used previously and referring to "this currish Jew" (4.1.289). Shylock in turn bemoans the fact that his daughter Jessica has married a Christian rather than a Jew. We are looking here at the moment immediately before Portia comes up with the solution that will save Antonio's life, namely the granting of the pound of flesh to Shylock, coupled with the strict warning that not a single drop of blood must be shed because this would be a transgression of the bond. It is no coincidence that the eth-

---

29 Korda also points out that "Shylock's hatred of Antonio leads him to succumb to a passion that privileges vengeance above profit or precision. Over the course of the play, this passion supplants the profit motive entirely."; Natasha Korda, "Dame Usury: Gender, Credit, and (Ac)counting in the Sonnets and *The Merchant of Venice*," *Shakespeare Quarterly* 60.2 (2009): 129–153, 149.

30 Stretton even claims that "her reliance on strict legalism exceeds Shylock's."; Stretton, "Conditional Promises and Legal Instruments," 71, and Kornstein refers to her "hypertechnical interpretation" of the law: Kornstein, "Fie Upon Your Law!," 38.

31 This potential, however, as will be shown, is not fulfilled. On poetic justice and *The Merchant of Venice* cf. Verena Olejniczak Lobsien, "'Richtet nicht, damit ihr nicht gerichtet werdet!' Biblische, säkulare und poetische Gerechtigkeit im England der frühen Neuzeit," *Poetica: Zeitschrift für Sprach- und Literaturwissenschaft* 37.3–4 (2005): 311–347, esp. 334–347.

nic identities of the characters involved are repeatedly stressed here because the conflict is thus turned into one between Christians and Jews. When Portia finally makes her point she does not merely warn Shylock that he should not spill any blood, but tells him that "if thou dost shed/One drop of Christian blood, thy lands and goods/Are by the laws of Venice confiscate/Unto the state of Venice." (4.1.306–309) Blood here comes with a religious denomination – it is *Christian* blood – and obviously marks the alterity of the protagonists.[32] Consequently, Gratiano, in his enthusiastic delight about Portia's legal trick,[33] addresses Shylock by not using his name, but an ethnic epithet: "Mark, Jew! O learnèd judge!" (4.1.310). The tables have now been turned on Shylock, and the way seems to be open for teaching him a lesson in equitable and legal behaviour as well as in mercy and justice beyond the mere following of formal regulations. When Portia tells him that "as thou urgest justice, be assured/Thou shalt have justice more than thou desir'st" (4.1.313–314), she turns Shylock's demand for justice into a threat against him because of his mechanistic and inequitable literal application of the law.[34]

This could turn into a moral lesson for Shylock, whose utter intransigence needs to be curbed even though we can see the history of discrimination and suffering at the hands of the Christians that lies behind him. However, what happens is much more than a reestablishment of the right measure and of proportionality in legal matters and rather constitutes a renewed perversion of the spirit of the law, which is why Isaac claims that "Shakespeare has posited a court ready to corrupt common rules of equity and jurisprudence in order to convict Shylock on the basis of a quibble."[35] When Shylock realizes that he cannot

32 Cf. Spinosa, "Shylock and Debt and Contract," 80: "The law has all along distinguished Christian blood from other blood. [...] At issue here is that Shylock, *an alien*, seeks to cut a *citizen's* flesh."

33 Cohen also refers to "Portia's famous 'quibble'"; Cohen, "The Quality of Mercy," 48, and so does Anna Maria Cimitile, "The (Un)Fixity of the Law: Modalities of Stasis in *The Merchant of Venice*," *anglistica* 1.1–2 (1997): 27–60, 40. Hartman similarly refers to the "tricksy-ness" of words in the play; Geoffrey Hartman, "The Tricksy Word: Richard Weisberg on *The Merchant of Venice*," *Law and Literature* 23.1 (2011): 71–79, 74. Bilello even talks about "Portia's con" and "Portia's fraud"; Thomas C. Bilello, "Accomplished with What She Lacks: Law, Equity and Portia's Con," *Law and Literature* 16.1 (2004): 11–32, 11, 12.

34 This is why Tucker speaks about "the equitable principles which explain Portia's pleadings in regard to Shylock's insistence upon the letter of the law."; E.F.J. Tucker, "The Letter of the Law in *The Merchant of Venice*," *Shakespeare Survey* 29 (1976): 93–101, 94.

35 Isaac, "The Worth of a Jew's Eye," 357. Similarly, Ojeda Alba reads the play as a "tale of effective injustice"; Isaac, "Justice and Injustice," 21, and Sáez states that "Shakespeare questions the moral validity of the Christian's attempt to impart justice."; Sáez, "Religion, Law and Justice," 267. Stretton therefore, joins "a growing number of scholars [who] argue that the equity

have Antonio's pound of flesh without shedding a drop of blood and thus jeopardizing himself, he accepts Bassanio's suggestion to be paid three times the amount owed by the merchant. However, not only does Portia insist on the bond being fulfilled literally by the cutting of exactly one pound of flesh, thus practising Shylock's earlier literal-mindedness back upon him,[36] but she also connects this with a threat to his life: "If thou tak'st more/Or less than just a pound, [..] if the scale do turn/But in the estimation of a hair,/ Thou diest, and all thy goods are confiscate." (4.1.323–329). Even now, if Portia relented at last and insisted on Shylock getting back no more than what he is owed, this could be understood as a lesson drastically taught. But even when Shylock himself says: "Give me my principal, and let me go" (4.1. 333), this does not happen. Instead, Portia remains adamant and states: "He hath refused it in the open court./He shall have merely justice and his bond." (4.1.335–336).[37] Once again, it is Shylock's alterity, his not being a Christian Venetian, that determines what happens, as becomes clear in Portia's words:

> It is enacted in the laws of Venice,
> If it be proved against an alien
> That by direct or indirect attempts
> He seek the life of any citizen,
> The party 'gainst the which he doth contrive
> Shall seize one half his goods; the other half
> Comes to the privy coffer of the state,
> And the offender's life lies in the mercy
> Of the Duke only, 'gainst all other voice –
> In which predicament I say thou stand'st,
> [...]
> Down, therefore, and beg mercy of the Duke. (4.1.354–360)

That Shylock now is forced to beg for mercy himself, having refused such mercy to Antonio before, could still be interpreted as part of a lesson in humane behaviour he is to be taught, but this becomes doubtful here because it is paired with the complete confiscation of his fortune, which does not only appear to be disproportionate but, coupled as it is with a rule applying to aliens only, takes on a

dispensed in the Court of Chancery, which served to mitigate the harsh effects of strict applications of common law, does not feature anywhere in the play (except perhaps in its absence)"; Stretton, "Legal Instruments," 72.

36 Isaac similarly says that "Portia too begins to do close readings of the text – and beats Shylock at his own game."; Isaac, "The Worth of a Jew's Eye,": 354.

37 This is why Sáez correctly claims that Portia "is not exactly merciful when turning the case against Shylock.": Sáez, "Religion, Law and Justice," 268.

xenophobic tinge and turns out to be an act of discrimination of the non-Venetian other.[38] This is apparent in the very choice of words when the Duke pardons Shylock and lets him live: "That thou shalt see the difference of our spirit,/I pardon thee thy life before thou ask it" (4.1.365–366). The difference referred to here is one that is used to construct the Jew into the position of a negative alterity that is used as a foil in front of which the positive identity of Christian Venice and its supposed clemency can be constructed. In view of the acts of discrimination, the racial slurs and the ethnically motivated slander in the first part of the play, this cannot be read as an act of Christian altruism, but must be seen as a strategic manoeuvre in the confrontation between Christians and Jews.

This is confirmed when the Duke asks Antonio to also show mercy to Shylock, which the merchant does in a very ambiguous way. On the one hand, he asks the Duke to let Shylock keep half his fortune, but on the other hand, this is linked to two conditions: that the Jew's fortune ultimately goes to Lorenzo and Jessica, who has converted to Christianity, and that Shylock himself "presently become a Christian" (4.1.384). The Other here is spared, but at the cost of ceasing to be an Other, i.e. at the price of annihilation. Alterity is thus done away with by force, and the notion of justice behind this can only be understood from an ethnocentric Christian point of view.[39] That ethnicity and otherness are indeed what is at stake here is confirmed by the way Portia asks for Shylock's reaction to Antonio's proposal. She once more uses the ethnic epithet to address Shylock rather than his name: "Art thou contented, Jew? What dost thou say?" (4.1.390). Shylock's answer, "I am content" (4.1.391), merely signals his agreement with the conditions stipulated by Antonio, but not his being satisfied with the outcome of the trial scene. He can only leave the scene as a loser and as a broken man with the following words:

---

38 Cf Sàez who reads this as a criticism of the Christians' ethos in the play and points out that "Shakespeare precisely denounces the inconsistency of the devotion to a faith that preaches love, mercy and charity when it encourages intolerance; intolerance based not only on religion but also on race."; Sàez, "Religion, Law and Justice," 270. Kornstein simply refers to the Alien Statute as "an outrage, at least to 20th century readers"; Kornstein, "Fie Upon Your Law!," 48.
39 Weisberg, in this context, quite aptly characterizes Antonio's behaviour as "Draconian 'mercy'."; Weisberg, "Antonio's Legalistic Cruelty," 16. Greiner also remarks on the annihilation of the Jewish Other and points out: "Dass das Stück [...] Bedürfnissen der Abwertung, ja der Auslöschung nicht allgemein des Fremden, sondern spezifisch des Jüdischen (mit der Zwangstaufe am Ende) entgegenkommt und so auch funktionalisiert worden ist, [...] lässt sich nicht leugnen." (Bernhard Greiner, "Is that the Law? Die Metaphorisierung des Rechts als Problem der Interpretation des *Kaufmann von Venedig*," in *Shylock nach dem Holocaust: Zur Geschichte einer deutschen Erinnerungsfigur*, eds. Zeno Ackermann and Sabine Schülting (Berlin: De Gruyter, 2011): 189–200, 194.

> I pray you give me leave to go from hence.
> I am not well. Send the deed after me,
> And I will sign it. (4.1.392–394)

Significantly, these are the last words spoken by Shylock in the play. He does not make an appearance any more and – even more importantly – he is practically not spoken of any more[40] although we are only in the first scene of Act four here, with one more scene and a whole act still to follow. This is why Isaac states that "the fifth act of *Merchant* has always been a problem, a challenge to any modern production" and refers to Morris Carnovsky who pointed out "that should he ever direct *Merchant*, he would either do it without the fifth act, or portray the Venetian lovers as obnoxious teen-age brats."[41] Shylock's "I am not well" (4.1.393) goes totally unheeded because the ethnic other simply does not count. The annihilation of the other through the forced act of conversion finds its outward and formal equivalent in the total disappearance in the play of the character that embodied alterity.[42] What follows is concerned with the playful bantering between Portia and Bassanio and the general tying up of the complications created by the various love interests. Shylock's feelings and thoughts, un-

40 Except in 4.2.1–2 where Portia makes sure Shylock fulfils the conditions of the doubtful partial pardon he has received by telling Nerissa: "Enquire the Jew's house out, give him this deed,/ And let him sign it." Shylock is briefly referred to one very last time by Nerissa again when, in 5.1.291–293, she hands over to Lorenzo and Jessica the signed deed in which Shylock bequeathes his whole remaining fortune to the couple after his death.

41 Isaac, "The Worth of a Jew's Eye," 351–352. Indeed, as Kornstein points out, "throughout much of the 19th century, English productions of *The Merchant of Venice* simply stopped the play after Shylock's humiliation at the end of the Fourth Act, dropping entirely the last act." He also, following Richard Weisberg's study of the play in *Poethics* (1992), argues in favour of the "overlooked legal significance" of Act five, but in terms of the play's treatment of the ethnic other, the fifth act is indeed only relevant with regard to its complete ignoring of Shylock; Kornstein, "Fie Upon Your Law!," 50. Geoffrey Hartman, therefore, comments on the play's ending in the following words: "If there should be an ethics here, it is too 'embedded' for me to discern it. No one at Belmont gives a thought to Shylock. [...] He who disturbs the peace has been purged."; Geoffrey Hartman, "The Tricksy Word," 78. Cavell also observes that "I have never satisfied myself about the ending of *The Merchant of Venice*, reading or attending it. Shylock's defeat has kept seeming to me to be abruptly pat and his thwarting and grief go insufficiently expressed"; Stanley Cavell, "Saying in *The Merchant of Venice*," in *Shakespeare and the Law: A Conversation Among Disciplines and Professions*, eds. Brian Cormack and Martha C. Nussbaum (Chicago and London: The University of Chicago Press, 2013): 221–230, 221.

42 This annihilation of the other graphically came out in a production of the play by George Tabori "where *Merchant* was being performed by the Jewish inmates as entertainment for the SS officers. [...] the Nazi guards [...] wrestle Shylock to the ground, and stab him to death with his own knife."; Isaac, "The Worth of a Jew's Eye,": 352.

like in the earlier scenes of the play, are not given any space here but are rather silenced.[43] As a human subject, Shylock has all but ceased to exist. He is left behind as a problem solved, an ethnic other reduced to sameness in a Venice that prides itself on its international trade connections but is not devoid of anti-semitism and the mechanisms of racial and ethnic discrimination of the other.[44] *The Merchant of Venice* is usually listed among Shakespeare's comedies, but from Shylock's point of view, it is much closer to tragedy.[45] What keeps us from seeing him as a fully tragic figure is the fact that he is not a noble character with a fatal flaw which, in a moment of hubris, causes his downfall. Rather, he does display a deeply human dignity, maybe even momentary grandeur, in his great soliloquy when he asks "If you prick us, do we not bleed?" (III.i.50 – 51), but he is also too greedy, too obstinate and too vengeful a character with too little sense of proportion to fully qualify for the status of a tragic character.[46]

---

43 It is not without some justification, therefore, that Sinsheimer refers to Shakespeare's play as "the most ingenious satire on justice and the courts of law in the literature of the world."; Hermann Sinsheimer, *Shylock: The History of a Character* [1947] (New York: The Citadel Press, 1963), 196.

44 To read the fact that Shakespeare's allowing us to see Shylock's perspective as well constitutes the basis for an interpretation in which "*The Merchant* can be understood as a pro-Semitic play" is one-sided because it ignores the all-too-facile dismissal of Shylock after Act 4.1; Ojeda Alba, "Justice and Injustice," 13.

45 Isaac argues that this is another reason why Shakespeare had to get rid of Shylock before the fifth act: "this man Shylock – this Jew – with his rage and a class-action cue for passion and revenge, almost ruined a romantic fairy-tale comedy; and Shakespeare had to get him off the set as quickly and as quietly as possible [...] so that the kids could have their fifth act moonlight and music."; Isaac, "The Worth of a Jew's Eye," 371. But "[i]t must have been hard for Shakespeare not to let Shylock have one last thunderous speech filled with curses and tears" which is why *The Merchant of Venice* can be regarded as "[a] problem play if ever there was one."; Isaac, "The Worth of a Jew's Eye," 372. Hadfield also refers to *The Merchant of Venice* as "a problematic play"; Hadfield, "Shakespeare and Republican Venice," 77. Mesquita therefore claims that the trial scene is the play's "point of crisis as a literary genre, determining its classification as a comedy or a problem play."; Filomena Mesquita, "Travesties of Justice: Portia in the Courtroom," in *Shakespeare and the Law*, ed. Daniela Carpi (Ravenna: Longo Editore, 2003): 117–125, 117.

46 Colley therefore also claims that "he [i.e. Shylock] is no tragic character."; John Scott Colley, "Lancelot, Jacob, and Esau: Old and New Law in *The Merchant of Venice*," *Yearbook Of English Studies* 10.(1980): 181–189, 181. Weisberg argues that "the play remains a comedy" and concludes that "Shylock must fall because ethical behavior [...] sits poorly on a religious outsider trying to exert himself lawfully in a comedic environment."; Weisberg, "Antonio's Legalistic Cruelty," 18. Kornstein aptly remarks that "[c]lassifying *The Merchant of Venice* has always been difficult. [...] There is nothing funny about this play [...]. It is, truly speaking, neither a comedy nor a tragedy nor a history. It is a dramatic crystal of many legal issues [...]."; Kornstein, "Fie Upon Your Law!," 54.

What this play, just as *Othello*, Shakespeare's other great Venetian drama, demonstrates, are the pitfalls and dangers of the mechanisms in which ethnic or racial alterity are constructed in multi- and intercultural legal contexts. *The Merchant of Venice*, in its depiction of both the Christian Venetians and of Shylock the Jew, anatomizes the processes of cognitive hostile delimitation between members of different ethnic groups, it provides and very tentatively criticizes examples of anti-semitism while at the same time it is wide open itself to the charge of anti-semitism in its total silencing and exclusion of Shylock after Act. 4.1.[47] To read the play as a deconstruction of and a warning against xenophobia and anti-semitism is easier from a twenty-first century point of view, and it can safely be assumed that most of Shakespeare's contemporary audience rather gloated over the subjection of the Jew.[48] We should not forget, on the other hand, that the very mechanisms of discrimination displayed and analysed in the play are still all too widespread today – recent events in Western Europe and the United States of America being a shameful example. It is this openness to interpretation and Shakespeare's artistry in showing up both the weaknesses and strengths of the Venetians' and Shylock's cases that has turned this text into a classic that has lost nothing of its topicality today, and it is to be hoped that future generations will see it as a warning against stereotypical constructions of alterity as a negative other rather than as a confirmation of their own xenophobic prejudices.

---

47 This is why Gross said about the play that "its complexities, ambiguities, and shifts confound interpretation."; Gross, *Shylock*, 386. This is not quite accurate, though, because rather than confounding interpretation, the play merely makes simplistic readings impossible: "Shakespeare was well aware of the pervasive injustice in the play and [...] in his view both Jews and Christians are in the wrong."; Ojeda Alba, "Justice and Injustice," 22. Weisberg is more careful and accurate when he says that *The Merchant of Venice* "is clearly one of Shakespeare's most complex and ironic plays." One can also read Shylock's complete disappearance as a strong marker of Venice's anti-semitism in the play, which could thus become the agent of the deconstruction of such a xenophobic attitude.

48 Ojeda Alba rightly concludes that "Elizabethan audiences laughed at Shylock and were steered to be as unconcerned with his fate as were all his fellow characters." Ojeda Alba, "Justice and Injustice," 11.

Paul Raffield

Shakespeare's Twin Brother: Foreigners, Outlaws, and *The Comedy of Errors*

1 Immigration and the imminence of death

It begins with a ship, negotiating choppy waters, traversing the Mediterranean Sea. On board is a family: a husband and wife, their twin sons, and adopted twin boys. The husband has paid the skipper for their passage. A violent storm suddenly erupts. The vessel is not up to the job. It sinks. The crew escapes in a small lifeboat, leaving the family clinging to the wreckage. A wooden mast is all that stands between them and death by drowning. Their lives are saved by fishermen, happening to be in the vicinity. Pirates abduct two of the boys, separating the family for years to come. But at least the parents and their children do not drown. The scenario is familiar. It is a tale we see played out on our television screens on a frequent basis, as news bulletins broadcast the latest instances of migrants, fleeing via the North African or Levantine coast persecution and poverty in their desolate homelands for what they hope will be a better life on the other (European) side of the Mediterranean. The camera pans across a capsized boat, its terrified passengers scrambling to gain a slippery foothold on its upturned hull.[1] They are the lucky ones. The presence of a camera crew means that their location has been identified. A naval vessel, as likely as not from Italy, is on its way and will rescue them. For the thousands who are not so lucky, the story ends in death by drowning.

Except that the scenario of the storm-tossed, sinking ship and its human cargo with which this essay opens is not another television news report of the latest doomed attempt at escape by Syrian, Libyan, or sub-Saharan-African refugees.[2] It is the story of a shipwreck, told by the merchant of Syracuse, Egeon, at the start of Shakespeare's *The Comedy of Errors*. Egeon is the father of the Antipholus twins, who were separated as babies when the ship bearing them to Syracuse from Epidamnum sank, and were united in Ephesus only at the end of the

1 See Justine Poon, "How a Body becomes a Boat: The Asylum Seeker in Law and Images," *Law & Literature* 30 (2018): 105–121.

2 According to the United Nations High Commissioner for Refugees, 2,510 refugees drowned in the Mediterranean between January 2016 and the end of May 2016: http://www.aljazeera.com/news/2016/05/unhcr-2500-refugees-drowned-europe-2016-160531104504090 (last access April 10, 2017).

https://doi.org/10.1515/9783110591514-008

play, some twenty-five years after they last saw each other. At the start of the play, Egeon has been sentenced to death for pitching up in Ephesus (after an extensive and unsuccessful search for his son, Antipholus of Syracuse), in breach of a statute passed by the Ephesian Parliament (the consequence of a trade war with Syracuse). The Duke Solinus informs Egeon that

> It hath in solemn synods been decreed,
> Both by the Syracusians and ourselves,
> To admit no traffic to our adverse towns;
> Nay, more, if any born at Ephesus
> Be seen at any Syracusian marts and fairs;
> Again, if any Syracusian born
> Come to the bay of Ephesus, he dies,
> His goods confiscate to the Duke's dispose,
> Unless a thousand marks be levièd
> To quit the penalty and to ransom him. (1.1.13–22)[3]

Thus, the dreadful doom of law intercedes. Egeon has neither money nor friends to pay the ransom, and therefore at five o'clock in the afternoon of the same day on which he arrived in Ephesus he will be executed. Time and the hours in the day are crucial factors not only in the action of the play, but are relevant also to the meta-theatrical significance of *The Comedy of Errors*, a point to which I shall return. Unknown to Egeon, one of his twin sons, Antipholus of Ephesus, has lived in Ephesus for the past twenty years. His other son, Antipholus of Syracuse, left his father's home seven years before the play began, at the age of eighteen, to search for his lost brother.[4] He too pitches up in Ephesus. Like his father, as a Syracusian in Ephesus, his life is in mortal danger. He is advised by an Ephesian merchant to deny his Syracusian provenance and "give out you are

3 All references to the text of the play are from William Shakespeare, *The Comedy of Errors*, ed. R.A. Foakes (London: The Arden Shakespeare, 1962).

4 After the shipwreck, Antipholus of Ephesus, his mother Emilia, and Dromio of Ephesus, were rescued "By men of Epidamnum" (5.1.355); but "rude fishermen of Corinth" (5.1.357) boarded their ship, abducted Antipholus and Dromio, and returned with them to Corinth. They left Emilia with the men of Epidamnum. Eventually, she too arrived in Ephesus. Menaphon, uncle of Duke Solinus, brought Antipholus to Ephesus (5.1.367–368). Antipholus of Syracuse (who was rescued from the shipwreck, along with his father and Dromio of Syracuse) left his home in Syracuse at the age of eighteen to search for his brother (1.1.125); according to Egeon, he has been gone for "seven short years" (5.1.309), making the twins twenty-five years of age when the play begins. The Duke informs Egeon that he has been "patron to Antipholus [of Ephesus]" (5.1.326) for twenty years; therefore Antipholus was five years of age when he was brought to Ephesus from Corinth.

of Epidamnum" (1.2.1). Egeon, Antipholus of Syracuse, and his servant Dromio (whom Egeon bought at birth, along with his twin brother,[5] who happens also to be called Dromio, and is the servant of Antipholus of Ephesus) are in effect illegal immigrants.

2 Shakespeare, racial tension, and the London apprentices

Shakespeare had first-hand experience of immigrants. He lodged with a family of French Huguenots, the Mountjoys, who had fled persecution in their native France and settled in the City of London. Like many of his exiled compatriots, Christopher Mountjoy (from Crécy in north-western France) became a successful entrepreneur in one of the textile-related crafts that flourished in Elizabethan and Jacobean London, that of the "tiremaker": "head-tires" or "attires" were a form of ornate headwear for women. In Charles Nicholl's study of Shakespeare's life as *The Lodger*, he adduces the strongest possible evidence that, while working in London, Shakespeare resided with the Mountjoys at their house in Silver Street between 1602 and 1604.[6] *The Comedy of Errors* predates this period by approximately ten years. References in the play to a French civil war suggest that at the earliest it was not written until late 1593, in July of which year Henry of Navarre became Henry IV of France.[7] By this date Shakespeare would have witnessed the often violent response in certain quarters to the influx of immigrants that was a notable and notably public feature of life in London in the 1590s: rising levels of immigration, severe inflation, and alarmingly low wages all contributed to the London apprentice riots of the 1590s.[8] In 1590, the crown responded to the Lon-

---

5 "Those, for their parents were exceeding poor, / I bought, and brought up to attend my sons." (1.1.56–57)

6 Charles Nicholl, *The Lodger: Shakespeare on Silver Street* (London: Penguin, 2007), 4, 17.

7 *Syr. Ant.* Where France? *Syr. Dro.* In her forehead, armed and revolted, making war against her heir. (3.2.120–122) See *The Comedy of Errors*, ed. Foakes, Introduction, xviii-xix. On the French civil war of this period, see Mack P. Holt, *The French Wars of Religion, 1562–1629* (Cambridge: Cambridge University Press, 2005). It is arguable that the title of Shakespeare's play derives from a line in Sidney's *The Defence of Poesie* (published in 1595, but written *c.* 1580): "[...] *Comedy* is an imitation of the common errors of our life [...]", Philip Sidney, *The Defence of Poesie* (London: W. Ponsonby, 1595), sig. E4.*r.*

8 For a collection of essays on the subject, see Ruben Espinosa and David Ruiter eds., *Shakespeare and Immigration* (Abingdon: Routledge, 2016). Manning records thirty-five instances of serious disorder in London between 1581 and 1602: Roger B. Manning, *Village Revolts: Social Protest and Popular Disturbances in England, 1509–1640* (Oxford: Clarendon, 1988), 187. The

don riots with a Proclamation, imposing curfews on apprentices.[9] But if the maintenance of public order was a preoccupation of the state authorities, so too was the perceived cause of civil unrest. So-called "Blackamoors" (from North Africa, as opposed to so-called "Negars" from West Africa) were the subject of opprobrium in the last years of Elizabethan rule, their numbers in England having increased following the capture of many Africans during the recent war with Spain. In 1601, a draft Proclamation of "Negroes and Blackamoors" demanded the deportation of black people,[10] on grounds that English "masters" should be encouraged to use their compatriots in service because English subjects were suffering "hard times of dearth."[11]

Shakespeare had addressed the issue of civil rebellion in one of his earliest plays, *Henry VI, Part 2* (*c.* 1590–91). Confusingly, this was almost certainly the first play that he wrote in the *Henry VI* trilogy, under the discursive title *The First Part of the Contention of the Two Famous Houses of York and Lancaster with the Death of the Good Duke Humphrey.* It was only with the publication of the First Folio in 1623 that the plays were listed as the *First, Second,* and *Third Parts of King Henry the Sixth. Henry VI, Part 2* contains the scenes of the Jack Cade Rebellion, and includes the line of one of the rebels, Dick the Butcher, which (for lawyers at least) has immortalised the play: "The first thing we do let's kill all the lawyers" (4.2.78).[12] Jack Cade's rebellion in 1450 was only periph-

London riots of 1595 "constituted the most dangerous and prolonged urban uprising in England": Manning, *Village Revolts*, 208. For a collection of essays on the subject of civil disorder, see also *Rebellion, Popular Protest and the Social Order in Early Modern England*, ed. Paul Slack (Cambridge: Cambridge University Press, 1984).

9 The 1590 Proclamation required that apprentices "tarry and abide within their several houses and not to be suffered to go abroad after nine of the clock at night, upon pain of imprisonment": "Enforcing Curfew for Apprentices," in *Tudor Royal Proclamations*, eds. Paul L. Hughes and James F. Larkin, 3 vols. (New Haven: Yale University Press, 1969), vol. 3, 60. See M.J. Power, "London and the Control of the 'Crisis' of the 1590s," *History* 70.230 (1985): 371–385; R.B. Outhwaite, "Dearth, the English Crown and the 'Crisis' of the 1590s," in *The European Crisis of the 1590s: Essays in Comparative History*, ed. Peter Clark (London: Allen & Unwin, 1985), 23–43.

10 On the draft Proclamation of 1601, see Andrew Dickson, "Multiculturalism in Shakespeare's Plays," available at http://www.bl.uk/shakespeare/articles/multiculturalism-in-shakespeares-plays (last access April 10, 2017).

11 Quoted in Emily C. Bartels, "Too Many Blackamoors: Deportation, Discrimination, and Elizabeth I," *Studies in English Literature, 1500–1900* 46.2 (2006): 305–322, 317. See also, Ania Loomba, *Shakespeare, Race, and Colonialism* (Oxford: Oxford University Press, 2002); Laura Hunt Yungblut, *Strangers Settled Here Amongst Us: Policies, Perceptions and the Presence of Aliens in Elizabethan England* (London: Routledge, 1996).

12 See Charles Hobday, "Clouted Shoon and Leather Aprons: Shakespeare and the Egalitarian Tradition," *Renaissance and Modern Studies* 23 (1979): 63–78. Philip Henslowe recorded receipts

erally related to the threat posed by immigrants to the indigenous population (or more specifically, the threat of military invasion by the French, following the loss of Normandy by the English). It was more overtly concerned with corruption and abuse of governmental power, although Shakespeare's depiction of events refers to causes of rebellion in London during the 1590s: inflation, and the price of corn and foodstuffs being two of them. Cade vows that, when he is crowned king, "There shall be in England seven halfpenny loaves sold for a penny" (4.2.67–68).

The theme of apprentices and their perceived injustices at the hands of their masters is evident in *Henry VI, Part 2.* The unnamed "Second Rebel," for example, complains that "The nobility think scorn to go in leather aprons" (4.2.13–14). Apprentices figure also in the *dramatis personae.* The unnamed "Third Prentice" proposes a toast to Peter Thump, apprentice to the armourer Thomas Horner: "And here's a quart for me, and be merry, Peter, and fear not thy master. Fight for credit of the prentices!" (2.3.73–75). But ultimately, the apprentices and rebels of *Henry VI, Part 2* serve the function (at least in part) of a comic interlude, albeit one that provides a satirical reflection on misgovernment by the ruling elite. These characters and the scenes in which they appear are peripheral to the main action of the play, which concerns the fatal dynastic struggle between the Houses of York and Lancaster. For a highly stylised depiction of the relationship between master and apprentice that is central to the drama, we must look elsewhere: to the relationship between master and servant in *The Comedy of Errors.* Indeed, in this virtuosic rendering of *The Menaechmi* by Plautus (d. 184 B.C.), the greatest dramatist of the Old Latin period, Shakespeare enhances the potential for comedy (especially and obviously through the device of mistaken identity) by doubling the number of twins in the play. Where Plautus created only the Menaechmus twins, Shakespeare created the Antipholus twins and their respective servants (also twins), the Dromios of Syracuse and of Ephesus. Antipholus of Syracuse refers to his servant as a slave – "I'll to the Centaur to go seek this slave" (1.2.104) – but this is more a derogatory and familiar term for his servant (as well as an allusion to the classical sources of the play: "Dromo" was a generic word in Roman drama for a slave), than an ac-

---

of £3 16s 8d for a performance by Lord Strange's Men of a "new" play at the Rose Playhouse in March 1592, which Henslowe entitled "harey the vj": *Henslowe's Diary*, ed. R.A. Foakes (Cambridge: Cambridge University Press, 2002), 16; Wells and Taylor argue that the play to which Henslowe refers was probably *Henry VI, Part 1*, the last in the trilogy to be written and performed: *William Shakespeare: The Complete Works*, eds. Stanley Wells and Gary Taylor (Oxford: Clarendon, 2005), 125. Specifically, on the line "Let's kill all the lawyers," see Paul Raffield, *Shakespeare's Imaginary Constitution: Late Elizabethan Politics and the Theatre of Law* (Oxford: Hart Publishing, 2010), 153.

curate description of Dromio's societal status when applied to late Elizabethan England.[13]

As Robin Blackburn noted in his study of slavery in Europe, at the time of the Domesday Book (1087) approximately ten per cent of the population of England were slaves, but soon after the Norman Conquest the feudal system led to the rapid attenuation of slavery in England, and the creation of a relationship between masters and servants, in which the latter became "specialist workers" and were not in a "fully servile condition."[14] This was the period in which apprenticeships were founded. In 1563, the year before Shakespeare was born, the formal structure of apprenticeships was defined by the *Statute of Artificers* (5 Eliz. I. c. 4).[15] Henceforth, the state arrogated to itself responsibility for regulating functions previously undertaken by feudal craft guilds. The apprenticeship was regulated by contract, subject to English common law. I emphasise the legal status of the master and servant relationship (employer and employee relationship, in modern parlance) because the presence of formal legal structures – of commercial contracts between individual parties, but also the social contract between governor and governed, and between citizen and citizen – is central to an informed understanding of *The Comedy of Errors.*

The farcical element of the plot is driven by a contractual dispute over the manufacture and delivery of a gold chain or necklace: the "carcanet" (3.1.4), which Antipholus of Ephesus has commissioned the goldsmith Angelo to make for his wife Adriana. *Laissez-faire* market forces and the enforcement of legally binding agreements are represented in the play by a long list of characters from the realms of commerce and law: Angelo (the goldsmith); Balthazar (the merchant); the First Merchant (who befriends Antipholus of Syracuse); the Second Merchant (Angelo's creditor); an Officer of the Law; a Jailer; and the supreme magistrate Solinus, Duke of Ephesus. But the conflict between characters is resolved at the end of the play only when they realise that there is another type of contract (less formal than that for the purchase of goods, but no less symbolic of agreement) that binds them into a civic relationship: a social contract based upon the bonds of friendship and community. In this respect, the gold chain or

13 Bartels notes that slavery "had been abolished from England and most of Europe by the sixteenth century": Bartels, "Too Many Blackamoors," 313.

14 Robin Blackburn, "The Old World Background to European Colonial Slavery," *The William and Mary Quarterly* 54.1 (1997): 65–102, 71.

15 See Chris Minns and Patrick Wallis, "Rules and Reality: Quantifying the Practice of Apprenticeship in Early Modern England," *The Economic History Review* 65.2 (2012): 556–579; also, Donald Woodward, "The Background to the Statute of Artificers: The Genesis of Labour Policy, 1558–63," *The Economic History Review* 33.1 (1980): 32–44.

carcanet is no mere prop. It has powerful juristic connotations, traceable to the Platonic description of public law as a "golden and holy" cord or chain, attached to citizens and connected to the gods, "tugging" at the populace to make it compliant with a prescribed and divinely ordained legal order.[16]

The contract between Antipholus of Syracuse and Dromio of Syracuse was of a different type: it was a contract of employment or service, rather than a contract for goods (the apprenticeship was sealed and made legally binding by the signing of indentures, which usually adhered to the same formula); but it was a contract all the same, and for an Elizabethan audience the implications of the threats made by both Dromios unilaterally to terminate their contracts of service with their respective masters would have been immediately apparent.[17] The *Statute of Artificers* 1563 provided that

> if any artificers be retained in service, or to work in great or for a time, do depart from his service or work without licence until the work is finished or the time be fully come up, the offender shall have one month's imprisonment and shall forfeit 20s. 0d.[18]

The roles of servant and apprentice often overlapped. An apprentice pledged to serve his master (there were small numbers of female apprentices during this period, mainly in the textile-related crafts, such as millinery and silk-work),[19] to

16 Plato, *The Laws*, trans. Trevor J. Saunders (London: Penguin, 2004), 31, Bk. 1.II.644e-645a. The Italian jurist Giambattista Vico observed in *La Scienza Nuova* (published in 1725) that the words for law derive from those for tendons or cords. Commenting on Vico's *magnum opus* (published in 1725), George Hersey notes that Vico developed tropes of the word *corda*, meaning variously tendons, sinews, lyre strings and musical chords, all of which implied (quoting Vico) "the union of the cords and powers of the fathers, whence derived public powers": George Hersey, *The Lost Meaning of Classical Architecture: Speculations on Ornament from Vitruvius to Venturi* (Cambridge, Mass.: MIT Press, 1988), 5. See also, Sir John Fortescue: "The Law, under which the People is incorporated, may be compared to the Nerves or Sinews of the Body Natural; for, as by these the whole Frame is fitly joined together and compacted, so is the Law that Ligament (to go back to the truest Derivation of the Word, *Lex à Ligando*) by which the Body Politic, and all its several Members are bound together and united in one entire Body," Sir John Fortescue, *De Laudibus Legum Angliae*, ed. John Selden (London: R. Gosling, 1737), 22. On the juristic symbolism of the carcanet in *The Comedy of Errors*, see Raffield, *Shakespeare's Imaginary Constitution*, 63–64.

17 When his master gives him money for safekeeping in the Centaur, Dromio of Syracuse says: "Many a man would take you at your word, / And go indeed, having so good a mean." (1.2.17–18) Threatened with a beating by his master's wife, Dromio of Ephesus remarks: "If I last in this service you must case me in leather." (2.1.85)

18 Quoted in Woodward, "The Background to the Statute," 43.

19 See Jennifer C. Ward, *Women in Medieval Europe: 1200–1500* (Abingdon: Routledge, 2016), 22; also, Ann Minister, "Pauper Apprenticeship in South Derbyshire: A Positive Experience?," in

keep his secrets, to do his commandments, not to commit fornication nor to marry, and not to run away. In return, the master was obliged to feed, lodge, and clothe his servant (regulations prohibited an apprentice from wearing clothes other than those provided by his master):[20] in all respects the Antipholus twins fulfil these obligations. The Dromios followed the established pattern of apprentices becoming part of their masters' respective households, living under the same roof, as they would have done with their own father had Egeon not paid money to buy them as babies.[21] He informs the Duke near the start of the play: "Those, for their parents were exceeding poor, / I bought, and brought up to attend my sons." (1.1.56–57) In this respect also, the act of payment to the parents of the Dromio twins bore similarity to the creation of a conventional apprenticeship. As Mihoko Suzuki notes in an article on the London Apprentice Riots of the 1590s, apprenticeships were (like marriages) often "arranged by parents and relatives," the main difference between the conventional arrangement and the action of Egeon in buying the Dromio twins being that parents often paid a substantial premium in order formally to create an apprenticeship.[22]

I have dwelt on the subject of apprenticeships because the topic leads me to the significant theme of violence, which was the most obvious feature of the apprentice riots of the 1590s, as it is also a notable aspect of *The Comedy of Errors*. There, the Ephesian Dromio complains that he has "some marks [of his master] upon my pate" and "Some of my mistress' marks upon my shoulders," (1.2.82–83) and throughout the play, at frequent intervals, we witness the two servants being beaten by their masters. The brutal beating of his servant by Antipholus of Ephesus, using a "rope's end" (SD 4.4.17), reflects not only the beating of apprentices by their masters (as Steven R. Smith notes, "there are numerous cases of apprentices suing their masters as a result of mistreatment");[23] it would

Experiences of Poverty in Late Medieval and Early Modern England and France, ed. Anne M. Scott, (Abingdon: Routledge, 2016), 63–84, 81–82; Ilana Krausman Ben-Amos, "Failure to Become Freemen: Urban Apprentices in Early Modern England," *Social History* 16.2 (1991): 155–172; Ilana Krausman Ben-Amos, "Women Apprentices in the Trades and Crafts of Early Modern Bristol," *Continuity & Change* 6.2 (1991): 227–252.

20 Steven R. Smith, "The London Apprentices as Seventeenth-Century Adolescents," in *Rebellion, Popular Protest*, ed. Slack, 219–231, 220.

21 Smith, "The London Apprentices," 221.

22 Mihoko Suzuki, "The London Apprentice Riots of the 1590s and the Fiction of Thomas Deloney," *Criticism* 38.2 (1996): 181–217, 190.

23 Smith, "The London Apprentices," 222. Smith quotes from the records of the Middlesex Sessions of the Peace and of the Mayor's Court; in one case, an apprentice "was beaten so severely

also recall for late Elizabethan audiences the whippings regularly doled out to those rioting apprentices who were apprehended and subsequently subjected to the full rigour of law. For example, on 27 June 1595, it was recorded that "certaine young men apprentizes and other, were punished by whipping, setting on the pillory, ec. for taking butter from the market women in Southwarke."[24] Those particular apprentices got off relatively lightly. In other instances, rioting apprentices were executed for their violent unrest: for example, John Stow records that on 22 July 1595, "five of those unruely youths that were on the Tower hill apprehended, they were condemned, and had iudgement to be drawne, hanged and quartered."[25] Michel Foucault famously opined that judicial punishment "belongs, even in minor cases, to the ceremonies by which power is manifested,"[26] and such is the case obviously with the punishment of the rioting apprentices, and indeed with the violent treatment meted out to the Dromios by their masters. But the power with which I am concerned in the present study is less the power of the sovereign than the power of the victim of oppression to subvert the authority of the sovereign by turning against the outsider, alien, or foreigner.

Much of the violence perpetrated by the apprentices was directed at foreigners, the presence of which in growing numbers on the streets of London was a major source of the apprentices' unrest. On 16 April 1593, members of the Privy Council signed a letter addressed to the Lord Mayor of London, the subject of which was a libellous, "lewde and vyle ticket or placarde set up upon some post in London purportinge some determynacion and intencion the apprentyces should have to attempt some violence on the strangers." Again, on 22 April 1593, the Privy Council lent its signature to a letter sent to the Master of Requests, Dr Julius Caesar, the subject of which was

> certaine libelles latelie published by some disordered and factious persons in and about the cittie of London, shewinge an intente in the artyficers and others who holde themselves prejudiced in theire trades by strangers to use some course of vyolence to remove the saide

---

that 'he could not go upright, and that he did spit blood for a fortnight after,'" Smith, "The London Apprentices," 222.

24 John Stow, *The Abridgement or Summarie of the English Chronicle, first collected by Master Iohn Stowe*, ed. Edmond Howes (London: John Windet for the companie of Stacioneres, 1607), 499–500.

25 Stow, *The Abridgement or Summarie*, 501.

26 Michel Foucault, *Discipline and Punish: The Birth of the Prison*, trans. Alan Sheridan (London: Penguin, 1991), 47.

strangers or by way of tumulte to suppresse them,
a matter very dangerous and with all deligence to be prevented.[27]

By far the most notorious of the libels posted in public places was the poem, written in blank verse and posted on a wall in the Dutch Churchyard in Broad Street in May 1593. Commonly known as "The Dutch Church Libel," the poem opens with the following lines:

Ye strangers yt doe inhabite in this lande
Note this same writing doe it understand
Conceit it well for savegard of your lyves
Your goods, your children, & your dearest wives
Your Machiavellian Marchant spoyles the state
Your usery doth leave us all for deade
Your Artifex, & craftesman works our fate,
And like the Jewes, you eate us up as bread [...]

The xenophobic theme persists uninterrupted for another forty-five lines, and includes the explicit threat:

Weele cutt your throtes, in your temples praying
Not paris massacre so much blood did spill
As we will doe iust vengeance on you all
In counterfeitinge religion for your flight [...]

The poem ends with the following stern injunction: "Fly, Flye, & never returne."[28] The signature at the bottom of the poem reads: "*per.* Tamberlaine," the eponymous Asiatic conqueror of Christopher Marlowe's play, which had been performed in London in 1587–88. In 1592, Marlowe dramatised the St. Bartholomew's Day Massacre of 1572 in a play entitled *Massacre at Paris*, to which the above poem refers. The finger of suspicion pointed indubitably at Marlowe. On 18 May 1593, the Privy Council issued a warrant for his arrest, after Thomas Kyd claimed under torture that heretical papers found in his lodgings belonged to the playwright. Marlowe was released after two days of questioning by the Privy Council. On 30 May 1593 he was killed in a pub at Deptford; stabbed in the eye, apparently by Ingram Frizer, a servant of Marlowe's patron, Sir Thomas Walsingham.

27 *Acts of the Privy Council of England* [1592–93], ed. John Roche Dasent, 46 vols. (London: HMSO, 1901), 24: 187, 200–201.
28 The poem was discovered by Arthur Freeman in the Bodleian Library, MS.Don.d.152f.4v. It is entitled: "A Libell, fixte upon the French Church Wall, in London. Ann° 1593°."

Whether Marlowe or Kyd was responsible for the Dutch Church Libel, or whether responsibility lay with agents of the Privy Council seeking to discredit either or both men, we shall probably never know for certain. But on 11 May 1593, soon after discovery of the Dutch Church Libel, the court of Star Chamber ordered officers of the City of London to arrest those suspected of its publication and to torture those who refused to confess the truth. Arthur Freeman attributes the extreme reaction of the court to the failure of the Lord Mayor of London on previous occasions to deal firmly with "unruly apprentices and journeymen."[29] Whatever the reason, the fear of state authorities that foreigners were capable of provoking sedition within the capital was palpable.

3 Xenophobia, riots, and *The Book of Sir Thomas More*

The narrative of alienation and retribution that characterizes the plot of *The Comedy of Errors* reflects contemporaneous events in London. As I have indicated, resentment at the rising level of immigration was a primary cause of the apprentice riots of the early 1590s. Shakespeare returned to the theme of immigrants and race riots in a later, multi-authored work on which he collaborated with no fewer than six authors. The contributors to *The Book of Sir Thomas More* (written *c.* 1600) were Henry Chettle, Thomas Dekker, Thomas Heywood, Anthony Munday, Edmund Tilney (who held the important government post of Master of the Revels: in effect, the state censor of dramatic works), an anonymous playhouse scribe, and Shakespeare himself.[30] As the title of the play suggests, the drama concerns the life of Sir Thomas More, up to and including his fall from royal grace and subsequent execution in 1535. More's relationship with Henry VIII, his elevation to the office of Lord Chancellor, his refusal to condone the annulment of marriage between the King and his first wife Catherine of Aragon, his further refusal to take the Oath of Supremacy (declaring the King to be Supreme Head of the Church in England), and his trial for High Treason, have all been well documented (and dramatized in Robert Bolt's play *A Man For All*

29 Arthur Freeman, "Marlowe, Kyd, and the Dutch Church Libel," *English Literary Renaissance* 3.1 (1973): 44–52, 45.

30 On the authorship and date of composition of *Sir Thomas More*, see "Sir Thomas More," in *William Shakespeare and Others: Collaborative Plays*, eds. Jonathan Bate and Eric Rasmussen, with Jan Sewell and Will Sharpe (Basingstoke: Palgrave Macmillan, 2013), 352–353.

Seasons).[31] For the purposes of the present analysis the play about More on which Shakespeare collaborated – *The Book of Sir Thomas More* – is distinctive for the concentration of its entire first half on the notorious May Day race riots of 1517, during the tenure of Thomas More as under-sheriff of London (by which time he had been appointed Privy Counsellor). More's role in these violent events was to address the rioters in his role as under-sheriff and (temporarily at least) to calm them. The occasion was also known as the Evil or Ill May Day, on account of the extraordinary levels of violence displayed by London apprentices towards foreigners in general, and immigrant Flemish workers, foreign bankers and merchants in particular. These people are described in the play as "Lombards." In the context of *The Book of Sir Thomas More*, the word refers in generic terms to foreign inhabitants of Lombard Street, near St. Paul's in the City of London, in which immigrant workers, bankers, and merchants congregated. The land on which Lombard Street was built had been granted by King Edward I (1272–1307) to emigrant goldsmiths from northern Italy – the Lombards themselves.[32]

The first half of *The Book of Sir Thomas More* is based on actual events (recorded by the chronicler Edward Hall), following a xenophobic speech made at the instigation of a city broker, named John Lincoln – the so-called "leader of the rebels" in the play. The speech (which was delivered by one Doctor Bele) enjoined all "Englishemen to cheryshe and defende themselves, and to hurte and greve aliens for the comon weale."[33] The writers of the play dramatised entire sections of Hall's description of the riot. For example, the play opens with a dispute between a "Lombard" called Cavaler and a carpenter called Williamson, the former seizing a pair of doves purchased by the latter on the grounds that doves were too dainty a dish "for a coarse carpenter" (1.1.17). This derives from a passage in *Hall's Chronicle*, in which

---

31 See for example, Peter Ackroyd, *The Life of Thomas More* (London: Chatto & Windus, 1998); John Guy, *The Public Career of Sir Thomas More* (New Haven: Yale University Press, 1980). The 1966 film of *A Man For All Seasons*, directed by Fred Zinnemann and starring Paul Scofield, won six Oscars, including those for Best Picture, Best Director, and Best Actor.

32 See John Timbs, *Curiosities of London* (London: Longman, Green, Reader, and Dyer, 1868), 530–532. The Germanic Lombards or *Longobardi* invaded the Italian peninsula in 568 A.D. and ruled until 774 A.D. when the Frankish King Charlemagne conquered Pavia, the capital of Lombardy, and annexed the Kingdom of Italy to his empire; see Neil Christie, *The Lombards: the Ancient Longobards* (Oxford: Blackwell, 1995).

33 Edward Hall, "The viii yere of Kyng Henry the viii" in *The Union of the Two Noble and Illustre Famelies of Lancastre & Yorke* (London: Richardi Graftoni, 1548): fo. lx.v; also quoted in Steve Rappaport, *Worlds Within Worlds: Structures of Life in Sixteenth-Century London* (Cambridge: Cambridge University Press, 2002), 15.

> a Carpenter in London called Willyamson whiche bought two stockdoves in Chepe [the market in Cheapside], and as he was aboute to paye for them a Frencheman tooke them oute of hys hande, and sayde they were not meate for a carpenter: well sayde the Englishman I have bought them and now payd for them, naye sayde the Frencheman I will have them for my lorde the Ambasador, and so for better or worse, the Frencheman called the Englisheman knave and went awaye with the stockdoves.[34]

In the play, the carpenter Williamson informs Cavaler that "I bought them [the stockdoves] in Cheapside, and paid my money for them," (1.1.13) whereupon Cavaler urges his fellow "Lombard," Francis de Bard: "let us go complain to my lord Ambassador" (1.1.48). And so it continues, the writers of the play adapting events and paraphrasing passages from *Hall's Chronicle,* thereby providing a realistic, dramatised documentary of the race riots of May Day 1517 (as far as we know, the play was never staged during Shakespeare's lifetime, its subject matter being deemed too contentious for performance in a public playhouse).[35]

Characters in the play speak in phrases that resonate with a twenty-first-century audience, the early modern idiom finding a peculiar echo in sentiments expressed during the United Kingdom's 2016 Referendum campaign on membership of the European Union. Lines such as "What, one stranger take thy food from thee, and another thy wife!" (1.1.22–23); "Shall strangers rule the roost?" (2.2.1–2); and "Shall these enjoy more privilege than we / In our own country?" (2.2.27–28) find parallels in the lexicon of certain "Brexit" affiliates. Even recent wars with neighbouring nation-states in continental Europe are invoked by characters in *The Book of Sir Thomas More* in defence of the riots: "I am ashamed that freeborn Englishmen, having beaten strangers within their own homes, should thus be braved and abused by them at home," (1.1.49–51) exclaims an outraged rioter. It will be remembered that during the 2016 EU Referendum campaign in the United Kingdom, some of the few surviving British veterans of the Second World War were wheeled out by various media outlets in the UK to air the collective opinion that they had not fought and defeated the Germans in a world war only to see their country subjugated to German rule in the iniquitous form of the European Union. In Thomas More's speech to the rioting apprentices (which was the principal authorial contribution of Shakespeare to the play), the humanitarian counterpoint to these xenophobic opinions was offered. More asked the rioters to "Imagine that you see the wretched strangers, /

34 Hall, "The viii yere of Kyng Henry the viii," fo. lix.*v.*

35 "Sir Thomas More," eds. Bate and Rasmussen, Introduction, 350. The editors note that one of the contributors to the play, Master of the Revels Edmund Tilney, wrote on the manuscript: "Leave out the insurrection wholly," 350. Nicholl notes that "The events depicted are parallel with the riots of 1593," Nicholl, *The Lodger*, 179.

Their babies at their backs, with their poor luggage / Plodding to th'ports and coasts for transportation" (2.4.70 – 72). For a modern audience these lines recall images both of the former Calais "Jungle" encampment for migrants and Alan Kurdi, the Syrian boy of Kurdish extraction, who drowned on 2 September 2015 in the Mediterranean Sea when the small inflatable boat in which his family hoped to reach the Greek island of Kos capsized, only a few minutes after setting sail from the Turkish port of Bodrum.[36]

The Book of Sir Thomas More provides a realistic depiction of the fractious relationship between wealthy "Lombards" residing in the City of London and the poor craftsmen and apprentices who lived alongside them. According to *Hall's Chronicle*,

> the multitude of straungers was so great aboute London, that the poore English artificers coulde skace get any lyvynge: And moost of all the straungers were so proude, that they disdayned, mocked and oppressed the Englishemen, whiche was the beginnynge of the grudge.[37]

Such was the fractious relationship between Williamson and Cavaler in *The Book of Sir Thomas More*. While the play (the first half anyway, which deals exclusively with London's race riots) may be read on one level as an insightful social history of race relations in sixteenth-century London, it does not tell us much about Shakespeare's treatment of the theme of foreigners in a hostile land. He wrote only one scene in the play: Act Two, Scene Four, where Sir Thomas More momentarily quells the rioting mob with a speech in which he reminds the rebels of the common humanity shared by indigenous subjects and foreign strangers alike. By asking the rioters to put themselves in the position of the immigrants – "What country would give *you* harbour?" (2.4.126) – he reminds them that "*you* must needs be strangers" (2.4.130).[38]

---

36 On 26 October, 2016 the French authorities announced that the Calais "Jungle" encampment had been cleared. For an account of quotidian existence in the Calais "Jungle," see Angelique Chrisafis, "'At night it's like a horror movie' – inside Calais's official shantytown," *The Guardian*, April 6, 2015: https://www.theguardian.com/world/2015/apr/06/at-night-its-like-a-horror-movie-inside-calaiss-official-shanty-town (last access April 10, 2017).

37 Hall, "The viii yere of Kyng Henry the viii," fo. lix.*v*.

38 Emphasis added.

4 Classical friendship and Christian community in *The Comedy of Errors*

"What country would give *you* harbour?" This is the same question that Shakespeare asks the audience throughout *The Comedy of Errors*. If you were to be placed in the precarious position of Egeon and Antipholus of Syracuse, what country would give you safe refuge? In this play, Shakespeare eschewed realism, incorporating instead a variety of styles and genres: farce, lyrical poetry, and romance (as in the late romances *Pericles*, *Cymbeline*, *The Winter's Tale*, and *The Tempest*)[39]. The effect is to create a non-realistic dreamscape in which mistaken identity drives a frenetic plot that manages to accommodate within its comedic mayhem the serious theme of alienation.

As indicated above, the action of *The Comedy of Errors* takes place in less than one day, and throughout the play the audience is reminded that the hour of Egeon's impending execution (five o'clock that afternoon) is approaching. The clock is ticking, and (as various characters apprise the audience) it is ticking very quickly: "Within this hour it will be dinner time," (1.2.11) Antipholus of Syracuse informs his servant upon arrival in Ephesus near the start of the play; a few moments later, "The clock hath stricken twelve upon the bell" (1.2.45); a few moments after that, Adriana tells her sister, "Sure, Luciana, it is two o'clock"[40] (2.1.3). The condensing of time in this fashion is a useful dramatic device, which drives the narrative to its expected conclusion, the death of Egeon: "By this I think the dial points at five; / Anon I'm sure the Duke himself in person / Comes this way to the melancholy vale, / The place of death and sorry execution" (5.1.118–121). This being a comedy, there is no public beheading, "Behind the ditches of the abbey here" (5.1.122). Egeon is reunited with his wife Emilia (who in the twenty-five years since they last saw each other has become Abbess of the Ephesian Priory, on the steps of which they meet), his twin sons,

39 Coleridge and Hazlitt both used the word "romance" to describe these plays: see William Shakespeare, *Cymbeline*, ed. Martin Butler (Cambridge: Cambridge University Press, 2005), Introduction 6–7. On Shakespearean romance as "the idea of a quest for discovery or self-discovery [...] a psychological journey," see William Shakespeare, *Cymbeline*, ed. Roger Warren (Oxford: Oxford University Press, 1998), Introduction, 16. Stephen Orgel states that in connection with a category of Shakespearean plays, the phrase "romance" was first used by Edward Dowden, in *Shakespeare: A Critical Study of His Mind and Art*, published in 1875: William Shakespeare, *The Tempest*, ed. Stephen Orgel (Oxford: Oxford University Press, 1987), Introduction 4, fn. 3.
40 On time and the making of contracts in *The Comedy of Errors*, see Raffield, *Shakespeare's Imaginary Constitution*, 65.

and their twin servants. Egeon is pardoned by a benevolent Duke, who also waives the ransom for his life: a higher, moral law – unwritten, other than in the hearts of men – supplants the authority of statute.[41]

In only one other of his plays, *The Tempest*, did Shakespeare compress the action of the drama into less than one day. And in none of his plays other than *The Comedy of Errors* did he confine the action to one specific location, an Ephesian street or "mart" in front of three houses: the house of Antipholus of Ephesus; the house of the Courtesan; and the House of God, the Priory (even in *The Tempest* the action is scattered across various parts of the island). This points us to interpretations in the early modern period of the Aristotelian classical unities (those of time, place, and action), as discussed in *The Poetics* of Aristotle, to which European dramatists of the sixteenth and seventeenth century tended to adhere. In none of the plays that he wrote before *The Comedy of Errors* (and in none that he wrote after, with the exception, as indicated above, of his last sole-authored play *The Tempest*) does Shakespeare demonstrate any interest in complying with the imperatives of the classical unities. Indeed, the action of each of the History plays in the First Tetralogy (*c.* 1591–94) covers several years, involves numerous sub-plots, and is located in various places in England and France. Of course, the restriction of the action to a single location in which one main story is enacted, in a timespan limited to a few hours, suits the farcical convention to which most of *The Comedy of Errors* subscribes.[42] But stylistic conformity with the classical unities is important also for the allusion inherent therein to the work of Aristotle, and it is in this respect that the meta-theatrical significance of *The Comedy of Errors* (to which I refer near the start of this essay) would have registered with the more astute (and classically educated) members of the late Elizabethan audience.[43]

---

41 Sir Edward Coke and Sir John Davies both described common law as a law "written only in the heart": the former in his report of *Postnati. Calvin's Case* in Part 7 of *The Reports* (1608), the latter in the Preface Dedicatory to *Le Primer Report des Cases* (1615); see Paul Raffield, "Common Law, *Cymbeline*, and the Jacobean *Aeneid*," *Law & Literature* 27.3 (2015): 313–342, 317.

42 See Richard Janko, *Aristotle on Comedy: Towards a Reconstruction of Poetics II* (London: Gerald Duckworth, 2002).

43 "[...] the plot being a representation of a piece of action must represent a single piece of action and the whole of it; and the component incidents must be so arranged that if one of them be transposed or removed, the unity of the whole is dislocated and destroyed": Aristotle, *The Poetics*, trans. William Hamilton Fyfe (Cambridge, Mass.: Harvard University Press, 1946), 33–35, c. VIII. On the particular form of classical education in Elizabethan grammar schools, see Carol Chillington Rutter, "Shakespeare and School," in *Shakespeare Beyond Doubt: Evidence, Argument, Controversy*, eds. Paul Edmondson and Stanley Wells (Cambridge: Cambridge University Press, 2013), 133–144. On the study of rhetoric at schools and the universities, see Peter

The Aristotelian allusion in *The Comedy of Errors* is confined not only to the classical unities and *The Poetics*. It extends to *The Politics* and *The Nicomachean Ethics*. In *Shakespeare's Imaginary Constitution* I argued that the ideal system of justice on which Shakespeare reflected in *Henry IV, Part 2* was Aristotelian, in the sense that the integration of the legal institution into the society it sought to regulate was contingent upon the recognition that community, association, or friendship was a crucial factor in creating and maintaining the polis.[44] In Book I of *The Politics*, Aristotle used the microcosm of the village community to demonstrate the interdependency of the various constituent members of the State. They were "homogalactic": literally, they suckled from the same source of milk, the communal cow.[45] Of equal relevance to *Henry IV, Part 2* and *The Comedy of Errors* is the political importance that Aristotle attached to friendship in Books VIII and IX of *The Nicomachean Ethics*. For Aristotle, friendship was the bond of communities and was also, he claimed, more important to lawgivers even than justice, simply because the primary objective of lawgivers was the attainment of concord and the elimination of faction, and concord was synonymous with friendship.[46]

The major theme of Aristotelian friendship in *The Comedy of Errors* is transcribed in the shared name of one set of twins: Antipholus. The name translates from the original Greek as "against friend" ("anti philos" or "αντι φιλοσ"). Antipholus of Syracuse is the lost brother, in search of friendship. He is the archetypal alien, thrust into an Ephesian society that is hostile towards Syracusians and whose citizens are divided by the commercial imperatives of monetary profit. The image of the stateless citizen in search of his identity not only as a sentient being

Mack, *Elizabethan Rhetoric: Theory and Practice* (Cambridge: Cambridge University Press, 2002), 76; also, Peter Mack, *A History of Renaissance Rhetoric 1380–1620* (Oxford: Oxford University Press, 2011).

44 Raffield, *Shakespeare's Imaginary Constitution*, 171.

45 Aristotle, *The Politics*, trans. T.A. Sinclair (London: Penguin, 1992), 58–59, 61, Bk. I.II.1252b15–27, 1253a29–b1. On the importance of cattle to communal existence in ancient Greece, see Jeremy McInerney, *The Cattle of the Sun: Cows and Culture in the World of the Ancient Greeks* (New Jersey: Princeton University Press, 2010). Regarding the commonwealth described in Sir Thomas Smith's *De Republica Anglorum*, Burrow argues that Smith (despite his claims to the contrary) presents "a single, Aristotelian model of what a commonwealth suited to the English temperament should be": Colin Burrow, "Reading Tudor Writing Politically: The Case of *2 Henry IV*," *The Yearbook of English Studies* 38.1/2 (2008): 234–250, 240.

46 Aristotle, *The Nicomachean Ethics*, trans. J.A.K. Thomson (London: Penguin, 2004), 200–201, Bk. VIII.I.1155a1–32. On the bonds of friendship, which form the basis of the Aristotelian *polis*, see Alasdair Macintyre, *After Virtue: a Study in Moral Theory* (London: Duckworth, 1981), 146.

but also as a person linked to his fellow man by their common humanity is conjured in Antipholus's description of himself soon after his first entrance, an image derived both from the shipwreck in which he almost drowned as a child and his more recent encounter with the Mediterranean Sea, in search of his lost twin:

> I to the world am like a drop of water
> That in the ocean seeks another drop,
> Who falling there to find his fellow forth,
> (Unseen, inquisitive) confounds himself. (1.2.35–38)[47]

His irascible (and occasionally deranged) twin, Antipholus of Ephesus, is for most of the play the personification of discord; he is literally *anti philos* or "against friend." All of his relations, whether with his wife, his servant Dromio, or the various merchants, moneylenders, and craftsmen with whom he deals, are characterised either by disharmony or violence (I refer above to the "rope's end," which he threatens to "bestow / Among my wife and her confederates / For locking me out of my doors by day" (4.1.16–18)).[48] Caught up in the maelstrom of farcical action, revolving around mistaken identity but driven by the relentless obsession of Ephesian citizens (and the Ephesian legal institution) with mercantilism, he finds some kind of spiritual, emotional, and social repose only at the end of the play, when he is reunited with his twin brother and they leave the stage, for the last time, together.[49] Their overjoyed mother Emilia speaks for the audience as well as herself when she announces: "After so long grief, such felicity" (5.1.406).

---

47 The image recurs when Adriana speaks of her love for her husband: "For know, my love, as easy mayst thou fall / A drop of water in the breaking gulf, / And take unmingled thence that drop again / Without addition or diminishing, / As take from me thyself, and not me too." (2.2.125–29) See *The Comedy of Errors*, ed. Foakes, 14, note to 1.2.35–38.

48 Kinney notes the "customary definitions and discussions" of the play, which comment on "the aggressive, hostile, and violent movement and sensing a basic theme the destruction of the family and of family values": Arthur F. Kinney, "Shakespeare's *Comedy of Errors* and the Nature of Kind," *Studies in Philology* 85.1 (1988): 29–52, 30; for an exemplar of this "customary" definition, see Bentley's *Life of the Drama*, in which the author argues that "Farce is perhaps even more notorious [than melodrama] for its love of violent images": Eric Bentley, *The Life of the Drama* (London: Methuen, 1965), 219.

49 Shakespeare was himself the father of twins: Hamnet and Judith (b. 1585); Hamnet died aged eleven in 1596. On the depiction and interpretation of twinship in early modern literature, see Daisy Murray, *Twins in Early Modern English Drama and Shakespeare* (Abingdon: Routledge, 2017).

As noted above, the golden chain or carcanet, purchased by Antipholus of Ephesus as a gift for his wife Adriana, has obvious Platonic connotations of public law and the legal order;[50] but the dispute over its purchase also performs the metaphorical function of signifying a society bound together only by the commercial pressures of the market, having broken the true bonds of friendship through which a political community may be recognised.[51] The emphasis on social harmony engendered by the bonds of friendship extends to the last lines of the play, when the Ephesian Dromio announces to his twin brother: "We came into the world like brother and brother, / And now let's go hand in hand, not one before the other" (5.1.425–26). The bonds of friendship (upon which the foundations of the Aristotelian polis were built) is the final, healing image of the play.

The first recorded performance of *The Comedy of Errors* was at Gray's Inn on 28 December 1594, described in the anonymous account of the revels *Gesta Grayorum* as *The Night of Errors*;[52] when revels turned to riot and the honoured guests of Gray's Inn – the Ambassador of the Inner Temple and his retinue – left in a huff.[53] Scholarship regarding the Gray's Inn revels of 1594 tends to concentrate exclusively on the riotous events of that fateful night;[54] but this is to overlook the thematic similarity between *The Comedy of Errors* and the Gray's Inn revels themselves. The overarching theme of the Candlemas revels of 1594 was friendship and the warm reception of foreigners by a host nation-state (a matter of striking contemporaneous relevance, given the race riots of the early 1590s discussed above). The hosts of the revels, Gray's Inn, had invited their "ancient Friend the State of *Templaria*" (the Inner Temple) to attend Gray's Inn (whose

---

50 See text to n. 16, above.

51 See Raffield, *Shakespeare's Imaginary Constitution*, 53; see also Ian Ward, *Shakespeare and the Legal Imagination* (London: Butterworths, 1999), 137.

52 Anonymous, *Gesta Grayorum or The History of The High and Mighty Prince Henry Prince of Purpoole Anno Domini 1594*, ed. Desmond Bland (Liverpool: Liverpool University Press, 1968), 32. *Gesta Grayorum* was first published in 1688 by William Canning.

53 *Gesta Grayorum*, ed. Bland, 31; after the departure of the Ambassador, "a Comedy of Errors (like to *Plautus* his *Menechmus*) was played by the Players," 32.

54 On *The Night of Errors*, see Raffield, *Shakespeare's Imaginary Constitution*, 51–52; also Paul Raffield, *Images and Cultures of Law in Early Modern England: Justice and Political Power, 1558–1660* (Cambridge: Cambridge University Press, 2004), 111–123; Bradin Cormack, "Locating *The Comedy of Errors:* Revels Jurisdiction at the Inns of Court," in *The Intellectual and Cultural World of the Early Modern Inns of Court*, eds. Jayne Elizabeth Archer, Elizabeth Goldring and Sarah Knight (Manchester: Manchester University Press, 2011), 264–285; William N. West, "'But this will be a mere confusion': Real and Represented Confusions on the Elizabethan Stage," *Theatre Journal* 60.2 (2008): 217–233.

ruler for the duration of the revels was "Henry, *Prince of* Purpoole, *Arch-Duke of* Stapulia *and* Bernardia, *Duke of* High *and* Nether Holborn, *Marquis of St* Giles's *and* Tottenham," among other noble titles) on the evening of Holy Innocents' Day (28 December).[55] The words "friendship" and "amity" recur throughout the account of the night's festivities. Following the indignity suffered by the Ambassador of the state of Templaria on *The Night of Errors* (the cause of which, according to the anonymous *Gesta Grayorum*, was "a great Witchcraft": echoing the malign presence of witchcraft and sorcery in the Ephesus of *The Comedy of Errors*),[56] the host "nation" (Gray's Inn) expressed its profound regret that "our dearest Friend, the State of *Templaria*" was "disappointed of their kind Entertainment."[57] A few days later, friendship was restored and reaffirmed. On the evening of Friday 3 January 1595 "an Altar to the Goddesss of Amity" was erected in Hall. Worshipping at the altar were members of the two Inns, dressed as archetypal "friends" from classical literature. These included Theseus and Perithous, Achilles and Patroclus, Pilades and Orestes, and Scipio and Lelius: "Lastly, were presented *Graius* and *Templarius*; and they two came lovingly, Arm in Arm, to the Altar, and offered their Incense as the rest." After this touching display of mutual love and affection, the High Priest or "Arch-Flamen" to the Goddess of Amity "did pronounce *Grayus* and *Templarius* to be as true and perfect Friends, and so familiarly united and linked with the Bond and League of sincere Friendship and Amity, as ever were *Theseus* and *Perithous*" and the other archetypes of male friendship who paid homage to the Goddess of Amity.[58]

---

55 *Gesta Grayorum*, ed. Bland, 23, 29.

56 *The Acts of the Apostles* describes Ephesus, as visited by St. Paul, as a place of "exorcists" and "evil spirits" (19.13), in which people "used curious arts" (19.19). The Biblical association of Ephesus with witchcraft is emphasised by Antipholus of Syracuse:

They say this town is full of cozenage,
As nimble jugglers that deceive the eye,
Dark-working sorcerers that change the mind,
Soul-killing witches that deform the body [...] (1.2.97–100)

See Richmond Noble, *Shakespeare's Biblical Knowledge and Use of The Book of Common Prayer, as exemplified in the Plays of the First Folio* (New York: The Macmillan Company, 1935), 106–107.

57 *Gesta Grayorum*, ed. Bland, 32.

58 *Gesta Grayorum*, ed. Bland, 35–36. On the symbolism of these rites, and the early modern legal profession as "a fraternity predicated upon the image of masculine friendship," see Paul Raffield, *The Art of Law in Shakespeare* (Oxford: Hart Bloomsbury, 2017), 57–58. The word "homosociality" is used by Mikkel Borch-Jacobsen to describe the nature of relationships in a professional or working environment. He uses the term "'political' zone" to describe this location, an area occupied (he posits) predominantly by men: Mikkel Borch-Jacobsen, *The Freudian Subject*, trans. Catherine Porter (Stanford: Stanford University Press, 1988), 76, 78. On the cult of masculinity at the early modern Inns of Court, see Lynne Magnusson, "Scoff Power in

In the plethora of classical references and allusions at the Gray's Inn revels of 1594, it should not be forgotten that *The Comedy of Errors* unites a Plautine plot with a profoundly Christian theme: that of birth and rebirth. Christianity emerges from paganism, just as comedy emerges from Plautine farce. The choice of play for performance on the evening of Holy Innocents' Day was not accidental: The Feast of Holy Innocents commemorated the slaughter of young, male children in Bethlehem, ordered by King Herod and recorded in *The Gospel According to St. Matthew* (2.16). In 1604, ten years after the performance of *The Comedy of Errors* at Gray's Inn, the play was again performed on Holy Innocents' Day, at the court of King James I.[59] Like Christ, both the Antipholus and Dromio twins – "the calendars of their nativity" (5.1.404) – were born in an inn (1.1.53); Antipholus of Syracuse declares himself to be "a Christian" (1.2.77); Dromio of Syracuse calls for his rosary – "O for my beads" – and crosses himself "for a sinner." (2.2.188); Act Four opens with a reference to Pentecost (4.1.1); the schoolmaster Doctor Pinch performs a Christian exorcism on the distraught Antipholus of Ephesus (4.4.52–55); and the play ends with an invitation to a feast, in celebration of reunion and rebirth: "Go to a gossips' feast, and joy with me" (5.1.405). The Epidamnum of Plautus's *Menaechmi* has been transformed into the Christian, specifically Pauline, setting of its mise-en-scène, Ephesus.[60]

In the classical world, Ephesus had been one of the twelve cities of the Ionian League, before coming under control of the Roman Republic in 129 B.C. It became the capital of pro-consular Asia in twenty-seven B.C. during the reign of the Roman emperor Augustus. Ephesus was also a cultural hub during the classical era: it contained the Library of Celsus, the Temple of Artemis (Diana), and a theatre.[61] In the post-classical period, Ephesus was the site of several Christian

Love's Labour's Lost and the Inns of Court: Language in Context," *Shakespeare Survey* 57 (2004): 196–208.

59 See Kinney, "Shakespeare's *Comedy of Errors*," 31–32.

60 Kinney, "Shakespeare's *Comedy of Errors*," 38. Epidamnum had a strong Middle Eastern, Islamic character, and was notable (among other things) for the number of its mosques. Captured by the Ottomans in 1501, it is now the chief seaport of Albania, known as Durrës (Durazzo).

61 See Guy Maclean Rogers, *The Mysteries of Artemis of Ephesos: Cult, Polis, and Change in the Graeco-Roman World* (New Haven: Yale University Press, 2012). Relevant to the theme of commerce in *The Comedy of Errors* is that St. Paul was briefly imprisoned in Ephesus, having clashed there with artisans selling statuettes of Artemis. For a collection of essays on the life, writings, and theology of St. Paul, see James D.G. Dunn ed., *The Cambridge Companion to St Paul* (Cambridge: Cambridge University Press, 2003); for specific discussion of *The Epistle of Paul the Apostle to the Ephesians*, see Andrew T. Lincoln, "Ephesians," in *Cambridge Companion to St Paul*, ed. Dunn, 133–140.

Councils in the Fifth Century A.D.[62] Of course, Ephesus was also the setting for *The Epistle of Paul the Apostle to the Ephesians* (St. Paul lived there from 52 to 54 A.D.), and one of the seven churches of Asia to which *The Revelation of St. John the Divine* was addressed.[63]

In her guise as the Abbess, before being reunited with her husband Egeon, Emilia embodies the Pauline injunction to perform charitable acts. "It is a branch and parcel of mine oath, / A charitable duty of my order," (5.1.106–107) she informs Adriana regarding her intention to make Antipholus of Ephesus "a formal man again." (5.1.105) It is a duty that she would be obliged to discharge for anyone in need, Ephesian subject and foreigner alike. Her charity did not, would not, and was not permitted to distinguish between races. She was herself an immigrant, like her husband, her two sons, and their two servants. If the play does contain a didactic message then it is that citizens and states are morally obliged (whether by the political philosophy of the classical world or the Pauline injunction to perform charitable acts, founded in the tenets of Judaeo-Christian theology) to extend the bonds of friendship not only to each other, but to all those who seek refuge and asylum because they have nowhere else to turn. In the words of St. Paul, from *The Epistle of Paul the Apostle to the Ephesians:* "And be ye kind one to another, tenderhearted, forgiving one another, even as God for Christ's sake hath forgiven you." (*Ephesians* 4.32)

---

62 Ephesus was the most important city of the Byzantine Empire, after Constantinople, before its conquest by the Ottomans in 1304. See Clive Foss, *Ephesus after Antiquity: A late antique, Byzantine and Turkish City* (Cambridge: Cambridge University Press, 1979); on political and commercial relations between early modern England and the Muslim world, see Jerry Brotton, *This Orient Isle: Elizabethan England and the Islamic World* (London: Allen Lane, 2016).

63 "I am Alpha and Omega, the first and the last: and, What thou seest, write in a book, and send *it* unto the seven churches which are in Asia; unto Ephesus, and unto Smyrna, and unto Pergamos, and unto Thyatira, and unto Sardis, and unto Philadelphia, and unto Laodicea." (*The Revelation of St. John the Divine* 1.11) All quotations are from the Authorized King James Version of *The Bible.*

Part Three **Legal Theory**

Jeanne Gaakeer

Fuss about a Footnote, or the Struggle for (the) Law in German Legal Theory

Overture: remembrance of times past

When I first started my research in *Law and Literature*, the then dominant debate was on Shakespeare's *The Merchant of Venice* and so I included an overview of the often diametrically opposed interpretations of the play in my 1994 Ph.D. thesis. My reading of Heinrich Heine's essays on female characters in Shakespeare's plays[1] with its strong defense of Shylock – in his analysis of Jessica, Heine refers to a Drury Lane performance that he attended, on which occasion a lady in the audience became passionate about the injustice that she perceived done to Shylock[2] –, combined with Richard Weisberg's reference, albeit in a note, in *Poethics*[3] to Rudolf von Ihering's view that Portia uses a foul trick to bring Shylock down, brought me to the fierce and rather odd attack in German legal theory of Rudolf von Ihering by Josef Kohler on the interpretive position taken by Portia.

In Anglo-American as well as European *Law and Literature* in the 1990s,[4] however, this debate if at all mentioned was mainly relegated to the footnotes, or used to denote controversies between scholars, and no extensive analyses

---

1 Heinrich Heine, *Shakespeares Mädchen und Frauen* [1838]. Translated into English as either *Shakespeare's Girls and Women* or *Shakespeare's Maidens and Women.*

2 Heinrich Heine, *Shakespeare's Maidens and Women*, in *The Works of Heinrich Heine*, trans. from the German by Charles Godfrey Leland, vol. I (London: Heinemann, 1906), 377, (last access November 1, 2016). https://archive.org/stream/worksofheinrichh01heinuoft/worksofheinrichh01heinuoft_djvu.txt: "WHEN I saw this piece played in Drury Lane there stood behind me in the box a pale British beauty who, at the end of the fourth act, wept passionately, and many times cried out, 'The poor man is wronged!'." Cf. Julius Hirschfeld, "Portia's Judgment and German Jurisprudence," *The Law Quarterly Review* (1914): 167–174, 167.

3 Richard Weisberg, *Poethics and Other Strategies of Law and Literature* (New York: Columbia University Press, 1992), 207, note 41.

4 See Uwe Diederichsen, "Shakespeares 'Kaufmann von Venedig'. Jurisprudenz auf dem Forum der Bühne," in *Literatur und Recht, literarische Rechtsfälle von der Antike bis in die Gegenwart*, ed. Ulrich Mölk (Göttingen: Wallstein Verlag, 1996), 186–228, who mentions Ihering and Kohler but mainly devotes his article to contemporary *Law and Literature* on the subject. Theodore Ziolkowski, *The Mirror of Justice, literary reflections of legal crises* (Princeton: Princeton University Press, 1997), 173–174, finds a dispute comparable to that of Von Ihering and Kohler in Richard Weisberg's and Richard Posner's on the topic of Portia's interpretation of the bond.

https://doi.org/10.1515/9783110591514-009

were offered. Neither was O. Hood Phillips' earlier *Shakespeare and the Lawyers*[5] very helpful, because he paid no attention whatsoever to the underlying theories of law espoused by Von Ihering and his critics. In my own thesis, too, I left it at some short paragraphs and then forgot about it. Now with the celebration of *Shakespeare 400* I think it fitting to return to the topic, not least because the whole German debate rests upon the different readings of one single footnote in Von Ihering's *The Struggle for Law*, so that the question to me at least is: Why the fuss about the footnote? Shakespeare's use in *The Merchant of Venice*, consciously or not, of the controversial concept of the laceration of a debtor by his creditor in the Roman Law of the Twelve Tables, as the background for the infamous bond, triggered extensive commentaries that, I suggest, not only prompted discussion about the prolonged, pervasive influence of Roman law on German jurisprudence but also projected a dark light on German law and legal theory in the early twentieth century. There is, therefore, a hiatus to be remedied in this proto-*Law and Literature* debate. That is why I aim to make a fuss about a footnote, though differently than my predecessors.

1 The modern use of Roman Law

The reception of Roman law throughout continental Europe was a gradual process that started with the rediscovery of the *Corpus Iuris Civilis* in the eleventh century. Suffice it to say for purposes of this article that in due course Roman law became the *ius commune* that superseded local law in that it became the starting point also for the interpretation of customary law. Its claim for legitimacy was generally accepted and eventually Roman law permeated all (sub)fields of law in that its tripartite conceptual framework of *res*, *persona*, and *actio* formed the basis for subsequent developments.[6]

With the onset of the view of natural law based on human reason, the *recta ratio*, as developed by the legal theorists of the seventeenth- and early eighteenth century such as Hobbes, Grotius, and Pufendorf, things already began to change. The Enlightenment view on rational law in the second half of the eighteenth century further brought the idea of law as a system of codified rules and the concept of democracy under the rule of law. The status and influ-

5 Owen Hood Phillips, *Shakespeare and the Lawyers* (London: Methuen, 1972), 91–118.

6 Cf., Helmut Coing, *Die ursprüngliche Einheit der europäischen Rechtswissenschaft* (Wiesbaden: F. Steiner, 1968), 12. For a more detailed treatment of the development of Roman law in the European context, see Jeanne Gaakeer, "Reverent Rites of Legal Theory: unity-diversity-interdisciplinarity," *Australian Feminist Law Journal* 36 (2012): 19–43.

ence of Roman law faded into the background in most European countries that embraced the concept of the nation-state and its consequence, the codification of national positive law.

In Prussia, however, the theorists of the Historical School of jurisprudence, Friedrich Carl von Savigny (1779–1861) and Georg Friedrich Puchta (1798–1846), vehemently opposed the very idea of codification. Von Savigny specifically attacked Prussian General Legal Code of 1794, the project initiated by Frederick the Great. The priority of human reason to understand law as advocated by Enlightenment thinkers was rejected because it was ahistorical, the French Revolution was viewed as a dangerous thing as was the codification ideal of the later Napoleonic era. In 1815 Von Savigny warned the German peoples not to follow the example of the French codification in his *Vom Beruf unserer Zeit für Gesetzgebung und Rechtswissenschaft.*[7] Romantic in its cherishing of the ideal of tradition as a source of knowledge, the Historical School aimed to understand law historically, i.e. it sought for the meaning of legal concepts in the context of their origin. To Von Savigny, then, the true legislator is found in the spirit of the people, the *Volksgeist*, a term coined by Johann Gottfried Herder. This thesis that the root of law is to be found in the people builds on Herder's views on the organic relation between language and culture.[8] Von Savigny then argued that the development of Roman law could be traced throughout the centuries and had therefore developed from the consciousness of the people. Thus German law was the natural synthesis of Roman law. Ironically, Herder himself, who had briefly studied under Kant's tutelage but of whose Enlightenment stance he was also critical, fulminated against the lack of originality of German literature, the cause of which he took to be precisely the Romanist influence pervasive in German society.[9] It should also at once be noted that the Romanist strand of the Historical School that is usually taken to have started with Von Savigny's 1803 study *Das Recht des Besitzes*, had a counterpart in the Germanist strand of those, Jacob Grimm among them, who saw the *Volksgeist* exemplified in medieval Germanic law. And, paradoxically, given that Roman law was case-based,

7 Translated by Abraham Hayward as *Of the Vocation of our Age for Legislation and Jurisprudence* (New York: Argo, 1975).

8 For an analysis of Herder's thought, see Jeanne Gaakeer, "Close Encounters of the 'Third' Kind," in *Diaspora, Law and Literature*, eds. Daniela Carpi and Klaus Stierstorfer (Berlin and Boston: De Gruyter, 2016), 41–67.

9 Johann Gottfried Herder, *Fragmente über die neuere deutsche Literatur* (1766–1767), in Johann Gottfried Herder, *Werke, Band I Herder und Sturm und Drang 1764–1774, erste Sammlung, zweite völlig umgearbeite Ausgabe (1768)*, ed. Wolfgang Pross (Munich: Carl Hanser Verlag, 1984), 71–90.

Von Savigny and his followers of the Historical School used the Roman *Digests* or *Pandectae* to build a strict, closed system of legal concepts. They were more interested in the nature of law than in its societal effects or goals. Thus the *usus modernus pandectarum* or *Pandektenwissenschaft* while pretending to be the modern legal garb of the *Corpus Iuris Civilis*,[10] soon became a deductive, formalist jurisprudence of concepts, the *Begriffsjurisprudenz*, one that was devoid of any ethical or social notion.

It should, however, also at once be noted that Von Savigny's position within legal theory was and remains pivotal. Not only did Von Savigny reject natural law and was instrumental in getting it removed from German legal curricula,[11] his success in building a Roman-law based system was amazing to say the least. If we consider the decline of Roman law in the rest of Europe and the fact that the Holy Roman Empire had collapsed in 1806, Von Savigny's 1815 *Geschichte des römischen Rechts im Mittelalter* (Part I) was provocative in a situation in which what we now call Germany was a patchwork of smaller entities with as a result a patchwork of civil law(s).[12] After all, it was not until 1871 that the nation came into being. This makes Von Savigny's plan to develop one all-encompassing legal *theory* for the whole of Germany remarkable and explains his aversion to, for example, the plan of Anton Friedrich Justus Thibaut (1772–1840) to construct a *general* German civil law *code* against which he also wrote his *Vom Beruf unserer Zeit für Gesetzgebung und Rechtswissenschaft*. Another reason perhaps for the combination by Von Savigny of a historical method and the legal precision of a highly conceptual level of systematization that culminated in *Begriffsjurisprudenz* can be found in the fact that Von Savigny had no experience whatsoever of legal practice, and no working knowledge of law in action. He did not incorporate any legal decisions in his theory. His was the scientific study of law, the law of university professors in their ivory towers. Its predominant influence resting on the authority of the system and ordering of concepts, however, was so impressive that as late as 1920 the National-Socialist Party in article 19 of their party manifesto demanded the substitution by truly German law of Roman law because that had too long served the materialistic

10 Cf. Klaus Riebschläger, *Die Freirechtsbewegung* (Berlin: Duncker und Humblot, 1968): chapter 1.
11 Paul Koschaker, *Europa und das römische Recht* [1947] (Munich: G.H. Beck Verlag, 4th ed. 1966), ch. XV.
12 Uwe Wiesel, *Geschichte des Rechts in Europa. Von den Griechen bis zum Vertrag von Lissabon* (Munich: G.H. Beck Verlag, 2010), 509.

world order only. They had failed to notice that Roman law had by then been obsolete in most parts of Germany for quite a few decades.[13]

The Historical School met with fierce criticism, from the inside as well as the outside. To start with the latter, it was the philosopher Georg Wilhelm Friedrich Hegel who led the attack. Hegel had great admiration for the idea of national codification projects. In contrast to the Romanists, he also admired Napoleon whom he had seen riding past after the decisive Battle of Jena in 1806 when Napoleon defeated the Prussian army. To Hegel, the emperor was "the world-spirit on horseback." Hegel rejected the idea of looking at laws only in their historical context when it comes to understanding their meaning and significance, because to him Roman laws "are positive in so far as their significance and appropriateness are *circumstantial* and their value is therefore entirely historical; they are accordingly of a transient nature."[14] In short, it will not do, as Von Savigny and his followers such as Gustav Ritter Von Hugo (1764–1844)[15] suggested, that historical meaning can be transposed to contemporary circumstances. To Hegel, sticking to such historical meaning is a matter of "supplying a good reason for a bad thing."

Enter Shakespeare, Enter Shylock. I humbly submit that the example Hegel then gives of such a bad thing may have been precisely the trigger for the later criticism by Joseph Kohler of Rudolf von Ihering's view on *The Merchant of Venice* laid down in that famous footnote that I turn to below, namely that of the debate between the Roman jurists Caecilius and Favorinus on the Twelve Tables' *Tabula III*, i.e. that "abominable law which, after a specified interval had elapsed, gave the creditor the right to kill the debtor or to sell him into slavery, or even, if there were several creditors, *to cut pieces off him and so divide him between them that, if anyone had cut off too much or too little, he should incur no consequent legal disadvantage* (a clause which would have benefited Shakespeare's Shylock in *The Merchant of Venice* and which he would most gratefully have accepted)."[16]

---

13 Koschaker, *Europa*, 246–248 and 299.

14 G.W.F. Hegel, *Elements of the Philosophy of Right*, ed. Allen W. Wood and trans. H.B. Nisbet (Cambridge: Cambridge University Press, 2003), paragraph 3 of the Introduction, 31 [italics in the original]. I also used G.W.F. Hegel, *Grundlinien der Philosophie des Rechts* [1820] (Hamburg: Felix Meiner, 1967), and the Dutch translation by Willem Visser, G.W.F. Hegel, *Hoofdlijnen van de Rechtsfilosofie* (Amsterdam: Boom, 2014) for purposes of comparison, not least because of the English edition's somewhat unusual title *Philosophy of Right*, rather than *of Law*.

15 Hugo wrote a textbook entitled *Lehrbuch de Geschichte des Römischen Rechts* (1790), that enjoyed many editions.

16 Hegel, *Philosophy of Right*, 32 [italics in the original].

The other great theorist of the jurisprudence of concepts, Rudolf von Ihering (1818 – 1892) eventually recognised its dangers. Initially he adhered to the Romanist strand of the Historical School and elaborated upon the *ratio scripta* of Roman Law and the Historical School's principles in the first three volumes of his *Der Geist des Römischen Rechts auf den verschiedenen Stufen seiner Entwicklung* (i. e. *The Spirit of Roman Law in the various stages of its development*, Part I 1852–Part III 1865), with the concept of the legal transaction as one of its most prominent features: it is the intent, the will of the legal actor to reach a desired result that is leading and that the law should then help carry out. Von Ihering endorsed the ideal of the jurisprudence of concepts, i. e. of refinement of concepts to such a degree of conceptual clarity that at the end of the day each and every legal decision could unquestionably and unambiguously be deduced from the system itself.

The turning point for Von Ihering came with the sequel to the third volume of *Der Geist des Römischen Rechts* in 1865 when he wrote: "Life does not exist in the service of concepts, but concepts are there to serve life. Not what logic demands but what life, social relations, the feeling what law ought to be postulate, be that logically deducible or not."[17] From then on Von Ihering began to develop a more sociological jurisprudence, more specifically in his 3-volume *Der Zweck im Recht* (i. e. literally *The Purpose of the Law*, 1877 – 1884, although it should be noted that the English translation of 1913 was *Law as a Means to an End*).[18] The starting point for this legal theory was found in the interests of individual persons in society, the so-called *Interessenjurisprudenz* that is comparable to the Benthamite sociological idea of law as a means to an end and is echoed in Oliver Wendell Holmes jr.'s "The life of the law has not been logic: it has been experience."[19] What is more,

17 As cited in Riebschläger, *Freirechtsbewegung*, 29, my translation of "Das Leben ist nicht die Begriffe, sondern die Begriffe sind des Lebens wegen da. Nicht was die Logik, sonders was das Leben, das Verkehr, das Rechtsgefühl postulieren, hat zu geschehen, mag es logisch deduzierbar sein oder nicht."

18 Rudolf von Ihering, *Law as a Means to an End* (Boston: Boston Book Company, 1913), trans. Isaac Husik.

19 Oliver Wendell Holmes jr., *The Common Law* [1881] (Cambridge (Mass.): Belknap Press, 2009), 3. Cf. G. Edward White, *Justice Oliver Wendell Holmes, Law and the Inner Self* (New York and Oxford: Oxford University Press, 1993), 130 note 8, that Holmes took an interest in German scholarship on legal history, read Von Savigny's *Das Recht des Besitzes* and Puchta's *Cursus der Institutionen* but disagreed with the Romanist notion of the importance of intent of the legal actor when it comes to matters of interpretation; cf. also Sheldon M. Novick, *The Honorable Justice, The Life of Oliver Wendell Holmes* (Boston: Little, Brown and Co., 1989), 134 note 32 for the remark that Holmes understood German school of idealist jurisprudence as saying that law is

Von Ihering's criticism also culminated in his satire on the heaven of legal concepts in which he exposes concepts as fictions, i.e. constructs, useful though they may be, that exist only because of the order that law imposes. This heaven's inhabitants, the first being Puchta, but soon followed by Von Savigny who "based a legal institute purely on the sources or the ideas therein without resorting to any real practical meaning,"[20] are taken to task for discussing jurisprudential problems without ever asking after their practical significance, one example being Von Savigny's analysis in *Das Recht des Besitzes* of the problem whether possession is a question of law or of fact.[21]

In short, Von Ihering's scholarly development may be viewed as a mirror of nineteenth-century German legal theory, from a jurisprudence of concepts to sociological views on law and, eventually, to the Free Law Movement. The latter, on the one hand, shared the jurisprudence of interests' rejection of the technicality of the purely conceptual thought, but, on the other hand, took its leave from the sociological starting point to view law as a whole with its concomitant idea that the judge should take into consideration the principles of justice as well as law including the lawgiver's intention in the sense of the purpose of a specific piece of legislation, in favour of a discretionary, i.e. free form of judicial interpretation. That is exactly what the German debate on Portia's interpretive position turns on.[22]

2 Equitable justice

To reach one's *Zweck* in law, one must be prepared to start one's *Kampf ums Recht*, one's struggle to attain one's ends, as Von Ihering explains in his book on the subject. *Der Kampf ums Recht* is Von Ihering's elaboration of a speech delivered before a Vienna audience of jurists-practitioners. Such was its success that within two months after its publication in 1872 a second edition was necessary, a year later a third and 1874 did not only see the fourth edition but also translations in Hungarian, Russian and Dutch. The fifth edition of 1877 was

---

the expression of the *Volksgeist*, a view Holmes attacked in *The Common Law*, but that it is uncertain whether Holmes had read Von Savigny when he started developing *The Common Law*.

20 Rudolf von Ihering, *In the heaven for legal concepts: a fantasy* [1884], tr. Charlotte L. Levy, foreword by John M. Lindsey, *Temple Law Quarterly* 58 (1985): 799–842, 804. I also used Rudolf von Ihering, *Scherz und Ernst in der Jurisprudenz* (Darmstad: Wissenschaftliche Buchgesellschaft, 1992).

21 Von Ihering, *Heaven*, 820.

22 Riebschlager, *Freirechtsbewegung*, 17 and 48.

translated into English. For this outstanding contribution to legal theory Ihering was also given a decoration, the Cross of the St. Annen Order, by the Russian emperor.[23]

As Von Ihering explains, his aim was not to further the scientific study of law but "the cultivation of the state of mind from which the law must ultimately derive its strength, viz.: the courageous and constant exercise of the feeling of right," an unfortunate translation of the original German term "Rechtsgefühl" which refers to the idea of law and justice rather than to an individual, subjective right.[24] This can be inferred from Von Ihering's definition of the struggle for law as "Der Kampf ums Recht ist eine Pflicht des Berechtigten gegen sich selbst" which is rather roughly translated as "The struggle for his right is a duty of the person whose rights have been violated, to himself,"[25] because what Von Ihering means to emphasize, next to any practical result in law because law and rights can only be said to exist when they are "realized" in the world,[26] is the ethical thrust: it is our existential duty to seek law and justice.[27] The English translation is therefore a bit ambiguous, no doubt given the civil-law setting of the production of Von Ihering's text as compared to the American translator's common-law setting.[28]

---

23 For purposes of citation I use the 4th edition in German and the 5th edition in English: Rudolf von Ihering, *Der Kampf ums Recht*, 4th edition, in *Rudolf von Jhering Ausgewählte Schriften*, ed. Christian Rusche (Nürnberg: Glock und Lutz Verlag, 1965); Rudolph von Ihering, *The Struggle for Law*, trans. from the 5th edition in German by John J. Lalor (Chicago: Callaghan and Co., 1879); for materials with respect to the speech version, I also consulted Rudolf von Ihering, *Der Kampf um's Recht*, 18th edition 1913, ed. Felix Ermacora (Berlin: Propyläen Verlag, 1992). The work is also translated as *The Battle for Right*, trans. Philip Arthur Ashworth (London: Stevens and Son, 1883). Cf. *Kampf um's Recht*, the introduction by Ermacora at 27–28, for the reference to the decoration.

24 Von Ihering, *Struggle for Law*, vii, *Kampf ums Recht*, 195 "weniger darauf gericht, die wissenschaftliche Erkenntnis des Rechts [...] zu fördern [...] [als] diejenige Gesinnung[...]: die der mutigen und standhaften Behauptung des Rechtsgefühls."

25 Von Ihering, *Kampf ums Recht*, 213, Von Ihering, *Struggle for Law*, 29.

26 Von Ihering, *Struggle for Law*, 12, *Kampf ums Recht*, 204, "The idea of law is an eternal Becoming"; cf. Benjamin Cardozo's "Law never is, but is always about to be" (*The Nature of the Judicial Process*, New Haven: Yale university Press, 1921), 126.

27 Von Ihering, *Struggle for Law*, 129–130, "It is [...] ethics which has to tell us what is in harmony with, and what contradicts, the idea of law." *Kampf ums Recht*, 272, "Die Ethik hat uns Aufschluss darüber zu geben, was dem Wesen des Rechts entspricht oder widerspricht."

28 Cf. *Kampf um's Recht*, the introduction by Ermacora, 46, which references the original speech that contains the wonderfully succinct remark on the duty not to be a coward when it comes to struggling for one's right: "Das Preisgeben eines verletzten Rechtes ist in meinen Augen ein Act der Feigheit, der, wenn er nicht durch die Einrichtungen des Staates zur Nothwendigkeit gemacht wird, der Person zur Unehre und dem Gemeinwesen zum höchsten Schaden gereicht. Der Kampf für das Recht ist ein Act der ethischen Selbsterhaltung, ist eine Pflicht gegen sich

So what matters, also in Shylock's case, is that one therefore always has to start the *legis actio* as it is called in Roman law, in order to invoke the law, "das Gesetz anrufen," for "The law itself is called in question; it is the law itself which is under discussion in a particular case [...] There is question not alone of a personal interest [...] but there is a question of the law itself which has been despised, trampled under foot, and which must be defended, if the law itself is not to become a mockery and a word without meaning. When the legal right of the individual is sacrificed, the law is sacrificed likewise."[29] This can also be seen in Shylock's remark "I stand for judgment" (IV.1.103),[30] immediately after he has said "The pound of flesh which I demand of him Is dearly bought. 'Tis mine, and I will have it. If you deny me, fie upon your law: there is no force in the decrees of Venice (IV.1.98–101)." It is this passage from the play that Von Ihering first cites, without clear references, however, so that we cannot be absolutely sure whether after this he refers to the "I stand for judgment" or to "I stand here for law" (IV.1.141) or the line "I crave the law" (IV.1.201) that follows Portia's "quality of mercy" speech, which is what the English translator chooses.

Not that it matters much since all citations qualify when it comes to the use Von Ihering makes of Shylock's standpoint, namely that

> It is hatred and revenge that take Shylock before the court to cut his pound of flesh out of Antonio's body; but the words which the poet puts into his mouth are as true in it as in any other. It is the language which the wounded feeling of legal right will speak, at all times and in all places; the power, the firmness of the conviction, that law must remain law, the lofty feeling and pathos of a man who is conscious that, in what he claims, there is question not only of his person but of the law. [...] 'I crave the law'. In these four words, the poet has described the relation of law in the subjective to law in the objective sense of the term and the meaning of the struggle for law, in a manner better than any philosopher of the law could have done it. These four words change Shylock's claim into a question

---

und gegen die Gemeinschaft," my translation "To relinquish a violated right is in my opinion an act of cowardice, that when not made necessary by the organizations of the state, brings disgrace to the individual and harm to the community." In the book versions, see the comparable but rhetorically weaker passages Von Ihering, *Struggle for Law*, 127, *Kampf ums Recht*, 217–271.

29 Von Ihering, *Struggle for Law*, 78–79; *Kampf ums Recht*, 242 "das Gesetz anzurufen [...] Das Gesetz selber ist in Frage gestellt, es is ein Streit ums Gesetz, der in dem einzelnen Fall entscheiden werden muss [...] es handelt sich bei dem Streit nicht bloss um das Interesse des Subjekts [...] sondern das Gesetz selber is missachtet, mit Füssen getreten; das Gesetz, wenn es nicht eitel Spiel und Phrase sein soll, muss sich behaupten – dem Recht des Verletzten, stürtzt das Gesetz selbst zusammen."

30 References are to William Shakespeare, *The Merchant of Venice*, in *The Norton Shakespeare*, eds. Stephen Greenblatt et al. (New York and London: W.W. Norton & Company, 1997).

> of the law of Venice [...] it is the law of Venice itself knocking at the door of Justice; for his rights and the law of Venice are one and the same; they both stand or fall together.[31]

As a result of Portia's interpretive strategy, not only Shylock but the law itself is broken. So when Shylock "finally succumbs under the weight of the judge's decision, who wipes out his right by a shocking piece of pleasantry,"[32] [...] "who can help feeling that in him the law of Venice is humbled; that it is not the Jew, Shylock, who moves painfully away, but the typical figure of the Jew in the middle ages, that pariah of society who cried in vain for justice?"[33] The tragedy, then, to Von Ihering, is not that Shylock's rights are denied in "the pathological moment" in which he seeks them,[34] but that his faith in the law as a firm rock is shaken by the judge who dispels the illusion that he has a right and teaches him that he is only "the despised medieval Jew to whom justice is done by defrauding him."[35] Onward now to the famous footnote attached to the passage "a shocking piece of pleasantry" which is a rather weak translation, I suggest, of Von Ihering's "schnöden Witz," "schnöde" being a far more negative connotation of disgraceful behaviour with the intent to cause harm. It re-

31 Von Ihering, *Struggle for Law*, 80–81. It should be noted that language is one of Von Ihering's metaphors for law, undoubtedly an influence of the Historical School. Cf. *Kampf um's Recht*, the introduction by Ermacora, 18, referencing the speaker who thanked Von Ihering after his speech, and specifically noted the Herderian idea that law, like the language of a people develops organically throughout the ages, "wie die Sprache eines Volkes, ein auch sich organisch werdendes, ein organisch gewordenes Product der Geschichte sei," my translation "like the language of a people, an organically developing, and organically created product of history." Cf. *Kampf ums Recht*, 243, for the same passage in German.

32 Von Ihering, *Struggle for Law*, 81; *Kampf ums Recht*, 243, "Und wenn er selber dann zusammenbricht unter der Wucht des Richterspruches, der durch schnöden Witz sein Recht vereitelt."

33 Von Ihering, *Struggle for Law*, 82.

34 Cf. *Kampf um's Recht*, the speech version in the introduction by Ermacora, 41, "pathologischen Momentes."

35 Von Ihering, *Struggle for Law*, 82–83, "His fate is eminently tragic, not because his rights are denied him, but because he, a Jew of the middle ages, has faith in the law – we might say as if he were a Christian – a faith in the law firm as a rock which nothing can shake, and which the judge himself feeds until the catastrophe breaks upon him like a thunder clap, dispels the illusion and teaches him that he is only the despised medieval Jew to whom justice is done by defrauding him"; *Kampf ums Recht*, 244, "Die gewaltige Tragik seines Schicksals beruht nicht darauf, dass ihm das Recht versagt wird, sondern darauf, dass er, ein Jude des Mittelalters, den Glauben an das Recht hat – man möchte sagen, gleich als wäre er ein Christ -, einen felsenfesten Glauben an das Recht, den nichts beirren kann und den der Richter selber nährt; bis dann wie ein Donnerschlag die Katastrophe über ihn hereinbricht, die ihn aus seinem Wahn reisst und ihn belehrt, dass er nichts ist als der geächtete Jude des Mittelalters, dem man sein Recht gibt, indem man ihn darum betrügt."

turns as "ein elender Winkelzug, ein kläglicher Rabulistenkniff," *rabula* being the Latin for "wrangling advocate, pettifogger,"[36]

> The eminently tragic interest which we feel in Shylock, I find to have its basis precisely in the fact that justice is not done to him; for this is the conclusion to which the lawyer must come. The poet is, of course, free to build up his own system of jurisprudence, and we have no reason to regret that Shakespeare has done so here; or rather that he has changed the old fable in nothing. But when the jurist submits the question to a critical examination, he can only say that the bond was in itself null and void because its provisions were contrary to good morals. The judge should, therefore, have refused to enforce its terms on this ground from the first. But as he did not do so, as the "wise Daniel" admitted its validity, it was a wretched subterfuge, a miserable piece of pettifoggery, to deny the man whose right he had already admitted, to cut a pound of flesh from the living body, the right to the shedding of blood which necessarily accompanied it. Just as well might the judge deny to the person whose right to an easement he acknowledged, the right to leave footmarks on the land, because this was not expressly stipulated in the grant. One might almost believe that the tragedy of Shylock was enacted in the earliest days of Rome; for the author of the Twelve Tables held it necessary to remark expressly in relation to the laceration of the debtor (*in partes secare*) by the creditor, that the size of the piece should be left to his free choice. (*Si plus minusve secuerint, sine fraude esto!*).[37]

Von Ihering compares Shylock's broken resistance after Portia's decision to the figure of Michael Kohlhaas in Heinrich von Kleist's eponymous novel. Kohlhaas is given a comparable treatment but he stays firm in his insistence on, and devotion to the law. In the end he accepts the consequence of his position with dignity: after his rights are honored he accepts the death penalty for his own violent acts. What matters to me here is that Von Ihering qualifies this decision as "Judicial murder is the deadly sin of the law"[38] and this is, I suggest, also Von Ihering's verdict of Portia's act.

How, then, did it come about that Von Ihering was so severely criticized for his footnote?[39] From a point of law it is well-balanced, both as far as the outcome of the case as authored by Shakespeare is concerned, for Von Ihering respects Shakespeare's authorial liberty and from his approving remark that "we have no reason to regret that Shakespeare has done so here,"[40] i.e. that the outcome in the sense of the denial of the validity of the bond is as such correct, and from

36 Von Ihering, *Kampf ums Recht*, 244. Cf. Julius Hirschfeld, "Portia's Judgment," 167 n.1.

37 Von Ihering, *Struggle for Law*, 81 note 1; *Kampf ums Recht*, 244 note.*

38 Von Ihering, *Struggle for Law*, 86, *Kampf ums Recht*, 247, "Justizmord ist die wahre Todsünde des Rechts."

39 Already after *Kampf ums Recht* was published in the speech version, Von Ihering was criticized, see Cf. *Kampf um's Recht*, the introduction by Ermacora, 28.

40 Von Ihering, *Struggle for Law*, 81 note 1.

a point of view of interpretation, i.e. his remark that if one pays careful attention to the legal aspects, the verdict would have been that the bond was void, is in no way out of the order with his legal theory. Von Ihering's view that the bond was null and void to start with fits with his jurisprudence of interests that takes into consideration principles of law when ascertaining what the lawgiver intended with a specific piece of legislation as noted above in paragraph 2. That would include, I suggest, equity in its original Aristotelian meaning of equitable justice as found in the *Nicomachean Ethics*, not least because in *Das Zweck im Recht* Von Ihering thinks in terms of mercy as justice in the individual case.[41]

In other words, this resembles the Aristotelian argument that "all law is universal but about some things it is not possible to make a universal statement which shall be correct." Thus, the error that arises from the universality of the law, is an omission to be corrected by saying, "what the legislator himself would have said had he been present, and would have put into his law if he had known," hence Aristotle's conclusion that, "this is the nature of the equitable, a correction of law where it is defective owing to its universality."[42] The equitable is therefore just not because it is legally correct; it is just because it is a correction of the justice provided by the system of law itself. It is here that Portia fails as the judge who interprets the lawgiver's texts: she has the technical acuity to understand that according to Venetian law the bond must be honored if she sticks to the letter of the law, but her solution to save Antonio's life is lacking in the practical wisdom necessary to apply the equitable correction of the law that the bond's content is contrary to the principle of good morals under-

---

41 See also the twentieth-century editor of Von Ihering's *Der Zweck im Recht*, Arthur Kaufmann's view that to Von Ihering mercy was the "Selbstkorrektur der Gerechtigkeit" (as noted in *Der Zweck im Recht*, vol.1, 6th and 8th German edition, 1923, 331) in "Recht und Gnade in der Literatur," in Arthur Kaufmann, *Beiträge zur Juristischen Hermeneutik* (Köln: Carl Heymanns Verlag, 1984), 227–245, 228. But see the different view of Gustav Radbruch, *Rechtsphilosophie* [1950] eds Erik Wolf and Hans-Peter Schneider (Stuttgart: K.F. Köhler Verlag, 1973), Besonderer Teil, par. 24 "Die Gnade," 275, i.e. "Mercy," "Die Gnade erschöpft sich also nicht darin, nach Iherings Wort "Sicherheitsventil des Rechtes" zu sein. Sie ist ein Symbol, dass es in der Welt Werte gibt, die aus tieferen Quellen gespeist werden und zu höheren Höhen aufgipfeln, als das Recht." To Radbruch, mercy is not the safety valve but a symbol of a universal value that is superior to positive law. From a point of view of legal theory, however, Von Ihering's view and Radbruch's are not essentially different; they differ in degree rather than kind since both agree on the function of mercy to bring about justice, and both agree that mercy is part and parcel of law as an ordering system, since as "*Selbst*korrektur," it is self-correction of law. Cf. Gustav Radbruch, *Kleines Rechts-Brevier* [1941] (Göttingen: Vandenhoeck & Ruprecht, 1954), nr. 59, referencing the "quality of mercy"-speech.

42 Aristotle, *The Nicomachean Ethics*, trans. and introduction by David Ross, revised by J.L. Ackrill and J.O. Urmson (Oxford and New York: Oxford University Press, 1991), 132–133, V.10.

lying all law, that it is unconscionable. I find support for this view also in Von Ihering's remarks in the Preface to the 5th edition where he says that those who disagree with him have to answer the question, "What should a man do when his rights are trampled under foot?" and continues by saying that "The person who can give a tenable answer to the question, that is an answer compatible with the existence of law and order and with the dignity of personality has refuted me,"[43] the inclusion of the principle of human dignity and legal personhood being indicative of the inclusion of principles in the *quidditas* or "whatness" of law.[44] And then he concludes,

> One word more, on a point which has been contested even by those with whom I otherwise agree. I refer to my claim that injustice was done to Shylock. I have not contended that the judge should have recognized Shylock's bond to be valid; but that, once he had recognized its validity he should not, subsequently, have invalidated it by base cunning. The judge had the choice of deciding the bond valid or invalid. He should have declared the latter, but he declared it to be the former. Shakespeare represents the matter as if his decision was the only possible one; no one in Venice doubted the validity of the bond; Antonio's friends, Antonio himself, the court, all were agreed that the bond gave the Jew a legal right. And confiding in his right thus universally acknowledged, Shylock calls for the aid of the court, and the "wise Daniel," after he had vainly endeavored to induce the revenge-thirsty creditor to surrender his right, recognizes it. And now, after the judge's decision has been

43 Von Ihering, *Struggle for Law*, xiii.

44 Von Ihering's views were praised by German legal theorist Georg Jellinek in his 1879 speech "Die Idee des Rechts im Drama in ihrer historischen Entwicklung," in Georg Jellinek, *Ausgewählte Schriften und Reden*, Band I, part II, *Zur schönen Literatur*, essay nr. 9 (Berlin: O. Häring Verlag, 1911), 208–233. Jellinek is Kantian in his own approach: only the rational wills of human beings together can form the law, i.e. laws are the boundaries that human beings impose on themselves, so that law in the objective sense draws the boundaries of human action and law in the subjective sense of the rights of the individual is the legal freedom to act. It is in the tension between the two aspects of law that the struggle for law originates. Significantly, Jellinke uses the term "Kampf ums Recht" when he writes that in ancient Greek drama, Sophocles' *Antigone* being the prime example, the struggle is for the legitimacy and ultimate predominance of the legal norms of the case, whereas in modernity, the first writer announcing that era being Shakespeare (220), the struggle focuses on the legitimacy of the legal claim (subjective law) versus the order of the legal system (objective law). Viewed this way, one would have to denote Portia as belonging to the ancient order or *cosmos* because her solution is to bend the law in the direction of the kind of mercy she imposes by introducing another legal norm, the one that helps destroy Shylock. Jellinek does not specifically address this issue but he explicitly refers to Von Ihering when he writes, "Da wird durch einen rabulistischen Kunstgriff, wie ein bedeutender Jurist der Urteil der Porzia treffend nennt das starre Recht geknickt zugunsten der Forderung der Gnade" (225, note 1), my translation "The strict law is there bent in favour of mercy, through an artificial act of pettifoggery, as one important jurist aptly calls it." Jellinek sees Shakespeare as one of the first playwrights who no longer portray the legal order as absolute and indisputable, as one who clearly shows that law is the work of men.

> given, after all doubt as to the legal right of the Jew has been removed by the judge himself, and not a word can be said against it; after the whole assembly, the doge included, have accommodated themselves to the inevitable decree of the law – now that the victor, entirely sure of his case, intends to do what the judgment of the court authorized him to do, the same judge who had solemnly recognized his rights, renders those rights nugatory by an objection, a stratagem so contemptible, that it is worthy of no serious attention. Is there any flesh without blood? The judge who accorded Shylock the right to cut a pound of flesh out of Antonio's body accorded him, at the same time, the right to Antonio's blood, without which flesh cannot be. Both are refused to the Jew. He must take the flesh without the blood, and cut only an exact pound of flesh, no more and no less. Do I say too much when I assert that here the Jew is cheated out of his legal right? True it is done in the interest of humanity, but does chicanery cease to be chicanery because practiced in the name of humanity?[45]

The latter rhetorical question enraged critics even more and the neo-Hegelians were in the majority to lead the attack.

3 Chicanery in the name of humanity?

3.1 Prioritizing the state

One of them, the sitting judge August Pietscher as early as 1881 devoted a study to Von Ihering's view on Portia. While granting that law in its actual appeareance does not always reflect the underlying idea and ideal of law, the "Rechtsidee," Pietscher initially praises Von Ihering for having drawn the attention to the urge of the human soul to struggle to get his right in *Der Kampf um's Recht* that Pietscher calls "A study equally excellent in content and form."[46] However, Von Ihering's "appellate review" of the lower-court judge Shakespeare does not meet with Pietscher's approval.[47] Already foreboding Josef Kohler's attack on Von Ihering, Pietscher claims that while the essence of law is to have universally applicable rules and norms, there may come a moment when the development of societal relations and new demands of human commerce can no longer be subsumed under the existing rules, i.e. when there is an antithesis between law and

45 Von Ihering, *Struggle for Law*, xiv-xvi.

46 August Pietscher, *Jurist und Dichter, Versuch einer Studie über Jhering's 'Kampf um's Recht' und Shakespeare's 'Kaufmann von Venedig'* (Dessau: Emil Barth Verlag, 1881), 5, my translation of "Eine Schrift gleich vortrefflich nach Inhalt wie nach Form."

47 Pietscher, *Jurist und Dichter*, 6, "einer oberrichtlichen Revision, die ein für den Dichter nicht eben günstiges Ergebnis liefert," my translation "a review by a higher judge that does not lead to a favourable result for the poet."

life.[48] Unlike Von Ihering whose Historical-School view that law in the objective sense of the legal norm has developed through the ages in a way comparable to law in practice, i.e. in the discursive courtroom situation of the struggle for meaning with a debate on meaning in legal use and a constant tension between *de lege lata* (what the law is) and *de lege ferenda* (what the law should be), Pietscher favours the idea that if the laws of Venice were of such poor quality that they suffered the good merchant Antonio to be destroyed by Shylock, the judge is indeed allowed to use "a chicanery" to respond to such villainy.[49]

In all fairness it should at once be noted that Pietscher has a keen eye for both the Shakespearean text and the demands of trial practice. He draws the attention to the fact that so far legal theorists have not noticed some crucial aspects of Shylock's character. For example, he refers to Shylock's remark to Tubal to bespeak him an officer of the court in a fortnight at the end of scene 3.1, "I will have the heart of him if he forfeit, for were he out of Venice I can make what merchandise I will"(3.1.105–107) as the sure indication of Shylock's motive of commercial competition; he also questions the validity of Shylock's remark "An oath, an oath, I have an oath in heaven. Shall I lay perjury on my soul?" (4.1.223–224) because it has not been mentioned so far; and as a true legal practitioner he asks why Shylock did not take the precaution of adding a clause to the contract to justify the spilling of blood, for we all know, don't we that what is not laid down in legal documents does not exist, any lawyer could have told Shylock that.[50]

But "our jurist" Von Ihering, as Pietscher condescendingly calls him, only has the defense for his client Shylock that the bond was *contra bonas mores* to start with and that is an insufficient argument, a *turpis causa* in Portia's legal theory, one that is bound to make Shylock lose the case.[51] While Pietscher is willing to acknowledge that in interpreting the trial scene we must take for granted that the laws of Shakespeare's Venice did not contain the rule that there can be no unconscionable contract, he contends that even if any legal system would contain such a rule, and that could only be a highly sophisticated

48 Pietscher, *Jurist und Dichter*, 4, "Widerspruch zwischen Leben und Recht, der Streit des lebendigen Menschen mit der abgezogenen Regel," my translation "Discrepancy between life and law, the struggle of the living being with the abstract legal rule."

49 Pietscher, *Jurist und Dichter*, 22.

50 Pietscher, *Jurist und Dichter*, 19, "Und was nicht in dem Akten isst, isst nicht in der Welt," my translation "What is not in the legal documents, does not exist in the world."

51 Pietscher, *Jurist und Dichter*, 19.

legal system,[52] this does not guarantee its correct interpretation, for after all much of what we now consider immoral laws were once generally accepted, with the acceptance of slavery until recently in the U.S. as a good example. So Von Ihering's argument is a failure since poetic justice is the prerogative of the playwright and while Shakespeare's Portia may not have been able to give good reasons for her decision, she intuitively felt that Shylock should be hoist with his own petard by sticking to the literal words of the bond. In truly neo-Hegelian vein, Pietscher then contends "Here rises the injured majesty of the idea of law, able to mete out punishment, destructive against the one who viciously dares to use the law to bring about injustice. The injured individual disappears behind the [...] state of Venice."[53] That is why to Pietscher Portia's presumedly legal ruse, "Tarry, Jew. The law hath yet another hold on you" (4.1.241–242) is totally acceptable, because while the idea of law may well originate from the struggle for law as both Von Ihering and Shakespeare understand so admirably, nevertheless "Law must remain law,"[54] i.e. positive law prevails because in the Hegelian view it originates from the state and serves to guarantee its existence. Pietscher's view did not augur well for the reception of Von Ihering's view but worse was yet to come.

3.2 The judge's discretionary power: over Shylock's dead body?

Significantly, Josef Kohler opens his analysis of *The Merchant of Venice*, the first chapter of *Shakespeare vor dem Forum der Jurisprudenz* with the name "Ihering." And while in the Foreword to the first edition he claims that he had long wanted to take up the subject of Shakespeare's plays in relation to law, it is clear from the start that Von Ihering's footnote is the trigger to Kohler who calls Ihering's views as internally contradictory as they are forcefully argued.[55] Although Kohler

52 Pietscher, *Jurist und Dichter*, 20, "seine Anerkennung im Rechte gehört immer nur den höchsten Kulturstufen," my translation "its acknowledgement in law always goes together with the highest level of culture."

53 Pietscher, *Jurist und Dichter*, 24, "Da erhebt sich also die verletzte Majestät der Rechtsidee, selbst strafend, vernichtend gegen den, der sich frech vermass, das Recht zum Unrecht zu gebrauchen. Der verletzte Privatmann tritt zurück hinter den [...] Staat Venedig."

54 Pietscher, *Jurist und Dichter*, 23 and 24, "Recht muss doch Recht bleiben."

55 Josef Kohler, *Shakespeare vor dem Forum der Jurisprudenz* (Würzburg: Verlag der Stahel'schen Universitäts Buch- und Kunsthandlung, 1883), 6 and iii, 'die ebenso kräftig durchgeführte, als innerlich unrichtige Auffassung Ihering's." The copy of Forum 1883 I used for this article is the li-

claims that he aims to distil the legal thoughts from the plays and that he will not look at the law in Shakespeare's days, but contribute to the universal study of law,[56] ironically, throughout the book his approach is specifically historical-comparative and geographically situated,[57] also in its attack on Von Ihering and his footnote on Portia's pettifoggery that bent the law of Venice. Kohler notes that no performance of the play that he attended was sympathetic to the character of Shylock, and that *although* he is a jurist, he has always watched the scene in which "the wise Daniel" curbed Shylock's revenge breathlessly.[58]

To Kohler, the trial scene offers an example of the development of law in all ages, a deeper form of jurisprudence than the one we find in *Pandectist* textbooks or the one offered in all the works of Von Savigny and Von Ihering taken together, an obvious sneer at the Historical School.[59] After such opening

---

brary copy of Harvard College dated 1901 which goes to show that Kohler too was widely known in his days.

56 Kohler, *Forum* 1883, iii-iv, "Mein Zweck, war es, die innern juristischen Gedanken, welche der grösste Dichter im Gewande der Poesie zum Ausdrucke gebracht hatte, in der Sprache der Jurisprudenz zu entwicklen und in ihrem universalgeschichtlichen Sein und Werden zu beleuchten," my translation "It has been my purpose to develop in the langauge of jurisprudence the intrinsically legal thoughts, that the greatest poet has expressed in the garb of poetry, and to throw a light on their universal-historical existence and values."; Kohler, *Forum* 1883, v, on the aim of the book, "Ich wollte einen Beitrag zur Universalgeschichte des Rechts geben," my translation "I wanted to contribute to the universal history of law."

57 Yet Kohler specifically rejects the historical method of John, Lord Campbell in *Shakespeare's Legal Acquierements considered* (London: John Murray, 1859). For a more compact treatment than Kohler's, see Uwe Diederichsen, "Das Fleischpfand," in *Literatur und Recht, literarische Rechtsfälle von der Antike bis in die Gegenwart*, ed. Ulrich Mölk (Göttingen: Wallstein Verlag, 1996):138–149.

58 Kohler, *Forum* 1883, 5, "habe ich, *obgleich* Jurist, immer und immer mit angehaltenem Athem dem weisen Daniel gelauscht [...] und der Kläger, der die heilge Stätte des Rechts beschmutzen wollte mit dem Schmutze seiner elenden Seele, der das Recht selbst in die Tiefe gemeiner Rachgier herunterziehen wollte, mit Schimpf und Schande von den Schranken des Gerichtes weggejagt wird."; my translation "have I, *although* [my italics] I am a jurist, on all occasions while holding my breath listened to the wise Daniel [...] and [how] the complainant, who dared stain the holy places of the law with the soil of his wretched soul, who himself wanted to pull down the law in the very depths of his mean revengeful state of mind, is chased away from the courtroom showered with scorn and disgrace."

59 Kohler, *Forum* 1883, 6, "ein typisches Bild der Rechtswentwicklung aller Zeiten [...] sie enthält die Quintessenz vom Wesen und Werden des Rechtes in ihrem Schoosse, sie enthält eine tiefere Jurisprudenz, als 10 Pandektenlehrbücher und eröffnet uns einen tiefern Blick in die Gechichte des Rechts, als alle rechtshistorischen Werke von Savigny bis auf Ihering." Cf. Ziolkowski, *Mirror*, 173, "the trial scene [...] is a typical image of the legal development of all times: it contains the quintessence of the nature and progress of law; it contains a more profound jurisprudence than ten vol-

lines, the reader would expect Kohler to delve into the contentious issue without further ado. However, it takes him some seventy odd pages of legal-historical and anthropological descriptions and explanations, with incredibly detailed[60] comparative analyses of the topic of the laceration of a defaulting debtor by his creditor ranging from the law in Padua to that in Avignon and even that in the Dutch town of Zutphen, before he arrives at the point he need to make to save the day for Portia. And that point is that in all legal cultures a development takes place from the literal taking of flesh to what Kohler later on in the book calls "a world-historical necessity"[61] to deny creditors like Shylock their rights. So what matters is to ascertain the level of development in the historical period in which Shakespeare situates his play, as if that would be a simple task to start with.[62] This view is odd to say the least, not least because it presumes a referential view on literature as the mirror of a specific era, one that finds its counterpart in the jurisprudence of concepts' ideal of the referential power of a language of concepts, i.e. once the system of concepts has reached its zenith, the solution to each and every legal problem will perfectly follow from it. And it is precisely the jurisprudence of concepts that Kohler despises. What is more, in hermeneutics viewed as the science of interpretation, the idea of referentiality was also already in decline, so we may consider this literalness a sign of Kohler's positivistic world view. It does fit in, however, with John Wigmore's later idea of reading literature as an historical source for legal professionals.[63]

Kohler emphazises that this development is a gradual one, because before a legal order starts rejecting a contract of the kind that Shylock has had Antonio sign, i.e. on the ground that such contract needs to be annulled, the legal con-

umes of Pandects and opens up a deeper view into the history of law than all works of legal history from Savigny down to Ihering."

60 Kohler, *Forum* 1883, 45, 51.

61 Kohler, *Forum* 1883, 94, "eine welthistorische Nothwendigkeit."

62 Kohler, *Forum* 1883, 71, "Wie weit diese Entwickelung in der rechtsgeschichtlichen Periode, in welche der Dicher das Stück verlegt, sich bereits vollendet hat, das ist der juristische Springpunkt in der Beurtheilung des Kaufmann von Venedig," my translation "To which degree this development has been completed in the periode of legal history in which the poet situates the play, is precisely the legal point that stands out in our view on The Merchant of Venice." Cf. Paul Huvelin, "Le Procès de Shylock dans Le Marchand de Venise de Shakespeare," *Bulletin de la Société des Amis de l' Université de Lyon* (1902): 173–198, 182 and 186, for the view that we should doubt that Shakespeare specifically intended the audience to understand that it was sixteenth-century Venetian law that was applicable, especially since Portia applies common law reasoning. Huvelin is one of the few critics of the Von Ihering- Kohler controversy who specifically mentions this common law orientation.

63 John Henry Wigmore, "A list of legal novels," *Illinois Law Review*, 2 (1908): 574–593.

sciousness of its people will have anticipated the necessity to do so. This, I suggest, already forebodes Kohler's adherence and contribution to the Free Law Movement, though differently than he himself later claimed when in the Foreword to the second edition he wrote, in a rather self-congratulatory vein,

> What are my explanations of Portia's decision other than the dawn of the Free Law Movement, that is brought to light here and in my essay on the interpretation of the laws? That through daring interpretations a law already obsolete is pushed back and a judicial customary law is created, as the as yet unconscious judicial feeling of right [...] breaks though [...] and that, next to the laws, the judge's [own] view comes to the fore as a factor of developing the law, these are the principles of my thought, that my work has introduced to jurisprudence for more than three decades, principles that today have not merely gained solid ground, but have become the foundations of the whole of our legal science.[64]

What matters to me here is that Kohler prioritizes the legal consciousness of a people, a society, as the starting point for a judicial decision. To Kohler, then, because Shylock is devoid of any ethical feeling and deaf to the plea for mercy, his insistance on his legal right and subsequent downfall is not tragic. Shylock himself is a pettifogger, a "rabulististic plaintiff"[65] and therefore his downfall is a signal that "the malignant bubonic growth is erased."[66] It's good riddance to bad rubbish, and we are glad to be rid of one who recklessly damaged our law. In other words, Shylock is the pariah that is excluded because he

---

64 Josef Kohler, *Shakespeare vor dem Forum der Jurisprudenz*, (Berlin: Rothschild, 1919), 2nd edition, iii, my translation of "Was sind meine Ausführungen über den Spruch der Porzia anders als die Morgenröte der Freirechtsbewegung, welche hier und in meinem Aufsatz über die Interpretation der Gesetze zuerst zu Tage getreten ist? Dass durch gewagte Auslegungen verlates Recht zurückgedrängt und ein gerichtliches Gewohnheitsrecht geschaffen wird, indem das unbewusste Rechtsgefühl des Richters [...] hindurchbricht [...], und dass neben dem Gesetze das richterliche Urteil als Faktor der Rechtsbilding hervortritt, das sind Grundgedanken, welche mein Werk vor mehr als drei Jahrzehnte in die Jurisprudenz hineingetragen hat, Grundgedanken die heutzutage nicht nur festen Fuss gefasst haben, sondern zu den Stützen unserer ganzen Wissenschaft geworden sind." See also Kohler, *Forum* 1919, i, for Kohler's view that the topic of law in literature was new when he wrote *Forum* in 1883, but that now it is good to see jurists paying attention to Goethe and Ibsen, because literature offers a piece of world history that any jurist would do well to recognize is its depiction of the progress of law, "Ein Stück Weltgeschichte ist es, was der Dichter bietet, und wehe dem Juristen, der in der Weltgeschichte den Rechtsfortschritt nicht zu erkennen vermag," my translation "It is a piece of world history that the poet offers and woe to the jurist who fails to recognize in world history the progress of law."

65 Kohler, *Forum* 1883, 79, my translation of "rabulistischen Kläger."

66 Kohler, *Forum* 1883, 76–77, my translation of "die wuchernde Pestbeule ausgeätzt ist." Note that the German "wucherend" contains the idea of Shylock being a usurer ("Wucherer") and the idea that, unless stopped, his point of view will grow rampant.

prioritizes his own legal and financial interest above the morals and values of the community. Immoral use of the law cannot be tolerated. The tragic character of the play is not Shylock but the judge who is the instrument in the hands of this scoundrel and who on the basis of the laws of Venice that she has to apply, does not know how to avoid the undesirable, bad solution that the law suggests.

To Kohler, this does not mean that Von Ihering was right when he wrote that cutting a pound of flesh implies the shedding of blood. On the contrary, this would mean sticking to the letter of the law, and ignoring, "the legal consciousness of the judge, the legal instinct that lives in him, that has not yet developed itself into a complete and clear insight and therefore hides itself behind the mock argument of the wise Daniel."[67] It is her legal consciousness that makes the judge aware of the fact that now is the time to set aside the old law. Obviously, the lawgiver should be aware of the instincts of the people and preferably change the law accordingly. But since this is not always possible, the judge should act as the intermediary between the lawgiver and the people. She should grasp the straw that she can use to legitimize her decision, i.e. her instinctive legal consciousness as the foundation of her decision, that she then clothes in the legal garb of interpretation, as Portia does. The judge is allowed to do so once the word of the law is too rigid. What Kohler does not tell us, however, is how the judge is at all able to sense that the law is rigid. Criteria for this decision are lacking so that the risk of arbitrary decisions, nourished by sentiments other than those of law's progress, looms large. What is more, Kohler's argument contains a shocking, and, I suggest, distinctively discriminatory remark to brush aside any comments that critics might voice. The answer he gives to his own rhetorical question whether or not at the end of the play we should take pity on Shylock whose very existence is threatened, is this: "every great advancement of society lets no one or nothing stand in its way, in the same way each healthy walk causes the death of a great amount of innocent animals."[68] The metaphor is as anti-semitic as it is false – the purpose of the walker, after all, is not to go out to kill -, with Shylock as an insect to be trampled, which is nothing to be worried

67 Kohler, *Forum* 1883, 83, my translation of "das Rechtsbewusstsein des Richters, der im Richter lebende Rechtsinstinkt, der sich noch nicht zur vollständig klaren Erkenntnis heraufgearbeitet hat und sich daher hinter den Scheingründen des weisen Daniels verbirgt"; cf. *Forum* 1919, 39.

68 Kohler, *Forum* 1883, 95, my translation of "jeder grosse Fortschritt der Gesellschaft schreitet über Leichen hinweg, ebenso wie jeder heilbringende Spaziergang einer Menge unschuldiger Thiere den Tod bereitet." Cf. Kohler, *Forum* 1883, 74, for a disparaging remark on Heinrich Heine's view that Shylock is the most respectable character of the play, which is odd if you read Heine who, while calling both Portia and Shylock brilliant figures, nevertheless calls Shylock "the terrible, unpitying Jew" (Heine, *Maidens and Women*, 394).

about, for, as Kohler insists, the devil Shylock, this enemy of law and justice, "has forfeited life."[69]

In his Afterword Kohler explicitly points to the two premises of his argument, once more by way of reaction to Von Ihering who in the seventh edition of *Der Kampf ums Recht* had referred to Kohler's view on Shylock, but, again, had not understood a thing. The first principle of Kohler's legal theory indeed heralds in the Free Law Movement: the decisive importance of judicial legal consciousness; the second is the explicit acceptance of (individual) injustice in the course of inevitable progress in and of law.[70] The "Shylock Problem" as Kohler later calls it remains central stage in his thought, and while in his Afterword he emphasizes that Von Ihering incorrectly presumed that he invited him to a debate,[71] his opposition to Von Ihering is what I would call a "pathological moment" in legal theory. Kohler, while admitting that Portia's legalistic turn is unacceptable from a point of view of the law "as it is,"[72] claims that it is acceptable because Portia understands that the law is about to change, and insists that his historical explanation shows how the judge with her discretionary power has the duty to annihilate "the bearer of the by now defeated level of civilization" that is Shylock.[73] This idea of the necessary annihilation of a "defeated level of civiliza-

69 Kohler, *Forum* 1883, 95, my translation of "hat das Leben verwirkt." Kohler also refers to the Faust legend in which the devil loses, despite of the pact. For Kohler's interest in literary-legal connections, see also Josef Kohler and Ernst Landsberg, "Fausts Pakt mit Mephistopheles in juristischer Beleuchtung," *Goethe Jahrbuch* vol. 24, II Abhandlungen, (1903): 113–131.

70 Josef Kohler, *Nachwort zu Shakespeare vor dem Forum der Jurisprudenz*, (Würzburg: Verlag der Stahel'schen Universitäts Buch- und Kunsthandlung, 1884), 1.

71 Kohler, *Nachwort*, 3.

72 Cf. Theodore Niemeyer who disagrees with the interpretations of Von Ihering, Kohler and Huvelin. Niemeyer dismisses Kohler's view that Portia's decision was correct: neither the result nor the arguments are sound law. While he agrees with Von Ihering about the pettifoggish character of Portia's ruse to save Antonio, he does not follow Von Ihering's argument that the contract was void because *contra bonas mores*, but calls Shylock's fate "the tragedy of a man who is made a sacrifice in a typical conflict, a conflict that lies not only in his own person, not only in the dissentient views of his own generation, but also in the discordant nature of all law." What it means that law's nature is discordant, Niemeyer does not disclose, and, comparable to Kohler, he loses himself in a description of contemporary German law. Theodore Niemeyer, "The Judgment against Shylock in *The Merchant of Venice*," *Michigan Law Review*, vol.14.nr.1 (1915): 20–36, 36, trans. Wandell Herbruck of *Der Rechtsspruch gegen Shylock im 'Kaufmann von Venedig': ein Beitrag zur Würdigung Shakespeares* (Munich and Leipzig: Duncker & Humbolt, 1912).

73 Josef Kohler, "Das Shylock-Problem," *Der Zeitgeist, Beiblatt zum Berliner Tageblatt*, 8 September 1902, nr. 36, 1, mt translation of "[D]er Träger einer überwundenen Kulturstufe." Again Kohler fulminates against Von Ihering whose interpretation was devoid of any historical insight and who keeps calling the way Shylock is treated as an injustice. To Kohler it is obvious that "whoever resists the Wheel of Progress, will be crushed by it," my translation of "Wer sich

tion" and the role of the judge in bringing this about (apart from the legal social Darwinism it seems to adhere to) sits uneasily with accepted principles such as the concept of the separation of powers and the idea(l) of fair trial. What is more, it augurs ill for the idea that law should be a bulwark to protect citizens against unjust intrusions by the state in whatever form.

In the second edition of *Shakespeare vor dem Forum der Jurisprudenz* in 1919 Kohler forcefully repeats his view that Shylock's downfall is anything but tragic. It cannot be tragic for that would mean that we would take his legal argument seriously and interpret it in a positive way as a contribution to legal discourse. This "cannot be; his downfall must itself portray the deliverance from a heavy epidemic that threatened to torture the world."[74] In short, it is "the dreadful struggle of the repressed Jewry, that wants to use the law."[75] And so we must indeed wonder what it means to Kohler that Shylock "stands on the boundary between two worlds," and that Kohler insists that Shylock knew from the very start that his case and his cause were unjust, that what he did was an intentional abuse of law.[76]

4 Gute Juristen, böse Christen?

So where's the rub? What moved Kohler whose long and distinguished career spans decades, whose list of publications is one hundred and fifty pages

gegen das Rad der Entwicklung aufbäumt, wird von ihm zermalmt." Cf. Josef Kohler, "Phantasie im Recht," *Westermanns illustrierte deutsche Monatshefte*, Band 97 (1906): 239–242, 242, that throughout the ages poets have given legal issues a literary form, the example Kohler gives is, once more, Shakespeare's *The Merchant of Venice* with its "subtile Rechtsfrage," its subtle *questio iuris*.

74 Kohler, *Forum* 1919, 6, "Das darf nicht sein: sein Untergang muss selbst die Erlösung bilden von einer schweren Epidemie, welche die Welt zu bedrängen drohte." It should be noted that the first and the second edition of Forum are actually two quite different books. The second edition has an enormous excursion on debtor's law in a comparative context; the second editon lacks the Introduction that the first has; Von Ihering who remains the culprit in the second edition, is nevertheless not mentioned in the name register. In the second edition Kohler also takes Julius Hirschfeld ("Portia's Judgement") and Frederick Pollock ("A Note on Shylock v. Antonio," *The Law Quarterly Rewiew* (1914): 175–177) to task for their views on Portia's verdict.

75 Kohler, *Forum* 1919, 6, my translation of "der furchtbare Kampf des unterdrückten Judentums, der sich des Rechts bedienen will."

76 Kohler, *Forum* 1919, 10, my translation of "steht an der Grenzscheide zweier Welten," and 45, my paraphrase and interpretation of "er war sich eben von jeher in seinem Innern bewusst, das sein Bestreben ein materiell unrechtes war."

long,[77] who co-founded the *International Association for the Philosophy of Law and Social Philosophy*, to engage in such an extended discussion on a single footnote in an equally distinguished scholar's work?[78] Why is his interpretation of *The Merchant of Venice* driven by an aversion to the theoretical views of his contemporaries or predecessors? Why the many antagonisms? In line with what Richard Weisberg in his *Poethics* has ingeniously denoted as the ressentiment of the jurist-verbalizer,[79] I suggest that Kohler with his one-sided emphasis on legal history, albeit in a geo-comparative context, favours a literal reading[80] and a scholastic hermeneutics of referentiality that is informed by professional jealousy of Von Ihering combined with a not too subtle form of anti-semitism.[81] Kohler's interpretation of both Portia's decisionmaking-process and his treatment of his colleagues is a good example of Martin Luther's saying "Gute Juristen, Böse Christen," good jurists, bad, i.e. malicious Christians.

To start with the first point, throughout his works Kohler contrasts his supposedly superior neo-Hegelian view with Von Ihering's legal amateurism.[82] That is strange, not only because Von Ihering and Kohler share the view that the study of law should be practical,[83] and they share an aversion to Von Savigny's emphasis on a jurisprudence of concepts and both emphasize the purpose of the law so that

---

77 Arthur Kohler, *Josef Kohler-Bibliographie* (Berlin: Rothschild, 1931). Kohler also wrote poetry, e.g. "Lebensweisheit," *Westermanns Monatshefte* 50 (1905), xlv.

78 For an overview of Kohler's career, see Andreas Gängel and Michael Schaumberg, "Josef Kohler, Rechtsgelehrter und Rechtslehrer an der Berliner Alma mater um die Jahrhundertwende," *Archiv für Rechts-und Sozialphilosophie* (*ARSP*), (1989): 289–312.

79 Richard Weisberg, *The Failure of the Word* (New Haven and London: Yale University Press, 1984) and *Poethics and Other Strategies of Law and Literature* (New York: Columbia University Press, 1992).

80 See also Kohler's reaction against Paul Huvelin's view, like Pietscher's, that Shylock should have added a clause on the spilling of blood, Kohler, "Shylock Problem," 1.

81 That we also see in other authors, cf. O. Hood Phillips, *Shakespeare and the Lawyers*, 93, "Ihering, *himself a Jew,* " [my italics].

82 Josef Kohler, *Philosophy of Law* [New York: Augustus M. Kelley, 1914] (New Jersey: Rothman, 1969), 11 and 26, "A phenomenal work like Hegel's *Rechtsphilosophie* was followed by amateurish platitudes like Ihering's *Zweck im Recht* in which Ihering only stammers a bit about law," and "Ihering's whole attempt came to grief on the rocks of a deplorable dilettantism; only an unphilosophical mind like that of Ihering himself could find satisfaction in it."

83 Gängel and Schaumberg, "Josef Kohler," 294, note 20, citing Josef Kohler, "Rechtsgeschichte und Culturgeschichte," *Grünhuts Zeitschrift* 12 (1885), 588, "Die Rechtswissenschaft soll praktisch sein, weil das praktische Recht das richtige Recht ist, weil ein Recht, das zu ungesunden praktische Resultaten führt, sich damit von selbst als ein falsches Recht, als ein Hirngespenst erweist," my translation "The science of law should be practical, because practical law is the right [form of] law, because a[n individual] right that leads to unwholesome results proves itself to be incorrect law, a chimaera."

it seems unlikely that Kohler begrudged Von Ihering his "turn" in legal theory,[84] but also in view of the fact that Von Ihering's scholarship was impressive and his interpretation of Roman law renowned. Calling Von Ihering an amateur is therefore blatantly ridiculous. Yet, while Kohler may have had no reason to complain about scholarly respect during his long career, one thing is obvious, namely that Von Ihering is still a household-name in legal theory, while Kohler is hardly ever mentioned, for, other than Von Ihering, Kohler had no pupils in academia, no successors who helped continue attention to his intellectual legacy.

What is insightful is that Kohler has Nietzsche's eponymous concept of the *Wille zur Macht* as an epigraph to his textbook on legal philosophy. In his more or less characteristic self-congratulary way, Kohler compares Nietzsche's views to his own, "It is striking that Nietzsche is often in agreement here [i.e. in *Wille zur Macht*] with the ideas that I have expressed since my *Shakespeare vor der Forum der Jurisprudenz*."[85] Kohler's view on the progress of a world-historical consciousness and the progress of nations and their levels of culture lead him to favouring the Nietzschean idea of the "Übermensch," a species he already perceived to exist in the cultured nations of the Occident, specifically if we look at his view on the figure and the power of the judge who when she discovers in herself the conviction that the law "as it is" should be discarded in favour of a law fit for that presumed higher level of civilization, should act accordingly.[86]

Kohler contrasts the great cultured nations, Germany being one of the more prominent among them, with "Peoples that must be brought down, so that world

84 In *Über die Interpretation von Gesetzen*, *Grünhuts Zeitschrift* 13 (1886): 1–60, Kohler explicitly notes that what matters is not the legislator's intent, but what the law wants to accomplish as an organical strife after a purpose, and that does not essentially differ from Von Ihering's concept of the purpose of the law.

85 Josef Kohler, "Nietzsche und die Rechtsphilosophie," *ARWP* (abbreviation of Archiv für Rechts-und Wirschaftsphilosophie)1 (1908): 355–360, 355, my translation of "Merkwürdig ist, wie Nietzsche hier [i.e. in *Wille zur Macht*] manchmal mit den Ideen übereinstimmt, die ich seit meinem *Shakespeare vor der Forum der Jurisprudenz* geäussert habe."

86 Josef Kohler, "Auf den Spuren Nietzsches," in Josef Kohler, *Aus Kultur und Leben* (Berlin: O. Elsner, 1904), 3–10 [orig. *Berliner Tagesblatt*, nr 45, November 10, 1902], 5, "Der Übermensch ist ja schon heute da: der Europäer und Angloamerikaner sind Übermenschen gegenüber den Wesen niedriger Rasse." The point is already noted by Girard who contends that while Kohler's historical approach is impeccable from a point of description of ancient laws, nevertheless, "M. Kohler prend, pour un appréciation du personnage de Shylock, un point de vue un peu bien antisémitique [...] qui l'a même conduit avec M. Ihering à une polémique fort acerbe, my translation " Mr Kohler takes, for an analysis of the character of Shylock, a rather anti-semitic point of view [...] that has even led him to a polemic with Mr Ihering," Paul Fréderic Girard, "Les travaux allemands sur l'histoire du droit comparé, le *Shakespeare vor dem Forum der Jurisprudenz* par Joseph Kohler," *Nouvelle Revue Historique du Droit* (1886): 224–238, 235.

culture does not suffer distress in its very essence.[87] After World War I, Kohler is nationalistic and somewhat reactionary in his remark that his second edition of *Shakespeare vor dem Forum der Jurisprudenz* is his contribution in hard times to prove that the Germans "are and will always be the first in science."[88]

Obviously, the idea of the judge as "Übermensch" is a dangerous concept. The subjective judicial consciousness as the decisive factor in the judicial construction of the applicable norm sits uneasily with the principles of equality before the law and legal certainty. And even though Kohler insisted that the judge's discretionary power was not absolute in the sense that it could go *contra legem*,[89] the Free Law Movement was increasingly criticized in the first decade of the twentieth century. Kohler's view on the matter has an uncanny resemblance to what Hermann Kantorowicz wrote in his 1906 work significantly entitled *Kampf um die Rechtswissenschaft*. In it, Kantorowicz argued that ultimately the progress of the law depends on the culture and will of the (individual) judge,

> We therefore demand that the judge [...] decide a case as much as a case can be decided according to the clear wording of the code. He may and should abandon this, first, the moment the code appears to him not to offer an undisputed decision; secondly, if it, according to his free and conscientious conviction, is not likely that the state authority *in power at the time of the decision* would have come to the decision as required by law. In both cases he ought to arrive at the decision that, according to his conviction, the present state power would have arrived at had it the individual case in mind. Should he be unable to produce such conviction, he should then decide according to *free law*. Finally, in desperately involved or only quantitatively questionable cases such as indemnity for emotional damages, he should – and he must – decide according to *free will*.[90]

---

87 Josef Kohler, "Ein letztes Kapitel zum Recht und Persönlichkeit," *ARWP* 8 (1915): 170, as cited in Gängel and Schaumberg, 302, n.66, my translation of "Völkern die niedergedrückt werden müssen, damit die Weltkultur nicht wesentlich notleidet."

88 Kohler, *Forum* 1919, iii, my translation of "dass wir in der Wissenschaft die Ersten sind und die Ersten bleiben werden."

89 Kohler, "Über die Interpretation." The point is elaborated upon by Hermann Kantorowicz in "Die Contra-Legem Fabel," DRiZ (abbr. of *Deutsche Richter Zeitung*, trans. *German Judicial Journal*) (1911): 258–263.

90 Published under the pseudonym Gnaeus Flavius, "The Battle for Legal Science," trans. Cory Merill, *German Law Review* 12.11 (2006): 2005–2030, 2025, http://static1.squarespace.com/static/56330ad3e4b0733dcc0c8495/t/56b71dcc01dbae3ec98a32bb/1454841292956/GLJ_Vol_12_No_11_Flavius1.pdf [my italics] (last access September 15, 2016). Cf. Gnaeus Flavius, *Der Kampf um die Rechtswissenschaft* (Heidelberg: Winter, 1906), 34, "Wir fordern deshalb, dass der Richter [...], den Fall so entscheidet, wie nach klarem Worlaut des Gesetzes zu entscheiden ist. Von diesem darf und soll er aber absehen erstens, sobald das Gesetz ihm eine zweifellose Entscheidung nicht zu bieten scheint; zweitens, wenn es, seiner freien und gewissenhaften Überzeugung nach, nicht wahrscheinlich ist, dass die zur Zeit der Entscheidung bestehende Staatsgewalt die Entscheidung

The German judges did not agree and reacted accordingly. At the second Conference of German Judges in 1911, they restricted the freedom that the Free Law Movement would give to judges. Firstly, they stated that all judicial power is subject to positive law, and that the judge is not allowed to deviate from positive law; secondly, that even when the content of the law is uncertain, the judge is not allowed to decide according to his own feeling, but is to solve any doubt by interpretation of the law according to its intended meaning and purpose, when need be by means of analogy; thirdly that in event that a law can be interpreted in different ways, the judge must give precedence to the interpretation that best fits the general legal consciousness and the demands of society.[91] In the latter, stricter requirement than the Free Law's unbridled subjectivism, we can see the turn to the sociological view espoused by Von Ihering. So it may well be that Kohler's diatribe kept feeding on the disappointment that Von Ihering's view, as had been the case since his turn to the jurisprudence of interests, prevailed. The Free Law Movement subsequently petered out and was discontinued in 1933.[92] The year is as significant as it is ominous, because by then what the Free Law theorists had propagated was trumped by the very instincts of the people (healthy as these supposedly are) as the new, formal and sole guideline for judicial decisionmaking, "das gesundes Empfinden des Volkes" as the National Socialist creed had it.

There the fuss about the footnote ended. And what a fuss it was if we consider that the Law of the Twelve Tables on the subject of debt enslavement had already been abolished in 326 BCE.[93] So this goes to show that uses and abuses

so getroffen haben würde, wie das Gesetz verlangt. In beiden Fällen soll er die Entscheidung treffen, die seiner Überzeugung nach die gegenwärtige Staatsgewalt, falls der einzelne Fall ihr vorgeschwebt hätte, getroffen haben würde.Vermag er sich eine solche Überzeugung nich herzustelen, so soll er nach freiem Recht entscheiden."

91 *Kampf ums Recht*, the introduction by Ermacora, 55–56, my translation of "1. Die richterliche Gewalt ist dem Gesetz unterworfen. Der Richter hat deshalb niemals die Befugnis, vom Recht abzuweichen. 2. Die Zweifelhaftigkeit des Gesetzesinhalt berechtigt den Richter nicht, nach seinem Ermessen zu entscheiden; vielmehr ist der Zweifel durch Auslegung des Gesetzes nach Sinn und Zweck und zutreffendenfals nach Analogie zu lösen. 3. Ist ein Gesetz verschiedener Auslegung fähig, so hat der Richter derjenigen Auslegung, welche dem Rechtsbewusstsein und den Verkehrbedürfnissen am besten entspricht, den Vorzug zu geben."

92 Riebschläger, *Freirechtsbewegung*, 89.

93 Cf. Mary Beard, *S.P.Q.R., A History of Ancient Rome* [2015] (London: Profile Books, 2016), 14, for the sobering view on the Twelve Tables that "later Romans looked on this motley collection of regulations as the beginning of their distinguished tradition of law," and 142 for the view that later on, as a result of paraphrasing the earlier texts, "In some cases, even learned Roman lawyers misunderstood what they read in the Twelve Tables. The idea that a defaulting debtor who had several creditors could be put to death and his body divided between them, in appropriately

of literature in the sense of out-of-context appropriations for purposes of the development of (a) legal theory, or for self-aggrandizement should be viewed critically. Sometimes there is already also something outside the text, pace Derrida. The example of the Kohler-Von Ihering controversy should also make us pause and reflect on contemporary interdisciplinary ventures lest we perpetuate ancient or new grudges to the detriment of the future development of *Law and the Humanities* and end up with a reductionist picture of both Shakespeare and the law, and our own field(s) of inquiry.

sized pieces, according to the amount owed, looks like one such misunderstanding (or so many modern critics have hoped)," and 563, the abolition of debt enslavement in 326 BCE.

François Ost

Measure for Measure: Are Criminal Laws Made to Be Applied?

1 Text and context

Shakespeare wrote *Measure for Measure*[1] in 1604, when James VI, King of the Scots, had just ascended the throne of England as James I.

The plot of this play, which shifts between tragedy and comedy and, as is often the case with Shakespeare, is overflowing with twists and secondary intrigues, is not easy to summarize. The following is an initial overview.

In an imaginary Vienna, a degree of licentiousness has grown roots. The Duke, who wields power in a somewhat carefree manner, decides to step aside and temporarily yield the regency to Angelo, a person of severe righteousness.

As soon as he is in charge, Angelo rushes to bring back into application a law that had been allowed to slumber and which punishes extramarital relations with death. He also orders that the brothels be closed, and arrests, and then sentences to death, an unfortunate gentleman, Claudio, whose only wrong is to have impregnated his fiancée, Juliet.

Claudio's friends spring into action; Lucio, who plays the part of a roguish clown, solicits the sister of the unfortunate man, Isabella, a novice preparing to enter the Order of Saint Clare. Lucio begs her to obtain a pardon for Claudio from the inflexible Angelo. At the same time, and parallel to the main plot, there is a subplot that unfolds in Vienna's clubs and brothels, and involves protagonists from a carnival of pimps, prostitutes and representatives of order who will act as the distorting mirror of the main characters facing one another in the palace.

Of course, Isabella does not succeed in persuading the regent until he, taken with a sudden, guilty passion for her innocent candour, proposes an "odious ransom:" her virginity for Claudio's head. As one might suspect, Isabella bridles, outraged. Even when her brother begs her, she cannot be brought to sacrifice her virtue.

1 I had the opportunity to work with three French translations of the play: that by René Galland (Paris: Éditions Les belles lettres, 1930); that by André Markowicz (Besançon: Éditions Les Solitaires intempestifs, 2008), with a Preface by Margaret Jones-Davies; and finally that by Jean-Michel Deprats (Paris: Éditions théâtrales, 2001), with an analysis and substantial notes by Anny Crunelle-Vanrigh.

https://doi.org/10.1515/9783110591514-010

At this point in the drama, the Duke, who had only apparently disappeared, comes back on stage (disguised as a friar) and from then on takes control of the plot. He remembers that, not long before, Angelo broke his own engagement with Mariana, considering her dowry insufficient. The rest of the plot, controlled behind the scenes by the Duke, leads to the thwarting of Angelo's plans and soon, in the final conclusion:

- Mariana takes Isabella's place during a nocturnal rendez-vous proposed by Angelo (the classical "bed trick");
- when Angelo, despite the sacrifice of what he thought was Isabella's virginity, breaks his word again and demands that he be brought Claudio's head, he will be presented with the head of a prisoner who died of natural causes (the "head trick").

The time is ripe for the Duke to make a public return. Immediately, he sets up a huge trial to deal with the complaint of the unfortunate Isabella, who has been kept in ignorance of the subterfuge that saved her brother's life. Angelo, whose moral turpitude is now exposed to the light of day, admits his wrongs and demands that he be sentenced to capital punishment. However, the Duke, faithful to his jurisprudence, has other designs: after getting Isabella to forgive Angelo, he also grants him grace, though not without first having forced him to marry Mariana. Similarly, this time intervening in the subplot, he forces Lucio, the roguish clown, to marry the prostitute he impregnated.

As is the case in many of Shakespeare's plays, the story is directly related to the current events of the time. When the play was performed before the King at Whitehall the day after Christmas 1604, James I (of the Stuart line) had just ascended the throne of England, thus ending Elizabeth I's long reign, and at the same time the Tudor domination. The situation was difficult, marked by wars of succession, famine and the ravages of the plague (36,000 dead in London, out of a population of around 200,000 at the time); there was also great uncertainty concerning the style and intentions of the new king. In London, the manual of political instructions (the *Basilikon Doron*) that the King had written for his son, Prince Henry, was circulating secretly, although it would soon be public. In it one could find in particular the exhortation to ensure that law be strictly applied for fear that licentiousness would take root and repression would become impossible or, if repression was nonetheless necessary, it would appear as arbitrary and discriminatory.

Another current event: the very recent order to close brothels (September 16, 1603). The measure was probably justified first out of concern to limit the spread of the plague – a scourge that also led to the postponement by six months of the coronation celebrations. However, this decision can also be interpreted as an opportunity to strengthen social control and raise the moral standards of a potentially seditious London mob.

Here again, Shakespeare takes control of this controversial question – at the crossroads of the requirements of social order and the necessities of desire – and he does not fail to frame it as a problem: is such a measure legitimate? Has it the slightest chance of being effective? We cannot eradicate the passions, yet can we regulate them?

2 Title and interpretation

We are gradually moving towards an understanding of the play by taking its title very seriously. The idea of *measure* is precisely both the guiding thread and its moral. This cannot fail to attract the attention of jurists, who know that law is, in its essence and function, the art of measure.[2]

The entire play never ceases questioning the idea of exchange: can everything be traded (Isabella's virtue for Claudio's life, for example, or Mariana's body for that of Isabella? – and this leads to the inevitable slide toward the theme of prostitution that makes itself felt as a continuous bass vibrato: the body of a woman for money?) Again, on the penal level this time, must we say that the punishment has to be equal to the crime? If so, how can that measurement be performed?

The measure referred to here is paradoxical in a drama in which so many cross the line; in fact, "Excess for Excess" could have just as well been the title.[3] Angelo's excess of legalistic rigor leads to Isabella's excessive indignation, who does not hesitate to sacrifice her brother to save her virtue. The disproportion of Claudio's punishment (death for having had carnal relations with his fiancée, who was perhaps already his wife according to certain interpretations of the law in effect at that time – cf. infra); the unbridled violence of Isabella, who calls death down upon her brother's head, accusing him of a kind of incest

2 François Ost, *Le temps du droit* (Paris: Odile Jacob, 1999), 333–334. The law is measurement in at least four senses: (1) It consists in a set of "measures" (norms, rules); (2) It is an instrument of measure, modelled after scales that establish the right proportions in human relations; (3) It expresses the middle way, targets balance and moderation, and is in opposition to excess; (4) In the ongoing adjustment, the law sets the measurement, this time in the temporal sense: it sets the appropriate rhythm, the choice of the right moment, the tempo given to the march of the social.

3 Anny Crunelle-Vanrigh, *Sur mesure. Documents et notes*, in the translation of *Measure for Measure*, J. M. Déprats, (Éditions théâtrales, 2001), 134, 144.

("Is't not a kind of incest to take life / From thin own sister's shame? [...] / Die; perish," 3.1.138 – 140).

The Duke will probably intervene to set things straight and re-establish measure. But exactly what measure? This is the fundamental question and also the moral of the story, which will come clear when the Duke subjects Isabella to her final ordeal in the last scene. Either it will be "one for one," which evokes the ancient *lex talionis*, restated in the Old Testament: "And thine eye shall not pity; but life shall go for life, eye for eye, tooth for tooth, hand for hand, foot for foot" (*Deuteronomy* 19:21). In this case, it will be "An Angelo for Claudio, death for death! / [...] Like doth quit like, and Measure still for Measure" (5.1.407 – 411).

Or else the Christological interpretation of the New Testament will prevail, which causes grace and mercy to triumph over the strict logic of the judgement of equivalence. "Judge not that ye be judged. For with what judgement ye judge, ye shall be judged: and with what measure ye mete, it shall be measured to you again. And why beholdest thou the mote that is in thy brother's eye, but considerest not the beam that is in thine own eye?" (*Matthew*, 7:1 – 5). We come closer to our story when we recall the episode of the adulterous woman pardoned by Jesus, after he first thwarts the legalism of the Pharisees: "He that is without sin among you, let him first cast a stone at her" (*John* 8:3 – 11). The point becomes even clearer when we remember that it was precisely in a commentary on these passages that Saint Augustine, for the first time it seems, referred to the "odious ransom" imposed on a young woman forced to choose between her virginity and her husband's life. Far from condemning her sacrifice, Saint Augustine saw it on the contrary as a proof of love. This lesson in tolerance must not have escaped Shakespeare since Saint Augustine's texts were known and appreciated by the contemporaries of Montaigne and Shakespeare. In this case – and this will be Isabella's choice – Angelo's life will be saved; in return for evil, he will receive good ("Well, Angelo, your evil quits you well," 5.1.495).

The play is thus divided between measure and excess, seeking the best "common measure." Sometimes, passions are unleashed, with all of their destructive excesses; sometimes there is strict equivalence, the logic of an eye for an eye, which still underlies our thought, even though we have the penal paradigm of retribution of which we will speak below. While it is vulnerable to the twofold criticism of being archaic and formalistic, the *lex talionis* has at least the merit of containing the excesses of punishment (which is all the difference between socially instituted vengeance and uncontrolled popular scapegoating); sometimes, lastly, there is the excess of grace and forgiveness that avoids give and take, but "from above" this time, through a free, gratuitous action.

With mercy, we come back to a form of "excess" that flows from a logic of "supplement" to which we will come back.[4]

These preliminary discussions concerning the exegesis of the title say enough about the difficulties involved in interpreting the play as a whole.[5] In Shakespeare's corpus, *Measure for Measure* is considered unclassifiable: it is neither a true comedy, nor a true tragedy. In short, it is a problem play, an enigma fed both by the composite style of the work and by the ambiguity of the characters, the ambiguity of its moral and the depth of its themes. (It has been argued, for example, that the true motif of the work is defamation, and that regulating sexual behaviour is only a screen.)[6]

Under these conditions, the commentators' perplexity is not surprising, nor is the fact that it continues to be staged in a wide variety of ways. Thus, while it is possible to give priority to a relatively positive, edifying interpretation of the play by drawing from it a lesson in juridical wisdom ("penal laws are not made to be applied wholesale, at least not systematically"), as we will do, or even a way to live and forgive in the face of death-dealing forces (which we will call the logic of "supplement"), there is nothing to prevent one, in contrast, from drawing from the drama a suspicious, Foucauldian logic that would see, in decadent Vienna, the theatre of re-establishment of control by a manipulative Duke, renouncing the ostentation of the show of public punishment for widespread social control, a prelude to full regulation.[7]

---

4 On the role of equity and mercy in the play, see Daniela Carpi, "Law, Discretion, Equity in *The Merchant of Venice* and *Measure for Measure*," *Cardozo Law Review* 5.6 (2005): 2325–2329.

5 For an overview of these various interpretations, see Ian Ward, *Shakespeare and the Legal Imagination* (London: Butterworths, 1999), 83*ff*.

6 In this sense, see Mariangela Tempera, "Slander and Slanders in *Measure for Measure*," in *Shakespeare and the Law*, ed. Daniela Carpi (Ravenna: Longo, 2003), 127*ff*. It is true that James I seemed obsessed with defamation and meant to punish it severely.

7 We find arguments in this sense in the notes, cited above, of Crunelle-Vanrigh, *Sur mesure. Documents et notes*, 140. The author refers, in parallel, to the slide of strategies of power, renouncing the theatre of politics in favour of panopticon mechanisms – a thesis supported by the Duke's omnipresence in all the shady corners of the city: jails, monks' cells, dens of iniquity. Going even further, the author suggests that the Duke encourages misconduct in order to regulate it better.

3 Legal issues: are criminal laws made to be applied?

As we have said, the repression has fallen upon the unfortunate Claudio, and now he is displayed, in his chemise, on the public square ("why dost thou show me thus to th' world?", 1.2.116); this was the first stage of the punishment for those who were guilty of extramarital sexual relations. (Only Juliet's pregnancy spares her for the moment.) Angelo's repressive policy is part of the classical "culture of shame" that Michel Foucault speaks about, a culture that also appealed to the crowd assembled at the foot of pillories, gallows and other execution venues.[8]

However, questions remain about the effectiveness of this type of legislation. On this point, the pimp Pompey does not tire of exercising his flair for mockery: Mistress Overdone is worried about the order to close the brothels? She should take comfort! "Though you change your place you need not / change your trade", 1.2.98–99). Escalus reminds him about the prohibition against prenuptial relations? Pompey retorts: "Does your worship mean to geld and spay all the / youth of the City? [...] / Truly, sir, in my poor opinion, they will to it then", 2.1.229–233).

This leads us to the central argument of the play: Was Angelo well advised – was he even authorized – to bring this repressive legislation out of relative obsolescence?[9] This question is developed at length: no less than four characters set out the stakes using a network very rich in images and metaphors.

Thus, the Duke reveals some of his intentions to a friar who is sheltering him:

> We have strict statutes and most biting laws,
> The needful bits and curbs to headstrong steeds,
> Which for this fourteen years we have let slip;
> Even like an o'orgrown lion in a cave,
> That goes not out to prey. Now, as fond fathers,
> Having bound up the threatening twigs of birch,
> Only to stick it in their children' sight

8 Michel Foucault, *Surveiller et punir* (Paris: Gallimard, 1975), 70.

9 On the question in general, see Harry Keushian, "Punishment Theory in the Renaissance: the Law and the Drama," in *Shakespeare and the Law*, eds. Gary Watt and Paul Raffield (Oxford: Hart publishing, 2008), 175*ff.* The author bases his analysis of the difference between strictness and fairness on the twofold nature of English jurisdictions: common law courts (stricter, fodder for tragedies) and jurisdictions of equity (more utilitarian, fodder for comedies).

> For terror, not to use, in time the rod
> Becomes more mock'd than fear'd; so our decrees,
> Dead to infliction, to themselves are dead,
> And liberty plucks justice by the nose. (1.3.24–29)

Finally, it is Angelo himself who states this penal philosophy in complete clarity:

> We must not make a scarecrow of the law,
> Setting it up to fear the birds of prey,
> And let it keep one shape till custom make it
> Their perch, and not their terror. (2.1.1–5)

We will soon see, in light of Michel van de Kerchove's analysis, what "criminal paradigm" Angelo's resolution belongs to. However, in order to gain a complete picture, we still have to identify two motivations that, while more discreet, nonetheless help to explain his attitude. Indeed, the regent does not seem to be content with re-affirming the law to ensure compliance with it after it has been violated; his concern is also to prevent future crimes:

> The law hath not been dead, though it hath slept
> Those many had not dar'd to do that evil
> If the first that did th'edict infringe
> Had answer'd for his deed. (2.2.115–118)

Likewise, the concern for a form of restorative justice with respect to victims is not foreign to him, at least on the rhetorical level (the scene places him in opposition to Isabella, who corners him):

> [...] I pity those I do not know,
> Which a dismiss'd offence would after gall [...] (2.2.101–102)

Let us accept, following Angelo's position, that it is necessary, for various reasons, to ensure the complete and entire strength of criminal law in general. Yet, could we not – this is Isabella's argument – make exceptions in certain cases in which there are duly substantiated reasons? Cannot in-principle penal rigor ever accommodate minor equity? Can we not "Condemn the fault and not the actor of it?"– Angelo sweeps the question away with the back of his hand: "Why, every fault's condemn'd ere it be done[...]" (2.2.38).

Isabella then has to raise the stakes: the appeal to mercy and forgiveness: "But you might do't [pardon him], and do the world no wrong." Too late, he has been condemned, replies the rigid Angelo – and so the beautiful novice refers, as a last resort, to the argument of divine justice: If the supreme judge pardons, He who knows all our failings, who are we to judge? (2.2).[10] Angelo's response it to take cover, once again, behind the law: "It is the law, not I condemn your brother."

Isabella is not the only one, far from it, to try to calm Angelo's repressive fervor. The Prevost himself, officer of justice, aware that "[a]ll sects, all ages, smack of this vice," tries to avoid rushing into anything; while he delays and Angelo presses him to take action, he protests: "Lest I might be too rash; / Under your good correction, I have seen / When, after execution, judgment hath / Repented o'er his doom" (2.2.7–10). Without succumbing to unwelcome anachronisms, we can think that arguments drawn from the procedural guarantees of due process of law are mainly what inspire the moderation of this professional of justice. Moreover, Escalus, the wise advisor to the Duke, who has remained at his post in Angelo's shadow, says nothing different: "Ay, but yet / Let us be keen, and rather cut a little / Than fall and bruise to death" (2.1.5–6).

Naturally, all of this prepares the way for the Duke to make his grand re-entrance on stage, during the "last judgment" (the term is not inappropriate since the Duke's justice is largely inspired by divine mercy) and his deluge of verdicts.

Angelo and Lucio, one in a serious mode, the other with a comical tone, will suffer comparable fates (5.1. 548–549): each one, after being forced to marry, will be condemned to capital punishment (in the case of Angelo: "We do condemn thee to the very block Where Claudio stooped to death"; in Lucio's case: "The nuptial finish'd Let him be whipped and hanged"). Next, however, it will be the pardon and commutation of the sentences (in Angelo's case: "I find an apt remission in myself"; in Lucio's: "Thy slanders I forgive; and therewithal Remit thy other forfeits").

Where does this "apt remission" come from? The Duke raises a corner of the veil, in which could very well be the final appraisal resulting from his experience as an observer-participant in the political life of his duchy: "I have seen corruption boil and bubble / Til it o'errun the stew: laws for all faults, / But laws so countenanced that the strong statutes / Stand like the forfeits in a barber's shop, / As much in mock as mark" (5.1.342–345). It is a valuable observation since it will escape no one that it rings in perfect counterpoint with the reasons justifying bringing the law back into effect. In the end, the Duke prefers sleeping law to law applied in a corrupt manner.

10 In fact, Isabella uses two other arguments during this confrontation. On one hand, she refers, not without finesse, to the argument of the arbitrariness of a condemnation that comes after two years of tolerance: "Who is it who has died for this offence? There's many have committed it." On the other hand, and we will come back to this, she invites, prophetically, Angelo to put himself in the place of the man he is condemning: "If he had been as you, and you as he."

Now let us return, in a more theoretical mode, to the central question: Are criminal laws made to be applied? Despite its apparently provocative nature, this question relays a concern that applies to law as a whole, as Dean Jean Carbonnier subtly points out: "The mundane phrase that the legal norms are made to be applied, although it seems like a truism, is not a truth. Or at least not a universal truth."[11] The author recalls the merits of *comminatory* orders, that "uncertainty of efficiency" that makes possible an economy of penal means and very often suffices to ensure the effectiveness of the penal system.

In an important and often cited article,[12] Michel van de Kerchove approaches the question from the following angle: with regard to the different functions assigned to punishment, what criminal model most easily accommodates purely selective application? Three models are considered. First, the axiological, retributive model, in which a punitive or repressive philosophy clearly dominates. Criminal law tends toward the protection of the social order itself and punishes attacks on goods that are considered essential. Legal vengeance is in question in this case, and sanctions are measured according to the seriousness of the offence. It is understandable that, of all the models, this is the one that has the most trouble accommodating partial ineffectiveness of penal law. Second, there is the preventive model, of utilitarian inspiration. In this case, the gaze turns from the past of the guilty action to the future, with a view to prevention in the broad sense (dissuasion, neutralization, rehabilitation). Application of the penal sanction is no longer considered a good in itself, but as an instrument in service to an external good: the prevention of the crime in the mind of the guilty party or any other potential offender. Only truly harmful forms of behaviour are established as offences and only truly dangerous individuals will have the punishment applied to them. Criminal law is applied with flexibility and discretion, in the name of a superior principle of effectiveness. Lastly, a third model flows from the concern for a symbolic reaffirmation of a prohibition. In this case, what is sought is a symbolic reaffirmation of values protected by the norm, not in the mechanical sense of the paradigm of retribution, but rather with a socio-pedagogical goal designed to inculcate, spread and reaffirm, on a symbolic level, the strong values that structure the collective consciousness. In this context, affirmation of the law is considered more important than the associated punishment, and we can speak of partial decriminalization.

11 Jean Carbonnier, *Flexible droit. Textes pour une sociologie du droit sans rigueur*, (Paris: LGDJ, 1971), 101. [Our translation.]

12 Michel Van de Kerchove, "Les lois pénales sont-elles faites pour être appliquées?," *Journal des tribunaux*, (1985): 239–334; Van de Kerchove, *Sens et non-sens de la peine* (Brussels: Presses de l'Université Saint-Louis, 2009).

What conclusions can be drawn from these observations for the analysis of *Measure for Measure?* Clearly, Angelo's attitude is inspired by the axiological-retributive model, including the anonymous, automatic aspect of the sanction, which takes the equivalence of the *lex talionis* as its model. Crime must be punished because it is crime, and the sanction is to be calculated in proportion to the seriousness of the offence. Angelo's point of view is at once legalistic, literal and backward-looking; his eye is turned to the past and he sees no further than the letter of the text – for these two reasons, he will not gain the stature of statesman.

In contrast, the Duke is quite comfortable with the relative material ineffectiveness of criminal law. Can his behaviour be explained through the reference to a single model? It is probably wiser to explain it using reasons drawn from each of them, since it is true that in practice the various paradigms are applied in a cumulative manner.

Thus, the Duke certainly must share some of the procedural scruples expressed by his lieutenants, the Prevost and Escalus (a self-restraint phenomenon with a view to the requirements of due process of law). As the statesman he is, he certainly does not seek a revengeful, mechanical application of criminal law. The way he applies it is instead flexible and discriminating, with a view to the future and with a general concern for prevention. Lastly, he is certainly more attached to the symbolic affirmation of the values underlying the prohibition than to its systematic application to offenders. We have seen that he is not stingy with pardons and that he employs with perseverance all of the resources for differentiating among punishment, sentencing and execution.

However, while he rather systematically evades penal prohibitions, he refrains from repealing them as he would have the power to do. Even better, we have not forgotten that his partial withdrawal was explained in particular by the concern to assign to an inflexible regent the unpopular task of recalling the prohibition at a time when libertinism was spreading dangerously in his states. This proves the observation that the symbolic effectiveness of the norm cannot survive over the long term unless it is, at least from time to time, reactivated by truly being applied.

4 Anthropological stakes: pardon and life, the logic of supplement

As pertinent as they may be, these socio-juridical analyses do not exhaust the meaning of the play. In order to try to do it justice, we have to take a more encompassing perspective, of an anthropological order. Its ultimate point, in line with the momentum that flows through the whole plot, is the celebration of life and pardon, according to a logic of free gift and supplement: a declaration of life despite the suffering of existence (the stench of the plague that was decimating the population of London at the time), the generosity of forgiveness despite the ravages of vice and corruption.[13]

However, the approach of this logic of supplement (d) implies a series of prior mediations: it presupposes the ethical capacity of decentring, which consists in placing oneself in another's shoes or, even better, discovering the other in oneself ((c) "If he had been as you, and you as he"). In turn, that capacity supposes that we become aware of the relativity of the separation of desire and the law – or, to speak more frankly, of the subversion of the law by desire (b). Lastly, this subversive theme is itself announced and performed in the work through a whole series of substitutions, subterfuges and confusions that we must first bring to light (a).

(a) *Substitutions*

In a fascinating chiaroscuro interplay (palace lights, the shadows of the jail cell and the brothels, the unreliable light of Lucio, the will-o-the-wisp rogue clown), coming and going between the high and the low (the summit of power, the dregs of the slums), and suspicious images (out of sync, doubled) reflected by a wide variety of distorting mirrors, the play deploys a twisting plot that moves ahead only through slides and substitutions, two-tongued talk and double games.

First, there is a topographical confusion in that upside down Vienna, with trap doors and secret passages that, from the convent cell to that of the jail, from the alcove in the brothel to the backroom of the executioner, and from those to the antechambers of the palace – not to mention the garden where the trick is played, to the great dismay of the fallen Angel.

Next, there is the slide in roles from the beginning of the play: the Duke puts on a friar's cloak (a prelude to a long series of masquerades) – which will soon be answered, at the end of the play, with the engagement of the pimp wearing the executioner's livery.

---

13 In the play, love itself appears largely corrupted: from the prostitution that dictates life in the slums to the venal nature of legitimate unions, largely conditional on the size of the dowry (both Claudio and Angelo explain the postponement or breaking of promises by questions of insufficient dowry, 2.1).

Moreover, as is natural, it is first language that is marked by the confusions. We laugh heartily at the clumsy retorts of the unfortunate Constable Elbow, who systematically uses one word when he means another. Yet, when we look at it closely, this clownlike confusion is only the out-of-sync reflection of the shiftiness affecting the language of the powerful: the Duke, who gives Angelo's "deputation all the *organs* of our own power" (2.1.20), and Angelo who, with complete ambiguity, discusses with Isabella the question of "to do it" or "not to do it" ("pleased you to do 't at peril of your soul", 3.4.68–69).

(b) *When desire subverts the law*

Shakespeare must be convinced of it: sex drive is as natural as it is universal; we can probably try to channel it, but trying to contain it is pure madness. We have already recalled the firm opinions of the wise Prevost in this respect ("All sects, all ages smack of this vice," 2.2.5) and there are also those of the dubious Pompey ("If you head and hang all that offend that way but for ten year together, you'll have to give out a commission for more heads," 2.1).

Angelo is also well convinced of this; therefore, to combat what he sees as a manifestation of the devil, he deploys energy proportional to the force of evil. However, we soon see that this zeal is not as innocent as he would have us believe, thus anticipating the words of Voltaire and Pascal. Voltaire: "Anyone who seeks to destroy the passions instead of controlling them is trying to play the angel" – like Angelo, precisely; but Voltaire must have had in mind Pascal's "whoever would play the angel plays the brute." This is the truth of Angelo: behind the incorruptible saint, the lustful ape. Let us understand this well: it is not enough to say that Angelo, the austere regent, is troubled by physical passions from time to time. This would be mundane and simplistic, and yet would make the man more human. What Shakespeare suggests – the lesson is much more troubling– is that Angelo is overwhelmed by his desires in the very exercise of power. This would not be, once again, in the mundane sense in which he uses his authority to achieve his ends, but in the sense that it is his puritan zeal that is itself entirely driven by sex. Claudio understands this well when, in scene 2, he reveals the truth about Angelo's obscure power with the help of a network of metaphors with explicit sexual connotations:

> Or whether the public body be
> A horse whereon the governor doth ride,

> Who, newly in the seat, that it may know
> He can command, lets it straight feel the spur; (1.2.156–160).[14]

Moreover, Angelo himself soon admits the disturbing enjoyment that he finds in exercising his authority over Claudio and thus having the innocent Isabella in his power. Lucid, the regent himself finds the words to express the turmoil he feels: not the very natural stirring of emotions at the sight of the young novice in tears, but instead, directly, the abjection, in other words, very precisely, the confusion of the most sacred with the most vile.

> [...] Having waste ground enough,
> Shall we desire to raze the sanctuary,
> And pitch our evils there? (2.2.20–22).

Later, when he sees Isabella again, the right words again come to him, perfectly aligned with the money metaphor that has been flowing throughout the play:

> Their saucy sweetness that do coin heaven's image
> In stamps that are forbid[...] (2.4.45–46).

Lastly, when Isabella finally understands his intentions and escapes them in the most energetic way possible, Angelo gives free reign to his libido, and this reveals sadistic aspects: torture, not only death for Claudio, Juliet's body subjection to all of his whims, and to crown it all, delectation of the impunity guaranteed by his high office. Thus, Angelo's perversion is brought to light: he is not content with ordinary corruption obtained through little arrangements with justice. Instead, under the cover of restoring common statutes, he plans to impose his own law: the dictatorship of his desire, transforming all of his partners into objects (Marianna rejected, Isabella raped, Claudio and soon Juliet killed) and asphyxiating all of his relationships in the rarified air of what Sade called "isolism."

Facing him, Isabella's character, while she initially attracts sympathy like Antigone's character, proves to be just as complex. Her fragile innocence is a poor veil for an excess of passion. When she appears in scene 4 of Act 1, are her first words not to call for "more strict restraint" in the Order of Saint Clare that she is preparing to enter? She never yields her horror of sexual sin to the terror Angelo threatens. Indeed, at no point does she contest the legality of the prohibition that strikes her brother or the seriousness of the crime of

14 Sexual connotations: *horse* and *whores* are homophones, and *ride*.

which he is guilty. When she speaks of flesh, she uses expressions such as "ahorr'd pollution" and "yield My body up to shame" (2.4.104). Moreover, while she does not lack courage when pleading for her brother, she does not consider for a second, even when he begs her, sacrificing her chastity for him.

In sum, she appears as the faithful reflection of the regent's strictness, the proud vestal virgin sacrificed on the altar of virtue. However, the parallel is troubling and requires us to take a closer look at it also. Is not this attachment to principles, which would take priority over the very life of a brother, not also suspect? Who will describe Isabella's dark sides?[15] She herself, perhaps; she reveals (another point in common with Antigone) a desire for death that is clearly sexually driven when she grasps the unworthy exchange she has been offered:

> [...] were I under the terms of death,
> Th'impression of keen whips I'd wear as rubies,
> And strip myself to death as to a bed
> That longing have been sick for, ere I'd yield (2.4.100 – 105).

That thing that she nonetheless "abhors to name" (2.1), the sexual desire that she suppresses so violently, does it not return in the absolutism of her resolutions?

(c) ***Moving away from self-centredness.*** **And if it were you?**

The aesthetics of substitutions (a) and the theme of subversion of the law by desire (b) produce a critical view and disclose, in short, a suspicious, passably disenchanted anthropology. However, we are also permitted (and our hypothesis is that Shakespeare actually invites us to do so) to draw from this the resources of an ethics of shared humanity that could very well soon lead to mercy and forgiveness.

What have we found so far? A horde of more or less carnavalesque metamorphoses, substitutions of roles, two-tongued discourses and double-dealing, dodgy principles, the duplicity of many characters. Beings who are masked, twisted, corrupted, disguised.

So be it. Yet, Shakespeare seems to suggest that we might be able to simply acknowledge this disturbing truth rather than suppress it. We would then discover the other in oneself, for better or for worse. We would know we are fragile, vulnerable, criss-crossed with many cracks, but also complex, human, probably

15 Erika Rackley, "Judging Isabelle: Justice, Care and Relationships in *Measure for Measure*," in *Shakespeare and the Law*, eds. Watt and Raffield, 65.

better able to listen, understand and interact. The poet said, "I is Somebody Else"; the philosopher went one further: "Oneself as Another."

We can make the hypothesis that this is the point of departure for any ethics worthy of the name (we are speaking of *ethics*, which is a question of values and standards; and not *morals*, which concern principles and prohibitions). It is based on a simple two-letter word: "if," a word that has the tremendous power of introducing a wedge into dogmatic certainties and contains the formidable potential to unleash the possibilities slumbering in reasons and minds.

"If he had been as you, and you as he." The proud subject is invited to look deep within his conscience: "He that is without sin among you, let him first cast a stone at her" and the Pharisee legalists disperse. In a word, the prophet managed to make them feel their sameness with the prostitute. *Do not do unto others*, continues the prophet, and suddenly the subject, who believed he was invulnerable is projected in his imagination into the possible situation of the other, vulnerable and dependant.

It is possible to argue – without risk of being contradicted – that the "if" strategy – "If he had been as you, and you as he?" – creates a rhythm in the play, like a leitmotiv, and is, from the beginning to the end, the instrument that both thwarts Angelo and finally saves him. This theme occurs innumerable times throughout the plot.

> For example, Escalus to Angelo:
> Whether you had not sometime in your life
> Err'd in this point which you now censure him. (2.1.20–21)

(d) *Logic of supplement. Excess of forgiveness. Stubbornness of life.*

Let us repeat: forgiving is a very special social institution: nothing should make it compulsory. As such, it is the manifestation *par excellence* of sovereign justice. Its essence is divine, as Isabella, who has run out of arguments, does not fail to remind Angelo: In your place, God would have pardoned (2.2).

Moreover, the play shows how narrow the path of forgiveness is, between laxity and corruption, two figures that are very present in the plot. Laxity produces a sort of slackening of the rule or obliteration of values that then encourages other transgressions. In support of Angelo's new policy, the wise Escalus recalls a time when his sinister consequences had not yet shown themselves:

> [Angelo's severity] is but needful:
> Mercy is not itself that oft looks so:
> Pardon is still the nurse of second woe. (2.1.269–271).

Corruption leads to forgiveness through complicity with the forgiven evil. Far from transcending the crime, it spreads it; far from strengthening the law by showing it capable of humanity, it waters it down by making it private, hijacks it by subordinating it to special interests. This is precisely the meaning that Isabella and the Duke give to the mercy (temporary and false, moreover) that Angelo pretends to accord to Claudio in exchange for the odious exchange that he imposes on Isabella.

This is therefore the narrow way of forgiveness, between laxity and corruption. This is also the ordeal that the Duke imposes on Isabella at the point when she is still unaware that Claudio has been spared. We know the outcome: not an Angelo for a Claudio, "Like doth quit like, and Measure still for Measure," but "Well, Angelo, your evil quits you well."

An edifying happy ending? The ultimate ruse of a Machiavellian Duke employing forgiveness as a recipe for power? And what if it were simply a salient mark of life? Life that stubbornly persists and that, despite debauchery and the plague, stronger than the silence of the monastic cells and the racket of capital punishment, claims the last word.

Such forgiveness, like life and love, seems to spare no one: from the unworthy regent to the pious novice, from the grotesque pimp to the gentle Mariana. Torrents of warm humanity, all classes together: this is what Shakespeare opposes to the cold reason of death. In a deafening pandemonium that shakes up both styles and conventions, he celebrates the hymn of life that triumphs over all.

Filippo Sgubbi

Measure in Penal Law

1 "O, it is excellent / To have a giant's strength; but it is tyrannous / To use it like a giant." (Isabella in *Measure for Measure*, 2.2.107–108)

Out of the many reflections triggered by Shakespeare's comedy, *Measure for Measure*, anyone such as myself who deals with criminal law will see in this phrase an effective conception of the power of the state *vis-à-vis* the governed – and one that is still valid today. The power of the State is ambiguous and often hypocritical, is not based on certain rules, and is often left to the arbitrary decision of one single person: and the criminal law is the main instrument for the specific exercise of sovereign power over citizens/subjects. This is the case today as it was 400 years ago, and may indeed remain so forever.

Obviously, a person who causes an unmarried woman to become pregnant will not today risk the death penalty; however, no such law existed even at the time as it was Angelo that re-exhumed an ancient law (Claudio, Act 1, Scene 2), perhaps entirely on an *ad personam* basis. The contemporary context is less gruesome; honour and virginity are not primary values, and social relations are structured in a more open and less hierarchical manner. However, the dynamics of power and authority remain similar. In fact, the great Enlightenment narrative that man must be governed by law and not by men is being progressively abandoned. Similarly, the distribution of powers has changed.

The Constitution in books is still rooted in the central role of Parliament as the sovereign lawmaker, along with the Government and the Judiciary as bodies that are subject to the law. The Constitution in action offers a different distribution of power: true, effective power lies in bodies not elected by the people. The judiciary first and foremost, the European institutions, the various agencies that carry out inspections, controls and checks in relation to private individuals and businesses in various areas (financial, tax, labour law, etc.) along with independent administrative authorities such as the CONSOB (the Italian Securities and Exchange Commission), the Bank of Italy and – of fundamental importance within the current climate in Italy – the National Anticorruption Authority, which is vested with practically unlimited powers over the economic and political life of the nation.

https://doi.org/10.1515/9783110591514-011

But in particular, power is vested in the judiciary, which is in the body charged with administering the criminal law. Political and social power lies with the body that can decide at its discretion to punish other individuals and to confiscate assets. The latter should limit these powers, but "the strong statutes stand like forfeits in a barber shop" (Duke Vincenzo, Act 5). We have slipped from the political to the criminal, moving from a democracy characterised by debate and representation to a democracy of inculpation. The widespread and arbitrary use of criminal law destroys people, businesses and political careers. Such tyranny is inherent within the role (Claudio, Act 1, Scene 2) and power acquired by the criminal courts.

Means of mass communication magnify these perverse effects: accusations proliferate and a simple indictment turns into a definitive judgment, fuelling the judge's vanity by promoting his fame and career, even in politics (Claudio, [Angelo revives and applies laws that had fallen into desuetude] – "surely for a name" – Act 1, Scene 2).

2 Second reflection

Power seeks consent, attributing unpopular political choices to someone else: "My nature never in the fight to do in slander" (Duke, Act 1, Scene 3).

This is a widely known way of yielding power. There is no doubt that, within the current world, unpopular decisions are pinned on others obviously by very different methods, which are in any case more sophisticated than the delegation to Angelo and the disguising of the Duke. Nowadays, there is a myriad of centres of sovereignty through which political decisions and rules are adopted. Consider the growing influence of unelected officials requiring a high level of technical expertise, the growing influence of court rulings or the political and social power of medicine, science and national and multinational finance. These constitute alternative and auxiliary governments, which influence the construction of society, both today and tomorrow. It is thus easier to hide within this forest of decision making powers and to govern from behind the scenes. And it is increasingly difficult to know who is responsible for a political decision.

At the same time, the decisions made within contemporary political life are becoming increasingly complex: it is often necessary to choose between different positive values, sacrificing one of them (a very topical example: taking in refugees as against avoiding disruption for citizens). At the same time, the social bodies with a blocking or veto power are increasing (consider for example the dissemination of the NIMBY attitude). Bodies vested with institutional sovereignty are increasingly unable to make decisions, amongst other things to avoid losing votes. This is especially the case if – as in Shakespeare's comedy – it is necessary to depart from a consolidated political stance of indulgence towards illegality in order to restore rigorous respect for the law: "We have strict statutes and most biting laws [...] which for 19 years we have let slip" (Duke, Act 1, Scene 3). And the Duke is right: tolerance of illegality over the long term morphs into the right to break the law.

The paralysis of decision making power that is characteristic of political authority results in a shift (or delegation) towards the judiciary, which for all intents and purposes becomes a deputy power. Citizens expect judicial procedures to lead to the specific results that cannot be obtained through elections.

3 Third reflection. Absolute power vested in an individual favours corruption

Angelo proposes to Isabella that they engage in sexual relations in exchange for her brother's life. This request was made possible by the absolute criminal power vested in Angelo: a *jus vitae ac necis* that is not limited by law or balanced by external powers capable of exercising effective control. This is an extreme example of criminal government by men.

Unfortunately, similar situations continue to occur to this day, even if it is not life that is at stake. In a large number of cases, the law vests individuals with far-reaching powers of inspection and control over private and financial activities. This, coupled with the legal uncertainty characteristic of the world of today, gives certain individuals complete discretion over individual rights. And this offers fertile ground for the development of corruption.

4 Conclusion

"Death for Death; Like doth quite like" (*Measure for Measure*, Duke, Act 5). The Duke's vision appears to draw inspiration from the law of an eye for an eye, typical of the ancient criminal law, which is however still today present within the irrational instinct and within the common sense of each of us. But this is not the real philosophy inspiring the Duke, as is shown by the clemency ultimately granted to Angelo.

A valid moral lesson can also be drawn for the modern political climate. The authorities, the bodies holding political power and above all those administering criminal law have the task of overseeing compliance with the law: but they must have the right measure when performing this highly difficult task. Criminal power is a matter for giants and it is an excellent thing; however, to use it as a giant amounts to tyranny. "O, it is excellent / To have a giant's strength; but it is tyrannous / To use it like a giant" (Isabella, Act 2, Scene 2).

Carlo Pelloso

Are the Conspirators Purgers or Murderers? Shakespeare's *Julius Caesar* and Roman *Ius Sacrum*

1 Introduction

"Let us be sacrificers, but not butchers, Caius [...] And, gentle friends, let's kill him boldly, but not wrathfully; let's carve him as a dish fit for the gods, not hew him as a carcass fit for hounds [...] This shall make our purpose necessary, and not envious; which so appearing to the common eyes, we shall be called purgers, not murderers."[1] In the tragedy *Julius Caesar*, Shakespeare depicts Brutus – the dictator's friend and protégé – as deeply anguished and, at the same time, firmly fascinated by the prospect of killing an extraordinary and noble Roman that, in his opinion, appears like a to-be king and ultimately deserves to die.[2] It is in Act II that Brutus pronounces such solemn, powerful, and visionary words.

In a recent analysis of the play, Garry Wills has interpreted these lines – alongside the so-called orchard soliloquies, as well as further speeches held by the conspirator – as proof of an intensive use of rhetorical strategies exclusively concerned with "how to present the action to others." According to this scholar, Brutus would be "performing a kind of transubstantiation, turning blood back into sacrificial wine;" he would just try "to cover up the ugly reality

1 William Shakespeare, *Julius Caesar*, ed. David Daniell (London: Arden Shakespeare, 1998), 2.1.166, 172–175, 180: the sole textual source of the tragedy (first performed in 1599) is the Shakespeare First Folio (London, 1623). See, moreover, the astonishing scene where the conspirators ritually wash their hands in Caesar's wounds: "Stoop, Romans, stoop, // And let us bathe our hands in Caesar's blood // Up to the elbows and besmear our swords. // Then walk we forth even to the market place, // And waving our red weapons o'er our heads, // Let's all cry, Peace! Freedom! and Liberty!," 3.1.105–110.

2 See Julia Griffin, "Shakespeare's Julius Caesar and the Dramatic Tradition," in *A Companion to Julius Caesar*, ed. Miriam Griffin (MA and Oxford: Wiley-Blackwell, 2009), 371–398, 383 (following the *communis opinio*): "At the beginning of Act II, he reveals his uncertainty in a long soliloquy about the killing, and how to justify it: the argument he reaches is that Caesar, though no tyrant at present, might later become one. However unsatisfactory this argument might appear [...] Shakespeare's concept of a brooding, hesitant Brutus was a dramatic innovation."

https://doi.org/10.1515/9783110591514-012

with ritual pieties," as well as, in order to contradict "the ugly realities of the plot," he would also refuse to treat it "as a contract."[3]

Although rhetorical artifices, tricks, and figures of speech are undeniable devices used in Elizabethan poetry in general, and in the work at issue in particular,[4] the above-mentioned interpretation completely disregards the historical, religious, and legal grounds of this Shakespearean play (strongly embedded in the Roman culture), and appears to be excessively simplistic. Differently from such one-dimensional approaches, Roman law may contribute to develop the studies of English literature and, specifically, to deepen our understanding of Shakespeare's dramas.

2 Murder: substance and procedure in Roman law

On the Ides of March, 44 BC, a group of conspirators, all members of the senatorial élite, cut down Julius Caesar in the Senate.[5] On the one hand, this dramatic episode was "the final main effort on the part of a still vital aristocratic tradition to turn the tide of events."[6] On the other hand, it can suggest that Caesar had become rather isolated, more than in the past, during his final months in office:[7]

3 Garry Wills, *Rome and Rhetoric: Shakespeare's Julius Caesar* (New Haven, London: Yale University Press, 2011), 71–72.

4 See Wolfgang G. Müller, "*Ars Rhetorica* und *Ars Poetica:* Zum Verhältnis von Rhetorik und Literatur in der englischen Renaissance," in *Renaissance-Rhetorik*, ed. Heinrich F. Plett (Berlin: De Gruyter, 1993), 225–243, 230; Brian Vickers, *Classical Rhetoric in English Poetry* (Carbondale: Southern Illinois University Press, 1970), 44; Wills, *Rome and Rhetoric*, 37–78.

5 App. *bell. civ.* 2.106–147, and, particularly, 2.114, 119–124; Plut. *Caes.* 60–68 and *Brut.* 1–20; Cass. Dio 44.21.2, 44.34.2–7; Nic. Dam. *Caes.* 25.91–94, 58–106; Suet. *Iul.* 76–85.

6 Luigi Capogrossi Colognesi, *Law and Power in the Making of the Roman Commonwealth* (Cambridge: Cambridge University Press, 2014), 229.

7 Andrew Lintott, "The Assassination," in *A Companion to Julius Caesar*, ed. Miriam Griffin (Malden, MA and Oxford: Wiley-Blackwell, 2009), 72–81, 72: "Among the immediate causes of the conspiracy listed were fears that his eastern expedition would lead to a relocation of Rome's capital to the East, his excessive honours, his manipulation of the elections, his failure to rise to meet a deputation of senators, his deposition of the two tribunes who imprisoned the man who crowned his statue with a diadem, the incident of the diadem offered by Mark Antony at the Lupercalia, and the rumour that it would be proposed in the senate that he should have the title of king on his Parthian expedition. Thus the story is one of an arrogant claim to supremacy, leading to the tragic fall of an otherwise good man."

even Antony and Lepidus, bound by oath to avenge Caesar's death, ended up observing any *consultum* passed by the Senate.[8]

The following notes deal with some challenging aspects concerning the legal qualification of the killing of Caesar, in order to appreciate the solemn words pronounced by Brutus. They are precise and clear: indeed, Shakespeare highlights that the 'assassination' of Caesar is a lawful act. What is the reason why such killing might not be considered – from a legal perspective – a murder?

In Rome, murder is an offence primarily governed by the ancient *lex Numae*, a royal provision stipulating that "if a person with wrongful intent and knowingly causes the death of a *homo liber*, he or she will be a *paricidas*"[9] (that is, according to the most persuasive interpretation of the sign *paricidas*, he or she will be put to death by the victim's relatives).[10]

---

8 See Stephen Weinstock, *Divus Julius* (Oxford: Clarendon Press, 1971), 221–225.

9 Paul.-Fest. *verb. sign.* s.v. *Parrici<di> quaestores* (Lindsay 247): [...] *ita fuisse indicat lex Numae Pompili regis his composita verbis: Si qui hominem liberum dolo sciens morti duit, paricidas esto* (see FIRA, ed. Salvatore Riccobono [Florence 1941], 13). There is a large modern literature on the original nature of homicide and on its penalty; on the text, see – among others – Duncan Cloud, "*Parricidium:* from the *Lex Numae* to the *Lex Pompeia de Parricidiis,*" *Zeitschrift der Savigny Stiftung für Rechtsgeschichte. Romanistische Abteilung* 88 (1971): 2–18; Geoffrey MacCormack, "A Note on a Recent Interpretation of *Paricidas Esto,*" *Labeo* 28 (1982): 43–50; Roberto Fiori, *Homo sacer. Dinamica politico-costituzionale di una sanzione giuridico-religiosa* (Neaples: Jovene, 1996), 62; Giorgio Agamben, *Homo Sacer. Sovereign Power and Bare Life* (Stanford: Stanford University Press, 1998), 81; Leonard Johanter Beek, *Dolus. Een semantisch-juridische studie* (Nijmegen: Katholieke Universiteit Nijmegen, 1999), 322–331; Luigi Garofalo, "*Homo liber* et *homo sacer:* deux archétypes de l'appartenance," *Revue historique de droit français et étranger* 87 (2009): 317–337; Leon ter Beek, "Divine Law and the Penalty of *sacer esto* in Early Rome," in *Law and Religion in Roman Republic*, ed. Olga Tellegen-Couperus (Leiden: Brill, 2012): 11–29; Marco Falcon, "*Paricidas esto.* Alle origini della persecuzione dell'omicidio," in *Sacertà e repressione criminale in Roma arcaica*, ed. Luigi Garofalo (Neaples: Jovene, 2013): 191–274.

10 *Pace* the *communis opinio* (see Bernardo Santalucia, *Diritto e processo penale nell'antica Roma* [Milano: Giuffré, 1998], 15–19), Marco Falcon has recently demonstrated that, during the archaic era, the negative consequences prescribed by Numa in case of homicide – either murder (*dare aliquem morti dolo sciens*) or manslaughter (*occidere aliquem imprudentia*) – did not restore the harmony and the state of peace between the community of the Romans, on the one side, and the community of the gods, on the other side (i.e. they did not reconstitute the so-called *pax deorum*). Indeed, homicide was not, at its beginnings, a *scelus* (crime), that is a wrong implying the state of collective 'impurity' and, as a consequence, the infringement of a public interest. The commission of this offence, according to the original legal-religious system of Rome, deserved neither 'atonement' (by means of an animal sacrifice: Serv. *Verg. ecl.* 4.43 *in Numae legibus cautum est, ut, siquis inprudens occidisset hominem, pro capite occisi agnatis eius in cautione offerret arietem*; see, moreover, XII tab. 8.24a), nor 'execution of the offender' (in terms of a human sacrifice: Paul.-Fest. *verb. sign.* [Lindsay 247]), depending on the *mens rea* of the offender. In other words, the penalties prescribed in the two *leges Numae* at issue

In early Roman law, this offence (as many other acts that in modern legal systems are treated as wrongs against the state and prosecuted by public authorities) was regarded as a private tort. The family of the dead was given a rightful claim and at the same time a religious duty to execute the wrongdoer, after the *quaestores* (so-called *parricidi*) had carried out the due inquiry.[11] Yet, such situation changed in the following centuries.[12] During the proto-republican period,

---

were not directed to eliminate the public impurity due to the unlawful killing of a human being. The legal term *paricidas* designated, for the murderer, a status of dependence under the victim's relatives. The former, as such being caught in the grip of the latter, lost his previous status and the consequent rights and prerogatives; the relatives were religiously compelled to 'avenge' the deceased or, rather, to 'restrain the anger of his ghost'. Likewise, the *subactio* of the *aries*, if the killer did commit the offence unknowingly (*imprudentia*), aimed at avoiding the return of the dead to haunt the living (see Marco Falcon, "*Paricidas esto*," 230 – 236, 237 – 272). These concepts were so deeply rooted in Roman culture, that long after homicide was labelled as a crime against the State, and religion played a less influent role in this area (see Plin. *nat. hist.* 18.12; Cic. *top.* 64, *Tull.* 51, *de orat.* 3.158, *rep.* 2.61; Liv. 33.9 – 10; on the topic, see Santalucia, *Diritto e processo penale*, 56, and ntt. 33 – 35), a kinsman was bound to initiate the public prosecution against the killer and, if he failed to do so, he could not obtain any of the deceased's inheritance.

11 As far as the primitive *regnum* is concerned, the *quaestores* (*parricidii*) were established to inquire into killings (above all on the *mens rea* of the killer) and, probably, even to give a final judgment on the behalf of the king (explicitly, see Tac. *ann.* 11.22.4; D. 1.13.1 pr.; Lyd. *mag.* 1.24; implicitly, Zon. 7.13; Varr. *l.L.* 5.81; Paul.-Fest. *verb. sign.* s.v. *Parrici<di> quaestores* [Lindsay 247]; *contra*, see Plut. *Publ.* 12.3 and D. 1.2.2.22 – 23, where the *quaestores* are considered only a republican institution); on a possible harmonization of the two views, see Luigi Garofalo, *Appunti sul diritto criminale nella Roma monarchica e repubblicana* (Padova: Cedam, 1997), 71 – 86; see, moreover, Roberto Fiori, *Homo sacer*, 387 – 388; Vera Dementyeva, "The Functions of the Quaestors of Archaic Rome in Criminal Justice," *Diritto@Storia* 8 (2009), available at http://www.dirittoestoria.it/8/Tradizione-Romana/Dementieva-Quaestors-Archaic-Rome.htm (last access May 20, 2017); Piotr Kołodko, "The Genesis of the Quaestorship in the Ancient Rome. Some Remarks," *Legal Roots* 3 (2014): 269 – 280.

12 See, *amplius*, Carlo Pelloso, "Sul diritto del cittadino al processo popolare dalla caduta del regno al decemvirato legislativo," *Revue Internationale des Droits de l'Antiquité* 62 (2015): 323 – 344; Carlo Pelloso, "Ai primordi del giudizio popolare: *poena capitis* e garanzie del *civis* nella prima età repubblicana," in *Regole e garanzie nel processo criminale romano*, ed. Laura Solidoro (Turin: Giappichelli, 2016): 83 – 120; Carlo Pelloso, "*Provocatio ad populum* e poteri magistratuali dal processo all'Orazio superstite alla morte di Appio Claudio Decemviro," *Studia et Documenta Historiae Iuris* 82 (2016): 219 – 264. Originally, criminal proceedings were totally inquisitorial. Once the magistrate was aware of a crime, he was entitled to initiate the investigation of the case, to file the charge against the suspected wrongdoer, to produce the necessary evidence, to give a judgment. The magistrate acted as a public prosecutor (either personally or by means of auxiliaries) and as a judge (very probably just personally): see Plut. *Publ.* 3 – 7, Zon. 7.12; Dion. Hal. 5.57.2 – 4; Cassiod. *var.* 6; Cic. *rep.* 2.53, 1.62, *acad. pr.* 2.5.13; Val. Max. 4.1.1; Dion. Hal. 5.19.4, 5.70.2, 6.58.2, 7.41.1; Plut. *Publ.* 11.2; D. 1.2.2.16, 23; Dion. Hal. 5.72.1 – 2; Liv. 2.8.2; Flor. 1.9.4; *vir. ill.* 15. Yet, according to the Roman tradition, the *lex Vale-*

the still existing capital trials by magistrates (which started embracing the cases of homicide, now labelled as authentic crimes) were gradually replaced by the so-called popular *iudicia* where, on the one hand, the supreme magistrates or the *quaestores*, as their representatives, initiated the legal proceedings and acted as mere public prosecutors, summoning the accused, holding the trial *in contione*, eventually presenting a motion in the form of a *rogatio* where he proposed the penalty (that is they were responsible just for *iudicare alicui*).[13] On the other hand, either according to the magisterial discretional choice, or on the grounds of a *provocatio* submitted by the Roman citizen affected by the magisterial proposal, the people as a whole gave final judgments (that is the *populus Romanus* operated as a court of justice whose *officium* was *iudicare aliquem*).

It is clear that such a system, based on adjudication of crimes by the Roman people, as a whole, could have been successful just in the context of a "face-to-face" *civitas*. As political, economic and social conditions got more complex, the so-called *iudicia populi* became gradually inadequate in dealing with criminal prosecutions: the questions implied were excessively hard; moreover, the escalating number of cases made comitial trials very problematic, as the procedure was too complicated, cumbersome and time-consuming.[14] A decisive moment

ria, that is the first centuriate statute passed in the 509 BC, stipulated that, had a Roman citizen submitted a *provocatio ad populum*, the magistrate, either as a judge, or as a police authority, was not allowed to put him to death. In other words, after the establishment of the Republic (or better in the first year of the *libera res publica Romanorum*), jurisdiction over the major crimes was still vested in the consuls, even if the *provocatio ad populum* was conceived of as a civic right and not as an act of grace. The Law of the Twelve Tables went even further: as of 451 BC, no magistrate had the power to pass a capital sentence (Cic. *Sest.* 30.65, 34.73, *rep.* 2.54, *rep.* 2.61, *leg.* 3.44; *leg.* 3.11; Salv. *gub.* 8.5; see, moreover, Plaut. *aul.* 200, *truc.* 819, *pseud.* 1232; Aug. *civ. Dei* 1.19; Pol. 6.14.6; Dion. Hal. 3.22.3).

13 The activities implied by this Latin phrase are well known: see Santalucia, *Diritto e processo penale*, 69–97. The magistrate, after summoning the citizen accused, held a trial in (at least) three successive *contiones* (that is public informal meetings). During this phase, he carried out investigations on the case; he determined matters of fact and law based on the evidence; had the accused been found guilty, an order summoning the popular assembly to meet on the expiry of the *trinundinum* was issued. During this period (corresponding to 24 days) the Roman citizens discussed the case. When the assembly took place on the appointed day, the magistrate presented a *rogatio* for condemnation. Without any preliminary debate, the citizens in favour of the magisterial *rogatio* (bill, proposal) voted '*condemno*', while those against it voted '*absolvo*'. Thus, if the majority voted in favour of condemnation, the magistrate, as president of the assembly, pronounced the final judgment.

14 In the early second century BC a gradual evolution took place: see, among others, for a summary, Richard A. Bauman, *Crime and Punishment in Ancient Rome* (London and New York: Routledge, 1996), 21–22. The people voted the creation of special jury-courts or commissions of inquiry (*quaestiones extraordinariae*) for the investigation of some offences characterized by a

in the history of Roman criminal procedure (*iudicia publica*) was the creation of a system of permanent courts (*quaestiones perpetuae*) entitled, by statute, to adjudicate crimes of a specific nature.[15] Thus, in the second half of the first century BC, trials for simple and aggravated homicide, as well as for parricide[16] – besides other crimes[17] – were held before a permanent court and not before the *comitia*.

---

political nature (such as abuse of power or dereliction of duty by magistrates and provincial officials, and conspiracies against public order and the security of the state). Moreover, the Senate, on occasions of emergency, started setting up, by its own authority and without the Roman people's authorization, special courts whose judgements were final. In the transformed background of the later Republic, such *quaestiones extraordinariae* provided more efficient instruments of prosecuting crimes than the archaic *iudicia populi* (see Santalucia, *Diritto e processo penale*, 97–102).

15 The first *quaestio perpetua* was instituted in 149 BC to deal with the 'abuse of power' (mainly in terms of extortion: *repetundae*), a crime perpetrated by magistrates charged with provincial administration and tax collection (see Cic. *Brut.* 106). The establishment of such *quaestio* later inspired the creation of other jury-courts. Thus, by the end of the second century BC, three further permanent *quaestiones*, aside the *quaestio de repetundis*, had been established for high treason (*de maiestate*), electoral corruption (*de ambitu*), and embezzlement of public money (*de peculatu*). Under Sulla's dictatorship (82–81 BC), the 'court system' was revised, renewed and improved. For the first time a very criminal legal system (the *ordo iudiciorum publicorum*) posed the administration of criminal justice on more consistent grounds. The jury-courts were in permanent session. Each statute defined a crime (or a group of crimes), and consequently laid down procedures and penalties. Any adult male citizen in good standing to bring a charge, if he became aware of a crime, could start the prosecution by making an accusation. If a relevant accusation was made, the magistrate in charge of a particular court for the year (a *quaesitor*-magistrate, usually a *praetor*, but sometimes an ex-*aedilis*, allotted by the Senate) was entitled to proceed to the enrolment of a *quaestio*, whose members were chosen from a yearly *album*. Condemnation required a majority verdict. See, for a concise overview, Duncan Cloud, "The Constitution and Public Criminal Law," in *Cambridge Ancient History* 9.2 (1994): 491–530, 530; Olivia F. Robinson, *The Criminal Law of Ancient Rome* (London: John Hopkins University Press, 1995), 2–3; see, for an exhaustive survey, Santalucia, *Diritto e processo penale*, 103–188.

16 As far as the pre-Sullan period is concerned, see Sen. *clem.* 1.23.1; Quint. *decl. min.* 377.1; Plut. *Rom.* 22.5; Val. Max. 1.1.13; Zon. 7.11; Cic. *Rosc. Am.* 11, 64–65, *inv.* 2.58–59. Even if Pomponius commits a mistake, his words testify that the Sullan *quaestio* also embraced this crime: see D. 1.2.2.32; CTh. 9.19.4.1, with Bernardo Santalucia, "Cicerone e la *nominis delatio*," *Labeo* 43 (1997): 404–417, 415–417.

17 According to the sources (see, for instance, D. 48.8.1; C. 9. 16), the first *caput* of the *lex* at issue gave the court capital jurisdiction over those who carried weapons (*ambulare cum telo*) with the wrongful intent of killing or stealing (*occidendi furtive faciendi causa*), and over the *sicarii* who killed (*hominem occidere*). The fifth chapter dealt with poisoning, that is the making up (*facere*), the selling (*vendere*), the buying (*emere*), and the keeping (*habere*) of a *venenum*, as well as its fatal administration (*dare*). This court also had jurisdiction over common and simple homicides (see Santalucia, *Diritto e processo penale*, 145–149, especially 148, nt. 137), urban

More precisely, by Sulla's time the *quaestio perpetua* based on the *lex Cornelia de sicariis et veneficis* (i.e. a "legge di circostanza" primarily directed to protect and to restore social peace)[18] had become a general unified murder court, by bringing together two older courts.[19]

Those who were found guilty by such *quaestio* – for instance the perpetrators of the crime already punished by Numa in his *lex*, by means of the imperative phrase *paricidas esto* (*hominem liberum morti dare dolo sciens*)[20] – were sentenced to death. Nevertheless, they were granted the *potestas effugiendi*, unless the accused was found guilty of *parricidium* and, accordingly, the penalty was the atrocious *poena cullei*.[21]

---

arson (D. 48.8.1 pr.), and in some cases the corrupt procuring of the condemnation of an innocent person on a capital charge (D. 48.8.1 pr.–1).

18 Santalucia, *Diritto e processo penale*, 147.

19 Cic. *nat. deor.* 4.74, *Cluent.* 148; D. 48.8; I. 4.18.5; Paul Sent. 5.23; Coll. 1.2–3, 8.41; see, on the statute, Jean Louis Ferrary, "*Lex Cornelia de sicariis et veneficis*," *Athenaeum* 69 (1991): 417–434; on the Sulla's unification of the two courts, see Erich S. Gruen, *Roman Politics and the Criminal Courts 149–78 BC*, 1968 (Cambridge, MA: Harvard University Press, 1968): 268; Wolfgang Kunkel, *Kleine Schriften. Zum römischen Strafverfahren und zur römischen Verfassungsgeschichte* (Weimar: Böhlaus, 1974), 58. Before Sulla's government, a court for hearing cases of poisoning (*quaestio de veneficis*) was established and this is confirmed for the year 98 BC (CIL VI 1283; see Cic. *inv.* 2.58–59). However, it probably was at least as old as the century if it did not date back even to the 120s BC. A court dealing with cases of assassination (*quaestio de sicariis*) had been created as early as 142 BC, but it is unclear if it operated only as a *quaestio extraordinaria* (Cic. *fin.* 2.54; see, moreover, for some cases of homicide in 127 BC, Asc. 45.22–26); the first attestation of a *quaestio perpetua de sicariis* is found in Cic. *Rosc. Am.* 11, 64–65 (concerning a case predating the Sullan reforms). Under Sulla's *lex Cornelia de sicariis et veneficis* of 81 BC, both forms of homicide (as well as other *species* of this crime and other crimes breaching the common peace) were dealt with by the same *quaestio*.

20 Indeed, the wording of the *lex Cornelia* did not exactly overlap Numa's provision, since the new statutory phrase was just *hominem occidere*. However, this expression did not embrace the killing of a slave (perpetrated by anyone) or of a *filius familias* (perpetrated by the *pater*); moreover, it did not punish only a mere *actus reus* (i.e. killing), but the killing perpetrated *dolo* (aforethought, with intent, knowing the effects of the conduct): see Santalucia, *Diritto e processo penale*, 145–148.

21 Cic. *Rosc. Am.* 30, 71–72, *inv.* 2.149, *Cluent.* 148; Coll. 1.3.1. According to Pol. 6.14.7, by the mid-second century BC, it had become customary to allow those condemned before the Roman people to go into exile, as long as even one *centuria* had not voted. Such a *mos* seems not abandoned in the *quaestiones perpetuae:* see Olivia Robinson, "Polybius on exile," *IVRA. Rivista internazionale di diritto romano e antico* 55 (2004): 19–27. See, moreover, Sal. *Cat.* 51.21–22 and 51.40: in these passages Sallust, through Caesar, maintains that exile is allowed for those condemned of a crime, while Polybius clearly assumes that exile is granted only before (and not after) formal condemnation. However, the former perhaps deals only with the system of the *quaestiones*, and with the short delay between the judgment and the execution of the sentence

3 Lawful homicide and "sacertas"

A possible answer to the riddle put forward in the previous paragraph is the following: Caesar was no longer a free man (*homo liber*) covered by the protections settled by the Roman *civitas*, at the procedural and substantive level. Had the *dictator* become a *homo sacer* (that is a sacred human being), the aforementioned *lex Numae* – as well as, *a fortiori*, the more recent *lex Cornelia* – could not have applied to the case at issue.

What does *homo sacer* mean? The adjective *sacer, -a, -um* belongs to the earliest level of the Latin language and it probably derives from the Indo-European root *sak-,[22] even if the precise determination of the features involved in the Latin adjective is still under debate. Nonetheless, it is undeniable that its original meaning (firmly connected to the legal-religious sphere), in archaic Rome, applied to anything – real property, animals, chattels, human beings – perceived as divine, or rather perceived as pertinent to the divine sphere and, consequently, separated from the human world.[23] The *sacrum*, in the most exact meaning, is

given to the condemned. The latter is without a doubt concerned with the *iudicia populi*, where such an interval *pro condemnato* was not allowed at all: see Gordon P. Kelly, *A History of Exile in the Roman Republic* (Cambridge: Cambridge University Press, 2006), 21–23.

22 See Fiori, *Homo sacer*, 66–72 (for a useful and complete overview); see, moreover, Giovanni Semerano, *Le origini della cultura europea*, II.2, *Dizionari etimologici. Basi semitiche delle lingue indoeuropee. Dizionario della lingua latina e di voci moderne* (Firenze: Olschki, rist. 2002), 454.

23 On the one side, Huguette Fugier, *Recherches sur l'expression du sacré dans la langue latine* (Paris: Belles Lettres, 1963): 109–125, has attempted to demonstrate that the original meaning of the root *sak– was "exister, être réel;" on the other side, Emile Benveniste, *Le vocabulaire des institutions indo-européennes*, 2, *Pouvoir, droit, religion* (Paris: Les Éditions de Minuit, 1974), 188–191, maintains that "c'est aussi en latin qu'on découvre le caractère ambigu du sacré: consacré aux dieux et chargé d'une souillure ineffaçable, auguste et maudit, digne de vénération et suscitant l'horreur. Cette double valeur est propre de *sacer.*" Moreover in the scholar's opinion: "la différence entre *sacer* et *sanctus* se voit en plusieurs circonstances. Il n'y a pas seulement la différence entre *sacer*, état naturel, et *sanctus*, résultat d'une opération;" [...] on dirait que le *sanctum*, c'est ce qui se trouve a la périphérie du *sacrum*, qui sert a l'isoler de tout contact; [...] Mais cette différence s'abolit peu à peu à mesure que la valeur ancienne du *sacer* se transfère à la sanction: *sanctus* n'est plus seulement le *murus*, mais l'ensemble du champ et tout ce qui est en contact avec le monde du divin. [...] Là s'achève l'évolution: *sanctus* qualifie alors une vertu surhumaine." Next, by emphasising that *sacer* is anything characterized by the quality *sak–, while *sanctus* is anything that has been made *sak–, James Rives, "Control of the Sacred in Roman law," in *Law and Religion in Roman Republic*, ed. Olga Tellegen-Couperus (Leiden: Brill, 2012), 165–180, 177, suggests that "in archaic Rome the word *sacer* (or *sakros*) was applied to anything spontaneously perceived as having some inherent connection with the divine." From a legal point of view, these three reconstructions fail to keep to the point. First, any etymological

anything *in proprietate deorum*, as the jurist Trebatius Testa clearly maintains.[24] Therefore, this concept, *per se*, bears no biased connotation, being just a neutral description of a legal-religious status, without any intrinsic ambivalence of meaning.

More specifically, the legal-religious imperative clause "*sacer esto*" designates a penalty to be applied if a person commits a wrong prohibited by the Roman system and perceived by the Roman community as an offense to a god or to a group of gods (even if the *actus reus* concretely harmed a human victim).[25] As

---

and primeval meaning remains a mere supposition (so that no *communis opinio* does exist: indeed, one must underline that the root *sak– is linked either to the verbs "to cut" and "to establish," or to the nouns "cause," "accusation," "dispute.") Second, the sources clearly attest that the adjective *sacer* is not constantly used to denote a natural status only. Third, the supposed ambivalence of the concept at issue is not an original feature at all. In short, the adjective *sacer*, from a legal and religious perspective, neutrally designates human beings, animals and things belonging to a god: see, *amplius*, Carlo Pelloso, "Sacertà e garanzie processuali in età regia e proto-repubblicana," in *Sacertà e repressione criminale in Roma arcaica*, ed. Luigi Garofalo (Neaples: Jovene, 2013), 64–66.

24 For an explanation of the so-called *sacertas* in terms of divine ownership (as clearly emerges from Macr. *Sat.* 3.7.3, that cites the jurist Trebatius Testa), see Bernardo Albanese, "*Sacer esto*," *Bullettino dell'Istituto di Diritto Romano 'Vittorio Scialoja'* 30 (1988): 155–177; Luigi Garofalo, *Studi sulla sacertà* (Padova: Cedam, 2005), *passim*; John Scheid, *An Introduction to Roman Religion* (Edinburgh: Edinburgh University Press, 2003), 23; *amplius*, see Pelloso, "Sacertà," 57–144.

25 Several *testimonia* link the phrase *sacer esto* to the *leges regiae*, where – in the majority of cases – the wrong prohibited by statute is committed against a human being, but the punishment (or, rather, the legal consequence) is described in terms of forfeiting to the gods (that is the wrongdoer is marked as divine property). Festus informs us of a law enacted by Romulus and Titus Tatius providing that "if a *nurus* had maltreated her *parens*, she was *sacer* to the gods of her parents." Dionysius of Halicarnassus assumes that Romulus enacted a law (also repeated in the Twelve Tables) which forbade a *patronus* to break the *fides*-bond existing with his *cliens*. The phrase *sacer esto* is also linked to the second king of Rome: Festus points out that the guarding of the fields was under Terminus's patronage. Thus, Numa provided that a person who had removed a boundary stone by ploughing was *sacer* (rather: both he himself and his oxen). Likewise, Dionysius of Halicarnassus maintains that this king decreed "if a person has removed or changed the position of the boundary stones, be the offender *hieros* to the god." Next, one finds a direct quotation from the laws of Numa in Festus: "if a person shall act otherwise (*aliuta*), he himself shall be *sacer* to Jupiter." Finally, Festus quotes a law enacted by king Servius Tullius: "if a *puer* shall have maltreated his *parens*, and this *parens* shall have uttered an *endoploratio*, the *puer* shall be *sacer* to the gods of his *parentes*." Also in the early Roman Republic one finds the phrase *sacer esto*. It is mainly connected with the *leges sacratae* prescribing that those who have done something contrary to the plebeian sworn provisions shall be *sacer* together with their slaves and property. See Fest. *verb. sign.* s.v. *Plorare* (Lindsay 260: *si parentem puer verberit ast olle plorassit paren<s>, puer divis parentum sacer esto*; *si parentem nurus verberit ast*

a result, the perpetrator, while and by committing such offence, would become the very object of divine ownership and *ipso iure*, that is to say automatically, would lose any human protection.[26]

In other words, as the offended god becomes the owner of the offender, the latter, as *homo sacer*, is neither a *liber civis* (that is a human being belonging to the community of the freemen and of the Romans), nor a *peregrinus* (that is

---

olle plorassit paren<s>, nurus divis parentum sacer esto); Fest. *verb. sign.* s.v. *Termino* (Lindsay 456: *Numa Pompilius statuit eum qui terminum exarasset et ipsum et boves sacros esset*; see Dion. Hal. 2.74.3), Fest. *verb. sign.* s.v. *Aliuta* (Lindsay 98: *si quis aliuta faxit, ipsos Iovi sacer esto*); Serv. *in Verg. Aen.* 6.609 (*ex lege XII Tabularum venit, in quibus scriptum est patronus si clienti fraudem fecerit, sacer esto*; see Dion. Hal. 2.10.3); Cic. *Tull.* 20.47 (*iubeat impune occidi*), concerning the plebeian *lex sacrata* that, enacted in 494 BC, introduced the Tribunes' inviolability (see Dion. Hal. 6.89.3, 10.35.2; Zon. 7.15); Liv. 3.55.6–7 (*eius caput Iovi sacrum esset*), concerning the *lex Valeria Horatia* of 449 BC, in the part where the Tribuns' *sacrosanctitas* was recognised by the whole *civitas* (see Fest. *verb. sign.* s.v. *Sacratae leges* [Lindsay 422]); Liv. 3.55.4–5 (*ius fasque esset occcidi*), concerning the above-mentioned *lex Valeria Horatia*, in the part where the creation of magistrates *sine provocatione* was prohibited (see Cic. *rep.* 2.54). For further (but controversial) cases, see Cic. *dom.* 17.43, *Sest.* 30.65; Dion. Hal. 5.70.2; Liv. 2.8.2 (with Plut. *Publ.* 12.1; Liv. 2.1.9, 2.2.5); Dion. Hal. 5.19.4 and Plut. *Publ.* 11.

26 Such an automatism represented a constant trait of the Roman regime concerning the *homo sacer*. Not only during the primitive *regnum* and in the early Republic, but even after the enactment of the Twelve Tables, neither a legal process against the supposed *sacer* was necessary, nor a judgment proclaiming the status of *sacer* and, implicitly, allowing anyone to kill the wrongdoer, once found guilty. Indeed, the decemviral provision *de capite civis* did cover the *cives Romani* only and who infringed a "*sacer esto*-statute" automatically lost the *status civitatis*, as well the *status libertatis* (Cic. *Sest.* 30.65: *cum* [...] *XII Tabulis sanctum esset ut neque* [...] *liceret, neque de capite nisi comitiis centuriatis rogari*; *Sest.* 34.73: *de capite* [...] *iudicari* [...] *nisi comitiis centuriatis*; *rep.* 2.61: *de capite civis Romani nisi comitiis centuriatis statui vetaret*; *rep.* 2.54: *ab omni iudicio poenaque provocari licere indicant XII Tabulae conpluribus legibus*; *leg.* 3.44: *tum leges praeclarissimae de duodecim Tabulis tralatae duae, quarum altera* [...] *altera de capite civis rogari nisi maximo comitiatu vetat; ferri de singulis nisi centuriatis comitiis noluerunt*; *leg.* 3.11: *de capite civis nisi per maximum comitiatum* [...] *ne ferunto*; Salv. *gub.* 8.5: *interfici* [...] *indemnatum quemcunque hominem etiam duodecim Tabularum decreta vetuerunt*; see Aug. *civ. Dei* 1.19; Dion. Hal. 3.22.3). See Pelloso, "Sacertà," 110–144: on the one side, Fest. *verb. sign.* s.v. *Sacer mons* (Lindsay 424: *at homo sacer is est, quem populus iudicavit ob maleficium; neque fas est eum immolari, sed, qui occidit, parricidi non damnatur; nam lege tribunicia prima cavetur, 'si quis eum, qui eo plebei scito sacer sit, occiderit, parricida ne sit'*) is read as a confuse and imprecise mention of the *lex Valeria Horatia* enacted in 449 BC, and, on the other side, the existence of *iudicia populi* directed to declare the status of *homo sacer* is ruled out. See, moreover, Leon ter Beek, "Divine Law," 28: "Being *sacer* means that all forms of protection enjoyed by all other people are lifted; in fact, a *homo sacer* is excommunicated from society and anyone may kill such a person without being punished. Moreover, the consequence of being *sacer* comes about immediately, without any kind of trial or judicial sentence. It is up to the gods to decide what will happen to the *sacer* person."

stranger, belonging to a non-Roman *civitas*), nor a *servus* (that is a slave, and as such, property of a human being). It is clear that the *homo sacer*, as such, does not belong to any human community, as he or she enters into the super-natural world. This way, the *sacertas*-mechanism reconstitutes the *pax deorum* (i.e. the situation of harmony and agreement existing between the divine and the human communities), thus granting life and prosperity to the *civitas Roma*.[27]

Since any owner, on the grounds of private law, can do whatever he or she wants with his or her properties, and since the god or the goddess, offended by the perpetration of the wrong, becomes the 'owner of the *homo sacer*, the former, on the grounds of sacred law, can do whatever he or she wants with the latter. The superhuman being can let the *homo sacer* live; it can make him or her crazy; it can make him or her die of disease or of other natural causes; it can even kill him or her by means of a human agent, that is an executor of the divine determination. Accordingly, from the human and legal point of view, no one who kills a *homo sacer* is punishable, since such killing is not prohibited and no crime is perpetrated.

So, keeping to the point, it is clear that Brutus seems totally aware that the plotters' *actus* does not fall into the limits established by the *lex Numae* and by the *lex Cornelia*; he is aware that killing Caesar, from the legal-religious perspective, is not an *actus reus*. Accordingly, he emphatically presents himself and the others as a very *longa manus* of the gods to avoid any suspicion of murder.

4 Caesar and the Republican order

How might Caesar have become a *homo sacer?* Why, therefore, could anyone lawfully kill him? The last steps along the path of his extraordinary career, if interpreted as a gradual, albeit implicit, subversion of the republican order, reveal a plausible answer.

In the years immediately before the civil war,[28] the *optimates*, on the one hand, were inclined to destabilize Caesar (whose popularity and wealth had increased after the conquest of Transalpine Gaul, and to whom the troops were more and more devoted). On the other hand, they intended to support and to im-

---

27 Francesco Sini, "Diritto e *pax deorum* in Roma antica," *Diritto@Storia* 5 (2006), available at http://www.dirittoestoria.it/5/Memorie/Sini-Diritto-pax-deorum.htm (last access May 20, 2017).
28 For the sources, see T. Robert S. Broughton, *The Magistrates of the Roman Republic*, 2 (New York and Atlanta: American Philological Association, 1951–1952): 233–271.

prove Pompey's standing (above all when the latter started siding with the senatorial oligarchy).[29]

Caesar, still in Gaul, was in an extremely problematic position.[30] He wanted to remain at the head of his army and to stand for his second consulship by proxy. His plan was to return to Rome only after he had entered the *honos*: this way, his person would not be vulnerable anymore. If he had respected Pompey's law and, therefore, he had come back as an ordinary citizen, he would have put himself at the mercy of his opponents. All this would have likely led him either to an inexorable political defeat (if prosecuted and condemned), or even to an immediate death (since assassinations were a normal *de facto* device to resolve disputes).

It was necessary to change the rules and to do so with all the rationality and firmness that had always inspired Caesar's political and military actions. The *imperator* crossed the Rubicon and, so, the *pomerium* itself. By placing himself

29 In 52 BC, Pompey entered the office of *consul* without a colleague. Therefore, he was in possession of an unprecedented *honos*. Moreover, it was more and more apparent that Caesar's position entirely depended on Pompey's authority, political friendship, and discretional choices. In 51 BC, Pompey did not contrast a motion that the Gallic provinces should be discussed in the Senate on March 1, 50 BC. In February, 50 BC, the tribune C. Scribonius Curio brought in the proposal that both Caesar and Pompey stepped down, surrendering their extraordinary commands. Consequently, Pompey shifted toward the position held by the senatorial oligarchy, endorsing the opinion that Caesar should leave Gaul on the Ides of November. In December, 50 BC, the Senate passed the proposal that Caesar should surrender his command, while the *consultum* on Pompey's resignation failed to pass. Curio's original proposal passed by a margin of 370 to 22. Anyway, no practical consequence took place. Finally, through a symbolic and powerful act, the consul Marcellus, together with the consuls-elect for the year 49, placed a sword in Pompey's hands, praying him to defend the Republic against Caesar. On January 7, 49 BC, the Senate passed a *consultum ultimum*. To Caesar, civil war was the only option.

30 If Pompey was supported by the *optimates*, Caesar enjoyed great influence amongst the tribunes. The plebeian magistrates of the year 52 proposed that he should be recalled to Rome as Pompey's colleague. Notwithstanding that, Caesar both refused this position and persuaded the tribunes themselves to present a bill that would allow him to stand *in absentia* for the consulship (that is an office he could legally hold only in 49 BC), once his command in Gaul had expired. Obviously, so long as Caesar possessed *imperium*, he could remain immune from any criminal prosecution and he could preserve his bodily safety. Thus, Caesar required either a further extension or a new proconsular command. However, campaigning for his second consulship in the normal way would have left him defenceless before entering the office. On the one hand, Pompey had proposed a law that required all candidates to stand for the office in person; on the other hand, after the law was passed and published, he added a codicil of exemption stipulating that Caesar was not deprived of his privilege. However, since this provision possessed no legal force, Caesar's safety depended on Pompey's alliance. However, the harmony between the two would not last too long.

outside the law, he intended to reshape the traditional notion of legality. With the repudiation of the traditional order, the rise to a tragic and incomparable power ineluctably starts.

The *antiquissimum pomerium* was, in fact, a legal-religious border around the city of Rome. Accordingly, Rome existed, in legal terms, only within its *pomerium:*[31] everything beyond it was merely territory belonging to Rome. What is more, inside the *pomerium*, that is *domi*, the republican magistrates who held *imperium* did not have full powers (as the *provocatio* and the tribunician *intercessio* worked as tools limiting *consules*' initiatives).[32] On the contrary, beyond the

---

31 See Gell. 13.14.1; Varr. *l.L.* 5.143; Gran. Lic. 28; Cic. *div.* 1.3, 1.95 and 2.77; Liv. 1.36.6, 6.41.4, 10.8.9; Fest. *verb. sign.* s.v. *Prohibere comitia* (Lindsay 268). The line of the *pomerium*, supposedly traced by Romulus himself, corresponding to the boundaries of the magisterial *auspicia urbana* (*finis urbani auspicii*) surrounded the urban space inaugurated by the founding auspices and, consequently, it delimited the area of the so-called *imperium domi*. Beyond the urban space, the magistrates were given the *imperium militiae* (that is a power that was either absolute or limited depending on the target pursued and on the measure carried out by the magistrate). During the republican period the most important popular assembly was convened outside the *pomerium:* Varro, indeed, did equate convening the people's *comitium* with commanding the centuriate army, and called the centuriate assembly itself the urban army (Varr. *l.L.* 6.88, 93). As a matter of fact, it was not possible to command the army within Rome's augural precincts (see Gell. 12.27.5). However, this boundary did not overlap the territorial limits imposed, during the Republic, to the *ius provocationis ad populum* (whose visive sign was the absence of the *secures*, that is the axes that in 509 BC Publicola removed from the magisterial *fasces:* Plut. *Publ.* 10.7; Val. Max. 4.1.1; *vir. ill.* 15.4; Cass. Dio 3.13.2) and to the *auxilium tribunicium*. As of fifth century, inside the *Urbs* as well as outside Rome till the *primum miliarum* from the walls (Liv. 3.20.6–7), any magisterial measure *de capite* (implying the *verberare fascibus* and the *necare securibus*) could be blocked by the Roman citizen affected by it; see Bernardo Santalucia, "*Longius ab urbe mille passum:* cittadini e *provocatio* in Italia prima delle *leges Porciae*" in *Praesidia libertatis. Garantismo e sistemi processuali nell'esperienza di Roma repubblicana. Atti Copanello 1992* (Neaples: Edizioni Scientifiche Italiane, 1994), 63–84. This spatial distinction is well explained by Roberto Fiori, "La convocazione dei comizi centuriati: diritto costituzionale e diritto augurale," *Zeitschrift der Savigny Stiftung für Rechtsgeschichte. Romanistische Abteilung* 131 (2014): 60–176, 171: if the *provocatio ad populum* was not in force, both *intra pomerium* and *extra pomerium* the magistrate would be allowed to prohibit any free discussion in the preparatory meetings, to force the citizens to approve his proposals, to put to death or to flog any opponent.

32 See, on the first *lex Valeria de provocatione* enacted in the 509 BC (Cic. *rep.* 2.53, 1.62, and *acad. pr.* 2.5.13; Val. Max. 4.1.1; Dion. Hal. 5.19.4 e 5.70.2; D. 1.2.2.16), Elena Tassi Scandone, *Leges Valeriae de provocatione. Repressione criminale e garanzie costituzionali nella Roma repubblicana* (Neaples: Jovene, 2008), *passim*. For the tribunician *intercessio*, susceptible to be used inside and even outside Rome, but not *longius ab Urbe mille passuum*, see Liv. 3.20.7 (the plebeian tribunes were allowed to exercise their negative power against any magisterial initiative conceived of as a damage to plebeians); in general, see Renzo Lambertini, "Aspetti positivo e neg-

pomerium, that is *militiae*, their military command was originally without any restriction (unless the acts carried out by the magistrates were civilian and not military in character).[33] Crossing the *pomerium*, in other words, represented a first serious infringement of the republican constitution. Better, it could even be understood as the actual subversion of the republican order as a whole.

In addition, the further grounds on which Caesar's supremacy rested implied an undeniable departure from the republican traditions and provisions. First, he concentrated on his person an extraordinary convergence of offices and powers never held by the same person at the same time. For instance, he combined the office of *dictator* with a ten-year term of consulship; he even took over some senatorial prerogatives, such as the *ius* to assign provinces, to start new wars, and to control the treasury. Second, he reunified civil and military powers. For instance, he acted as *consul*, although – through his proconsular *imperium* – he retained

ativo della *sacrosancta potestas* dei Tribuni della plebe," *Diritto@Storia* 7 (2008), available at http://www.dirittoestoria.it/7/Memorie/Sini-Diritto-pax-deorum.htm (last access May 20, 2017).

33 However, the high magistrates, empowered to convene and preside over the *comitia centuriata* by means of the *ius agendi cum populo*, could also carry out acts directed to achieve civilian targets, even though *militiae*. Thus, when a *consul* summoned the Roman people and submitted bills either to seek approval for new *leges*, or to propose a penalty, or to elect supreme magistrates for the following year, his power was not absolute. On the problems concerning nature and limits of the magisterial *imperium* in the space included between the original *pomerium* and the first mile from the Roman walls, see Theodor Mommsen, *Römisches Staatsrecht*, 1^3 (Leipzig: Verlag von S. Hirzel, 1887), 61–71, 98–105; André Magdelain, *Recherches sur l'imperium, la loi curiate et les auspices d'investiture* (Paris: Presses Universitaires de France, 1968), 45–68; Fiori, "La convocazione dei comizi centuriati," 60–176. On the gradual extension of the guarantees against the military and civic *imperium* to curb the consuls' authority over soldiers and citizens even outside the *pomerium*, see Santalucia, *Diritto e processo penale*, 52–53, 71–72. In short, one can assume that, until the second century BC, the *imperium* carried out *militiae* (that is outside Rome, both beyond and before the *primum miliarum*) authorized the magistrate – through a very summary procedure – to flog and put to death the Roman *milites*. On the contrary, between the original *pomerium* and the *primum miliarum* (as well as inside Rome), as far as the civilian sphere was concerned, any magisterial initiative implying either capital punishment or severe pecuniary fines (and, from the second century on, even corporal punishment by means of *fasces*) could be blocked. In the first century BC, not only did Sulla intend to sharpen the divide existing between civilian and military offices, as well as to reaffirm the rule banning the exercise of the *imperium militiae* within the *pomerium*. He also replaced the original line at the northern boundaries of the Italian Peninsula, making it illegal to conduct any kind of military command within its confines. This way, he practically deprived the consuls of their *imperium militiae* (since they had to reside in Italy) and gave the pro-magistrates the command of the army: see Capogrossi Colognesi, *Law and Power*, 203–204. Obviously, after these reforms, the above-mentioned problems, depending on the divide between augural boundaries and *primum miliarum*, were annihilated.

command of the army; moreover, he was granted the life title *imperator*, i.e. a title bestowed by the troops on magistrates who led them to victory. Third, he gradually and *de facto* acquired other republican powers. For instance, he was vested with the *potestas censoria*, even if *de iure* he did not hold any correspondent office.[34]

However, the singular nature of Caesar's personal status became even more obvious as a result of the absolute and plenipotentiary position he acquired by appointing himself as *dictator.*[35] To be more precise, in 49 BC, he took his first dictatorship under the guise of *comitiorum habendorum causa et feriarum Latinarum causa* (i.e. the office was held in order to convene the popular assemblies and to conduct the Latin festivals).[36] Next, he held five consecutive annual dictatorships *rei publicae constituendae causa,*[37] that is he was *dictator* for the purpose of establishing the *res publica:* the office was still temporary, although far exceeding the old republican six-month term. Finally, in 45 BC Caesar assumed the title of *dictator perpetuus,*[38] that is to say, he became *dictator* with no fixed terminal date. This, being an unprecedented figure in the republican tradition, turned out to be an apparent misjudgement, as it is likely to have accelerated his killing.

---

34 See, *amplius*, Capogrossi Colognesi, *Law and Power*, 221–225, underlying (at page 223) the following: "On the symbolic level as well, a number of innovations worked to exalt his person beyond the limits prescribed by tradition: from the purple toga that magistrates wore only on the day of a triumph but which was eventually granted him without restriction, to the laurel wreath, also originally a symbol of military triumph but which he had the right to wear at all times, to his personal retinue of bodyguards made up of senators and equestrians."

35 Mathias Gelzer, *Caesar: Politician and Statesman* (Cambridge, MA: Harvard University Press, 1968), 320–321; Ronald Syme, *The Roman Revolution* (Oxford: Oxford University Press, 1960), 50–56; Elizabeth Rawson, "Caesar: Civil War and Dictatorship," eds. John Anthony Crook, Andrew Lintott, Elizabeth Rawson, *The Cambridge Ancient History* 8 (1994): 424–467; Heinrich Siber, "Caesars Diktatur und das Prinzipat des Augustus," *Zeitschrift der Savigny Stiftung für Rechtsgeschichte. Romanistische Abteilung* 55 (1935): 99–58, 103; Jane Gardner, "The Dictator," in *A Companion to Julius Caesar*, ed. Miriam Griffin (Oxford: Wiley-Blackwell, 2009), 57–71.

36 In mid-49 BC the *praetor* M. Lepidus was allowed, by statute, to nominate a *dictator* (Cic. *Att.* 9.9.3, 9.15.2; Caes. *bell. civ.* 2.21.5). He nominated Caesar, while the latter was still at Massilia.

37 T. Robert S. Broughton, *The Magistrates of the Roman Republic*, 3 (New York and Atlanta 1952), 107–108. According to Plutarch *Caes.* 51.1 and Dio 42.20.3, Caesar held his second dictatorship for a full year: he returned to Rome from the East in September, 47 BC, for a short period, before leaving for Africa. There is a gap between the end of the second dictatorship, and the start of the third. The latter was supposed to last ten years, initially renewed annually (*Bell. Hisp.* 2.1; Cass. Dio 43.14.3), then held continuously. This seems to be a step taken to assure continuity of authority: Roman government was in danger under the demands of a general civil war.

38 App. *bell. civ.* 2.442; Plut. *Caes.* 57; Cass. Dio 44.8.4; 46.17.5; Suet. *Iul.* 76.1; Flor. 2.13.91; *vir. ill.* 78; Liv. *perioch.* 116; Zon. 10.11.

Caesar, employing, strengthening and even overcoming Sulla's model,[39] embodied the concept of '*dictator* with supreme power'. This new office represented the very paradigm for any commentator, even though it was inconsistent with the way in which dictatorship had thus far been employed and understood as a polyvalent feature.[40] In short, his role did not simply look like an anomaly or an exception with respect to the republican system whose negation was embodied by Caesar since the conspicuous monopoly on powers and honours gave him the appearance of a tyrant or a *de facto* monarch.[41]

All this was an intolerable hyperbole, above all to the men who felt right in deeming themselves to be his peers and thought that there seemed no limit to his *hybris*. Finally, in the last months of his life Caesar himself impressed a fatal acceleration on a process that seemed to be inevitable *per se*.[42]

---

39 See Broughton, *The Magistrates of the Roman Republic*, 2, 66–67; Broughton, *The Magistrates of the Roman Republic*, 3, 74–75; Arthur Keaveney, *Sulla: The Last Republican* [1983] (London: Routledge, 2005), 148–203; Ronald T. Ridley, "The dictator's mistake: Caesar's escape from Sulla," *Historia* 49 (2000): 211–229; Florian Ingrisch, *Sullas 'dictatura rei publicae constituendae' und Caesars 'dictatura rei gerendae'. Ein Vergleich* (Berlin: WVB, 2007). Late in 82, special legislation authorized the *interrex* L. Flaccus to name Sulla *dictator* – the first in 120 years, since the last dictatorship before Sulla occurred in 202 – with extraordinary powers to make laws and reorganize the constitution. He was completely free to settle the Roman polity (and without time limit, though he abdicated after about a year). His position was genuinely unrestricted: he was, in practice a king or a tyrant: see Plut. *Sull.* 32; App. *bell. civ.* 1.97–103; Dion. Hal. 5.77.4. Mostly in 81, he enacted a coherent, if questionable, program to stabilize the nobles' traditional system.
40 See Pol. 3.87–89, 6.12.5, 6.12.9; Dion. Hal. 5.73.1–2; Liv. 2.18.4–8. Indeed, the canonized view of the Roman dictatorship (grounded on the examples given by Sulla and, above all, by Caesar) maintains – seemingly without nuances and distinctions – that such an extraordinary office was granted unrestricted *imperium* and plenipotentiary jurisdiction. It moreover states that dictators administered the Roman polity autonomously and with supremacy over the consuls. On the one hand, in the period between the beginning of the fifth century and the end of the fourth century BC, the office at issue, in its original form, was given a power that resembled the consular *imperium militiae*, since the dictators served above all for consular military functions (*dictator rei gerundae causa:* literally, dictator for conducting military affairs). On the other hand, from the beginning of the third century BC up to the end of the third century BC, the office was used far less abundantly than in the previous centuries. Moreover, the *causae* attested in the sources reveal a deep change: in most cases, the *dictatores* performed just civic and religious tasks (such as the dictator for driving the nail into the temple of Jupiter; such as the dictator for holding elections, supervising sacrifices, handling the enactment of laws). See Andrew Lintott, *The Constitution of the Roman Republic* (Oxford: Oxford University Press, 1999), 109–113.
41 See Francesco De Martino, *Storia della costituzione romana*, 3 (Neaples: Jovene, 1972): 273.
42 See, *amplius*, Lintott, "The Assassination," 76, 78, 80. Caesar planned an Eastern campaign against the Parthians and, if some believed that Caesar's strategy entailed shifting the political balance of the Empire in an Eastern direction, others even suspected that he intended to conquer what was left of the world. What is more, his love affair with Cleopatra, whom Caesar himself

5 Caesar and the "lex Valeria de adfectatione regni"

The above-described conducts carried out by Caesar are susceptible to be qualified in terms of *adfectatio regni*, that is to say the crime of attempted tyranny. The details regarding the prosecution of such a crime is highly controversial. On the one hand, those who attempt to re-establish the primitive *regnum* are regularly charged with *perduellio* (that is treason) and brought to trial before the competent criminal courts.[43] On the other hand, Plutarch and Livy seem to attest the existence of a *lex Valeria* enacted in 509 B.C. that provides the status of *homines sacri* for the perpetrators of a crime statutorily labelled as *adfectatio regni*.[44]

---

had restored to Egypt's throne, was an open secret. Cleopatra's presence in Rome together with Caesarion, the son born of their relationship, and the dissolution of Caesar's previous marriage were aspects that, together with the exaggerated public exaltation of his person, made him resemble a king. Actually, many senatorial decrees heaped quasi-religious and quasi-regal honours on Caesar, before his death. Such honours did not give any real political power; however – as Dio points out (Cass. Dio 43.44–46, 44.3–8) – Caesar, whether he accepted or rejected them, was put in an invidious position: and this may have been the actual intention of the proposers.

43 See, on the prosecution of this crime, Santalucia, *Diritto e processo penale*, 47, 80, 152, 169.

44 Liv. 2.8.2: *Latae deinde leges, non solum quae regni suspicione consulem absoluerent, sed quae adeo in contrarium verterent ut popularem etiam facerent; inde cognomen factum Publicolae est. Ante omnes de provocatione adversus magistratus ad populum sacrandoque cum bonis capite eius qui regni occupandi consilia inisset gratae in volgus leges fuere*; Liv. 2.8.5: *ibi omnium primum ius iurandum populi recitat neminem regnare passuros nec esse Romae unde periculum libertati foret*; Plut. *Publ.* 12.2: ἔγραψε γὰρ νόμον ἄνευ κρίσεως κτεῖνια διδόντα τὸν βουλόμενον τυραννεῖν κτείναντα δὲ φόνου καθαρὸν ἐποίησεν, εἰ παράσχοιτο τοῦ ἀδικήματος τοὺς ἐλέγχους. See, on the *lex Valeria de adfectatione regni*, Fiori, *Homo sacer*, 325, and Tassi Scandone, *Leges Valeriae de provocatione*, 269, endorsing the view that the perpetrator of the crime became automatically a *homo sacer* and as such susceptible to be killed lawfully by anyone; *contra*, see Roberto Scevola, "L'*adfectatio regni* di M. Capitolino: eliminazione *sine iudicio* o persecuzione criminale?," in *Sacertà e repressione criminale in Roma arcaica*, ed. Luigi Garofalo (Neaples: Jovene, 2013), 275–344. See, moreover, Claire Lovisi, *Contribution à l'étude de la peine de mort sous la république romaine [509–149 av. J.-C.]* (Paris: De Boccard, 2000), 55, who maintains that the trial takes place *a posteriori* if the crime is attempted tyranny, while if the *adfectator regni* establishes a tyranny, "dans ce cas, on pouvait tuer le coupable sans attendre le jugement." See, on the republican right to put to death, *sine iudicio*, anyone who attempted to a establish a tyranny, Luis Rodríguez-Ennes, *Realidad historica y elementos legendarios en la seditio Manliana*, in *'Sodalitas'. Scritti in onore di A. Guarino*, 1 (Neaples: Jovene, 1984): 55–74; André Magdelain, *Remarques sur la 'perduellio'*, *Historia* 22 (1973): 405–422, 410. On the shadowy line dividing the *perduellio* (roughly translatable with 'treason', that is a crime usually tackled by the *tribuni plebis* since the middle of the third century BC, while the appointment of the ancient *duoviri* became virtually

Did Caesar really intend to subvert, as a tyrant, the republican order? Did he really attempt to re-establish the reign, and thus to enslave the Roman people?[45] On the one side, it is undeniable that Caesar formally refused the royal crown (even though someone suspected him as the planner of the solemn and subversive gesture carried out by the consul M. Antony on behalf of the Roman people during the festival of the *Luperci*, i.e. offering the diadem).[46] He also declined the title of king (even though the *tribuni plebis* who accused the citizens who had addressed him as *rex* were condemned and deprived of their office, notwithstanding their *sacrosanctitas*).[47] On the other side, despite the absence of any actual intention on his part to restore, *de iure*, the primitive *regnum*,[48] it is plausible that his outrageous and untraditional conducts led both the plebeian magistrates and the *optimates*[49] to consider him as a real *adfectator regni.*[50]

Indeed, the title of king and the royal crown are just exterior signs of a power that, in its substance, is conceived of as annihilation of the republican order (at least according to the *optimates*' view).[51] As a matter of fact, the crime of *adfec-*

---

obsolete) and the *adfectatio regni* repressed by the above-mentioned *lex Valeria* (through the religious-legal mechanism of the *sacertas*), see Pelloso, "Sacertà," 116–118, nt. 90.

45 As for Brutus's and Cassius's ideas (focused, first, on the violation by Caesar of the plebeian *sacrosanctitas*, and, secondly, on the early republican oath against the *adfectatores regni*), see App. *bell. civ.* 2.137–139, 144, 4.90–98. Cicero depicts Caesar's consulship of 59 BC as an actual *regnum* and maintains that Caesar had already had this in mind as early as his aedileship (Suet. *Iul.* 9.2). Finally he describes him in terms of *rex* in correspondence of 45 BC (Cic. *Att.* 13.37.2, *fam.* 6.19.2).

46 Cic. *Phil.* 2.84–7, 3.12, 5.38, 13.17, 13.31, 13.40, 13.31; Liv. *perioch.* 116; App. *bell. civ.* 2.108, 2.456–458; Cass. Dio 44.10.1–3, 44.11.2–3, 45.31.3; 46.49.2; Vell. 2.56.4; Suet. *Iul.* 79; Plut. *Caes.* 61; Flor. 2.13.91. It must be highlighted that Caesar used the episode *pro se*, ordering Antony's offer, and his refusal, to be recorded in the Fasti.

47 Cic. *Phil.* 13.31; Nic. Dam. *Caes.* 20.69–70; Liv. *perioch.* 116; Vell. 2.68.4–5; Val. Max. 5.7.2; Suet. *Iul.* 79–80; Plut. *Caes.* 61 and *Ant.* 12; Cass. Dio 44.9.3–44.10.4; 46.49.2; App. *bell. civ.* 2.108, 109, 122, 138; Iul. Obseq. 70; Zon. 10.11. Actually, the two tribunes, Caesetius and Marullus, were deposed from office not directly by the dictator himself, but on the proposal of a fellow tribune, that is C. Helvius Cinna.

48 De Martino, *Storia della costituzione romana* 3, 271–273.

49 App. *bell. civ.* 2.107; Liv. *perioch.* 116; Suet. *Iul.* 78; Nic. Dam. *Caes.* 22.76–79; Cass. Dio 44.8.6.

50 Liv. *perioch.* 116: [...] *quod Epidio Marullo et Caesetio Flavio tr. pl. invidiam et tamquam regnum adfectanti*; Val. Max. 5.7.2: *is tribunus plebis cum Marullo collega invidiam ei tamquam regnum affectanti iecerat*; Vell. 2.68.4: *immodica et intempestiva libertate usos adversus C. Caesarem Marullum Epidium Flavumque Caesetium tribunos plebis, dum arguunt in eo regni voluntatem* (see, moreover, App. *bell. civ.* 2.108; Nic. Dam. *Caes.* 20.69); Suet. *Iul.* 80: *Brutus, quia reges eiecit, consul primus factus est: // hic, quia consules eiecit, rex postremo factus est.*

51 Isabelle Cogitore, *Le doux nom de liberté. Histoire d'une idée politique dans la Rome antique* (Bordeaux: Ausonius Éditions, 2011), 108; Valentina Arena, *'Libertas' and the Practice of Politics*

tatio regni encompasses any wrong perpetrated against the republican *libertas*. This is a syncretic concept implying, at the constitutional level, that all the powers (*potestates*) come, directly or indirectly, from the *populus Romanus:* this, as an electoral assembly, votes the magistrates; as a lawgiver, passes the laws; as a judge, is allowed to sentence to death.[52] If during the (Etruscan) *regnum* the *res* had belonged to a single plenipotentiary, if not even capricious, 'magistrate' (*res regis*), during the Republic the *res* belonged to the people as a whole (*res populi*).[53] Accordingly, the magistrates, *in potestate populi*, were representatives of the Roman people (that was, on the contrary, *in sua potestate*)[54] and the senators, who were ex-magistrates, embodied the ruling oligarchy invested with powers and functions of coordination, supervision, and advise (by means of their *consultum* and *auctoritas*).[55]

From the beginning of the Republic, therefore, those who stepped outside the boundaries of the new constitutional order (that is the system replacing the primitive kingdom where there was no *res publica*, but a *res regis*) were labelled as *adfectatores regni*. When someone's power threatened to disrupt the balance in the new free order (as establishing the *regnum*, by statute, was not necessary), an accusation of *perduellio* (in terms of attempted subversion of the popular power) could be brought against him.

Notwithstanding that, according to the *lex Vaeleria* and under particular (and so far unknown) conditions, such criminals could even be put to death *sine iudicio*.[56]

Accordingly, out of his *de facto* tyrannical behaviour, Caesar could be qualified as a *homo sacer*, whether he had intended to modify formally the shape of the *res publica*, or not. The penalty "*sacer esto*," as we already know, removed the wrongdoer from any human community and consigned him to the sphere

in the Late Roman Republic (Cambridge: Cambridge University Press, 2012), 6, 26, 81, 116; Carlo Venturini, *Studi di diritto delle persone e di vita sociale in Roma antica* (Neaples: Satura Editrice, 2014), 483.

52 See, *amplius*, Giovanni Lobrano, *Res publica res populi. La legge e la limitazione del potere* (Torino: Giappichelli, 1996), *passim*.

53 Cic. *rep.* 1.39, 2.23; Liv. 2.1.1; Tac. *ann.* 1.1.1. See Francesco De Martino, *Storia della costituzione romana*, 3, 138: the predominant idea lying behind the noun *libertas* was not the so-called 'democratic freedom'; indeed, *libertas* (i.e., etymologically, 'belonging to the people') meant denial of *regnum* and, thence, absence of any tyrannical domination. See, moreover, Giuseppe Valditara, *Saggi sulla libertà dei romani, dei cristiani e dei moderni* (Soveria Mannelli: Rubbettino, 2007), 27.

54 D. 49.15.7.1; Varr. *l.L.* 9.6; Cic. *off.* 1.124, *de orat.* 2.167; Sen. *ep.* 14.7.

55 Cic. *rep.* 2.56, *rep.* 3.37, *leg.* 3.28, *dom.* 130, *Sest.* 137.

56 On tyrannicide, in general, see Andrew Lintott, *Violence in Republican Rome* (Oxford: Oxford University Press, 1999), 53–58.

of the gods. As such, Caesar would have lost any protection afforded by membership in the Roman *civitas*; he would have become property of the gods of Freedom and anyone, as a divine *longa manus*, could have killed him with impunity. His killers would not have been prosecuted.[57] His body would not have been buried, his goods would have been sold, his provisions, acts, and measures would have been considered void.[58]

This reconstruction[59] seems to be less sound in regard to the events occurring after Caesar's death. Since protecting the conspirators represented an ultimate need, qualifying Caesar's conducts in terms of tyranny turned out to be the easiest way to achieve this goal. A different way was taken, and what actually happened after Caesar's death is certainly remarkable, both from a political and a legal perspective.

First, in the Senate meeting of March 17, after a troubled session of the assembly,[60] an amnesty, supported by Antony, was voted: the *consultum* proclaimed that the plotters had committed murder (this implying that the Senate assumed that *lex Numae* and the *lex Cornelia* applied to the case), but, at the same time, it stipulated that they were not punishable. Second, it did not formally qualify Caesar as a tyrant (this implying that the Senate assumed that the *lex Valeria* did not apply to the case): thus, even against the opinion endorsed by some, in the same session the Senate voted to ratify Caesar's appointments to office and all his other measures (whether enacted or merely planned).[61] Third, after Piso's speech, the Senate authorised solemn funeral and burial for Caesar, as well as the public reading of his will.[62]

The senators did not rule out, from a legal perspective, the grounds for the *sacertas*-mechanism; they just decided, from a political perspective, to follow an-

---

57 App. *bell. civ.* 4.94: ἐπεὶ δὲ ἐγένετο, αὐτίκα ἡ βουλὴ τὴν κοινὴν γνώμην ἐξέφηνε, σαφῶς μὲν ὅτε καὶ γέρα τυραννοκτονικὰ ἐψηφίζοντο εἶναι: ἐπισχόντος δὲ αὐτοὺς Ἀντωνίου καθ' ὑπόκρισιν ἀταξίας καὶ οὐδ' ἡμῶν ἀξιούντων διὰ γέρα τῇ πόλει μᾶλλον ἢ δι' αὐτὴν τὴν πατρίδα βοηθεῖν, τοῦδε μὲν ἀπέσχοντο, οὐκ ἐθέλοντες ἐφυβρίζειν τῷ Καίσαρι, ἀλλὰ μόνης τῆς τυραννίδος ἀπηλλάχθαι, ἀμνηστίαν δὲ ἁπάντων ἐψηφίσαντο εἶναι καὶ σαφέστερον ἔτι, φόνου μὴ εἶναι δίκας.
58 Suet. *Iul.* 82: *corpus occisi in Tiberim trahere, bona publicare, acta rescindere* (see App. *bell. civ.* 2.128, 133–136, 3.18; Cass. Dio, 44.35.1; Plut. *Brut.* 20).
59 See Fiori, *Homo sacer*, 458, on the basis of App. *bell. civ.* 3.18.
60 App. *bell. civ.* 2.127–134.
61 App. *bell. civ.* 2.135: τοιαῦτα εἰπόντος τοῦ Ἀντωνίου σὺν ἀνατάσει τε καὶ ὁρμῇ βαρυτέρᾳ, γίγνεται δόγμα, ἡσυχαζόντων ἤδη καὶ ἀγαπώντων ἁπάντων, φόνου μὲν οὐκ εἶναι δίκας ἐπὶ τῷ Καίσαρι, κύρια δὲ εἶναι τὰ πεπραγμένα αὐτῷ πάντα καὶ ἐγνωσμένα, ἐπεὶ τῇ πόλει συμφέρει.
62 App. *bell. civ.* 2.136: θορύβου δὲ καὶ ἀγανακτήσεως γενομένης παρὰ πάντων, καὶ μάλιστα τῶν τι καὶ ἐλπιζόντων ἐκ τῶν διαθηκῶν αὐτοῖς ἔσεσθαι, τάς τε διαθήκας ἐς τὸ μέσον ἔδοξε προφέρειν καὶ θάπτειν τὸν ἄνδρα δημοσίᾳ.

other way. Nevertheless, it is apparent that this was a solution of mere convenience, rather than a legally and religiously grounded answer. Before the Senate, Antony pragmatically emphasizes that, if the killing of Caesar was to be considered as a 'tyrannicide', all the legal acts concluded by Caesar in the last five years should have been considered void and each public office should have been dismissed. This utilitarian approach gains the support of the majority. Hence, the Senate again annihilates the republican order: the same order that, first, Caesar had allegedly breached and, then, the conspirators had intended to re-establish. Paradoxically, the senatorial pardon – notwithstanding its internal and external coherence *de iure* – is, *de facto*, both a denial of the republican values and an acknowledgement of the order infringed by Caesar. Indeed, in accordance with the views of the Senate's majority, on the one hand, the regime shaped in the *lex Valeria* is not enforced; on the other hand, the killing is qualified in terms of murder, even though it is firm belief that the perpetrators do not deserve any punishment.

6 Some conclusions

During Caesar's funeral, Shakespeare presents all the ambiguity of the situation, reconfiguring Caesar's assassination as "the foundational violence of the Roman empire."[63] This is a dramatic event presented as unlawful (in contrast with the view supporting the enforcement of the traditional sacral law), but historically necessary (in order to found a new order that will turn out to look as formally homogeneous and practically heterogeneous with the republican tradition). Shakespeare celebrates the contingency of the codes of conduct, as well as the dialectics existing between antagonistic forces: and he does so, by emphasizing the ambivalence implied in the main character of the tragedy, Caesar, his life and his death.[64] He presents the inescapable run of history, and conceives of the historical *processus* in the path toward the future as recognition, inclusion, and

63 Richard Wilson, *Shakespeare in French Theory: King of Shadows* (London, New York: Routledge, 2007), 180, quoting from René Girard, *A Theatre of Envy: William Shakespeare* (New York, Oxford: Oxford University Press, 1991).

64 As Julia Griffin, "Shakespeare's Julius Caesar and the Dramatic Tradition," 371, underlines: "every major event in which he was involved might be regarded in two ways: was he merciful or corrupt in his attitude to Catiline? Were his conquests in Gaul and Britain to be admired or abhorred? How far was he responsible for the Civil War? Was his assassination a murder or a tyrannicide?"

transfiguration of the past: the republican thesis, symbolized by Brutus and Cassius, and the Caesarean antithesis will merge into the Augustan synthesis.

Antony, in line with the targets achieved by means of the *senatus consultum* of March 17, openly ratifies the order represented by the *dictator.* Caesar is depicted as a man who loved his people and hated any royal power; the crowd is even inclined to revenge Caesar's death, overcoming the senatorial settlement. Caesar is not a criminal who, by attempting to dissolve the republican *libertas*, becomes property of the gods (*sacer*); he is a noble hero, a god.[65] Accordingly, Brutus is not a divine agent; he is, formally, a murderer. Nevertheless, Antony himself has no hesitation in praising the enemy, Brutus, as one of the noblest Romans and as a man aiming at the common good and worthy of the rites of burial. This is a subtle and implicit recognition: the words pronounced by Brutus, in Act II, are not vain rhetorical devices. The latter had addressed the conspirators as real purgers (not as butchers and murderers), had urged them to kill Caesar with no wrath and envy, and had qualified the project as necessary.

Through this powerful picture, Shakespeare does not treat Brutus simply as a rhetorician who tries to deny the dreadful realities of the plot and to idealize a cruel assassination by describing it in religious terms. Through this powerful picture, Shakespeare describes – and, according to Roman law, quite correctly so[66] – the republican regime, entailing the so-called *sacertas* for those who attempted to dissolve the Roman *libertas*.

---

65 Antony had even called him "the noblest man // That ever lived in the tide of times," 3.1.256–57. Stephen Weinstock, *Divus Julius*, 411, points out, Caesar was "as an imaginative and daring religious reformer, who planned and created new cults, accepted extraordinary honours and died when he was about to become a divine ruler – a reformer who did not want to appear as an innovator [...] but to be guided by tradition; and yet one who in the end radically broke with it."

66 From a legal-religious perspective, the conspirators are not sacrificers, as Brutus erroneously maintains. Festus clearly attests that the *immolatio* of the *homo sacer* is *nefas:* Fest. *verb. sign.* s.v. *Sacer mons* (Lindsay 424): *at homo sacer is est, quem populus iudicavit ob maleficium; neque fas est eum immolari, sed, qui occidit, parricidi non damnatur; nam lege tribunicia prima cavetur, 'si quis eum, qui eo plebei scito sacer sit, occiderit, parricida ne sit'.* In other words, since such a *homo*, being *sacer*, already belongs to a god and since the sacrifice is a ritual implying the transfer of the *victima* "du domaine humain à celui des dieux" (Francesca Prescendi, *Décrire et comprendre le sacrifice*, [Stuttgart: Franz Steiner, 2007], 35), it is not *fas* (i.e. it is impossible from a religious and legal point of view) that who kills a *homo sacer* performs a sacrifice: "Was *sacer* ist bildet schon den Besitz der Götter, wird nicht erst gemacht", as Karol Kerényi, *Die antike Religion. Ein Entwurf von Grundlinien* (Düsseldorf and Körf: E. Diederichs, 1953), 84, remarks (see Garofalo, *Studi sulla sacertà*, 117; Pelloso, "Sacertà," 131).

Part Four **Performance**

Gary Watt

Notes on *A Strange Eventful History*

"Shakespeare didn't write this stuff to be read. It's like sheet music. You don't just look at it; it's just a bunch of notes on a page. This was meant to be played."

The actor Kevin Kline speaking on John Barton's *The Shakespeare Sessions* (Storyville Films, Dir: Jacoby, 2003)[1]

This paper retells the story of a strange event. In the summer of 2016, I joined The Song Company of Australia (described on its website as "the continent's leading vocal ensemble")[2] in rehearsing and performing a Shakespeare-themed show that I had co-written with their Artistic Director, the composer Antony Pitts.[3] The idea behind *A Strange Eventful History* ('*ASEH*') was to mark the four-hundredth anniversary of Shakespeare's death with a symphony of famous Shakespearean speeches and musical pieces connected by a playful narrative. The narrative, which was loosely structured according to the "seven ages of man" as presented by Jaques in Shakespeare's *As You Like It* (2.7.140–67),[4] was threaded throughout by the conceit that The Song Company had assisted scientists in recovering snippets from the original soundscape of Shakespeare's London. Thus the narrator introduces the show as "a journey back to Shakespeare's London and the journey of a lifetime from birth to the last scene of all" (*ASEH*, prologue). Another idea, at least for my part, was to experiment with some of the performance theories and practical techniques that I had written about in a book – *Shakespeare's Acts of Will: Law Testament and Properties of Performance* – that was published around the time of the show.[5]

1 Kevin Kline might have been recalling Harley Granville-Barker's words in the Introduction to his *Prefaces to Shakespeare:* "The text of a play is a score waiting performance" (London: Batsford, 1930), 5.

2 See http://song.company (last access September 6, 2017).

3 I am grateful to Antony Pitts, Marc Stauch and Sean Mulcahy for their helpful comments on a draft of this paper. I am to blame for duff notes that remain. My thanks also to Daniela Carpi, Chiara Battisti and Sidia Fiorato for the invitation to present these reflections at the conference *As You Law It: Negotiating Shakespeare* (Verona, 2016). I also want to take this opportunity to record my thanks to all members of The Song Company, those on stage and off, who did so much to entertain me and organise me and make me welcome.

4 William Shakespeare, *As You Like It*, The Arden Shakespeare, 3rd series, ed. Juliet Dusinberre (London: Bloomsbury, 2006). All references to Shakespeare are to the most recent editions in The Arden Shakespeare unless otherwise stated.

5 Gary Watt, *Shakespeare's Acts of Will: Law, Testament and Properties of Performance* (London: Bloomsbury Arden Shakespeare, 2016). See, further, Sidia Fiorato, "Gary Watt's *Acts of Will:* A

https://doi.org/10.1515/9783110591514-013

One of those techniques is a poetic method that is subtly at work in much of Shakespeare's dramatic writing. I call it "fractional inference." In essence, it is a method of scattering fragments of sound throughout a passage of a text and then combining the fragments to produce a recognizable word. The fragments provoke the subconscious to seek a resolution that at first eludes the ear (and eye, if the text is being read) until it finally finds completion in some word or phrase that combines an audible sense with the intended literal (dictionary) sense of the target word. I call this target word the "tenor" word. The term "tenor," with its obvious musical overtones, is actually borrowed from the vernacular of literary critique in which it describes the meaning or sense carried by the "vehicle" of a metaphor (in the phrase "love is like a red, red rose," love is the tenor and rose is the vehicle). In a case of "fractional inference," the tenor word combines the scattered sound fragments into a pleasing whole. The satisfaction of the resolution can be heightened by postponing the express presentation of the tenor word by using homonymic or homophonic forms of the word. Homophones tease the subconscious to within tantalizing proximity of the tenor word so that the final presentation of the true tenor becomes all the more pleasing. Occasionally the tenor word never appears, but is left to the imagination to create.

By way of illustration, I will repeat, in brief, an example of the phenomenon that I discuss in *Shakespeare's Acts of Will.* (A further, new, example is presented later on in this paper). Set out next are four lines from Shakespeare's *Julius Caesar* which feature in Antony's rhetorical effort in the funeral scene to stir the mob against Brutus. I have curtailed the passage for present purposes at the word "stir." "Stir" is the tenor word, and the reader will note how sound fragments of the word are scattered through the four lines and on two occasions the sound sense (but not the dictionary sense) of the word appears homophonically in "ye-ster-day" and "ma-ster-s," thus the culminating appearance of the word "stir" is the rhetorically satisfying third iteration in the tricolon "ster" – "ster" – "stir." I have underlined and bracketed the relevant sound fragments to show how Shakespeare sometimes encloses one fractional version of the word within another to produce a layering or amplification of sound effect:

> But ye**ster**day the word of Caesar might
> Have [**st**ood again{**st** the w**or**}rld. Now lies he th**ere**],
> And none [**s**o poor **t**o do him rev**er**]ence.
> O ma**ster**s! If I were disposed to **stir** (*Julius Caesar* 3.2.119–123)

Consummate Performance," *Cardozo Electronic Law Bulletin* (2016): 1–19; and Daniela Carpi, "Review of *Shakespeare's Acts of Will: Law Testament and Properties of Performance*," *Pólemos* 10.2 (2016): 453–457.

The reader will note that within the tricolon "ster" – "ster" – "stir" three fractional versions of the "stir" sound are sandwiched between the homophonic pair "ster" and "ster." The fact that one of these homophonic versions is enclosed within another means that there is a three-fold layering: a fractional "stir" sound inside a fractional "stir" sound inside the pair "ster" and "ster." We have then a tricolon of tricolons – the first is "ster" – "ster" – "stir," the second is the three fractional versions of the "stir" sound, the third is the three layers in which the sound is enclosed within the sound. As with the musical tricolon of melody, harmony and rhythm, the overall effect is rhetorically stirring stuff indeed.

The technique of "fractional inference" – by which the audience is prompted to infer a whole from fractional parts – is a sound effect which has equivalents or close comparators in musical theory. One such is so-called "thematic transformation" or "thematic metamorphosis." It is a common technique of musical composition whereby the composer produces a pleasing resolution or reiteration of a theme by scattering its component motifs and other elements throughout the work. The musical theme may be stated in complete form early in the piece so that it becomes the subject of subsequent fragmentation and variation; or the fragments may come first, to be combined later in a climactic statement of the theme; or the two sequences ("whole followed by fractions" and "fractions followed by whole") may be employed together in the same work. It may seem strange to commence these notes with reference to a single technical point of comparison between music and literary text, but the broader point is that the techniques in both arts are united by their pleasing effect upon the ear. It is my argument that such pleasing sound effects are the most direct point of connection between the arts of music and dramatic text and the arts of law, for they share a rhetorical concern to persuade through pleasing sensual, including auditory, effects. As the classical rhetorician Quintilian wrote:

> Composition, therefore, as it seems to me, plays the part of a sort of...bowstring in giving direction and force to our thoughts. This is why the best scholars are all convinced of its great value, not only for pleasure but also for its emotional impact, first because nothing can penetrate to the emotions if it stumbles at the ear – at the threshold, as you might say; and, secondly, because we are naturally attracted by harmony.
>
> The best judge of Composition is the ear, which senses completeness, feels the lack when something is incomplete, is offended by unevenness, soothed by smoothness. (Quintilian, *Institutio Oratoria*, 4.9–10, 116)[6]

6 Donald A Russell (trans.), *The Orator's Education*, Volume IV, Loeb Classical Library (Cambridge, MA: Harvard University Press, 2014).

Rhetoric is the most substantial justification for the inclusion of these performance notes in the present set of essays, concerned as they are with Shakespeare and the law. A less substantial, more circumstantial, link between *A Strange Eventful History* and the law is the fact that the fifth age in Jaques' seven ages of man is the age of "the justice." I want to suggest that Jaques' seven ages of man can be appreciated in a new acoustic sense as a series of seven notes on sound and silence. In *ASEH*, each of the six singers was allocated one of the first six ages. We have the "mewling" infant;[7] the "whining schoolboy";[8] the "sighing" lover;[9] the swearing soldier ("full of strange oaths") whose fiery instinct is to "quarrel" even in the cannon's mouth;[10] the justice "full of wise saws and common instances"[11] ("common instances" alludes to rhetorical commonplace sayings, such as Justice Shallow's "death is certain to all, all shall die" (*2 Hen IV*, 3.2.27)); and, the pantaloon whose "big manly voice" has turned again "to childish treble, pipes / And whistles in his sound" (2.7.163–4).[12] The seventh age is the age of oblivion, with its deathly decline into silent nothingness. His is the scene "[t]hat ends this strange eventful history" (2.7.165). The seventh age was allocated to the musical director Antony Pitts who throughout the entire show accompanied the singers on a Fender Rhodes electric piano on which he also intermittently played dances including the charming *Mal Sims* by Giles Farnaby (c. 1560–1640). The Fender Rhodes wonderfully evoked the tripping, daintiness of a Shakespearean virginal whilst simultaneously playing up to the conceit that the performers were sharing a soundscape revealed by space-age scientific instrumentation. The seventh age of man is a dance of death. His voice is silent.

Jaques' justice represents the life of man at its zenith before things start to go downhill. He is in all respects a full figure. Physically he has his "fair round belly with good capon lin'd"; intellectually he is "[f]ull of wise saws and modern instances" (2.7.157). After the age of the justice, Jaques informs us that the "sixth age shifts." The man wanes thin. The trousers have to be tightened at the waist ("His youthful hose well sav'd, a world too wide / For his shrunk shank" (2.7.161–2)); and eventually he wastes away to nothing. Jaques' depiction of the justice is a de-piction indeed; it is highly visual – we have his "eyes severe and beard of formal cut" in addition to the sight of his "fair round belly." The mouth is framed by the beard, and although both mind and mouth are full of

7 Played by Anna Fraser (soprano).

8 Played by Andrew O'Connor (bass baritone).

9 Played by Hannah Fraser (mezzo soprano).

10 Played by Mark Donnelly (baritone).

11 Played by Richard Black (tenor).

12 Played by Susannah Lawergren (soprano).

sayings, our imagined sense of sound is arguably drowned out by the overpowering sense of sight. I hear a warning here about the overpowering influence of the visual in law – a theme on which many law and humanities scholars have reflected.[13] It is said that justice must be seen to be done. Is it not equally true that justice must be heard?

The sense of sound – even the lack of sound and the strain to achieve a fair hearing – takes us back to rhetoric. Shakespeare's playhouse dramas and the performance of law are deeply connected to each other by their shared origins in the classical arts of rhetoric. The word "rhetoric" ultimately derives from Proto-Indo-European for the spoken word (**wretor*), and related to it is the Greek *rhetra*, which came to denote a ceremonial or authoritative utterance. Today we think of the "writ" – the written word – as an epitome of stated legal power, but a different and deeper authority emanates from the word spoken. Audible speech adds an appealing sense of sound to the silent rhetorical qualities of script, notwithstanding that silent script may acquire an imagined auditory quality by means of the mind's inner voice. Rhetoric of the spoken sort may be called the art of persuading through the music of sweet sound. For Shakespeare, music is the food of love, but lover's words also have a "silver-sweet sound" that is "like softest music to attending ears" (2.2.165–6). An appreciation of the audible quality of Shakespeare and law in performance will bring us closer to a sense of sound justice than can be achieved by a silent appreciation of the logic – the *logos* – of the written word alone. As David Levin put it, the "development of our capacity for listening exercises and develops our (bodily felt) sense of justice. The primary sense of justice is not seeing, but hearing."[14]

There is a difference between the word on the page and the word spoken. When I teach my student advocates how to speak well, I never focus exclusively upon the logical sense of the words used or even upon formal stylistic features of the script. I emphasize the musicality of pleasing speech and the moderation –

---

13 See Leif Dahlberg, ed., *Visualizing Law and Authority: Essays on Legal Aesthetics* (Berlin: de Gruyter, 2012); Peter Goodrich, *Legal Emblems and the Art of Law: Obiter Depicta as the Vision of Governance* (New York: Cambridge University Press, 2014); Ruth Herz, *The Art of Justice: The Judge's Perspective* (Oxford: Hart, 2012); Paul Raffield, *Images and Cultures of Law in Early Modern England: Justice and Political Power, 1558–1660* (Cambridge: Cambridge University Press, 2004); Richard K. Sherwin, *Visualizing Law in the Age of the Digital Baroque: Arabesques & Entanglements* (Abingdon: Routledge, 2011); Anne Wagner and Richard K. Sherwin, eds., *Law, Culture and Visual Studies* (Heidelberg; New York; London: Springer, 2014).

14 David Levin, *The Listening Self: Personal Growth, Social Change and the Closure of Metaphysics* (Abingdon: Routledge, 1989), 184; cited in Richard Dawson, "Listening," in *Justice as Attunement* (Abingdon: Routledge, 2014), 163–169.

indeed, the musical modulation – of the voice, which should be tuned to produce ease of speech and hearing so as to bring out with fidelity the sound quality of the script. Equally important is to learn to listen well and not merely to rely upon what is written down. There are, as has been said, "difficulties [...] in the tendency to reduce [...] sensory knowledge to visual terms[...] A word is more than a sign of something [...] It is a cry, a voice."[15] The appeal to human well-being and the human psyche in pleasing sound is so deep that justice silenced must surely amount to justice lost. We might have our day in court, but unless we are free to speak and to voice our concerns audibly we will not have had our hearing. Might it be that the sounding out of arguments and the hearing of voice are together absolutely essential to our sense that justice has been done? Richard Dawson and James Parker, legal scholars from New Zealand and Australia respectively, have recently and separately called for greater attention to the acoustic quality of justice.[16] It may be that the aural sense figures more prominently as a concern in common law jurisdictions due to the adversarial mode of trial procedure, but even in countries with a more documentary or inquisitorial system the call should not fall on deaf ears. One of the pillars of due process and of a fair trial – the hearing of both sides to an argument – has been telling us, since it was first rendered in the Latin *audi alterem partem*, that audition is the key sense in a judicial hearing. To an Anglophone ear the auditory connection between forensic rhetoric and other species of performative rhetoric is pronounced in the French word "audience," which the French lawyer hears as a legal hearing and an English speaker hears as the body of theatrical playgoers. In Anglophone jurisdictions we sometimes talk of judicial "hearings," but even the more usual word "trial" has a strained, perhaps strange, connection to audition. The verb "to try" seems to have its origins in ideas of sieving or separating, which ideas equally underlie such judicial words as "discern" and "discriminate." (Shakespeare uses "sift" in a judicial sense in *All's Well That Ends Well* where the king, having put material, written and oral evidence to the proof, states "We'll sift this matter further" (5.3.124)). Thus trial and audition can, at a strain, be understood to be connected by a sense of straining – the sense that a judge is called upon to discern the sweet voice of justice from the general noise of the debate or, to put it another way (and to make another etymological connection), to sift the true note from the general "clamour" of the claims. The

---

15 Walter J. Ong, *Ramus, Method, and the Decay of Dialogue: From the Art of Discourse to the Art of Reason* (Chicago: The University of Chicago Press, 1958), 109–110; cited in Richard Dawson, "Rhetoric," in *Justice as Attunement*, 220–226.

16 Dawson, *Justice as Attunement*; see especially the chapters on "Listening" and "Rhetoric"; James Parker, *Acoustic Jurisprudence* (Oxford: Oxford University Press, 2015).

judge's task of hearing or attunement becomes, therefore, the task of being able to tell which account rings true, and, in response to what is heard, to sound a new note in their judicial speech. Juris-diction is, after all, the necessary start and conclusion to any fair hearing that claims to give sound judgment.

These linguistic correspondences between sound and law are something more than puns. The metaphor of the legal hearing may be a dead metaphor but when it is disinterred a sound can be heard in it. Let me pause on that pairing "dis-in-terred" and "heard-in-it." As is the case with so many rhetorical and poetical devices, that pairing seduces our ear and our sense of sound before it seeks to reason with our sense of logic. In the pairing "dis-in-terred" and "heard-in-it" assonance is amplified by a structural palindromic technique that may be considered a species of chiasmus. Paired sounds move one way and then the other, as if echoing off a wall. "Dis-in-terred" bounces back as "heard-in-it" so that, through the assonance of paired sounds, the paired words become in the most literal sense resonant of each other. This echo-effect captures our attention and makes us attend to other reverberations created in the mind through sound. For example, we become aware, albeit subconsciously, that the echoing pair has produced a pleasing structural sense of balance. This sound sense of balance has numerous musical equivalents – for example juxtaposed crescendo and diminuendo or the use of ascending and descending scales. The idea of scales and balance can be playfully productive in our appreciation of the musical sweetness of sound justice. In *A Strange Eventful History*, each of the seven ages of man is introduced by a stanza written as a variation on Shakespeare's (Jaques') version and delivered by the narrator. For the age of the justice, we have the following iambic pentameter lines:

> See the justice keep score with scales and notes
> Ignoring weighty planks while sawing motes
> When sharp indentures the innocent bite
> The judge's jaw should set all things aright
> With evident eyes and fair-hearing ears
> Speaking sound judgment and drowning down tears (*ASEH*, the justice)

When the forms of law bite, the jaw of the law should speak substantial justice. Indenture is an old form of legal document that was typically cut down the middle to produce corresponding part and counterpart containing identical script, so that the two parties each had a portion of the original whole and a complete copy of the document's terms. The line of the cut was deliberately jagged like the intersecting teeth of a jaw, so that the original part was a true and perfect fit for none other than its original counterpart. It was an early technological method of fraud-prevention.

Let us dwell a little longer and more deeply upon the musical metaphor. Music is made up of melody, harmony and rhythm. It is most pleasing and persuasive to human sense when it is rhetorically constituted by the trinity of these elements, but each of the three can be played with; indeed the highest art – the discretionary and equitable aspect – consists in the judicious bending of the formal rules. Regular scales played in metronomic strict time are no more pleasing or humane than formal rules strictly and unwaveringly applied in law. A series of scale exercises is hardly more musical than a strict law is just. Justice, in music as in law, requires art as well as technical skill. The rhythmic metre of Shakespeare's verse, especially his iambic pentameter, is no doubt a large part of what makes it pleasing. The pairing of unstressed and stressed beats in the iambic foot ("dee-DUM") is said to be resonant of the "lub-DUB" of a human heartbeat. Commenting on iambic pentameter, Peter Groves observes that "Shakespeare's meter informs the actor's production of emotional meaning through rhythm… the rhythm can seem an echo to the sense."[17]

In addition to melody, harmony and rhythm, there is a fourth or master element – one that constitutes and combines and transcends all other elements. In a sense it is an anti-element. In both music and law it goes by the name of "silence." It is telling that justice systems based on juris-diction nearly always enshrine a right to silence. In English law, a criminal accused's right to silence is now exercised with this official caution: "You do not have to say anything, but it may harm your defence if you do not mention, when questioned, something which you later rely on in court. Anything you do say may be given in evidence."[18] Silence is very often more eloquent than words.[19] To take a musical example, each section of Pärt's setting of the Latin translation of the St John Passion in the Vulgate is "allocated a certain constant set of notes and durations throughout" and "Even the silences between sections have a precise duration specified by the number of syllables in the final word of the preceding sen-

17 Peter L. Groves, "'My heart dances': Performing Emotion through Shakespeare's Rhythms," in *Shakespeare and Emotions: Inheritances, Enactments, Legacies*, eds. R. S. White, Mark Houlahan and Katrina O'Loughlin (Palgrave Shakespeare Studies: Palgrave Macmillan, 2015), 84.

18 The Criminal Justice and Public Order Act 1994 ss.34–37 deals with "Inferences from accused's silence" including the effect of the accused's "failure to mention facts when questioned or charged" (s.34); "silence at trial" (s.35); "failure or refusal to account for objects, substances or marks" (s.36); failure or refusal to account for presence at a particular place (s.37). The right to silence is discussed in Annabelle Mooney, *Language and Law* (Basingstoke: Palgrave Macmillan, 2014), 68–73.

19 See, generally, Deborah Tannen and Muriel Saville-Troike, eds., *Perspectives on Silence* (Norwood, NJ: Ablex, 1985); Michal Ephratt, "The functions of silence," *Journal of Pragmatics* 40 (2008): 1909–1938. Ephratt adopts the term "Eloquent Silence."

tence."[20] Pärt's formula provides that "if the final word in a section (with a full stop) has one or two syllables, then the following silent bar should be of the same duration (as in the printed score); if the final word has three or four syllables, then the silent bar should be exactly half as long."[21]Actors know that silence fills the theatre in a way that can hardly be attained even by shouting. When one shouts, the sound immediately dies away, whereas silence gets louder and louder and louder the longer it lingers.[22] It is not emptiness, but a solid thing that demands our attention. It is not for nothing that we speak of a pregnant pause. The silent pause may be an anti-element to sound and it may be considered an absence, but it is by no means an emptiness or a vacancy. It is a full thing that seems to strike the ear physically almost as sound does.

To attend and to be attentive one must first be called to attention. In Shakespeare's London, church bells summoned congregations to hear sermons and trumpet and drum summoned playgoers to the theatre. The ear must be excited, incited, invited to hear. A clamour awakens the ear as a prelude to attentive hearing. Rhetorician's have long appreciated this need to excite auditory engagement, thus the rhetorician Thomas Wilson lauded the "plaine beginning" wherein "the hearer is made apt to giue good eare out of hande."[23] Shakespeare was highly likely to have been familiar with Wilson's work and it might even have inspired Mark Antony's famous plain beginning to his speech in Caesar's funeral where he expressly invites the "Friends, Romans, countrymen" to lend their ears (3.2.74). That said, the call to give or lend the ear had long been a staple of theatrical practice just as it had long been a staple of the rhetorical tradition. In fact, the earliest surviving play script in the canon of English theatrical drama – *The Castle of Perseverance* (c. 1420) – begins with a similar call to friends to lend their hearing: "Farewel, fayre frendys, / That lofly wyl lystyn and lendys."[24] In another example of the tradition, Shakespeare has the Vice figure, Rumour,

20 Arvo Pärt *Passio* (*Passio Domini Nostri Jesu Christi Secundum Joannem*), The Song Company; St Mary's Cathedral Choir; Omega Ensemble St Mary's Cathedral, Sydney, Friday 10 March 2017 (Programme Notes).

21 Antony Pitts, "A Brief Introduction to Pärt-writing: Arvo Pärt and his unique musical formula," *Church Music Quarterly* (March 2004): 1–7, 7.

22 See, further, Sean Mulcahy, "Acting Law | Law Acting: A Conversation with Dr Felix Nobis and Professor Gary Watt," *Exchanges: The Warwick Research Journal* 4.2 (2017): 189–200. Available at http://exchanges.warwick.ac.uk/index.php/exchanges/article/view/146/276 (last access September 6, 2017).

23 Thomas Wilson, *Arte of Rhetorique* [1560], ed. George H. Mair (Oxford: Clarendon Press, 1909), 99.

24 Frederick J. Furnivall and Alfred W. Pollard, eds., *The Macro Plays* (London: Oxford University Press, 1904), 75–188, lines 153–1544.

call upon the audience to engage their acoustic sense at the start of *Henry IV, Part II:* "Open your ears; for which of you will stop / The vent of hearing when loud Rumour speaks?" (*The Induction*). Similarly, *Coriolanus* opens with these words of a citizen speaking in the streets of Rome "Before we proceed any further, hear me speak" (1.1.1).[25]

The impressive quality of such lines, by which I mean that aspect of these lines that makes the fullest impression on the mind, is the fact that spoken words strike the ear and make an initial demand to be heard. Thus the call to hear operates in a curiously oxymoronic way by calling a listener to listen. The effect of this, I would suggest, is to make the audience reflexively self-aware of its own auditory engagement with the words of the script. It therefore invites a more acute and critical engagement with the sense of the words – hearing becomes *a* hearing. Shakespeare indicates elsewhere that the same effect can be achieved in combination with music. At the beginning of *Twelfth Night*, for example, the opening line ("If music be the food of love, play on…") makes express reference to music that we can presume was being played by musicians on stage or in one of the adjoining spaces. (*ASEH* included Antony Pitts' own setting of "If music be the food of love.") In Shakespeare's play the on-stage music, combined with the express textual overture to "music," would have excited the ear of the audience, and perhaps, by focusing their attention on stage sounds, would have prompted playgoers to hush their own chatter at the outset of the play. *Henry V* through its prologue invitation to the audience "gently to hear, kindly to judge our play" (1.prologue.34) more expressly and directly than any other of Shakespeare's plays invites the audience to engage in a critical hearing of the ensuing drama, but it also contains within it a more subtle and primordially effective appeal to the audience's sense of hearing. The opening line of that prologue – "O for a Muse of fire, that would ascend" – contains at least two significant auditory notes. The reference to "muse" is one, for it might awake a musical sense of hearing in readiness for the ensuing verse, but more potent is the very first word of the play – the exclamation "O." This is the shape of an open mouth and the sound that an open mouth makes, and it is also the shape of the open ear against which the sound strikes. It is in every sense a portal through which the play is presented, and this is quite apart from its resonance with the "wooden O" of the theatre structure.[26] That

25 I am grateful to Sean Mulcahy for directing me to the intensity of sound references in the opening and closing scenes of *Coriolanus*.

26 In *A Strange Eventful History*, I liken Shakespeare's Globe theatre to the instrument of the human voice: "But how did the scientists find the thread of a single voice strung out somewhere between the earth and the moon? Here Shakespeare helped us in ways he could not have fore-

opening "O" is not so much a word as an attention-grabbing alarm. *Beowulf*, the earliest surviving poem in the Anglo-Saxon language, begins with another example of an ear-seizing monosyllable, which Dr Felix Nobis describes as "the classic Anglo Saxon call" – "Hwæt."[27] It is frequently translated "listen!" or "lo!," although recent scholarship suggests that it should perhaps be read (in the context of the line) as "what we have learned."[28] The first line in full is "*Hwæt. We Gardena in geardagum*," which Seamus Heaney translates "So. The Spear-Danes in days gone by." In a note on his own translation he makes an interesting observation connecting Anglo-Saxon speech to legal speech: "when the men of the family spoke, the words they uttered came across with a weighty distinctness, phonetic units as separate and defined as delph platters displayed on a dresser shelf […]. They had a kind of Native American solemnity of utterance, as if they were announcing verdicts rather than making small talk."[29]

Techniques for acquiring an attentive ear, whether in express or more subtle forms, create a sense of acoustic anticipation whose combined effect is something similar to that produced by the biblical injunction – "those who have ears, let them hear."[30] In the context of a musical concert a similar effect is achieved by the tuning of the instruments. It is not just that the musical instruments are being tuned, but also that the auditory instruments of the audience – their ears – are being attuned to the acoustic context of the musicians' instruments in this place. It was with such techniques and considerations in mind that the advance publicity for *A Strange Eventful History* sought to strike a playful note calculated to invoke a critically engaged mode of hearing. The hope was the standard one of enticing through intrigue, but at the same time it sought to encourage acoustic appreciation of the resonance between the musicality of Shakespeare's words and the musical compositions that inspired him and which his works in turn inspired. The paragraph of advance publicity – the teaser – read as follows:

---

seen. His Globe theatre was a huge wooden model of the human vocal tract – a vast wooden cylinder for a throat and the sounding board of a hollow wooden stage thrust like a voice box into its very centre […] and Shakespeare kindly left the lid off for us, so the great mouth of the playhouse could shout out into thin air […] into the thin air of space, and of time" (*ASEH*, narrative).

27 See https://vimeo.com/108538344, at 8.38–46. See, further, http://artsonline.monash.edu.au/performance/beowulf-dr-felix-nobis (last access September 6, 2017)

28 See http://www.independent.co.uk/arts-entertainment/books/news/listen-beowulf-opening-line-misinterpreted-for-200-years-8921027.html (last access September 6, 2017).

29 See http://www.wwnorton.com/college/english/nael/beowulf/introbeowulf.htm (last access September 6, 2017).

30 Matthew 13:9.

> For decades, scientists have been straining to hear alien voices in outer space. Now traces of speech have been found. Are they extra-terrestrial, or could they be human voices trapped in time? The rumour is that scientists have found the sounds of Elizabethan London and have recovered the voices of actors in the original Globe theatre. Twenty-score years since the death of William Shakespeare (1564–1616), *A Strange Eventful History* marks time with a journey through a sweet soundscape of Shakespeare's words and the music he has inspired... Lend us your ears, and hear that strain again...

Bridging this preamble to each evening's performance, I opened the show by welcoming the audience whilst wearing a lab coat. This gave time for the six singers to warm up back stage and at the same time gave the playful illusion of scientific veracity and thereby continued the framing conceit – introduced by the advance publicity – that scientists had discovered or recovered actual sounds from Shakespeare's original Globe Theatre (from 1599 when it opened to 1613 when it was destroyed by fire).

The performance proper began with a prologue that in the printed paper programme was subtitled "roll-call." This was a playful reference to the fact that the paper programme was itself in the form of a large single-sheet designed to be rolled and therefore to evoke the paper scrolls on which the early modern player received his section of the playscript – his roll, it will be recalled, was the practical (and etymological) origin of the actor's "role." The word "call" was also intended to evoke the auditory cues, discussed earlier in this paper, by which audiences have historically been summoned to congregate as witnesses to a performance. Even such homonyms as roll and role were placed in the script not just for punning, but with a desire to engage and excite the ear. The prologue or roll-call of *A Strange Eventful History* comprises four elements – a song, a section of narration, a Shakespearean speech and another song. The first song, which served as an overture to the entire work, was "The isle is full of noises" (Paul Ayres b.1970) which was sung by the six singers as they gradually entered the scene from various points off-stage. The express reference to "noises" in the title of this song alerts the listener to the overall theme of the show, which is to connect speech and music and sounds of all sorts at the primal level of noise. The fact that the phrase "isle is full" is full of the lulling sound of the letter "l" fits with the lulling quality of the tune, which, like a lullaby, lulls the listener into a dreamlike state. Shakespeare's text promises that noises will be audible in the isle, but the busy, buzzing "s" and "z" sounds in the word "noises" are in fact inaudible when the word "isle" is pronounced – the same was probably true of pronunciation in Shakespeare's day, so his "isle" turns out to be curiously *empty* of noises. We are left, instead, with an isle (pronounced "I'll") that enhances the lulling, dream-like quality of the soundscape and in which the feeling that the isle is alien and unreal may be heightened because the "s" of the written word is not present. Shakespeare's line "the isle is full of noises" is taken from Shakespeare's play about a colonized island *The Tempest* (3.2.135), and this serves to open up a suggestive and intriguing set of acoustic allusions to the continental island of Australia in which the performances of *A Strange Eventful History* were taking place. Even in the suburbs of modern Sydney one is wonderfully assailed by a clamour of cockatoos, mynahs, parakeets and occasionally the lyricism of the elusive Lyre bird. One can easily imagine how raucous must have been the African and American islands on which early modern explorers first set foot in Shakespeare's day. The beautiful music of the opening song, coupled with Shakespeare's beautiful words, awakens the ears of the audience and stirs their attention even as it induces a somewhat soporific, dreamlike state. It is into this that the narrator's opening speech intrudes:

> The isle is full of noises and tonight we will be full of play. Welcome to *A Strange Eventful History* – a journey back to Shakespeare's London and the journey of a lifetime from birth to the last scene of all.

At this point the pseudo-scientific framing narrative is picked up, as it is throughout all of the narrator's speeches:

> Scientists have found strange sounds in space: historical remnants of human voices. They call them "Light Amplified Radio Cords" – L.A.R.C.s for short; and they have asked the Song Company to help turn these LARCs into human voices. Tonight we share our findings. You've heard the speculation....
> Shh...shh...Shakespeare's voice has been found!
> It's just a rumour, but who can "stop the vent of hearing when loud Rumour speaks?"

The narrative sections serve to articulate the songs and the speeches by connecting them whilst keeping them distinct from one another. The first of Shakespeare's speeches to be introduced is the famous prologue to the first Act of *Henry V*, spoken (as befits a strange form of choral concert) by the character called "Chorus." It begins with a couplet that brings in the musical and extra-terrestrial themes of the show: "O for a Muse of fire, that would ascend / The brightest heaven of invention" (1.prologue.1–2). One highly pertinent couplet later in the prologue directly urges the audience to visualise horses: "Think when we talk of horses, that you see them / Printing their proud hoofs i' the receiving earth" (1.prologue.1.26–7). These lines expressly urge the audience to see horses, but they also encourage the horses to be heard in the imagination's ear. The percussive "pr" sound that is rapidly repeated in the phrase "printing their proud" has an onomatopoeic quality that is calculated to make an impression on the ear of the mind even as the mind's eye is called upon to witness horses snorting and hooves impressing the soil. The narrator interrupts the speech immediately after the phrase "receiving earth" to amplify the playful conceit that scientists have detected signals of Shakespearean sounds that centuries ago had emanated into space. The interruption – which required me as narrator to interrupt myself in the middle of my own delivery of the prologue to Act One of Henry V – was deliberately designed to alienate and to create a sense of the alien. An instance, perhaps, of what Brecht called the *Verfremdungseffekt* ("alienation effect").[31] The interruption took the form of a question addressed to the singers and, obliquely, addressed to the audience: "Are you receiving earth?" The hope was that the audience might enter more fully as participants in the play and that their ears, alerted and alienated, would be more acutely attuned to the sound play connecting the songs and the script.

The prologue to the first Act of *Henry V* acquires the ear of the audience by means of another poetic technique that Shakespeare was profoundly adept in. The technique I am referring to is a playfulness with related vowel sounds. In particular, the vowel sound of "or." It should be noted that in the following passage the "hour" in hour-glass would also have been pronounced with an "or" sound in the Elizabethan pronunciation and the possessive pronounce "our" would have been closer to "or" than to our modern bisyllabic pronunciation.[32] I have underlined in bold the "or" sound and underlined related sounds to show how loudly the passage is loaded with this audible refrain:

F**or** 'tis y**our** th**ough**ts that now must deck **our** kings
Carry them here and there; jumping **o'er** times,
Turning the accomplishment of many years
Into an h**our**-glass: for the which supply,
Admit me Ch**or**us to this hist**or**y;
Who prologue-like y**our** humble patience pray,
Gently to hear, kindly to judge, **our** play (1.prologue.28 – 34).

31 John Willett, trans., *Brecht on Theatre* (London: Methuen, 1964), 144.

32 See David Crystal, *The Oxford Dictionary of Original Shakespearean Pronunciation* (Oxford: Oxford University Press, 2016). The 'or' sound ɔ: would have generally sounded ɔ˞: In his English Grammar, Ben Jonson likens it to the growl of a dog: "R is the dog's letter, and hurreth in the sound." Compare *Romeo and Juliet*, 2.4.190. In the original Elizabethan pronunciation, Hamlet's "words, words, words" (2.2.189) would have been filled with the sound of "or", as in modern Received Pronunciation of "swords, swords, swords." I have engaged elsewhere in an extended appreciation of the sound of "or" in *Hamlet* (Watt, *Shakespeare's Acts of Will*, Chapter 5, "'His will is not his own': Hamlet downcast and the problem of performance," 191 – 198).

Shakespeare is not the only great rhetorician to employ the sound of "ore" poetically to acquire the ear of his audience. The most famous example from politics is surely the opening clause of Abraham Lincoln's Gettysburg Address: "Four score and seven years ago our fathers brought forth." There are four "ores" in that one clause, and the rich "r" sound resonates further as it echoes around full vowel sounds in such words as "years," "our" and "Father." The "ore" sound fills the mouth and fills the ear. Repeated and amplified with further vowel and "r" sounds it has a roaring quality. In *A Strange Eventful History*, the prologue speech from *Henry V* is followed by *The Cries of London* by Orlando Gibbons (1583–1625) that was written around the time of the original Globe playhouse. The choral quality of the "or" sound features in the opening line of the song (as indeed it features in the composer's Christian name): "God give you good morrow, my masters, past three o'clock and a fair morning." In the original early modern pronunciation the repeated "r" sounds would have awakened the ear like a drum roll. ("God give you good morrrrow, my ma[r]sters, past thrrree o'clock and a fairrr morrrrning"). The song celebrates the musicality of the streets especially in the cries of street vendors who would have crowded the lanes outside the playhouse and mingled with the crowd inside.

For *ASEH*, it was hoped that the down-to-earth music of street voices would join with the hooves printing the earth to produce a concrete sense so that, despite the intangible quality of time and imagined time-travel, the listener would be located in a present felt experience. These are, of course, precisely the same effects that Shakespeare aimed at and so successfully achieved in the time-traveller prologues to the Acts of *Henry V* delivered by the Chorus. For example, in the prologue to the third Act we have the tangible call to 'Grapple your minds to sternage of this navy' (3.prologue.18) and in the prologue to the fifth Act the audience is invited (in reference to the king) to 'Heave him away upon your winged thoughts' and 'fetch' him in (5.prologue.8, 28), and, most tangibly of all, to 'behold / In the quick forge and working-house of thought' (5.prologue.22–3).

After the prologue part of *ASEH*, the show proceeds to the seven ages of man as Jaques describes them, starting with the age of the infant. To begin with, Jaques' entire speech was spoken to allow each singer to introduce themselves to the audience. All parts having been introduced in the overture, the show then proceeded to journey through the seven ages one-by-one. The format for each age contained, with occasional slight variation, the same structural elements. First, the narrator introduced the age with a poetic stanza newly written for this production. In writing these stanzas, I took Jacques' words as a starting point for a playful riff designed to emulate some of the techniques of sound play discovered in Shakespeare's writing. The new stanza for each age therefore operated as an amplification, and maybe an exaggeration, of Shakespeare's own poetic methods. For example, the stanza written to introduce the first age, began with the couplet "In expectation here begin fantastic / scenes and phantom sounds of ages past." This couplet makes straightforward sense as an introduction of the show's pseudo-scientific conceit concerning the recovery of an Elizabethan soundscape. Less obvious is the fractional arrangement of the word "infant" within the couplet; not just once, but twice. Here I copied Shakespeare's technique of bracketing or echoing a sound within a repetition of the same sound, as follows: "**[In** expectation here beg**{in fant}**astic / scenes and **phant]**om sounds of ages past." The effect of the closely concentrated **{in fant}** at the centre of the more sparsely spaced **[In ... phant]** seems to produce concentric waves of sound sense, akin to the waves produced by dropping a pebble in a pond. There is a large ripple in the middle that fades out to a more gentle ripple as the ring widens. Perhaps the concentric sense causes sound waves to ripple through the mind. The stanza for the age of the lover was a playful take on the "sigh" sound which Shakespeare's Jaques associates with this age. Thus the first couplet of the lover's stanza contains four homophonic repetitions of the "sigh" sound: "The lover's eyes for signs shoot swift to sight / As high in hope as cupid's darts in flight." The word "sigh" itself is never in its dictionary sense expressly stated in the couplet or the stanza as whole, but its absence might foster a lovesick sense of longing, and the quick repetition hopefully engenders a bodily sense of lovesick lament – as sighing does. Each stanza was merely the first feature in the performance of each age. Second, as I spoke the words of the stanza for each age, I handed a prop to the singer playing that particular age. In return each singer handed me the labcoat that they had been wearing up until that point, and which, removed, revealed clothes in some colour on the rainbow spectrum – one for each of the seven ages, starting with red for the infant and ending with violet. Third, having introduced the individual performer, he or she sang a solo piece (usually with other performers accompanying in the role of chorus). The prop was in each case appropriate to the age being represented and was in each case capable of being played as an instrument – a rattle for the infant, a hoop and stick for the schoolboy, a (violin) bow for the lover, a drum for the soldier, a pair of brass scales (miniature cymbals) for the justice, and a spectacles case for the pantaloon. Antony Pitts, representing the seventh age, the age of oblivion, had his instrument and prop throughout in the form of the Fender Rhodes electric piano. With its cover removed the audience saw a skeletal array of metal ribs and electric sinews which simultaneously evoked musical instrument, scientific instrument and something like an emaciated corpse in a lid-less coffin or sarcophagus. It was present throughout the entire performance, like a memento mori.

On that note, this might be the appropriate point to elucidate a further instance of "fractional inference" in Shakespeare's dramatic works. This example, like the earlier one, is taken from *Julius Caesar*. The following lines appear in a longer passage of speech that was spoken to exemplify the age of the soldier in *A Strange Eventful History:*

> O, p**ar**don m**e**, thou b**lee**ding p**iece** of **ear**th,
> That I am m**ee**k and **ge**ntle with th**ese** butch**ers**!
> Thou **ar**t the **ruins** of the noble**s**t man
> That ev**er** lived in the tide of time**s** (3.1.254–57)

As before, I have highlighted the relevant sound fractions to bring out the tenor more clearly, even though there might be some slight variation between Elizabethan pronunciation and modern. The subject of the passage – he who is the "bleeding piece of earth" – is none other than Julius Caesar himself, and the tenor word that may be inferred from the constituent sound fragments is "Caesar," perhaps (more tenuously) "Julius" also. Caesar's name appears towards the end of the full speech, but in this case the word "Caesar" is sufficiently inferred without needing to state it expressly. It is, after all, the title of the play and everyone knows to whom Antony is referring as he addresses the corpse. In fact, the inference is arguably all the more powerful through the absence of any express reference to the name, for this has the effect of confirming Caesar's absence in the listener's mind. Without the resolving satisfaction of an express reference to "Caesar," the audience will also be encouraged to hold in mind Caesar in his broken form. The fractional representation of "Caesar" in scattered sounds fits perfectly with an idea that is expressly stated in these lines, namely that the statuesque colossus that was Caesar is now a "ruin," fragmented into a rubble of parts (a few lines later Antony even muses in connected vein that Caesar's blood shall "cumber all the parts of Italy"). Note that the salient lines start with the declaratory "O," one effect of which is, as we have already observed, to engage the playgoers' auditory attention. The sound of Caesar is palpable, echoed especially in the endings of the first two lines "p**iece** of **ear**th" and "th**ese** butch**ers.**" These lines present the bleeding ruins of Caesar. Caesar chopped up.

This might seem to be pushing the point. Surely Shakespeare did not intend the audience to hear or sense Caesar's name in these lines. Perhaps not. Who can know what Shakespeare intended, and how much of his craft was instinctive. What is clear is that earlier in the play, Shakespeare makes great play of Caesar's name and expressly engages the audience's ear to hear the sound quality of "Caesar." Cassius asks:

"Brutus" and "Caesar": what should be in that "Caesar"?
Why should that name be sounded more than yours?
Write them together: yours is as fair a name;
Sound them, it doth become the mouth as well. (1.2.141–144)

Caesar himself speaks of his own name at the start and end of a seventeen-line passage that mentions hearing, music, the ear and deafness and in which we find in two adjacent lines two instances of fractional inference of the name "Caesar" (highlighted in the following abridgement):

Yet if my name were liable to fear,
I do not know the man I should avoid
So soon as that spare Cassius. He reads much,
[...]
[...] he hears no music;
[...]
Such men a**s he** be nev**er** at heart**'s ease**
Whiles they behold a great**er** than themselves,
[...]
[...] for always I am Caesar.
Come on my right hand, for this ear is deaf. (1.2.198–200, 203, 207–208, 211–212)

Shakespeare was fond of the set-piece eulogy spoken over the body of a Great One fallen. Julius Caesar is not the only one of his titular characters to receive the honour. Coriolanus is another, whose "eulogist" Aufidius cues the play's closing music with his words: "Take him up. / Help, three o' the chiefest soldiers; I'll be one. / Beat thou the drum, that it speak mournfully: / Trail your steel pikes" (5.5.147–50). This, of course, is an echo of *Hamlet.* In Hamlet's case the general Fortinbras, like the martial Antony, speaks formal honours for the fallen prince while Horatio takes Antony's part in speaking of his friend. The intervention of Fortinbras brings the play to a close with a crescendo of sound and auditory elements. When Horatio promises an oration on the sad events, Fortinbras commands "Let us haste to hear it, / And call the noblest to the audience" (5.2.370–71). His next passage of speech, the very last lines of the play, contains a cue, surely, for gunpowder effects (of the sort that would later cause the fire that destroyed the Globe playhouse) and a concluding fanfare of martial trumpet:[33]

33 See http://www.independent.co.uk/arts-entertainment/sound-the-trumpet-1249715.html (last access September 6, 2017).

Let four captains
Bear Hamlet, like a soldier, to the stage;
For he was likely, had he been put on,
To have proved most royally: and, for his passage,
The soldiers' music and the rites of war
Speak loudly for him.
Take up the bodies: such a sight as this
Becomes the field, but here shows much amiss.
Go, bid the soldiers shoot. (5.2.395–403)

The cacophonous climax brought in by Fortinbras is in marked contrast to the hush of Hamlet's passing. In his dying words, Hamlet had alluded to the audience (on-stage or playhouse, perhaps both). However noisy and distracted the playgoers might have been upon entering the playhouse they were surely silent for his last words; with which he resigned himself to the inevitable law of death. Hamlet did not live long enough to play the justice, for the sergeant Death has come:

You that look pale and tremble at this chance,
That are but mutes or audience to this act,
Had I but time (as this fell sergeant, Death,
Is strict in his arrest), O, I could tell you—
But let it be. (5.2.339–43)

Hamlet's final speech is a study in the sound of "o" that echoes until it dies away into a silence that fills the wooden "o' of the playhouse:

O, I die, Horatio.
The potent poison quite o'ercrows my spirit.
I cannot live to hear the news from England.
But I do prophesy the election lights
On Fortinbras. He has my dying voice.
So tell him, with th'occurrents, more and less,
Which have solicited. The rest is silence.
O, O, O, O. *(dies)* (5.2.306–313)

Hamlet's silence inspired the closing words of *A Strange Eventful History*. Perhaps those closing words provide a just and fitting note to finish on:

The rest is silence? No. The rest is sound.
The rest is peace? Yes. But not quiet.
True rest is the song of birds, the company of sweet words, the soothing chorus of friends.
And when we think that the light is fading and the colours are dying away...we are mistook.
The light is merely sleeping beneath the layers of a life laid down: it lies within a blanket of

enfolding dreams. The colours of life do not die, but dye...and deeply too. Ever deeper.
For mixed with the shades of me are the memories of you.
All hue. No cry...but a tone.
The end is not darkness, but beautiful black. Not silence, but a full forever sound.
Life ends in perfect pitch. (*ASEH*, epilogue)[34]

34 The words "a tone" were the cue for Antony Pitts to play 52 keys descending the length of the keyboard – one key for each completed year of Shakespeare's probable lifespan (he is known to have died on 23rd April 1616 and is romantically reputed to have been born on the same day in 1564, based on his baptismal date of 26th April that year). 23rd April was, even then, the Saint's Day of England's patron St George. The standard modern grand piano has 52 white keys and a total of 88 keys, as do some models of Fender Rhodes, although in this case the Fender Rhodes was of the smaller 73 key variety.

Marett Leiboff

"Stir Up the Australian Youth to Merriment": *A Midsummer Night's Dream*, Summer 1989–1990 (Sydney, Australia) and the Theatrical Transmutability of Law's Texts

1 Transmuting law and the theatrical

As You Law It. A pun that plays on and invokes a title that is so well known it almost goes without saying: *As You Like It.*[1] There are jokes aplenty in the catachresis and pun – *law* and *like* – can law be liked, what is law like, what is like law? This play of words takes us to the play of law, and plays on law. This play of words transmutes – from one thing into another, a conversion into something different, an alteration, a transformation.[2] Transmutation also conceives of the concept of *exchange*,[3] in an obsolete or archaic meaning of the word. It is also alchemical, literally and figuratively. The OED tells us that *trasmutabilità* or "transmutability" first surfaced in English in 1611,[4] in J. Florio's *Queen Anna's New World of Words*,[5] just a few years after *As You Like It,* and *A Midsummer Night's Dream*,[6] were first reputed to have been staged.[7] The advent of this active, adverbial form of the word carries with it an imposition of liveness, and liveliness. For although each play was thought to have been written during the last decade of the sixteenth century (Elizabethan and Jacobean performance meth-

---

1 William Shakespeare, *As You Like It: Updated Edition*, ed. Michael Hattaway (Cambridge: Cambridge University Press, 2009): further references in the text.

2 "transmutation, n." "b. *Law.* Transfer: usually transmutation of possession, transfer or change of ownership." *OED Online* (Oxford University Press, March 2017).

3 OED, "transmutation": *The Merchant of Venice* "exchange" denoted transmutation.

4 "transmutability, n." *OED Online* (Oxford University Press, March 2017).

5 This source derives from an English/Italian Dictionary, dedicated to the wife of James I, Anne of Denmark, by John or Giovanni Florio, also touted as a possible Shakespeare. *John Florio*, available at: https://en.wikipedia.org/wiki/John_Florio (last access March 20, 2017).

6 William Shakespeare, *A Midsummer Night's Dream*, ed. Burton Raffel (New Haven: Yale University Press, 2005): further references in the text, abbreviated as *Dream*.

7 *As You Like It*, in 1603, the year Elizabeth I died; *A Midsummer Night's Dream* in the second year of James' reign, in 1605.

https://doi.org/10.1515/9783110591514-014

ods aside),[8] it is only at a point of exchange, when words on the page are transformed through the liveness of the theatrical encounter, that their transmutation is made truly manifest, in the same way that law, too, is only made manifest, through the act of reading, interpreting and living law.

To begin thinking about how this exchange of transmutation, through the play of law, is made manifest, I will stay with *As You Like It*, for it is through one of the most famous of Shakespearean lines that we can find an exemplary instance of transmutation *as exchange* at play. After an encounter with the outlaw lords in the forest, the hapless Duke Senior remarks:

> Thou seest we are not all alone unhappy:
> This wide and universal theatre
> Presents more woeful pageants than the scene
> Wherein we play in. (*As You Like It*, 2.7.142–145)

to which Jaques most famously responds: "All the world's a stage And all the men and women merely players" (As *You Like It*, 2.7.145–146). Puns aplenty permeate Duke Senior's quip, an hilarious jape as sight gag for an audience who heard these words within the walls of *The Globe* theatre, that "wide and universal theatre," as identified through name and motto.[9] And of course, the puns ran deeper and longer, into the thick allusion of the *theatrum mundi*, the remnant classical and medieval concept of the Divine as author, director and spectator of the lives of humans on an earthly stage.[10] A commonplace divorced from its religious connotations by the sixteenth century, and so too a reference to a theatre building and a literary trope,[11] the world as stage, and stage as world, takes on a new significance for the early modern self, seeking to understand their place in the word.[12] Thus, as Quiring observes, Jaques' remark functions at a "purely immanent level of existence, without any reference to transcendent au-

8 Farah Karim Cooper and Tiffany Stern eds., *Shakespeare's Theatres and the Effects of Performance* (Bloomsbury: The Arden Shakespeare, 2013); David Bevington, *This Wide and Universal Theater: Shakespeare in Performance, Then and Now* (Chicago: University of Chicago Press, 2007).

9 *The Globe*'s motto was *Totus mundus agit histrionem.*

10 Lynda Gregorian Christian, *Theatrum Mundi: The History of an Idea* (New York: Garland, 1987), 7, 89, cited in Björn Quiring, "Introduction" to *"If Then the World a Theatre Present ...": Revisions of the Theatrum Mundi Metaphor in Early Modern England,* ed. Björn Quiring (Berlin: de Gruyter, 2014), 1–23, 4, 5.

11 Quiring, "Introduction," 5.

12 Quiring, "Introduction," 5.

thorities,"[13] and one that is deeply mired in the problems of existence in a changing world.

We lose this reading, however, when Jaques' response to Duke Senior is cut loose from its surrounding text. This untethering of the call from the response reads as lofty sentiment, rather than a mordant moan about the progress of being through the seven ages Jaques identifies. But cut adrift, a very particular complaint of and about law and lawyers, judge and judging, loses its sting entirely:

> And then the justice,
> In fair round belly with good capon lined,
> With eyes severe and beard of formal cut,
> Full of wise saws and modern instances;
> And so he plays his part. (*As You Like It*, 2.7.160 – 164)

Of course, this is a literal and figurative judge (the middle-aged as prosperous and reproving), but read with Duke Senior's opening gambit, presents a more synchronous saw of its own.[14] This is a far from flattering portrait of law and the judge, which echoes the far from flattering literal and figurative device of theatre to demonstrate the impediments that would intrude upon clear reason and analysis by a legal figure – the lawyer philosopher Francis Bacon.[15] 1603 is a very particular year in this respect. It is more than a small coincidence that Bacon was knighted by James I in 1603, the same year that the first staging of *As You Like It* can be traced,[16] and it was the same year that Bacon's unpublished *Valerius Terminus: Of the Interpretation of Nature* first circulated, originally to a closed circle, though it quickly became known more widely.[17]

---

13 Quiring, "Introduction," 6.

14 Richard J. Ross, "The Memorial Culture of Early Modern English Lawyers: Memory as Keyword, Shelter, and Identity, 1560 – 1640," *Yale Journal of Law & the Humanities* 10:2 (1998): 229 – 326.

15 1561 – 1626; *Contra* the postulation of the Baconian cipher, the hypothesis that Francis Bacon wrote the works of Shakespeare.

16 *As You Like It* was one of the few plays included in the *First Folio* of 1623 that had not been already been published in some other form. The text was possibly written between 1598 – 1600: Hattaway, in *As You Like It: Updated:* 49 – 53. Textual changes could come at any of seven stages up until publication: Hattaway, in *As You Like It: Updated*, 215, 216.

17 There are clues that the manuscript was finished in1603: Richard Serjeantson, "Communication: The Philosophy of Francis Bacon in Early Jacobean Oxford, With an Edition of an Unknown Manuscript of the *Valerius Terminus*," *The Historical Journal* 56 (2013): 1087 – 1106, 1090 – 1092.

Valerius Terminus inaugurates some of the ideas that Bacon would later develop, albeit in amended form, but for now he specifically identified his concern about "the internal and profound errors and superstitions in the nature of the mind," created through four "idols or fictions which offer themselves to the understanding in the inquisition of knowledge":[18]

> Of the inherent and profound errors and superstitions in the nature of the mind, and of the four sorts of Idols or false appearances that offer themselves to the understanding in the inquisition of knowledge; that is to say, the Idols of the Tribe, the Idols of the Palace, the Idols of the Cave, and the Idols of the Theatre. That these four, added to the incapacity of the mind and the vanity and malignity of the affections, leave nothing but impotency and confusion. A recital of the particular kinds of these four Idols, with some chosen examples of the opinions they have begot, such of them as have supplanted the state of knowledge most. [19]

As Rossi makes plain, the Idol of the Theatre was, at this stage of Bacon's thinking, an internal impediment to proper forms of judgment and reason.[20] Later, it would be reshaped as an external impediment to proper thought. With these two concepts in mind, the quip about "wise saws and modern instances" takes on a potentially potent meaning – by speaking to Bacon's emerging philosophy, coded deep in this exchange between Jaques and Duke Senior. Contemporary figures made their way into *As You Like It*, in the form of Jaques himself,[21] so this nudge and wink targeting this lawyer and politician, and Bencher of Gray's Inn,[22] who was now in early middle-age – could be easily decoded, a small barb as a perfect riposte in the hands of those whose profession was derided by Bacon's device.

There was more to come. In 1605, the same year that *A Midsummer Night's Dream* was first presented, Bacon published *Of the Proficience and Advancement of Learning, Divine and Human*, or *The Advancement of Learning*. The Idol of the Theatre was omitted from this publication, though he maintained the other idols,

18 Francis Bacon, *Valerius Terminus: of the interpretation of Nature* (eBooks@Adelaide, 2014), Ch. 11, available at: https://ebooks.adelaide.edu.au/b/bacon/francis/valerius/#chapter11 (last access March 20, 2017).

19 Bacon, *Valerius*, Ch. 16.

20 Paolo Rossi, *Francis Bacon: From Magic to Science* [1957], trans. Sacha Rabinovitch (London: Routledge and Kegan Paul, 1968), 157–158.

21 Jaques was identified, for instance, as a satire of the godson of the Queen (Elizabeth), Harington, mooted as one potential reason for its non-publication: Hattaway, *As You Like It: Updated*, 215.

22 Jayne Archer, Elizabeth Goldring and Sarah Knight eds., *The Intellectual and Cultural World of the Early Modern Inns of Court* (Manchester: Manchester University Press, 2013).

albeit in modified form.[23] However, theatre did not escape his attention; if anything, he added further barbs to his views of theatre, on a properly formed and functioning mind, now extended, too, to the practices of theatre-going. The literary device of poetry might be acceptable up to a point, but theatre is another thing entirely to a properly functioning mind:

> In this third part of learning, which is poesy, I can report no deficience [...] But to ascribe unto it that which is due, for the expressing of affections, passions, corruptions, and customs, *we are beholding to poets more than to the philosophers' works*; and for wit and eloquence, not much less than to orators' harangues. *But it is not good to stay too long in the theatre.* Let us now pass on to the *judicial place* or palace of the mind, *which we are to approach and view with more reverence and attention.*[24]

Thus properly formed judgment is corrupted by theatre, to wit, Jaques' sardonic remarks about the justice's saws is enlivened – in concert with Duke Senior's quip, for Bacon, too, is ill-disposed towards the place as communal.[25] Moreover, Bacon's conception of judgment is *law's* method, as Shapiro has revealed,[26] meaning the quips in *As You Like It* are more than a little apt as a play on law. And even if not directed towards Bacon, it is not had to see, given the opprobrium theatre received at the hands of justices of the peace,[27] how this exchange between Jaques and Duke Senior spoke to a world of law at play beyond, as well as within, the place of theatre, and a more than little disdain for law, and that which is proper.

But there is one more small point. In the *Novum Organon* of 1620, published just three years before Shakespeare's First Folio, Bacon expands on his complaints about the Idols, with the Idol of the Theatre now reinstated. *Truth and reality, as literal accounts of being are acceptable,* but not, it seems, fancy and fantasy.Asserting now that this Idol is one of philosophy and inherited systems of knowledge, the adoption of theatre – or stage plays – as a trope is far from accidental:

---

23 Rossi, *Bacon*, 161.

24 Francis Bacon, *The Advancement of Learning* [1893], ed. Henry Morley (The Project Gutenberg ebook), Book 2, Aphorism V, [my emphasis].

25 Allison P. Hobgood, *Passionate Playgoing in Early Modern England* (Cambridge: Cambridge University Press, 2014), 188–189.

26 Barbara J. Shapiro, *A Culture of Fact England, 1550–1720* (Ithaca: Cornell University Press, 2000); compare Barbara J. Shapiro, "Law and Science in Seventeenth-Century England," *Stanford Law Review* 4 (1969): 727–766.

27 Hattaway, *As You Like It: Updated*, 52–53.

> Lastly, there are Idols which have immigrated into men's minds from the various dogmas of philosophies, and also from wrong laws of demonstration. These I call Idols of the Theater, because in my judgment all the received systems *are but so many stage plays, representing worlds of their own creation after an unreal and scenic fashion.* [...] which by tradition, credulity, and negligence have come to be received.[28] [...] And in the plays of this philosophical theater you may observe the same thing which is found in the theater of the poets, *that stories invented for the stage are more compact and elegant, and more as one would wish them to be, than true stories out of history.*[29]

Theatre, then, represents error and mistake, as laziness, prejudice and a desire for a lack of complication and complexity. Yet what is instantiated here is a mistrust of the imagination, and the possibility of asking *how* reality is observed and processed – that is, Bacon's confidence in the possibility of the rational and scientific, "the true stories out of history" and how they are shaped and understood, are assumed to be perfectible. For he also remarks, of knowledge (science): "The human understanding is no dry light, but receives an infusion from the will and affections; whence proceed sciences *which may be called "sciences as one would." For what a man had rather were true he more readily believes...* [my emphasis].[30] When applied to law, rather than signalling an intellectual emancipation, Bacon's formula turns inwards, the condemnation of imagination becomes a means by which injustice could be made manifest, for a literal reading of Bacon takes us into analytically closed interpretative methods. Law closed its eyes to the narrowing of its interpretative universe, relying on this logic; law as play and the play of law and the possibilities that derive from exchange, as a mark of transmutation, as *"sciences as one would,"* represent an unacceptable break into law and rational, even in the face of injustice.

"Sciences as one would"? Bacon is complaining about selfish or self-oriented assumptions in the place of clear, rational judgment, but this is not Bacon's turn of phrase. He wrote, as all scholars of the time did, in Latin. Translation (itself an exchange and transmutation) is far from clear-cut. Two other scholars, Derham and Stewart each translates Bacon's Latin into – *"as-you-like-it"* science.[31] The

28 Francis Bacon, *The New Organon, or True Directions Concerning the interpretation of Nature* [1863], trans. James Spedding, Robert Leslie Ellis, and Douglas Denon Heath (eBooks@Adelaide, 2014), Book 1, Aphorism XLIV, available at: https://ebooks.adelaide.edu.au/b/bacon/francis/organon/chapter1.html (last access March 20, 2017).
29 Bacon, *New Organon*, Book 1, Aphorism LXII.
30 Bacon, *New Organon*, Book 1, Aphorism XLIX.
31 Stanley Stewart, *Shakespeare and Philosophy* (Abingdon: Routledge, 2010), 132; Daniel Derrin, *Rhetoric and the Familiar in Francis Bacon and John Donne* (New Jersey: Fairleigh Dickinson University Press, 2013), 120.

then-contemporaneous "saws" of *As You Like It* now read as a retort of Bacon's complaints of theatre and imagination. Jaques' justice could well be any judge, or any self-satisfied judgmental middle-aged man, but this now starts to take on the attributes of a specific individual. This takes the text into an entirely different direction. So too law inherited into the twenty-first century, for what had been inherited into law through Bacon's influence on its interpretative practices, loses precisely the complaint of theatre and the play of imagination within law. Law thus becomes a self-referential system, and one that instructed itself to disregard the world beyond its black letter rules and case precedents. Reason and judgment operated by closing itself off from the world for centuries to protect itself from "as you like it law." I now turn to Australia, to the 1980s, where law as a practice began after critical agitations through legal scholarship and politics, to turn its gaze beyond the books, and back into the world, into the *theatre* of the world, as a *theatrum mundi*, seemingly rupturing the Baconian logics in law by taking on a scintilla of "*as-you-like-it*" thinking that turned to imagination as a condition precedent of justice.

2 From Bacon to 1980s Australia – from cultural cringe to a new assertiveness

Common lawyers, including Australian lawyers, are the inheritors of the Baconian approach towards legal reasoning, method and concepts, through the later seventeenth-century judge and legal scholar, Sir Matthew Hale and the eighteenth-century codifier of legal concepts, Blackstone.[32] Legal doctrine was inherited through case law, containing precedents themselves sourced from the judges. Legislation was a rarity, though in the latter part of the twentieth-century, it burgeoned, including in Australia. Though law is now understood to mean legislation, law inherited through the cases remains foundational. Courts would "read down" socially progressive law in the name of doctrine and existing legal principle. Critical scholarship, particularly that which took shape in the 1960s and 1970s, charted the outdated logics and historical verities that were maintained by the courts, in entirely inappropriate circumstances, such as retaining doctrines created in England in the eighteenth-century that had been overturned in the 1930s, only to be revived in Australia in the 1970s, in entirely different social, geographic and temporal circumstances, some instances of

32 William Blackstone, *Commentaries on the Laws of England, Book II: Of the Rights of Things*, ed. Simon Stern (Oxford: Oxford University Press, 2016).

which were documented by the renowned Australian lawyer Geoffrey Robertson QC in his book *The Justice Game.*[33] Law, as a discipline and profession, was considered to be captive to a conservative political agenda, aided by the logics, reasoning and methods of analysis inherited through Bacon. Of course, there had been individuals and groups within the field whose politics and social attitudes were far from conservative, but the practices, procedures and methods of law cannot function as sites of political engagement. Challenges to conventional legal approaches required the creative redeployment of doctrine and legal principle – something that could only happen by looking outside the confines of law itself, drawing on imagination, that unacceptable "as-you-like-it" science – in part triggered by social changes themselves.

If anything typified the Australia of the 1960s and earlier, it was a concept, now largely lost, of a "cultural cringe." This infamous Australian state of mind could be summed up in one idea – that nothing in Australia was good enough, and the rest of the world, the United Kingdom in particular as the so-called mother country, was the source of proper and appropriate culture and law. Voices and accents were to mimic, as best they could, the "received pronunciation" of BBC English. Though it had its own superior court, the High Court, the final court of appeal was located in London, largely comprised of members of the Judicial Committee of the House of Lords, though some members of the Australian courts might sit from time to time. Local culture was considered inferior, by and large. Pressure started to be exerted, however, by the late 1960s and early 1970s, where this obeisance to an external presence started to be resisted, and a reiteration of an Australian identity was actively pursued. The election of a left-wing national government in 1972, led by the Prime Minister Gough Whitlam, kick-started or instantiated change, some of which had to wait until after that government was dismissed in 1975.

By the 1980s, small symbols of change took effect, such as changing the national anthem from *God Save the Queen* to the present *Advance Australia Fair,* cutting a symbolic tie to the "mother country," and the move to end legal links with the UK, through the eventual passing of the *Australia Acts* 1986 throughout the country, removing the final appellate function of the Privy Council for Australia, and inaugurating Australia as a sovereign independent nation, 85 years after it had been created. In 1988, the 200th year after Britain invaded the land that indigenous Australians had inhabited for at least 40,000 years, was a

33 Geoffrey Robertson, *The Justice Game* (London: Chatto & Windus, 1998).

Bicentennial celebration or a mark of shame as a result of the consequences of invasion.[34]

Though there had been some small shifts in the 1970s, by the 1980s, arguments that sought to overcome social and political injustice started to be accepted by the courts, using law's methods. Some judges and courts slowly began to adapt and change their positions – some, but not all. Those that did looked beyond the limits of law on the page, and to read those words within time and place, as Ann Genovese and Shaun McVeigh have recently charted, of two key decisions of the Australian superior court, the High Court, in the 1980s, when it started to shift its focus and look beyond the law in its narrowest sense.[35] As the description of Genovese's collection, *Australian Critical Decisions*, notes:

> The 1980s was a time of significant social, political and cultural change. In Australia, the law was pivotal to these changes. The two High Court cases that this book explores – *Koowarta v Bjelke-Petersen* (1982) and the *Tasmanian Dams* case (1983) – are famous legally [...] Yet these cases also offer a significant marker of Australia in the 1980s: a shift to a different form of political engagement, nationally and internationally [...] *to reflect on how Australians experience their law in time and place, and why those experiences might require more than the usual legal records.*[36]

These decisions reveal that the courts were now willing to shake off the Baconian yoke, to look beyond the limits of the law. A High Court decision of 1989 confirmed that 200 years of legal, political and social obeisance to the United Kingdom had ended with the passage of the 1986 *Australia Acts*,[37] regardless of the emotional or other ties Australia had to Britain. But there were changes afoot too, for Australia's indigenous people. Though it had started to take shape since 1982, and was subjected to numerous legal setbacks, in December 1988, right at the end of the Bicentennial year, in the case of *Mabo v Queensland No. 1.*,[38] the High Court of Australia laid the groundwork for the decision in 1992 that removed the doctrine of *terra nullius* from Australian law, the famous

---

34 Frank Bongiorno, *The Eighties – The Decade that Transformed Australia* (Carlton: *Black Inc. Books, 2015).*

35 Ann Genovese and Shaun McVeigh, " Nineteen eighty three: A jurisographic report on *Commonwealth v Tasmania,*" *Griffith Law Review* 24 (2015) 68–88; Ann Genovese ed., *Australian Critical Decisions: Remembering Koowarta and Tasmanian Dams* (Abingdon: Routledge, 2017)

36 Australian Critical Decisions available at: https://www.routledge.com/Australian-Critical-Decisions-Remembering-Koowarta-and-Tasmanian-Dams/Genovese/p/book/9781138692053 (last access March 20, 2017), [my emphasis].

37 *Sue v Hill* [1999] HCA 30.

38 *Mabo v Queensland (No. 1)* [1988] HCA 69.

Mabo decision, or *Mabo v Queensland No. 2.*[39] This decision looked beyond doctrines that had grounded the idea that, in law, Australia had simply been settled and not conquered. The case overturned law that had supposedly been inviolable doctrine – by applying imagination to that doctrine, and looking beyond the pages of the books. Starting from the position of "as-you-like-it science," the court looked into the world beyond the internalised assumptions of doctrine, and into the historical, social, political injustices that law had imposed upon indigenous Australians – and by looking at the evidence of their ownership and relationship to land. The decision in *Mabo* only went so far and not far enough to rectify 200 years of dispossession and harm, but to think *beyond* limits in this way takes law into the realm of theatre, looking beyond the interiority of inherited dogma and doctrine to consider the operation of law in time and place – to notice injustice and to reshape doctrine and principle.

Australian law was ripe for change at the end of the 1980s, but some of the most profound changes like *Mabo* had to wait a few more years. Australia, in the 1980s, had transformed itself, its understanding of its position in the world, and its sense of self-awareness. And as the clock ticked on the end of the 1980s, that most transmutable of Shakespearean plays, *A Midsummer Night's Dream*, was about to transmute again in Sydney, reminding us that theatre is there to insist that times and places matter, and that reason, without love, is an altogether dangerous thing. That most amusing of plays, perhaps poking a Puckean pole at Bacon (for it is to be remembered that the *Advancement of Learning* was published in 1605, the year *A Midsummer Night's Dream* was reputed to have been first staged), where Bacon warned that it "is not good to stay too long in the theatre," preferring to "now pass on to the *judicial place*," reminds us that law without justice is a dangerous thing. For as we know, the judicial place is overborne by real justice – "Egeus, I will overbear your will" (*Dream*, 4.1.179). Theseus admonishes, a position he came to belatedly, through the most theatrical of devices – that which is lived and experienced, in his case through that which Hippolyta experienced.[40] For *A Midsummer Night's Dream* has much more to tell us about justice than its historical frothy exterior might have led us to believe.[41]

---

39 *Mabo v Queensland (No. 2)* [1992] HCA 23.

40 A conventional legal analysis tells a fundamentally different story, taking eyes back into law and missing the consequences of action: "Theseus and Hippolyta are Royals, and they open the play; yet they are perhaps the least important figures we shall consider, and they present the least challenging legal questions. For they are basically bystanders. It is Theseus's job as Duke to apply the law to resolve the dispute between the young lovers": David P. Currie, "A Midsummer Night's Dream – The Legal Issues," *Green Bag* 2 (2003): 381–387.
Compare an interdisciplinary panel held in 2010 at Texas Law School, which takes a far more

3 Transmuting *A Midsummer Night's Dream*

Of all of Shakespeare's plays, *A Midsummer Night's Dream* has a most curious history of disappearance and transformation across time, as the visuals contained in an exhibition mounted by the British Library reveals.[42] The *Dream* has been constantly changed and transformed according to taste and social attitudes – even its words have changed from time to time, but how the play becomes theatre is another thing entirely. Whatever and however we see this play, we can take it for granted that it alters according to time and tide. Plays are meant to be seen and experienced. It needs to be remembered, too, that there is no authentic production of Shakespeare, unless we were to reincarnate his players and were prepared to have boys play the role of women characters, with bare stage and musical interlude. Even the text, now considered sacrosanct, has been subjected to variation and change, as the rule, rather than the exception. Bottom and the mechanicals have spawned offshoot productions, including the 1661 piece, *The Merry conceited Humors of Bottom the Weaver,*[43] (like the 1987 Australian *The Popular Mechanicals* "By Keith Robinson, William Shakespeare and Tony Taylor").[44] Indeed, *A Midsummer Night's Dream*, in its entirety, was out of fashion less than 60 years after it was first staged. In 1662, Pepys famously remarked that he had "never seen before, nor shall ever again, for it is the most insipid ridiculous play that ever I saw in my life. I saw, I confess, some good

---

nuanced view of the conduct of law at the outset of the play: "'According to our Law,' is taken from the play's first scene, when the harsh patriarch Egeus demands that his daughter marry the man of his choice or be executed 'according to our law.' The play's actions find a way to reconcile 'harsh Athenian law' and the erotic desires of the young lovers." *Shakespeare and the Law: Scenes and a Panel on Legal Issues from A Midsummer Night's Dream* (September 22, 2010), available at: https://law.utexas.edu/news/2010/09/20/shakespeare-and-the-law-scenes-and-a-panel-on-legal-issues-from-a-midsummer-night%E2%80%99s-dream/ (last access March 3, 2017).

41 Peter C. Herman, "Equity and the Problem of Theseus in *A Midsummer Night's Dream:* Or, the Ancient Constitution in Ancient Athens," *Journal for Early Modern Cultural Studies* 14.1 (2014): 4–31, holds to a narrow legal interpretation that asserts that the Duke reached his ultimate decision contrary to law.

42 Emma Smith, *Dream, Illusion and Doubling in A Midsummer Night's Dream*, (British Library, undated), available at: https://www.bl.uk/shakespeare/articles/dream-illusion-and-doubling-in-a-midsummer-nights-dream (last access March 3, 2017).

43 Published in 1661, London, Robert Cox [adaptor], available at: https://www.bl.uk/collection-items/the-merry-conceited-humors-of-bottom-the-weaver-1661#sthash.VuX9JCIC.dpuf (last access March 3, 2017).

44 Keith Robinson, William Shakespeare, Tony Taylor, *The Popular Mechanicals: a Funny Old (New) Play* (Paddington, N.S.W. : Currency Press in association with Belvoir Street Theatre, Sydney, 1992).

dancing and some handsome women, which was all my pleasure."[45] The play then took an altogether different shape in the form of an opera, *The Fairy Queen*, written as a series of masques in 1692 by the English composer Henry Purcell – though it was then lost until the early twentieth-century. The actor-manager, David Garrick, created his own operatic version, *The Fairies*, in 1755, effectively an entirely different creation made up of a pastiche of material, based in and around the lovers and the fairies.

By the early nineteenth-century *A Midsummer Night's Dream* had become a burlesque, subject to fashion and whims of staging, until, at mid-century the play itself was restored, and the formula of the play in production, inherited even into the twenty-first century, took shape. Now laden with musical interludes, formularised through Mendelssohn's score, this now "standard" *Dream* was a pastiche of lush spectacle and cute fairies, of balletic interludes featuring large *corps de ballet*, and reimagined as a romantic fantasy. Attempts by the theatrical *avant-garde* to unpick the layers of tulle and forest glen began in the early twentieth century, with Harley Granville-Barker's 1914 production that attempted to return the play back to facets of Shakespearean performance styles, including the use of English folk music; and forty years later, in 1954 a production by the RSC attempted to work with the image of the production Granville-Barker began, in a production that worked with the abstract, including features such as stylised metal trees to denote the forest. Despite this, the pantomimic *Dream* remained as the expected form.

But all that changed in 1970, when Peter Brook utterly transformed *A Midsummer Night's Dream*,[46] for good. Brook's *Dream* was profoundly influenced by the work of Polish scholar, Jan Kott, whose seminal book *Shakespeare Our Contemporary*,[47] first published in Polish in 1961, and then in English in 1966,[48] stripped the play back to its text and the deep coding of the unconscious within it. Kott's return to the texts provided the insight that Brook, through the Royal Shakespeare Company, would take to the stage. It had been fundamentally

---

45 Samuel Pepys, *Diary: Monday 29 September 1662*, available at: http://www.pepysdiary.com/diary/1662/09/29/(last access March 3, 2017).

46 Royal Shakespeare Company, *A Midsummer Night's Dream: Some of our Past Productions of A Midsummer Night's Dream* available at: https://www.rsc.org.uk/a-midsummer-nights-dream/past-productions (last access March 3, 2017); Alan W. Bellringer, "The act of change in *A Midsummer Night's Dream*," *English Studies* 64.3 (1983): 201–217.

47 Jan Kott, *Shakespeare our Contemporary*, 2nd ed., trans. Boleslaw Taborski (London: Routledge, 1988).

48 That is not to say that Kott was completely comfortable with all aspects of Brook's production: Jan Kott, "The Bottom Translation," *Theater* 18.1 (1986): 74–90.

and profoundly reorientated through a theatrical reimagining that shifted the play from its imagined exterior world of fairies and revel to one grounded in the interior, the sub-conscious, and in doing so profoundly changed the play's grammar and coding. Theseus and Oberon, Hippolyta and Titania were one and the same, the woods and forest the locale of the sub-conscious, the text no longer read literally but through its time and place and encounter between actor and spectator. With nods to the conventions of the Elizabethan and Jacobean stage, the production was utterly grounded in its time and place, at the same time triggering a renewed sense of how this play ought to appear in production.

The text was now unmoored from the staging conventions that had been ossified across time, and now an explosion of *Dreams* appeared throughout the world, taking its cue from this profound shift. *Dreams* appeared in public gardens and in parks, as the Women's Institute, as punk, as the *Dream* appeared in an entirely new vernacular, literally and figuratively, stripping itself of the layers of expected theatrical presence, and doing something new and having something to say, even productions that claim to return to "Renaissance" staging.[49] That wasn't to say that the other romantic *Dream* had run its course – it is still hankered for, and produced.

But like law's interpretative limitations using the logics of Baconian reason and judgment, combined with a disdain of the imaginative ability needed to turn to justice, this play reminds us how injustice can occur – through its *text*. If *As You Like It* criticised the logics and economy of an antitheatrical reason, then this play put it into effect, from the blackest of black letter legal logic at the beginning of the play (*Dream*, 1.1.21–90) to the shift at the end, where Egeus' demands for the exercise of his rights are quashed, allowing rightness and fairness to take its course (*Dream*, 4.1.135–179).

But this literal black letter logic also results in nonsense, where the *law really is an ass* – as revealed in one of the most intensely disturbing scenes of the play. It might be imagined that this denotes the opening scene of the play, when law is dispensed harshly, resulting in the flight from Athens by the lovers. But instead it is the situation where the incredulous Bottom responds to Titania's abject declaration of love, itself perversely engineered by Oberon. The hapless

49 Shakespeare's Globe, *A Midsummer Night's Dream* [2014], (undated), available at: http://www.shakespearesglobe.com/discovery-space/previous-productions/a-midsummer-night-s-dream-7 (last access March 20, 2017): "This production employed Renaissance costumes and staging." The cast list includes women. The Titania/Hippolyta, Oberon/Theseus doubling was deployed. There are significant clues to indicate that this doubling was the practice at the time, however.

Bottom, the captive dupe, responds to this extraordinary declaration, along the way congratulating himself on his cleverness:

> Methinks, mistress, you should have little reason
> for that: and yet, to say the truth, *reason and*
> *love keep little company together now-a-days; the*
> *more the pity that some honest neighbours will not*
> *make them friends.* Nay, I can gleek upon occasion. *(Dream*, 3.1.126–130, [my emphasis])

This ordinary man reminds us that reason and love *should keep company* and not function in different arenas, that reason on its own results in harshness. He, of course, is making sense of what seems to be Titania's nonsense and her abusive demands on him. But by the end of the play, Titania's *alter ego*, Hippolyta, seems to have learnt from him, acknowledging that reason, on its own, might lead to wrong conclusions. In speaking to Theseus of the strange experiences the lovers recount, she remarks: "Tis strange my Theseus, that these lovers speak of" (*Dream*, 5.1.1).

But this is not "strange" as in unbelievable; it is an account worthy of notice because of its singularity. Theseus, on the other hand, dismisses their story, speaking as a Baconian – and as a perpetrator (as Oberon), who, if the story of the night were to be attended to, would implicate him in its debasement. Better to blame Puck for this error than admit responsibility (*Dream*, 3.2. 88–101) and it is easy to turn attention towards a surplus of fantasy and imagination and a lack of reason (and thus judgment) on the part of the lovers:

> *More strange than true: I never may believe*
> These antique fables, nor these fairy toys.
> Lovers and madmen have such seething brains,
> Such *shaping fantasies*, that apprehend
> *More than cool reason ever comprehends.*
> The lunatic, the lover and the poet
> Are of imagination all compact:
> One sees more devils than vast hell can hold,
> That is, the madman: the lover, all as frantic
> [...]
> Such tricks hath strong imagination,
> [...]
> Or in the night, imagining some fear,
> *How easy is a bush supposed a bear!* (*Dream*, 5.1.2–22, [my emphasis])

This speech functions as a warning against the Idol of the Theatre and the danger of "as-you-like-it" science – but is self-serving in the extreme. It reveals, too, the danger of "cool reason" and "judgment" for justice. It is not, as Theseus,

Bacon, and generations of lawyers assumed, an unimaginative endeavour. Rather, "cool reason" that sits upon a mind grounded in prejudice or bias or self-protection, is the epitome of "as-you-like-it" law that then becomes embedded within doctrine and dogma. But if the Baconian promise of rationality and reason is to mean anything, then it might be expected that a fair judge will overcome their own prejudice through open eyes and minds – that can only come from looking out from within, from the books into action, as the American Legal Realists of the 1930s had it, and from experience. So when Hippolyta responds with logic and rational thinking, observing and analysing what the lovers say and do that niggles with her because of her own experience, she ever so cleverly countermands what his eyes presume, because, as she observes, their stories are confirmed by each other. There is corroborative evidence:

> But all the story of the night told over,
> And all their minds transfigured so together,
> More witnesseth than fancy's images
> And grows to something of great constancy;
> But, howsoever, strange and admirable. (*Dream*, 5.1.23–27)

Her arguments must have had some effect, because Theseus, as we already know, overturns his earlier edict of marriage or death, overbearing Egeus. True, he might just have been in a good mood, but Hippolyta/Titania, belatedly, was able to see and respond to their story, as advocate for truth and justice. The play, in this register, speaks to justice based in experience, and encourages challenges to convention and the forms in which law takes and how it operates.

Productions of *A Midsummer Night's Dream*, too, have challenged convention at least since Brook's seminal production of 1970, now to speak better to time and place, and to respond to joys and fears, criticisms and celebrations, and to define a sense of identity – or challenge it, asking audiences to pay attention to the world around them.[50] The play, regularly in production, seems to now take the temperature of the social and political world about it, and for it to *do* something, not just entertain. Of a new 2016 production by the Sydney Theatre Company, the artistic director of the company remarked: "For us to do the umpteenth production of it in Sydney, we had to have something new to say."[51] And that production had lots to say about justice and fairness, and the harshness of law, reflecting the tenor of the times.

---

50 Rob Conkie, *Writing Performative Shakespeares: New Forms for Performance Criticism* (Cambridge: Cambridge University Press, 2016).

51 Andrew Upton, "'A Message from Andrew Upton' Program: *A Midsummer Night's Dream*," (Sydney: Sydney Theatre Company, 2016).

It might have been thought that a production of the play in Australia in the late 1980s would also have been politically aware. Now self-confident, aware of its history and its mainstream obtaining some idea of injustices affecting indigenous Australians through popular music, such as through the politically aware band, *Midnight Oil,* fronted by lawyer and soon to be politician Peter Garrett, who made even the most unaware Australian familiar with injustices accorded to Aboriginal people in their 1987 hit *Beds Are Burning*, demanding land rights and justice at a time that it looked like *Mabo* might not come to fruition. And by 1991, Australians were soon humming along to a song, called *Treaty*, by the band *Yothu Yindi*. In 1988, its Yolngu members,[52] had famously handed the then prime minister of Australia a document created out of bark called the Barunga Statement, seeking a treaty between indigenous and non-indigenous Australians. The then prime minister set a date of 1990 for a treaty – which at 2018, is still unfulfilled. The song, however, had a huge success, and in 1992, a dance version became a global hit.[53] *Yothu Yindi* had people around the world dancing to a claim for indigenous rights – by a band comprised mostly of indigenous people and mostly sung in *language*,[54] that is the language of the Yolngu people who made up *Yothu Yindi* and embedding law and culture within it– but including parts in English that people could sing along to "Treaty yeah, treaty now," without any awareness of this unrealised promise and continued injustice "back in 1988."

Sitting between these two immensely powerful instances of popular culture, the still relatively new Sydney Theatre Company,[55] began work on a production of *A Midsummer Night's Dream*. It would form part of the annual summer Sydney Festival, from December 1989 until January 1990.[56] Yet this *Dream* did not take its audience into a politics of reconciliation, or challenge convention. In its own way, it chose to celebrate an Australian vernacular and place in the world, but

---

52 Dhimurru Aboriginal Corporation, *Yolngu Culture*, available at: http://www.dhimurru.com.au/yolngu-culture.html (last access March 20, 2017).

53 *Treaty (song)*, available at: https://en.wikipedia.org/wiki/Treaty (song), (last access March 20, 2017), reaching a position of No. 6 on the Billboard Hot Dance Club Play singles charts.

54 Trevor Marshallsea, "Why doesn't Australia have an indigenous treaty?" (London) *BBC News (Online)* (May 24, 2017), available at: http://www.bbc.com/news/world-australia-40024622 (last access March 20, 2017).

55 It was formed in 1979 out of antecedent organisations. The Company is funded as the flagship state theatre of the Australian state of New South Wales. There are numerous smaller companies throughout the state, and the other Australian states.

56 Sydney Theatre Company, "Archive: STC Productions of A Midsummer Night's Dream" (Sydney) *Magazine* (July 28, 2016), available at: https://www.sydneytheatre.com.au/magazine/posts/2016/july/archive-a-midsummer-night-dream (last access March 20, 2017).

through a new version of a Victorian Romantic expectation of the play, dressed differently and with different music, some local and some from the rest of the world, but now spoken as Australians in an Australian accent – and vernacular, that tried to keep up with the kids, with too many "modern instances" that ignored its text – at its peril.

4 *A Midsummer Night's Dream*, Sydney 1989–1990

It is mid-summer in Sydney in 1989, and a hugely controversial production of *A Midsummer Night's Dream* opens, directed by the supreme figure of Australian and Sydney theatre, Richard Wherrett. If anyone had been paying close attention, they might have noticed that the advertisement for the new production that would run from 7 December 1989 to 20 January 1990 was a little anomalous. "Stir up the Australian Youth to Merriment," the newspaper advertising said.[57] Purists would have realised that this might have been a play on the original text "Stir up the Athenian youth to merriments" (*Dream*, 1.1.12) and perhaps conceived as an advertising gimmick.

Wherrett's new production turned "Shakespeare's fairy festooned forest becomes a 1980s style dance club called The Wood; the funny, fond and foolish "mechanicals" performing Pyramus and Thisbe become a rather gritty group of kids."[58] With dramaturg and "translator," May-Brit Akerholt, Wherrett's *Dream* not only reimagined the place, locale and shape of the production of the *Dream*, but rewrote it: "So what we've done amounts, in fact, to a major change in the text. But I don't think the audience will even realise. The language just rolls off the tongue more easily than the original."[59] But the audience – and critics – did notice, and though the production was wildly successful, it went down in Australian theatre history as a fundamentally controversial and not entirely successful production. And his hope "If I'm right in this decision, I think it will be a pointer to where Shakespeare may go in the future,"[60] was not entirely unfounded, because textual changes to this and other Shakespearean plays have

57 "Sydney Theatre Co. presents A Midsummer Night's Dream," (Sydney) *The Sydney Morning Herald* (November 29, 1989), 34.

58 STC, "Archive."

59 Pamela Payne, "Dream of the Future," (Sydney) *The Sydney Morning Herald* (December 8, 1989): Metro.

60 Payne, "Dream Future."

become common, but as we have seen, there was nothing new in this kind of transmutation. What was missing was the exchange – between text and time and place, as Annette Fraser of Oxford Street, Newtown said in her letter of 4 January 1990, published in Sydney's main newspaper:

> SIR: Recently, I saw the Sydney Theatre Company's production of A Midsummer Night's Dream. I sat through the performance dazzled by the set, fascinated with the concept, disappointed with the acting (except for the brilliant Helen Buday) and strangely unsatisfied with the text.
> As I read through the program after the performance, I saw that the director, Richard Wherrett, had seen fit to alter many of Shakespeare's expressions to clarify meaning and to remove ambiguous, archaic terms. The examples provided confirmed my fears. In my opinion, the changes were ugly, clumsy and completely unnecessary.
> Much of the beauty and poetry of Shakespeare's language had been removed for nothing. Richard Wherrett must assume that his audience has all the intelligence of a deranged tarantula. Shakespeare is like music – it should not have to be translated. If the actors are competent and the direction clear, then the meaning will be obvious.
> When I pay $29 to see a Shakespeare play, I expect to see a Shakespeare play, not an abridged version.[61]

She was perhaps too kind. It was tedious, but maybe a few weeks into the production, things had improved. I had seen the production in "preview" just before it opened and it was big on style and short on substance. Richard Wherrett watched anxiously just behind where I sat with my friends, right at the back of the theatre, and couldn't help but have noticed our irritation and impatience. He might have been a little unhappy with us, but we were all part of that party scene at the time and some of us, me included, had theatre backgrounds. We would always be harsh critics.

But there was one really exciting feature of the production which was transfixing – and memorable. The set by Brian Thompson featured a globe on a vast blue geodesic dome (playing of course on Shakespeare's theatre), featured a world sat upside down, with Australia on top of the world, albeit inverted. It spoke to a new antipodean self-confidence, with Australia subverting its place in the world at the bottom of the globe, right on top. But along with that Australian sense of identity was an image of the play that sat firmly in New York City, at a nightclub called Nell's, owned by an expatriate Australian, Little Nell.[62] This was Wherrett's vision, a celebration of a sexual politics that challenged conven-

61 Annette Fraser, "Bastardised Bard," (Sydney) Letter to *The Sydney Morning Herald* (January 6, 1990): 16.

62 Payne, "Dream Future."

tions of conduct that released the unbuttoned self, to be revealed in its real sense at night time.[63] It was a *Dream* that spoke to Sydney's famed Oxford Street, via New York, drag queens included, relocated to a pub owned by Theseus, who commissions a party to celebrate this wedding. This was familiar territory for Wherrett, who also staged drag acts. He was an accomplished director who was about to turn 50, who succumbed to an HIV illness 10 years later. It was *this* politics, not the broader political agenda swirling around at the time, that imbued this *Dream*.

One of Sydney's prominent critics was kind, but firmly insisted that this was an adaption – and the much vaunted discussion of the "translation" an irrelevancy:[64]

> THIS is video-clip Shakespeare. It has every indication of being designed and executed – quite brilliantly – for a generation for whom sound, image, colour and movement mean virtually everything, while the text is of little account.
>
> The result is diverting, amusing, inventive and above all energetic, but it is not Shakespeare, any more than the Nimrod's extremely successful The Venetian Twins a decade ago was Goldoni.
>
> That will reassure many people. There is nothing in it to be afraid of; it does not matter in the least if the audience does not understand the text because that text is only the trigger, the springboard – even the excuse – for the action.
>
> It is curious, therefore, that Richard Wherrett's interesting program essay concerns itself so diligently with the question of what he cleverly calls"translating" the text for our times, yet the text is of such nugatory importance in this extravaganza.

There really was very little that was new, technology and time apart, and he also quietly remarked on its association with Wherrett's other interests – and scolded him for his lack of historical awareness of the transmutative character of the play. Adaptation, yes, Shakespeare, a firm no:

> It is part-pantomime, part drag-show, part rock-opera, in other words, part of a long English tradition of flamboyant Shakespearean adaptation. The composer Henry Purcell did it in collaboration with Dryden, with Shadwell (The Tempest) and also with Elkanah Settle in The Fairy Queen, a florid adaptation of A Midsummer-night's Dream.[65]

But it was one of the best and most scholarly of theatre critics in Sydney who picked it for what it was. Also noting its antecedents as a critical backdrop,

63 Payne, "Dream Future."

64 John Carmody, "Dream Night for a Midsummer Sydney," (Sydney) *Sun Herald* (December 10, 1989): 122.

65 Carmody, "Dream Night."

Bob Evans remarked that "Perhaps because of its emphasis on magic in an increasingly rational world, *Dream* has borne so many of the changes wrought in the theory and practice of theatre this century."[66] This prescient remark spoke to future *Dreams*, but for now, in noting some of the key productions of that century, he tied this production to the excess of Beerbohm Tree's extravaganza of the turn of the twentieth century (rabbits included), and then turns the screw:

> There is more of Tree's conspicuous consumption and tricksy populism than Brook's or Granville-Barker's [noted earlier] radical sensitivity in the Sydney Theatre Company's production [...] Wherrett's 21st-century production echoes the excesses of a century ago. Where Tree and Irving had lashings of Mendelssohn's *Sommernachtstraum* music, *corps de ballets* and children as fairies, Wherrett substitutes Malcolm McLaren's vogueish Waltzing Darling and Phillip Glass with hot dance club numbers.[67]

And here's the rub. Though focussing on the Kottian elements of the play – sex, the unconscious:

> What's missing from the performances and the production is heart and soul and a sense of what's at stake. The cast do not always manage the text, even in translation (which passes for the real thing and still may offend the purists) [...] It is the substance of the play which has been glossed over[68].

This inability to manage the text, missing what's at stake. This was no transmutation, despite the attempt to find the play in place. But as theatre history goes, this wasn't the end. *Dream* has now had four Sydney Theatre Company outings, and the one following Wherrett's was altogether different. In 1997, a *Dream* that celebrated Indigenous Dreaming, "understood by their diverse Aboriginal adherents to be reality, religion, and the Law,"[69] took to the stage. Directed by Aborigi-

---

66 Bob Evans, "Glitter Outshines Substance," (Sydney) *The Sydney Morning Herald* (December 11, 1989): 16.
67 Evans, "Glitter."
68 Evans, "Glitter."
69 Christine Judith Nicolls, "'Dreamtime' and 'The Dreaming': who dreamed up these terms?" *The Conversation* (January 29, 2014), available at: https://theconversation.com/dreamtime-and-the-dreaming-who-dreamed-up-these-terms-20835 (last access March 20, 2017). See also Christine Black, "Maturing Australia through Australian Aboriginal Narrative Law," *South Atlantic Quarterly* 110.2 (2011): 347–362; Christine F. Black, *The Land is the Source of the Law: A Dialogic Encounter with Indigenous Jurisprudence* (Abingdon: Routledge, 2010).

nal actor and director Noel Tovey and a stellar cast of Indigenous actors,[70] it changed the language of the *Dream* forever. It made small changes to the text,[71] to remind non-Indigenous Australians of harms caused to them, but Tovey intended that the production *not* be political.[72] Regardless, the transmutation of the production that mattered, and that is how it was read.[73] This new exchange, however, reminded that in the *Dream* and *Dreaming* law imbues life and justice matters, and law comes from land and place, the perfect manifestation of law grounded in life, place and justice.

However, injustice for indigenous Australians remained, in all facets of life. And the protection of law was also about to be radically confined. The last of the key judicial changes to land rights, the *Wik* case,[74] was decided just before Christmas 1996. Political disapproval followed, even though the legal principles on which the case was decided were sound.[75]In 1998, a so-called conservative judge was appointed to the High Court, and slowly the court would soon be predominantly populated by justices who would be less likely to "look beyond" the books and more likely to narrowly interpret law, as true Baconians. The promise of the 1980s seemed extinguished, but now, the court is made up, in part of judges who were only learning law in the 1970s and 1980s, and even now in the 1990s. What had changed then is now part of law. Turning back into the books now looks different, and the court is very different too. Even if eyes do not look up and out too often, it is harder now to ignore the world around.

And so too, *A Midsummer Night's Dream*. In the 2016 production mounted by the Sydney Theatre Company, the Tiwi Island actor, Rob Collins, was cast as Lysander.[76] Discussing his place as the only indigenous actor in the production he remarked:

---

70 Emma Cox, "'What's past is prologue': Performing Shakespeare and Aboriginality in Australia," *Multicultural Shakespeare: Translation, Appropriation and Performance* 8.23 (2011): 71–92, 80–85.

71 Emma Cox, "Negotiating Cultural Narratives: All-Aboriginal Shakespearean Dreaming," *Southerly* 64.3 (2004–2005): 15–27.

72 Cox, "Negotiating Cultural Narratives," 18.

73 Cox, "Negotiating Cultural Narratives"; Cox, "What's past is prologue."

74 *Wik Peoples v Queensland* [1996] HCA 40.

75 Maureen Tehan, "A Hope Disillusioned, an Opportunity Lost? Reflections on Common Law Native Title and Ten Years of the Native Title Act," *Melbourne University Law Review* 27.2 (2003): 523–571.

76 *Tiwi Islands* available at: https://en.wikipedia.org/wiki/Tiwi_Islands (last access March 20, 2017).

> The ideal scenario is to have an actor, regardless of race, creed or colour, picked for his ability [...] Mr Collins said he is drawing on his background to interpret A Midsummer Night's dream, comparing Shakespeare's fairies to similar mythologies in his own culture. "We have a wealth of stories of little men who steal children into the bushes. [77]

This exchange, the transmutation of Shakespeare as part of a modern Australia, in its own way reflects the position of law now. We were left knowing that law, and the challenges to law in the absence of looking and seeing and being aware of justice was not just a problem, but a danger to a properly functioning polity. A few weeks later, Donald Trump was elected President of the United States of America.

77 David Spicer, "Indigenous artists taking centre-stage at Sydney Opera House," (Australia) Australian Broadcasting Corporation (September 9, 2016), available at: http://www.abc.net.au/news/2016-09-09/indigenous-artists-taking-centre-stage-at-sydney-opera-house/7832542 (last access March 20, 2017).

Contributors

Heinz Antor is Chair of English Literatures and Head of the Department of English at the University of Cologne. He is editor of the journal *Anglistik: International Journal of English Studies*. He has published widely on anglophone literature from the sixteenth to the twenty-first century, postcolonial, inter- and transcultural studies, Canadian and Australian literature.

Chiara Battisti is Associate Professor of English Literature at the Department of Foreign Literatures and languages of the University of Verona. Her research interests include literature and the visual arts, with a particular focus on literature and cinema, literature and science, law and literature, food and literature, gender studies and fashion studies. She is a member of the European Society for the Study of English (ESSE), of AIA (Associazione Italiana di Anglistica) and of AIDEL (Associazione Italiana Diritto e Letteratura).

Gilad Ben-Nun is a historian of modern international law, and an EU - Marie Curie Individual Fellow at Verona University's Law Faculty, where he is currently writing up a drafting history of the 4th Geneva Convention for the Protection of Civilians of 1949 (EU Grant Award # 701275 - project REQUE 2) . Between 2001 and 2002 he was Ford Foundation's Middle East Fellow at the United Nations Institute for Disarmament Research (UNIDIR) in Geneva. From 2002 to 2009 he served as a diplomatic Middle East Program Officer with UNDP. In 2017, his monograph on the history of the international refugee regime, *Seeking Asylum in Israel: Refugees and the History of Migration Law* (I.B. Tauris, 2017), was nominated as the single finalist of the US National Jewish Book Award (writing based on archival material - The JDC-Herbert Katzki Award).

Daniela Carpi is Full Professor of English Literature at the Department of Foreign Literatures and Languages, University of Verona. Her fields of research are: Renaissance theatre, critical theory, postmodernism, law and literature, literature and science, literature and visual arts. She is in the scientific board of the journals *Symbolism: a Journal of Critical Aesthetics* (New York), *Anglistik* (Heidelberg), *La torre di Babele* (Parma), *Law and Humanities* (Warwick), *Cardozo Law Bulletin* (University of Trento), *CoSMo: Comparative Studies in Modernism* (Torino). She is a member of Academia Europaea, ESSE, AIA. She is the managing editor of *Pólemos: Journal of Law, Literature and Culture*. She is the founder and president of AIDEL (Associazione Italiana di Diritto e Letteratura) and a member of the Advisory Board of the series "Edinburgh Critical Studies in Law, Literature and the Humanities"; she edits the series "Law and Literature" for De Gruyter.

Sidia Fiorato is Researcher of English Literature at the Department of Foreign Literatures and Languages, University of Verona. Her fields of research include detective fiction and the legal thriller, literature and the performing arts, Shakespeare studies, the fairy tale. Among her publications, *Performing the Renaissance Body. Essays on Drama, Law and Representation* (edited volume with John Drakakis, Berlin, De Gruyter 2016), and essays on the contemporary novel, Shakespearian adaptations, Victorian Literature, postmodern fairy tales.

https://doi.org/10.1515/9783110591514-015

Jeanne Gaakeer is endowed Professor of legal theory at Erasmus School of Law, Rotterdam. The focus of her research is on interdisciplinary movements in legal theory (specifically Law and Literature and Law and the Humanities) and their relevance to legal practice. She is the 2013 recipient of the J.B. White Award (bestowed by the Association for the Study of Law, Culture and Humanities). She also serves as a justice in the criminal law section of the Appellate Court in The Hague.

Marett Leiboff is Associate Professor at the School of Law and Legal Intersections Research Centre, University of Wollongong Australia. Her research and scholarship centre on the legal theories of cultural legal studies, law and humanities and theatrical jurisprudence, with a particular focus on how the non-legal formation of the lawyer affects and influences practices of legal interpretation. She works with history, biography, and different cultural forms, and how they are experienced and encountered in order to understand how lawyers interpret legal texts through time, and how non-legal experience through generational change affects that interpretation, and what this means for legal integrity.

François Ost is Full Professor at the University Saint-Louis, Brussels. He is the president of the group FNRS Law and Literature. His publications include *Raconter la loi. Aux sources de l'imaginaire juridique* (2004), *Sade et la loi* (2005), *Shakespeare. La Comédie de la Loi* (2012). Since 2004 he has been a member of the Académie Royale des Sciences, des Lettres et des Beaux Arts de Belgique. He received the honorary title of Baron by the King of Belgium in 2014.

Carlo Pelloso is Associate Professor of Roman Law at the Department of Law of the University of Verona; he lectures in Ancient Greek Legal Systems at the University of Padua. Among his recent publications, "Protecting the Community: Public Actions and Forms of Punishment in Ancient Athens," in *Oxford Handbook of Ancient Greek Law*, eds. E. Harris, M. Canevaro (Oxford, 2015), and "Ephesis eis to dikasterion: Remarks and Speculations on the Legal Nature of the Solonian Reform," in *Symposion. Conferências sobre a História do Direito grego e helenístico* (Coimbra, 2016).

Paul Raffield is Professor of Law at the University of Warwick, where he teaches Tort Law, Origins of English Law, and Shakespeare and the Law. He is the author of *The Art of Law in Shakespeare* (2017); *Shakespeare's Imaginary Constitution: Late Elizabethan Politics and the Theatre of Law* (2010) and *Images and Cultures of Law in Early Modern England: Justice and Political Power, 1558–1660* (2004). He is consultant editor and co-founder of the journal Law and Humanities, and a member of AIDEL, the Italian Association for the Study of Law and Literature. Paul Raffield is a UK National Teaching Fellow, a Fellow of the UK Higher Education Academy, and a recipient of the Warwick Award for Teaching Excellence.

Filippo Sgubbi is Emeritus of Criminal Law at the University of Bologna. His research interests are mainly in the fields of corporate criminal law and financial criminal law. Among his publications: *Il reato come rischio sociale – Ricerche sulle scelte di allocazione dell'illegalità penale* (1991); "Il mercato della legge penale", IUS17 (2008): 27–28; "L'exemple en droit italien en matère boursière et de la protection de l'épargne," *Les Petites Affiches, La Loi* 396.134 (2007): 36–39.

Gary Watt is Professor of Law at the University of Warwick. He is the co-founding editor of the journal *Law and Humanities* and his books on law and literature include *Equity Stirring: The Story of Justice Beyond Law* (2009), *Dress, Law and Naked Truth* (2013) and the collection *Shakespeare and the Law* (2008, co-edited with P. Raffield). His latest monograph is *Shakespeare's Acts of Will* (2016). He was named UK "Law Teacher of the Year" in 2009 and was awarded a National Teaching Fellowship (2010).

Index of Names

https://doi.org/10.1515/9783110591514-016

Subjext Index

https://doi.org/10.1515/9783110591514-017

Bei Fragen zur Produktsicherheit wenden Sie sich bitte an:
If you have any questions regarding product safety,
please contact:

Walter de Gruyter GmbH
Genthiner Straße 13
10785 Berlin
productsafety@degruyterbrill.com